ROMAN WILTSHIRE AND AFTER

PAPERS IN HONOUR OF KEN ANNABLE

edited by

Peter Ellis

with contributions by

Mark Corney, Bruce Eagles, Anne Foster, Peter Fowler,
Nick Griffiths, Martin Henig, Ian Hodder, Sam Moorhead,
Paul Robinson, Jane Timby, and Bryn Walters

WILTSHIRE ARCHAEOLOGICAL AND NATURAL HISTORY SOCIETY

First published in the United Kingdom in 2001 by
Wiltshire Archaeological and Natural History Society (Wiltshire Heritage)
41 Long Street,
Devizes, Wilts SN10 1NS
Telephone 01380 727369
Fax 01380 722150

Registered Charity Commission No. 1080096

Publication of this Monograph has been grant aided by the Audrey Barrie Memorial
Fund of the Roman Research Society for which the Society expresses its grateful
acknowledgement.

ISBN 0 947723 08 0

Typeset in Garamond by Peter Ellis
and produced for the Society by
Avonset, 11 Kelso Place, Upper Bristol Road, Bath BA1 3AU
Printed in Great Britain

KEN ANNABLE

Ken Annable (left) receiving the Museum of the Year award in 1984 from a representative of the Illustrated London News

Ken Annable was born in Derby. From 1942 to 1947 he served in the Middle East, West Africa and Germany with the Royal Corps of Signals, the Royal Scots Greys and the Household Cavalry. He gained a degree in Classics and English Literature at Reading University and later studied under Sir Mortimer Wheeler at the Institute of Archaeology in London. In 1952 he did three months voluntary work at Guildford Museum and took part in the excavation of an Anglo-Saxon site in Essex. The following year he helped to excavate the Roman pottery kiln site at Cantley, Doncaster.

He was appointed Assistant Curator at Devizes Museum in January 1954 and succeeded Nick Thomas as Curator in 1957. He was curator for 28 years until his retirement in 1986. During this time he supervised large scale extensions and improvements, which included the construction of the Bonar Sykes wing, the conversion of the cellars as stores, very necessary for the growing museum collections, and the erection of two outside stores. He re-displayed in his time virtually the entire museum, bringing to the galleries his considerable artistic flair. The display labels with his delicate watercolour drawings of prehistoric sites in their landscape are delightful miniatures in their own right. A highlight of his time as curator was the presentation of the Museum of the Year Award in 1984.

Ken was fortunate to live in a time when curators who specialised in archaeology were encouraged to undertake excavation and fieldwork and were given full facilities for this. He carried out a number of important research excavations, notably of the Romano-British kilns at Savernake Forest and of the west gateway of the Roman town at *Cunetio* on the outskirts of Mildenhall. In addition he also undertook rescue excavations of several sites including a Roman well at *Cunetio*, a Roman lead coffin, also from *Cunetio*, and, perhaps his most important project, the early Saxon cemetery at Blacknall Field, Pewsey.

He was a firm believer in prompt and proper publication of his excavations in the Society's journal (and in the case of Pewsey cemetery has completed a catalogue and manuscript that will be a firm basis for a full publication of the excavation, hopefully shortly). He believed too in the great importance of museum catalogues. 'Annable and Simpson (1964)' has for nearly 40 years been required reading for generations of students of British prehistory. (Incidentally it has recently been reprinted and still sells well.) He planned and drafted with colleagues a succeeding volume cataloguing the museum's Iron Age collections.

Ken acquired a considerable reputation as a scholar and curator and was highly respected in the archaeological field. He is a Fellow of the Society of Antiquaries and in 1969 was awarded a Fellowship also by the Museums Association. He always emphasised the importance of the Society's museum and library as a centre for the serious study of archaeology in Wiltshire and gave unstinting help and support to budding historians and archaeologists studying the collection. At a ceremony in 1978 to celebrate his 25 years at the museum, he was praised for maintaining high standards of scholarship and courtesy towards students and the public. Bonar Sykes, the Society's chairman said of him 'Ken became an institution within an institution: bringing to his work artistry and sensibility, and a resolute defence of high standards'. He enjoyed a reputation among ordinary Wiltshire people too. When a Swindon workman engaged on digging a drain dug up a bone, the foreman said 'we must send for Mr Annable'. The workman asked 'will he come on an elephant?'

Ken was knowledgeable about many periods and fields. Above all, however, he was deeply interested in Roman archaeology, particularly pottery and its manufacture, the Roman army and the archaeology of *Cunetio*. These essays, principally on Roman themes, are a fitting tribute to him from his colleagues and friends who have benefitted from his work and the help and encouragement he has shown them in his career.

CONTENTS

LIST OF ILLUSTRATIONS

LIST OF TABLES

ABBREVIATIONS USED

BAR   British Archaeological Reports
CBA   Council for British Archaeology
JRS   Journal of Roman Studies
MCNHSR   Marlborough College Natural History Society Report
SSWM   Salisbury and South Wilts Museum
WANHM   Wiltshire Archaeological and Natural History Society Magazine
WHM   Wiltshire Heritage Museum (Devizes)
WILTM   Wiltshire Museums
VCH   Victoria County History

THE CONTRIBUTORS

Mark Corney is Lecturer in Landscape Archaeology at the University of Bristol as well as a consulting archaeologist specialising in topographic and aerial survey, and Iron Age and Roman artefacts.

Bruce Eagles is a Visiting Research Fellow at Bournemouth University. His publications include *The Anglo-Saxon Settlement of Humberside* (1979) as well as a number of papers in books and academic journals.

Peter Ellis is a freelance editor specialising in reports on backlog excavations, including the Society's recent monograph on Ludgershall Castle. He is an Honorary Research Fellow at the University of Birmingham.

Ann Foster has an MA in Classical Art and Archaeology from the State University of New York. She has published on various aspects of Roman Britain and has been an active member of WANHS since 1983.

Peter Fowler is a writer, archaeologist and historian. Since the 1950s, he has been much involved with Wessex, Wiltshire in particular. His first book (1967) was on the former. his latest, *Landscape Plotted and Pieced* (2000), is about Fyfield and West Overton, two parishes in the latter.

Nick Griffiths is an archaeological illustrator and an expert on finds. He has co-authored books on medieval finds from London and has illustrated many archaeological reports. He is a Fellow of the Society of Antiquaries.

Martin Henig lectures on Roman art at the University of Oxford where he is a Fellow of Wolfson College. He has been Hon. Editor of the British Archaeological Association since 1985. His books include *Religion in Roman Britain* (1984) and *The Art of Roman Britain* (1995).

Ian Hodder is a Fellow of the British Academy and teaches at Stanford University. His main publications are *Reading the Past* (CUP 1986), *The Domestication of Europe* (Blackwell 1990), and *The Archaeological Process* (Blackwell 1999).

Sam Moorhead is a staff lecturer at the British Museum. He was educated at the University of North Carolina, Durham University and the Institute of Archaeology in London. He has excavated in Britain, Italy and the near East.

Paul Robinson is curator of Wiltshire Heritage Museum - having taken over from Ken Annable in 1986, whose assistant he had been for the previous 12 years.

Jane R. Timby pursues a freelance archaeological career specialising in pottery. She has undertaken a range of work including writing up backlog excavations, preparing pottery reports for publication, illustration, excavation and teaching.

Bryn Walters is a freelance consultant and Director of the Association for Roman Archaeology. His career has concentrated on fieldwork in North Wiltshire having discovered several major sites and excavated on villas in that area.

ACKNOWLEDGEMENTS

The contributor's individual acknowledgements are presented with their respective chapters. Here it is a pleasure to record grateful thanks to them for their patience, to the staff of Wiltshire Heritage Museum, especially Paul Robinson, and to the Roman Research Trust for their grant towards the publication costs. The book was initiated by Paul Robinson and an early stage of editing was undertaken by Kate Fielden. The profile of Ken Annable was written by Paul Robinson and Lorna Haycock. The illustrations in Chapters 2, 3 and 4 are by their respective authors. Those in Chapter 7 are acknowledged there. Figures1.1, 5.1, 5.2, 5.3, 10.1, 10.4, 10.11, 10.12, 11.1, 11.2 and 11.3 were prepared by Alejandra Gutiérrez. Finally, John Chandler kindly advised on many aspects of the text and its presentation and scanned all the illustrations. I am most grateful to him for his assistance.

Peter Ellis

1 INTRODUCTION: A PERSONAL ACCOUNT

by Ian Hodder

I well remember driving down to Devizes in 1972, and looking for the museum where I was to have my first appointed meeting with its curator, Ken Annable. As a PhD student from Cambridge working on a theoretical topic, I knew painfully little about Roman Britain. Rather, my head was full of abstract ideas that I had obtained from human geographers about markets and Central Place Theory. I wanted to 'test' these on Roman Britain by finding distributions of pottery that might have been marketed through towns. The idea was to compare these distributions with the theoretical predictions of gravity models and the like. But I had not been successful in finding easily identifiable wares that I could plot.

So there I was, a young, rather lost and blinkered graduate student, entering the museum. In this volume, Peter Fowler talks of 'an attractive streak of unconformity' in Ken Annable, and perhaps it was this that encouraged him to respond warmly to my rather unorthodox questions and inadequate knowledge. He seemed to understand immediately what I wanted and he provided avuncular advice that was to stand me in good stead in the years to come. His kindness and generosity were very striking. He pointed out exactly what I needed – Savernake ware, since this was relatively well-provenanced and easily identifiable. He suggested I plot this and study its relationship to Mildenhall, the Roman *Cunetio*. He gave endless help in identifying sites at which it occurred, and assisted me in its identification, later confirmed by thin-section analysis. He showed considerable patience in dealing with my ignorance and youthful expectations.

Later I was to expand these same ideas and approaches to other types of Romano-British pottery (Hodder 1974), but it was the Savernake ware study which demonstrated to me the potential for identifying marketing patterns around Romano-British centres. Ken Annable was of course the ideal guide to the Savernake material. He had excavated the Savernake kilns (Annable 1962) after making the first positive identification of the kilns through fieldwork and excavation in 1957-8. Two kilns were excavated near Bitham Pond beside Column Ride in Savernake Forest and others have since been identified. As Jane Timby notes in her chapter, the kilns are about 0.8km west of the Roman road from Old Sarum to *Cunetio*, and about 1.25km south of that town. This was an ideal context for me – it allowed me to examine the way in which a distinctive type of pottery might have been marketed through an adjacent Romano-British centre. It was Ken Annable's work on the Savernake potteries that was a starting point for understanding the nature and spread of a regional pottery industry.

Our understanding of *Cunetio* itself also depended on the pioneering work of Ken Annable. During the 1950s and 1960s he had, with Tony Clark, conducted geophysical prospection and excavation in Black Field, and his engagement with the site has continued over the years (Annable 1966; 1974; 1980). This work, together with air photographs, demonstrated the importance and chronological range of this defended centre. As Bryn Walters notes in his chapter, Ken Annable's work at Mildenhall with Tony Clark in the 1950s contributed substantially to our understanding of this small town.

As many authors in this volume point out, the county of Wiltshire does not correspond to any known Roman administrative unit (Fig. 1.1). Rather, the importance of Wiltshire in Roman Britain attests to a long tradition of archaeological research in the county. In no small way, this research has been encouraged and inspired by Ken Annable's activities and enthusiasm. This volume is an outstanding collection showing the enormous range and coherence of work that follows on from Ken Annable's interests in Romano-British Wiltshire. The volume pays tribute to his work on the archaeology of the county and it honours his interest in Roman Britain. As Bryn Walters writes in his chapter: 'Ken Annable unquestionably laid the modern foundations of Roman archaeology in the county'.

There have of course been many changes in our understanding of Roman Wiltshire over recent years, and this volume provides a wonderful summary of these new developments. A good example is provided by changes in the interpretation of Savernake ware. An initial shift was towards an emphasis on the influence of the initial military impact (Swan 1975). But in this volume, Jane Timby provides an interesting account of how Savernake ware does not need to be seen as introduced and related to military markets. Rather, it can be better understood as a local development with some military influence. Of course, the military presence discussed in this volume by Nick Griffiths gave some boost to the industry, but, as Jane Timby writes, 'in form Savernake ware appears to be a direct continuation of local indigenous traditions'. She is surely right to point to the many and widespread early sites, often with no military component, with Savernake ware. In my view this account of a local industry working through local mechanisms of dispersal makes much better sense of the distribution of the ware.

The notion of strong continuity from the Iron Age runs as a distinctive theme throughout the volume. For example, in discussing the art of the region, Martin Henig demonstrates a strong development from the local Iron Age traditions. Equally, it has become clear that there are important shifts through time in the status and economic wealth of sites in the county. In his chapter, Sam Moorhead summarises the evidence from coin data in Wiltshire. He shows lower than average numbers of coins for the early centuries (relating to a lack of major military presence) but especially high rural economic prosperity in the 4th century.

This theme of change through time is an important component that complicates our understanding of Romano-British settlement patterns in the county. For example, the stone wall at *Cunetio* is late 4th century, while Savernake pottery production is concentrated

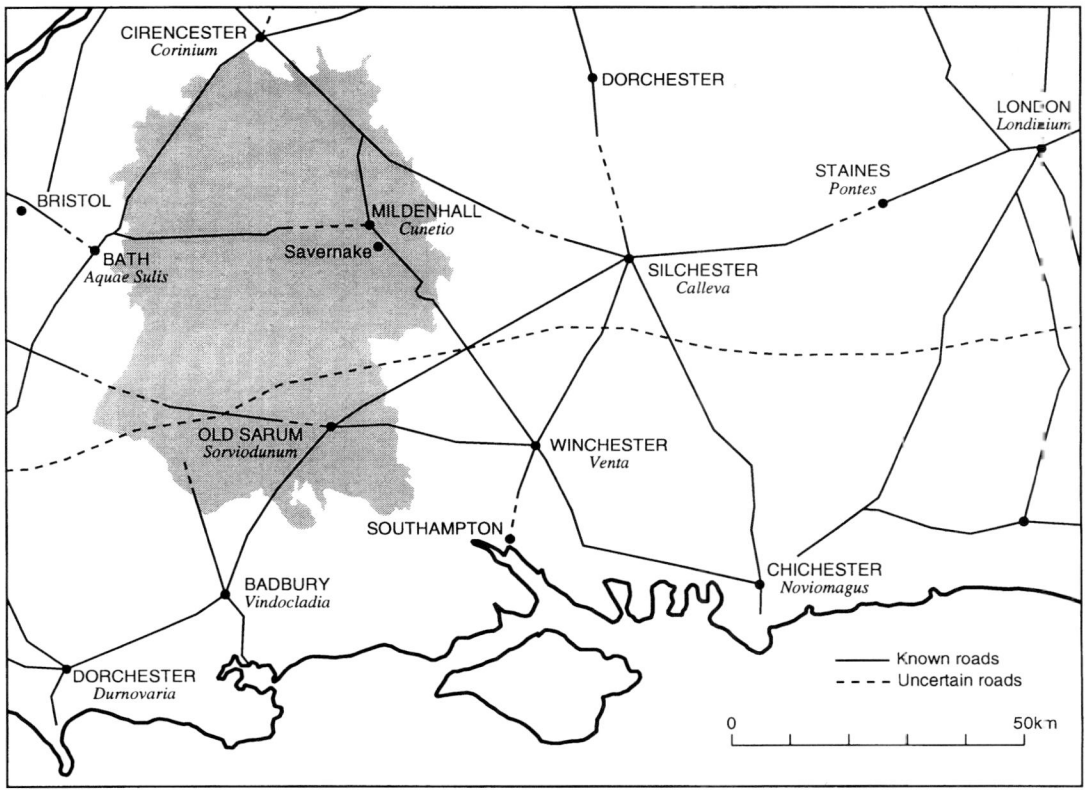

Fig. 1.1 Southern Britain with Roman sites and roads, area of Wiltshire outlined

in the 1st and 2nd centuries. This situation raises the problem of how to define the status of 'market' centres, and which ones to include in settlement pattern and pottery distribution analyses (Burnham and Wacher 1990).

Indeed, one of the most satisfying changes in thinking about Roman Wiltshire concerns the ways in which the study of settlement patterns has been transformed. When I did my work on marketing distributions in the early 1970s, a settlement pattern was a unified and coherent distribution of points on a map. Today, settlement patterns are seen as multi-layered, complex and perhaps even 'contested'. As Mark Corney shows in his chapter, there is a wide range of urban and nucleated settlement in Wiltshire, and he demonstrates their great diversity in form and function, including ritual functions. Substantial agricultural settlements set within rural economic systems may not be overly influenced by the system of roads and defended towns. The use of prehistoric ritual sites such as Silbury Hill perhaps comprises an 'alternative' landscape. Bryn Walters, in his chapter, provides a wonderful review of the villas in the county and their social and economic status, especially as linked to the small towns. Here we can see the individuality and diversity of the villas in Wiltshire.

Conclusions

This is an impressive volume. It covers an enormous range of material from burial (discussed by Anne Foster) to villas, from towns to pottery production, and so on. There is a fascinating chapter by Peter Fowler on Wansdyke as a military work in Roman mode, intended to face a military threat from the north, and there is a chapter by Bruce Eagles on the Anglo-Saxon presence in Wiltshire. This breadth and depth reflect the long period of archaeological research in the county to which Ken Annable has so significantly contributed. The volume is thus a fitting homage to Ken Annable and to his influence on the archaeology of Wiltshire.

As I drove out of Devizes after my first visit working in the stores in the museum, I remember being terribly excited that I had made my first breakthrough in identifying marketing patterns in Romano-British pottery. Of course, much more needed to be done in other museums to identify the wider distribution of Savernake ware, and much more needed to be done on other coarse and fine wares, but this first step indicated to me that the approach was feasible. We now realise more fully the difficulties involved in such claims, and this volume provides much indication of the complexity of Romano-British Wiltshire as we now understand it. But perhaps most importantly, my 'new idea' was not so new after all, and it was hardly 'mine'. In fact the idea had been suggested to me by a kind and generous man, whose remarkable knowledge of and engagement in Roman Wiltshire had set me on my way. I suspect that many in this volume, and many others who have worked in Wiltshire or have talked with Ken Annable, have had similar experiences. In these informal and personal ways he assisted and inspired us, and in his scholarship he guided us. For these reasons I, and so many, owe him an enormous debt of gratitude and respect.

References

Annable, F. K., 1962, 'A Romano-British pottery in Savernake Forest, kilns 1-2', *WANHM*, 58, 142-55

_____ , 1966, 'A late first-century well at *Cunetio*', *WANHM*, 61, 9-24

_____ , 1974, 'A bronze military apron mount from *Cunetio*', *WANHM*, 69, 176-9

_____ , 1980, 'A coffined burial of Roman date from *Cunetio*', *WANHM*, 72/3, 187-91

Burnham, B., and Wacher, J., 1990, *The Small Towns of Roman Britain*, London

Hodder, I., 1974, 'The distribution of Savernake ware', *WANHM*, 69, 67-84

Swan, V. G., 1975, 'Oare reconsidered and the origins of Savernake ware in Wiltshire', *Britannia*, 6, 36-61

2 THE ROMANO-BRITISH NUCLEATED SETTLEMENTS OF WILTSHIRE

by Mark Corney

Introduction

This paper is offered to Ken Annable as a small token of respect in recognition of the pioneering work that he, in company with the late Tony Clark, undertook on the Romano-British 'small town' at *Cunetio*, the modern village of Mildenhall near Marlborough. Although the historic county of Wiltshire does not boast a Roman town of *civitas* status or higher, it does have a number of important nucleated settlements that form a potentially informative regional group. Few have been investigated in detail, but the current available data for the Roman landscape of Wiltshire shows the broad distribution of sites discussed here (Fig. 2.1). The following is intended to bring the sites to a wider audience and, hopefully, stimulate further debate and work.

The choice of sites selected for discussion in this paper may be considered by some to be arbitrary. There are other settlements of Roman date that cover very large areas that have been excluded. On Salisbury Plain there are at least seven substantial settlements that in at least one case cover an area in excess of 20ha (50 acres). They are set in an extensive agricultural landscape, and a largely rural-based economic context seems most appropriate. In the south of the county a further four large settlements are known on the Great Ridge and in Grovely Wood. All appear to have developed from major Late Iron Age settlements (Corney 1989). Of these, three are of considerable extent – Hamshill Ditches, Ebsbury and Stockton Earthworks. However, despite their close proximity to the Roman road from Old Sarum to Charterhouse-on-Mendip, the settlements remained firmly fixed to their Iron Age predecessors and there is no evidence of any shift towards the road. Again, as on Salisbury Plain, these settlements are set within extensive field-systems and a predominantly agrarian economic setting seems certain. In contrast, all the sites featured in this paper, with the exception of The Ham at Westbury, are on the known Roman road network.

The county of Wiltshire in the Romano-British period was crossed by a network of major Roman roads, many of which met at important junctions within our study area (Fig. 2.1). Substantial settlements developed at three of these junctions, *Durocornovium* (Wanborough), *Cunetio* (Mildenhall) and *Sorviodunum* (Stratford-sub-Castle/Old Sarum).

In addition to these sites situated on nodal points of the local communication infrastructure, a number of other nucleated settlements developed both along the road network and beyond. In form they vary greatly and our knowledge of most of them is frustratingly meagre. Modern excavation on Roman urban and nucleated sites in the county has been limited and in many cases has only served to underscore the difficulties we are confronted with in attempting to categorise and interpret them. All fall into the rather convenient but ill-defined 'catch-all' category of 'small towns' (Burnham and Wacher 1990).

The Late Iron Age political structure and settlement pattern (Fig. 2.2)

The modern county covers an area that conventional Romano-British studies (Frere 1967; Ordnance Survey 1978) ascribe to at least three pre-conquest 'tribes': the Atrebates, the Dobunni, and the Durotriges. In addition to these three 'tribes', the Roman name for the 'small town' at Wanborough, *Durocornovium*, suggests a further otherwise undocumented unit called the Cornovii in the area of modern Swindon (Rivet and Smith 1979, 350). Based on a single reference by the 2nd-century AD geographer Ptolemy to the tribal affiliation of Bath, the territory of the Belgae, a *civitas* centred on modern Winchester (*Venta Belgarum*), has been claimed to extend across central Wiltshire and into north Somerset (*ibid.*, 121). This last point is controversial, by no means certain, and, although beyond the scope of this paper, is in urgent need of critical re-appraisal.

Using the distribution patterns of pre-Roman coinage in Wiltshire (which does not necessarily reflect a rigid political or economic situation) it can be seen that Dobunnic numismatic influence dominates the north and north west of the county (Selwood 1984; Van Arsdell 1994). Durotrigian coins extend across much of the southernmost part of the county and as far north as Salisbury Plain, and Atrebatic issues occur on the extreme eastern edge of Wiltshire but rarely occur west of the River Avon (Selwood 1984; Robinson forthcoming).

In addition to these primary distributions, Robinson (1977) has also identified a further distinctive range of Iron Age coins, stylistically linked to Dobunnic issues, that occur as a discrete cluster in central Wiltshire with a focus upon the Vale of Pewsey and Marlborough area. It is quite possible that these coins are associated with the major Late Iron Age complex centred upon Forest Hill, immediately to the south-east of Marlborough (Corney 1997a). Apart from the Forest Hill complex, major settlements of the Late Iron Age are surprisingly rare in northern Wiltshire. This may, in part, reflect the extensive modern urban sprawl of Swindon, although a more important factor is likely to be the local geology. Once off the chalk, the Jurassic deposits of clays and brash are not renowned for their sensitivity to crop-mark formation. Further, much of this region has been used for pasture in recent centuries thus reducing the opportunities for chance discoveries. In addition a number of RAF airfields, Lyneham, Colerne and Kemble, had restrictions on access to airspace (of these only Lyneham remains active).

In recent years a number of distinctive enclosures of rectilinear form have been recorded in the Malmesbury region (Ian Powlesland and Richard Wykes, pers. comm.) but evidence of widespread land division is still lacking. It is only in the far north of the

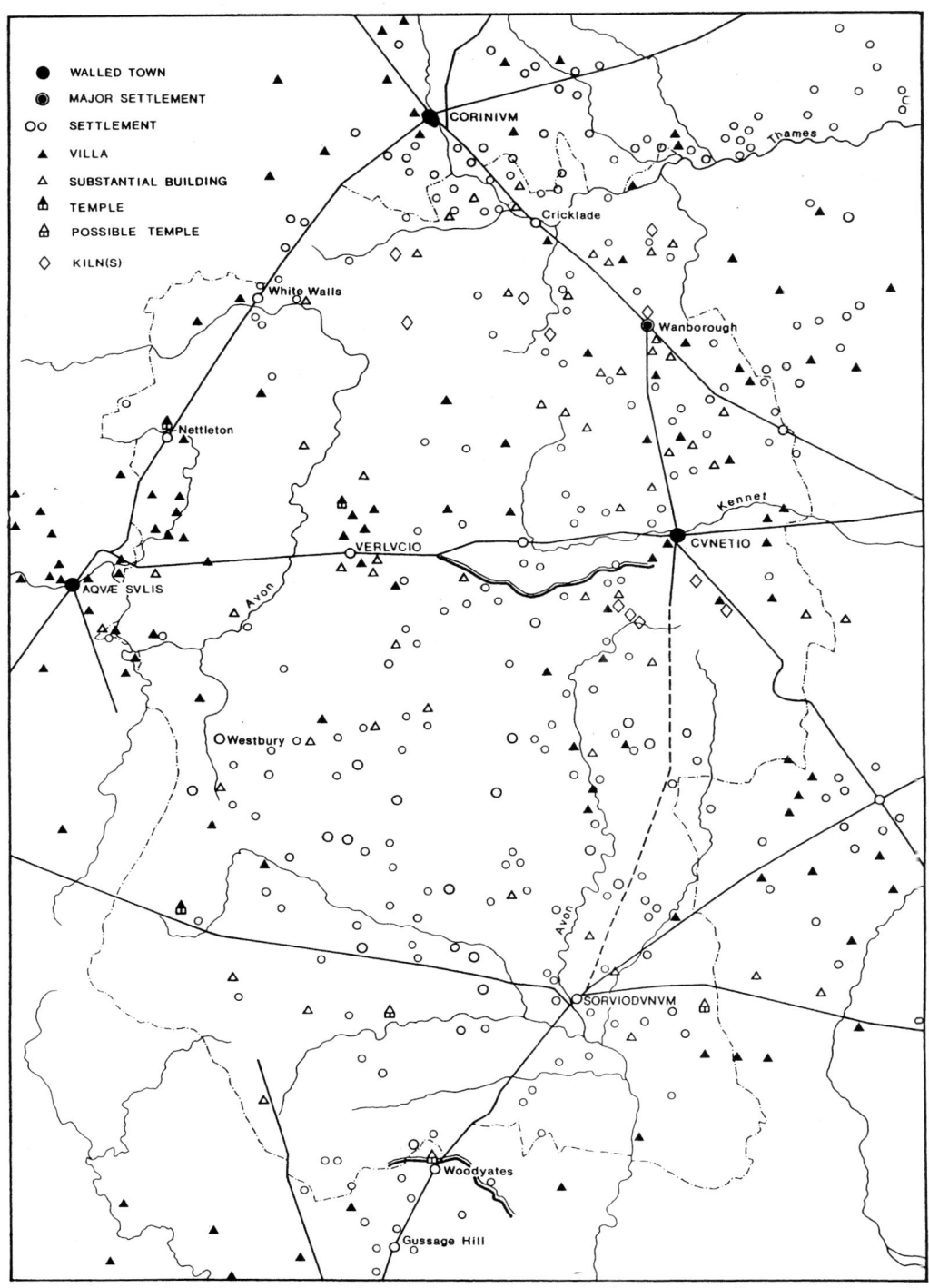

WALLED TOWN
MAJOR SETTLEMENT
SETTLEMENT
VILLA
SUBSTANTIAL BUILDING
TEMPLE
POSSIBLE TEMPLE
KILN(S)

CORINIVM

Thames

Cricklade

White Walls

Wanborough

Nettleton

Kennet

VERLVCIO

CVNETIO

AQVÆ SVLIS

Avon

Westbury

Avon

SORVIODVNVM

Woodyates

Gussage Hill

Fig. 2.1 Roman Wiltshire, the distribution of known sites clearly demonstrates the extent of Romano-British settlement; based on various sources

county on the gravel deposits of the Upper Thames Valley, that air photography has revealed an extensive and dense pattern of past settlement and other activities (Leech 1977). Excavation of a number of sites has demonstrated an intensively used landscape in the Late Iron Age, especially in the vicinity of Ashton Keynes and Latton. Excavations in advance of gravel extraction have identified a number of settlements such as Cleveland Farm (Morse and Richards 1989; Coe *et al.* 1991) where a sequence from the later Iron Age to early post-Roman has been identified. Sites of this type are typical of the Upper Thames Valley and have many parallels in neighbouring Gloucestershire and Oxfordshire (*cf.* Roughground Farm, Lechlade, Allen *et al.* 1993).

The evidence for a Durotrigian area in the south of the county is further defined and possibly reinforced by the distribution of characteristic Durotrigian ceramic styles as far as the valley of the River Wylye and the southern edge of Salisbury Plain. This is associated with a distinctive nucleated settlement form represented by multiple ditch systems that can encompass large areas and are frequently associated with 'banjo' enclosures. The most notable concentration of these settlements, Ebsbury, Hamshill Ditches, Hanging Langford Camp, and Stockton Earthworks, is along the Great Ridge and in Grovely Wood, between the River Nadder and the River Wylye. All four sites continued as nucleated settlements in the Romano-British period (Corney 1989).

On the extreme eastern edge of the county there are a number of morphologically distinctive Late Iron Age sites that belong to a broad group extending onto the central Hampshire chalk. No examples are known to the west of the River Avon. These sites are characterised by large, double-ditched enclosures, associated in some cases with extensive and contemporary unenclosed settlement beyond. The best known example is the Boscombe Down West complex recorded by Richardson (1951) located within RAF Boscombe Down airfield, near Amesbury. Other examples of this type are known on Salisbury Plain at Coombe Down (Entwistle *et al.* 1994) and on Upavon Down, the latter being known only from air photography and as yet untested by excavation. These sites are of very similar form to Suddern Farm, Hampshire (Palmer 1984, 44; Cunliffe 2000), and Steepleton Hill, near Stockbridge, Hampshire, and are regarded as being a distinctive component of 'Atrebatic' Late Iron Age settlement (Cunliffe 2000). Boscombe Down, Coombe Down, and Suddern Farm continued to be occupied into the Roman period, whilst the complex on Steepleton Hill is known only from air photographs and has yet to be more thoroughly investigated.

In the southern and eastern areas of the county the nucleated settlements described are set within highly ordered landscapes comprising extensive field systems associated with enclosed and unenclosed settlements (Bowen 1990; Palmer 1984). In both areas we can see a range of later 1st millennium BC settlement forms that are typical of the Wessex chalk (*ibid.*). The settlement pattern of the same date in the northern area is still far from clear, being restricted primarily to the Upper Thames Valley gravels where air photography has provided a wealth of data (Leech 1977). There are, however, a number of common links, with all three regions having a number of morphologically distinctive later Iron Age 'banjo' type enclosures.

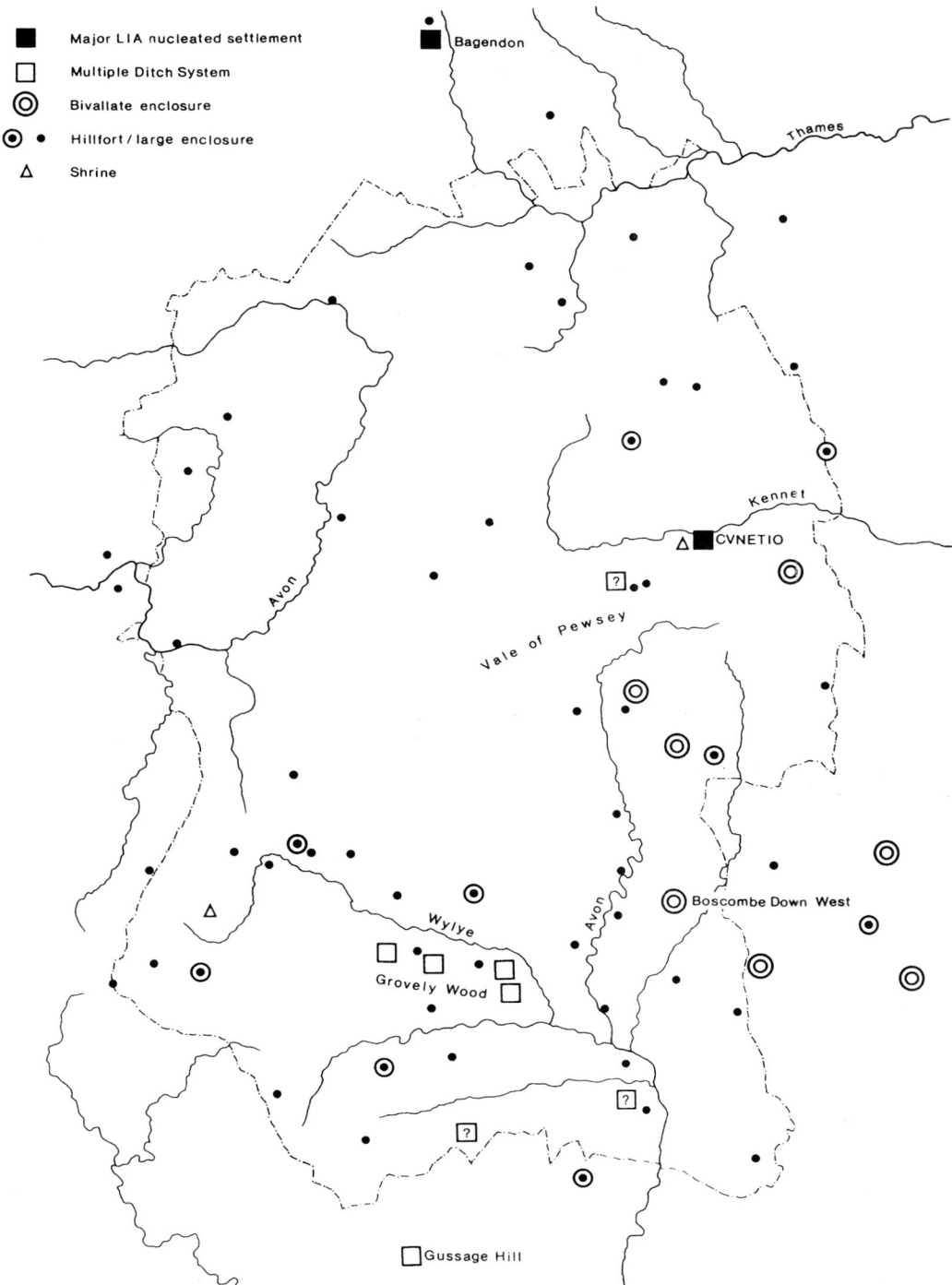

Fig. 2.2 Iron Age Wiltshire, showing selected sites to demonstrate the morphological diversity of pre-Roman settlement and other monument forms; source author

Urban sites with evidence for planning and public buildings

The nucleated settlements of Romano-British date fall into two morphologically distinct categories – urban-style sites and roadside settlements – although in a number of cases the sites are poorly understood and categorisation is at best tentative.

At present there are two sites that fit into the first category, Wanborough and Mildenhall. Both are located on major Roman roads that traverse the county. Wanborough appears in the Antonine Itinerary as Iter XIII (Rivet 1970) and its Roman name, *Durocornovium*, translates as 'fort of the Cornovii people' (Rivet and Smith 1979, 350). The Cornovii of *Durocornovium* are in all probability an otherwise unrecorded unit of the Dobunnic *civitas* and are not to be confused with the Cornovian *civitas* centred upon Wroxeter in Shropshire. The second site, Mildenhall, *Cunetio*, appears in the Itinerary as Iter XIV (Rivet 1970), although the derivation of the name, taken from the adjacent River Kennet, is still unresolved (Rivet and Smith 1979, 328).

Wanborough

The site of Wanborough, *Durocornovium*, is located on the eastern edge of the ever-expanding Swindon (Fig. 2.3). This partially excavated site is centred upon a planned core covering at least 16ha (although occupation may extend over an area of 25ha – 60 acres). A survey of the site published in 1821 by Colt Hoare shows that extensive earthworks marked the position of the town with a notable concentration in the angle formed by the junction of the roads from Mildenhall and Silchester (Hoare 1821, pl. facing p. 94). The current known extent of the site suggests that it is centred on the north-east side of Ermin Street, the Roman road linking Silchester (*Calleva Atrebatum*) with Cirencester (*Corinium Dobunnorum*), just to the north of the junction with the Roman road leading to Mildenhall (*Cunetio*) and Winchester (*Venta Belgarum*). The evidence of excavation and air photography suggests that the core of the planned area has an orthogonal grid laid out parallel to Ermin Street (Anderson and Wacher 1980; Burnham and Wacher 1990; Wacher 1975). The name *Durocornovium* suggests that there ought to be a substantial Late Iron Age settlement in the immediate vicinity but to date the evidence for this has not been forthcoming. The origins of the Roman settlement remain obscure and although a Claudio-Neronian military presence has been postulated on the basis of ceramics, coins, and other finds, no structural remains have been identified (Anderson and Wacher 1980, 117). The topographic location of the site does not appear to be especially advantageous. It is low-lying, located on Kimmeridge Clay, very poorly drained and prone to flooding. Despite the locational disadvantages, the extensive planned street grid and the identification of at least one substantial public building (see below) make it clear that *Durocornovium* was of some regional importance, most probably a *pagus* centre for the Cornovii.

All of the recorded modern excavations at Wanborough have been in advance of major road construction and flood prevention schemes. These have provided details of buildings along the frontage of Ermin Street where it passes through the heart of the settlement (Anderson and Wacher 1980; Wacher 1975). The initial construction of Ermin

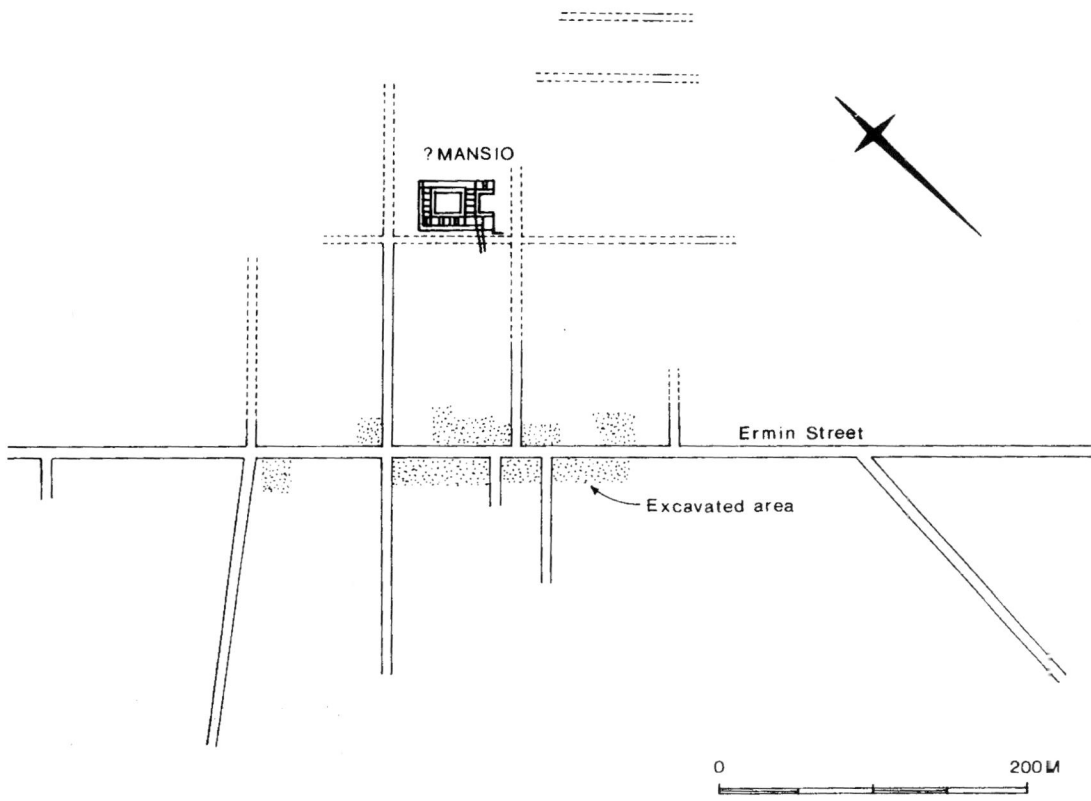

*Fig. 2.3 The settlement at Wanborough (*Durocornovium*). The possible* mansio *is known only from air photographs, excavation being restricted to the Ermin Street frontage (after Burnham and Wacher 1990)*

Street is dated to the Neronian period and at least one rectangular timber structure aligned on the road and contemporary with it has been recognised (Anderson and Wacher 1980, 117). The excavators postulated a possible break or change in the character of the occupation *c.* AD 80 with large quantities of pottery and industrial debris including glass and iron slag being deposited in a side-ditch of Ermin Street (*ibid.*). By the end of the 1st or early in the 2nd century, new buildings appeared beside Ermin Street. These were mainly of timber, although at least part of one building had sarsen footings and daub walls that overlay the earlier side-ditch.

The excavations have not established a date for the laying out and construction of the street grid, but air photographs taken in 1975 recorded a substantial stone courtyard building on the same alignment as the grid (Phillips and Walters 1977). Interpreted as a *mansio*, the building measures 48m by 34m and features a central courtyard surrounded by an ambulatory (Fig. 7.2). Across an adjacent street, to the south west of the building, further faint crop-marks may indicate the presence of an associated bath-house. The plan of the courtyard building compares favourably with other *mansiones* in Britain dated to the Hadrianic period (Black 1995, 32). If this date should prove to be correct, and the orthogonal street grid is contemporary with the postulated *mansio*, Wanborough may have been replanned on an ambitious scale during the second quarter of the 2nd century AD.

In the 3rd and 4th centuries AD, the Ermin Street frontage was flanked on both sides of the road by a number of buildings employing a variety of construction techniques. Some had stone foundations (although the nature of their superstructure is not certain) whilst others were of sleeper-beam construction, but of greatest interest was the recognition of alignments of packed stone settings. These appear to have been carefully levelled and have been interpreted as supports for floor-joists to which the walls could have been attached (Anderson and Wacher 1980, 119). This identification appears to be reinforced by the correlation between these buildings and the distribution of a range of small objects that could easily have fallen through gaps in the floorboards. This form of construction, effectively raising the timber building above the contemporary ground level, would appear to be highly appropriate at a low-lying site that was prone to flooding.

Wanborough appears to have had a short-lived, or even possibly unfinished, defensive circuit provisionally dated to the late 2nd or 3rd century AD. The evidence is both confused and complex but appears to include traces of footings for a stone gateway, possibly with an associated curtain wall and ditch. The history and archaeology of the decline and abandonment of the site are still far from clear.

Mildenhall

The Late Iron Age and Romano-British settlement of *Cunetio*, close to the modern village of Mildenhall, represents one of the most extensive and interesting Roman urban complexes in the county (Fig. 2.4). Unlike Wanborough, the site has not been built on since its abandonment and the only threat – albeit a very real one – comes from continued cultivation. The first detailed description of Mildenhall was given by Colt Hoare (Hoare 1821) who divided the site into 'Upper Cunetio' and 'Lower Cunetio'. He erroneously located the latter in the centre of the present village, the main focus of Roman settlement in reality being centred on Black Field on the south side of the River Kennet, where evidence for occupation spreads over an area of at least 18ha (44 acres). Little remains to be seen of the Roman town today, most of our data concerning the site being derived from air photography (Corney 1997a; Wilson 1975), limited excavation (Corney 1997a, n7), and a pioneering geophysical survey (Clark 1990, 14). During the Roman period the site was at a pivotal point in the road system with at least six routes converging on the crossing of the River Kennet. The town is also famous for the '*Cunetio* Treasure', the single largest find of *antoniniani* from Roman Britain (Besly and Bland 1983). In the 1st, 2nd and early 3rd centuries, the site appears to have been the principle marketing centre for the local coarse ware potting industry based in Savernake Forest (Hodder 1974; Swan 1975; Timby this volume). In contrast to Wanborough, *Cunetio* has very good evidence for a large Late Iron Age predecessor and although the status of the Roman town is unknown, it is a distinct possibility that the settlement was also the centre for a *pagus*.

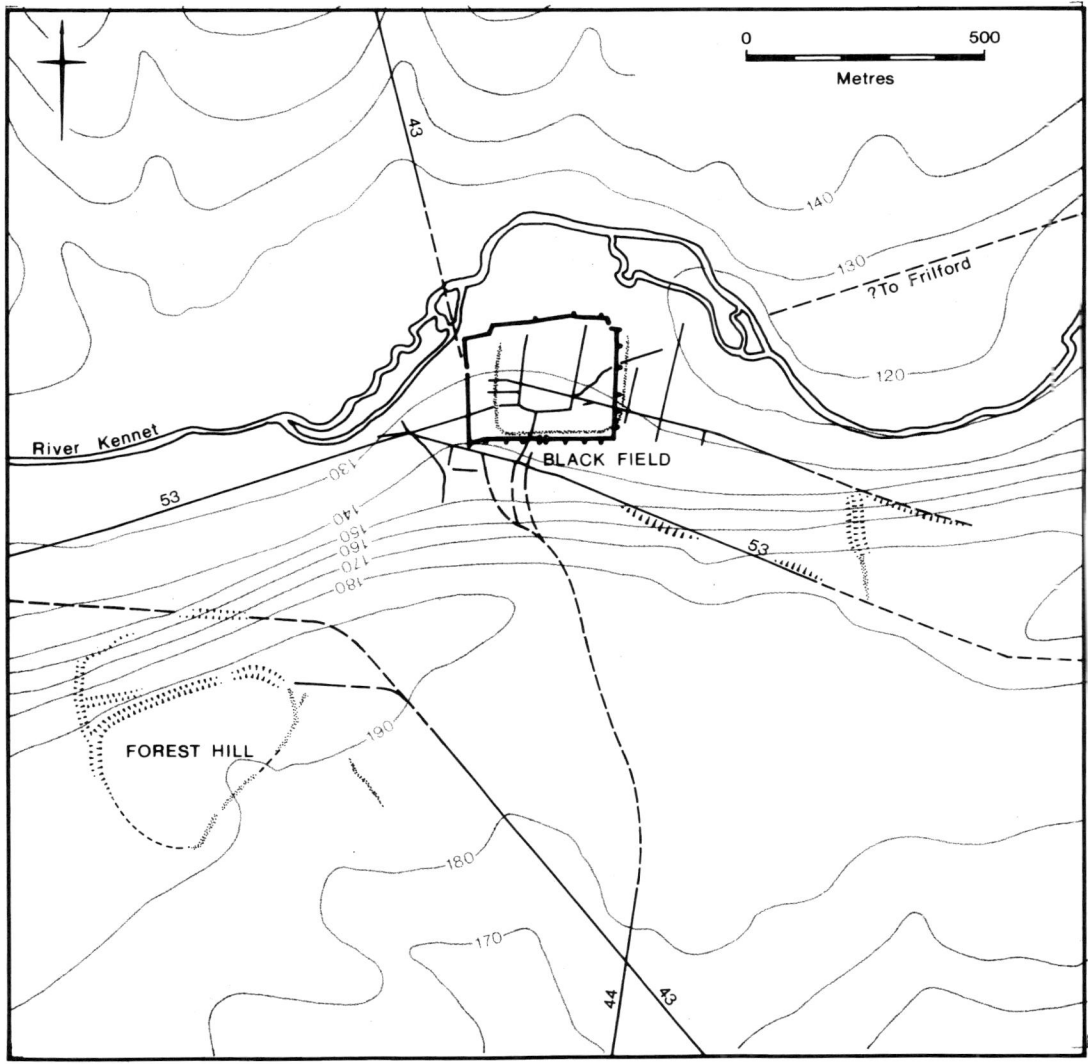

Fig. 2.4 The location of Cunetio *(Black Field) and Forest Hill, with the Roman road network in the immediate vicinity; source author*

FOREST HILL

There is little doubt that *Cunetio* was a major pre-Roman centre. Much Late Iron Age material has been recorded from the region, including rich burials and numerous finds of Iron Age coins (Corney 1989; 1997a; Cunliffe 1991, 136; Robinson 1993). On Forest Hill – Colt Hoare's 'Upper Cunetio' – to the south of the present village of Mildenhall, is a univallate enclosure encompassing an area of approximately 11 ha, 27 acres (Fig. 2.5). The south-west corner of the circuit is lost, but is probably marked by the cutting followed by the present A4 road. One original entrance is known on the east side. This appears to be associated with

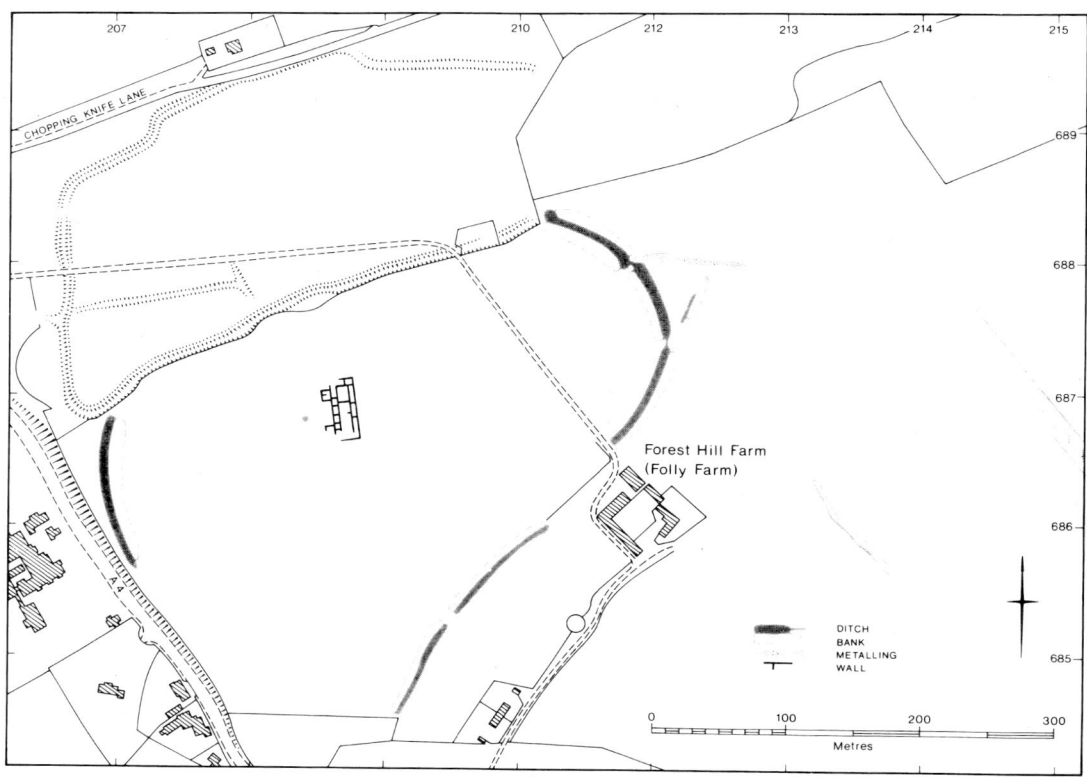

Fig. 2.5 The probable Late Iron Age and Romano-British complex on Forest Hill; source author

an isolated length of plough-levelled bank and ditch that may represent an outwork. On the north side of the enclosure further earthworks extend down the steep scarp. The general feel of the complex and the associated sites in the vicinity suggests that the Forest Hill complex was the regional *oppidum* at the time of the Roman invasion of AD 43 (Corney 1989). The eastern entrance of the Forest Hill enclosure also appears to be the original destination of the Roman road, Margary 43 (Fig. 2.4), approaching *Cunetio* from *Venta Belgarum* (Winchester). Cropmarks show that the road was metalled and defined by side ditches 10m apart. This road was probably later diverted via Margary 44 to lead into *Cunetio* at Black Field. It is possible that the original course was associated with a short-lived military presence within the *oppidum*. A Roman well excavated within the enclosure in the 1880s produced a probable early Roman military mount (Annable 1976). The detailed arguments concerning a possible short-lived Claudian military presence on Forest Hill have been discussed in greater detail and at length elsewhere (Corney 1997a, 339) and will not be repeated here. The site continued to be occupied after the Roman conquest, and air photography has revealed a substantial Roman building, west-facing with a pair of projecting wings, within the enclosure (Fig. 7.15). The location of a villa-like building within a large Iron Age earthwork can be paralleled at a number of sites in southern Britain as at Tidbury Ring, Hampshire (St Joseph 1953; Wilson 1974) and The Ditches, North Cerney, Gloucestershire (Trow 1988). Colt

Hoare also records and illustrates a bronze spoon and a figurine, probably of Venus, found on Forest Hill (Fig. 6.5; Hoare 1821, 71).

BLACK FIELD

Finds of pre-Flavian coins, pottery and items of 1st-century military equipment at Black Field (Annable 1966; 1976; Soames 1878; Griffiths 1983; this volume) indicate that occupation adjacent to the crossing point of the River Kennet began soon after the Roman conquest (Fig. 2.6). Given the locally strategic position of the site, it is tempting to postulate the presence of an early fort here, possibly succeeding a temporary occupation of Forest Hill. Despite the presence of pre-Flavian material no structures have yet been located that could form part of such an establishment, and if such a fort exists its remains may lie buried deep beneath the later town (Frere and St Joseph 1983, 167; Corney 1997a, 347).

Modern investigation of the site was initiated by the late Tony Clark and Ken Annable, who undertook a series of geophysical surveys and excavations in Black Field during the 1950s and 60s. These were focused upon a succession of defensive circuits revealed by aerial reconnaissance in 1949 and subsequent years (St Joseph 1953, pl. xiii, 2). Since the Annable and Clark campaign there has been no further systematic fieldwork at Black Field although 'rescue' excavation recorded a coffined burial (Annable 1980) and the 'Cunetio Treasure' was discovered by metal detectorists (Besly and Bland 1983). Most recently Corney (1997a) has plotted all of the available air photographic data for Black Field and summarised the current state of knowledge.

The air photographs show clear traces of a regular, planned street grid over much of the central and eastern parts of the town. This is centred on a road approaching the site from the east with a number of irregularly spaced side streets laid out at right angles. A further road parallel to this and 160m to the south is probably the main road from Silchester (Margary 53). One side street, to the east of the later defences, can be traced as far as the flood plain of the River Kennet. A number of stone buildings visible on the air photographs are aligned on this grid (Fig. 2.6, nos 3, 5, 7, 12, 14, 15, 17, 19 and 20), but none have been investigated. Of these structures one, no. 7, is of particular note. This building, measuring approximately 35m x 15m, has large areas of metalling to the north and east and is very close to the findspot of the 'Cunetio Treasure'. The western part of the town, by contrast, displays an irregular plan with a number of metalled streets or lanes converging on a point 100m west of the south-west corner of the later stone defences. Air photographs of this area also show a dense pattern of pit clusters and linear features that probably indicate property plots associated with mainly timber structures.

There are two especially large stone structures visible on the air photographs (Fig. 2.6, nos 1 and 8). One of these (no. 1) is of winged corridor form with a large apse on the north side and was partially investigated by Annable and Clark (*WANHM*, 58, 245). The building is either contemporary with or later than the construction of the stone defences of c. AD 360-380 (see below). In the centre of the town a large courtyard building (no. 8) is known. This building, measuring approximately 60m by 40m, has at least 24 rooms grouped in three ranges on the west, north and east sides and a south-facing court. The central position of this structure would suggest an official or public function, possibly as a *mansio*.

THE DEFENCES

Two defensive circuits are visible on the air photographs, one apparently consisting of an earthwork only; the other comprising a substantial free-standing wall with projecting bastions and a monumental south gate (Fig. 2.6).

An earthen circuit, known from air photography, forms a double-ditched sub-rectangular enclosure with rounded corners at the south-west and south-east angles. The position of the north side is unknown but it may underlie the stone circuit on the edge of the River Kennet floodplain. This would give a maximum enclosed area of approximately 6ha (14.7 acres). The enclosure shows most clearly along the southern and western sides where a pair of parallel ditches is visible. A trench cut across the eastern line of the circuit, close to the south-east corner, located a ditch which had either been deliberately backfilled or had the upper fill consolidated, prior to the construction of the stone defences (*WANHM*, 57, 235). Four possible entrances are known. The clearest is that on the south side, 60m east of the south-west corner, where a 10m wide causeway interrupts the ditches. This carries a

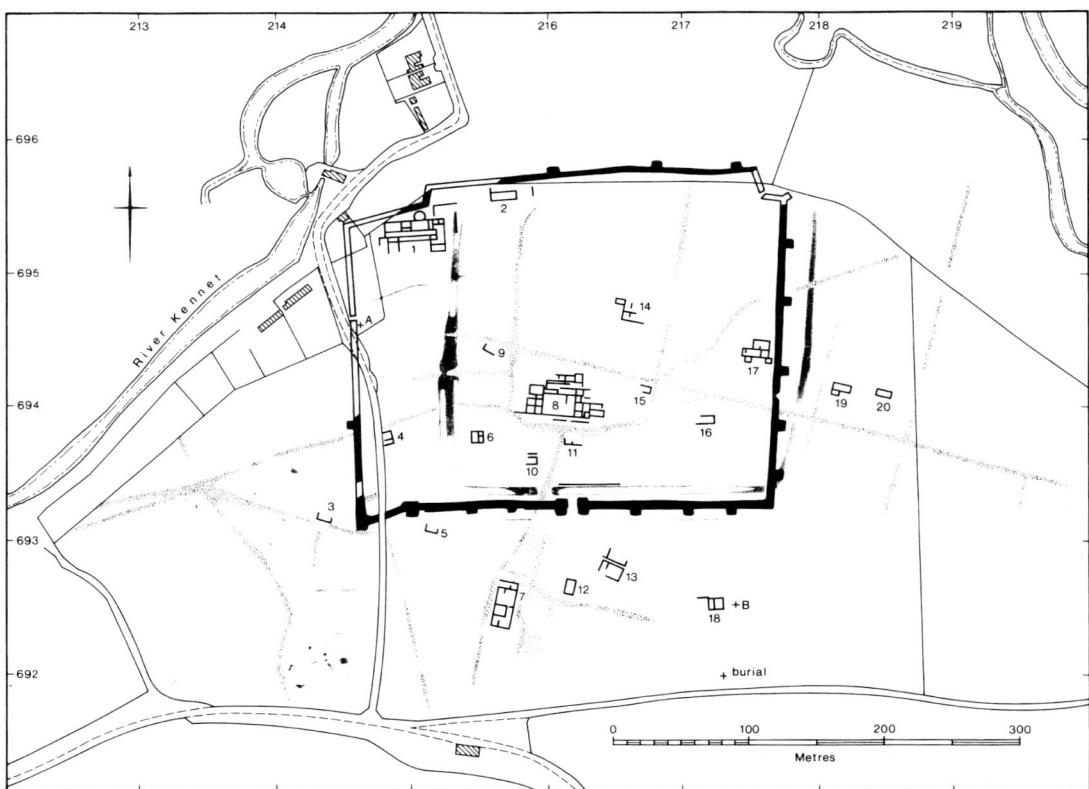

Fig. 2.6 Cunetio *(Mildenhall); plan largely derived from air photographs with additional detail of the stone defences from the work of Annable and Clark; source author*

metalled street which aims for the large stone building (no. 7) and links with the roads (Margary 43 and 44) approaching the site from Winchester (*Venta Belgarum*) and Stratford-sub-Castle (*Sorviodunum*). On the western side, an entrance is visible 85m north of the south-west corner. South of the causeway a third ditch appears to supplement the double-ditch system for a distance of 50m. On the eastern side there are two possible entrances. The most convincing is located 50m north of the south-east corner where a *c.* 8m-wide causeway carries the road (Margary 53) from Silchester (*Calleva Atrebatum*). Ninety metres north of this, a further road approaching from the north-east crosses the ditch although no causeway is visible.

The dating evidence for this circuit is meagre, but a possible context may be indicated through comparison with other sites in southern Britain where *mansiones* of 2nd-century date are frequently associated with the provision of an earthwork defence. At neighbouring Wanborough the defensive circuit is provisionally dated to the late second or early third century (see above). At Neatham, Hampshire (Millett and Graham 1986), a double-ditched circuit is also dated to the 2nd century, as is a triple-ditched enclosure at Crab Farm, south of Badbury Rings, Dorset (Papworth 1997). It is possible that the earthwork circuit at *Cunetio* is part of a widespread system of *mansiones* associated with defences and, possibly, having a local administrative function (Black 1995). The earthen defences at *Cunetio* appear to be relatively short-lived – by the time the stone-walled circuit was constructed their position had been forgotten and the south wall had been placed partly over the outer ditch and the east wall across both ditches.

The earthen defences were replaced by a free-standing stone wall on a new alignment associated with projecting bastions and at least one gate of monumental form. Only on the south side can an associated single ditch be seen. This is clearest from the south gate to the south-east angle. No trace of the ditch can be discerned on the west and north sides. This new circuit enclosed an area of approximately 7.5ha (18.5 acres). Small scale excavations on the line of the south and east sides of the circuit revealed the heavily robbed remains of the wall. The footings varied in width from 5m (east wall) to 5.9m (south wall), with evidence for an internal offset reducing the width to 3.8m. Where best preserved the wall was built of mortared flint rubble faced with dressed oolitic limestone blocks.

A total of seventeen bastions are now known, six on the east wall, seven on the south (excluding the pair which flank the south gate), one on the west, and three on the north. Spacing of the bastions is not regular, varying from 30m (south wall) to 80m (north wall) apart. If the average interval for the south wall – 37m, and the east wall – 39m, is applied to the north and west walls it becomes highly probable that further bastions await discovery.

Three gates are known, to the west, south and north-east. The south gate, located 145m west of the south-east corner is of monumental style and, curiously, lay some 20m east of the causeway across the earlier circuit carrying the road from Winchester and Stratford-sub-Castle. In form the gate is flanked by massive projecting towers similar to the west gate of the late 3rd-century stone fort at Richborough (Bushe-Fox 1926) and, possibly, the period VIII (late 3rd-century) north gate at Brough-on-Humber (Wacher 1969).

The west gate, a single carriageway opening 70m south of the north-west corner, was excavated in 1959-60 and 1964 (*WANHM*, 57; 58; 60) although its form remains uncertain.

The carriageway showed little evidence of use and had subsequently been reduced to a narrow passage suitable only for pedestrian traffic. An intriguing aspect of the late 4th-century defences of *Cunetio* is the apparent lack of a gate on the east side. The cropmarks clearly show the east wall crossing and apparently blocking the line of the road approaching from the east. However if there was a gate here of similar form to that on the west with a paved carriageway, it would not necessarily show as a cropmark. Only excavation could resolve this problem. All previously published plans show a probable gate in the curious dog-leg that forms the north-east corner of the circuit. The evidence for this is ambiguous and a full assessment must await the publication of the final report.

The clearest evidence for the date of the stone defences came from a coin hoard deposited *c.* AD 360 found during the excavation of the west gate. In addition, a ditch pre-dating the gate produced a coin of *c.* AD 354-8 from the primary silt. This strongly points to a construction date after *c.* AD 360 and it is most likely that the stone circuit at *Cunetio* is of Valentinianic date.

The apparent disregard for the existing lay-out of the site with which the stone defences were laid out would suggest that late 4th-century *Cunetio* underwent a radical change of function. The provision of a massive and monumental wall can only have been undertaken by the state. There must be a strong case for arguing that *Cunetio* became a regional administrative centre and, perhaps, a base for a component of the *Comitatensian* forces in the province of *Britannia Prima*. The site is also strategically sited close to areas of attested late Roman intensive agricultural production on Salisbury Plain, the Marlborough Downs (Fowler 2000), and the western Berkshire Downs (Gaffney and Tingle 1989). There is also a significant concentration of late Roman military metalwork known from the hinterland of *Cunetio* that would support this argument (Corney and Griffiths forthcoming; Griffiths this volume).

Roadside settlements

The majority of the remaining known nucleated Roman settlements in the county are located on the known or suspected road system. Some, such as *Sorviodunum*, are sited at a major junction of the road network and may be reasonably expected to have a local administrative function. Others, such as Nettleton or Silbury, may be closely associated with religious activities. Further sites are still poorly understood and in urgent need of greater study. In the latter category the sites at The Ham, near Westbury, *Verlucio*, and Easton Grey stand out.

Stratford-sub-Castle/Old Sarum (Sorviodunum)

Recorded in Iter XII and Iter XV of the Antonine Itinerary (Rivet 1971; Rivet and Smith 1979, 461), this extensive but poorly understood settlement was located at a major nodal point on the Roman road system that passes through southern Wiltshire (Fig. 2.7). Although the -*dunum* element of the name clearly refers to the hillfort of Old Sarum, the meaning of the *Sorvio* prefix remains unclear (*ibid.*). Although Roman material and possible structural remains (see below) have been recorded from within Old Sarum hillfort, the main areas of settlement appear to centre upon two areas outside the ramparts. The first lies to the south west of the hillfort along the line of the 'Portway', the Roman road from Silchester to Dorchester (Margary 4b and 4c) at Stratford-sub-Castle, and the second along Bishopdown, south-east of the hillfort and beside the presumed course of the Roman road (Margary 424) running towards the New Forest and Southampton region (Stone and Algar 1955).

Iron Age activity and settlement in the region is dense (Hampton and Palmer 1977, fig. 7). Details of the chronology of Old Sarum hillfort are lacking and it is by no means clear if the site was actually occupied at the time of the invasion of AD 43. Observation of pipeline work and rescue excavation on Bishopdown and beyond the East Gate of Old Sarum has recorded evidence of middle and later Iron Age occupation over a considerable area although no coherent plan has yet emerged (Borthwick and Chandler 1984; Musty 1959; Musty and Rahtz 1964).

Structural remains of the Roman period are fragmentary and widely scattered across the areas described above. Within the hillfort, two substantial walls, one still standing approximately 5 feet (1.5m) high and constructed of flints with an ashlar face, were found at a depth of 17 feet (5m) within the Norman castle mound (Fig. 2.7, a; Montgomerie 1948, 132). The floor of this structure sealed an Iron Age pit and although a Roman date could not be conclusively established, it must be considered a strong possibility. Otherwise, finds of Roman material from within the hillfort are sparse (Stone and Algar 1955) and it has been suggested (*ibid.*, 103) that Norman and later occupation has removed much of the evidence. Whilst this is a possibility, it is far more probable that any Roman period activity within the hillfort is likely to have been of a more restricted and specialised nature. The suggestion by Shortt (*ibid.*, 104) that the remains encountered within the Norman castle mound are those of a Romano-Celtic temple remains an attractive one.

On Bishopdown, Roman material, including stone roofing tiles, coins and pottery ranging from the 2nd to late 4th centuries, has been recorded over an area of at least 4ha, 10 acres (Stone and Algar 1955, 106). The area is now covered by the northern suburbs of modern Salisbury and is unlikely to become available for systematic archaeological investigation in the foreseeable future (Borthwick and Chandler 1984). Despite the presence of this modern development, the distribution of material would suggest that occupation took the form of a ribbon settlement, possibly flanking a road along the Bishopdown ridge. This postulated route would most likely have formed a junction with Margary 4b and Margary 44 just outside the eastern entrance to Old Sarum and have then headed towards the New Forest and Southampton Water area to form the northern end of Margary 424.

The best body of evidence for the core area of *Sorviodunum* comes from the village of Stratford-sub-Castle along the line of the Roman road from Old Sarum to Dorchester (Margary 4c). The line of the Portway has been confirmed both by excavation and a series of remarkably clear parchmarks recorded by air photography in the late 1980s and early 1990s. Observation and small-scale excavation during the 1960s can now be correlated

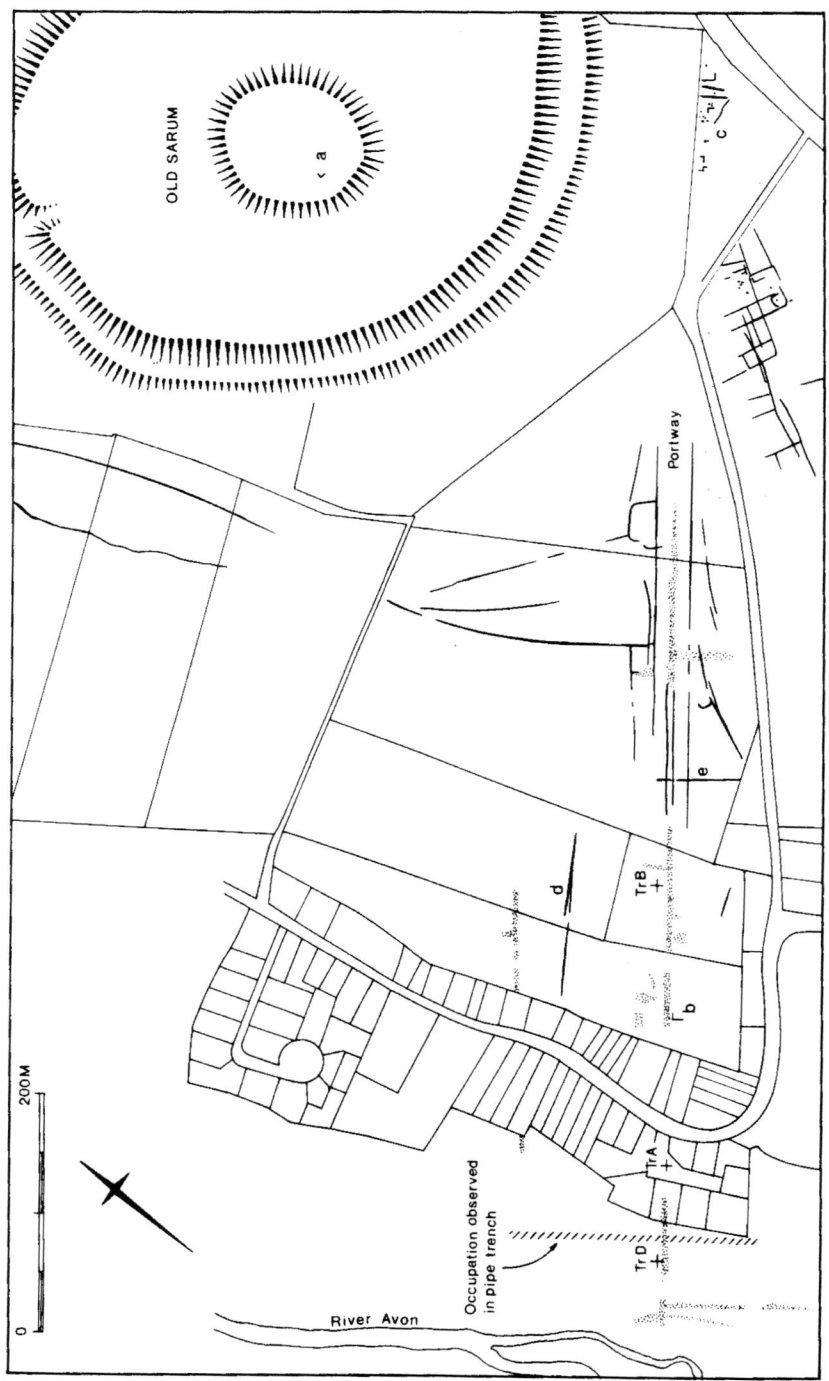

Fig. 2.7 Stratford-sub-Castle (Sorviodunum), plan based on air photographs showing the location of small-scale investigations and observations referred to in the text; source author

with the evidence from recent air photographs to give an outline picture of the settlement in this area (Fig. 2.7). None of the excavations have been fully published but brief summary accounts can be found in *WANHM*, 58, 471; *WANHM*, 61, 106, and *WANHM*, 65, 208 (no detailed plans accompany any of these reports). The main concentration of material comes from an area to the east of the River Avon, (Fig. 2.7: Tr A, Tr B and Tr D) although one trench on the west side of the river produced evidence for Roman-period occupation and a late 1st-century AD construction date for the Roman road (*WANHM*, 61, 106). At a number of locations east of the River Avon evidence for substantial structures has been recorded including box-tiles, ceramic and stone roof tiles, plaster and rammed surfaces. Most of the recorded structures front onto the Portway and in one area stone buildings were seen to have collapsed onto the road metalling (*WANHM*, 65, 208). At one point between the present village of Stratford-sub-Castle and the River Avon, observation of a pipeline cutting the Portway at right angles recorded Roman building debris extending for a distance of 213m (700 feet). Pottery spanning the 1st to 4th centuries was recorded and a succession of four floors (*ibid.*).

The plot of cropmarks and parchmarks (Fig. 2.7) coupled with the above observations now allow a tentative re-interpretation of the extent and character of *Sorviodunum*. The parchmarks are clearest in the open grassland to the north east and south west of Stratford-sub-Castle village and are dominated by the course of the Roman road, the Portway. The metalling of the road shows as a band up to approximately 5m (17 feet) wide. Towards the north east it can be seen to be positioned between side-ditches approximately 28m (92 feet) apart, a spacing in close accordance with the 26m (84 feet) width recorded by excavation (*WANHM*, 61, 106). The course of the road can be traced as far as the crossing of the River Avon at Tadpole Island. The air photographs also show a number of probable side streets or lanes set at right angles to the Portway. Between Stratford-sub-Castle and the River Avon, one side street can be seen extending south east from the road for at least 150m. Immediately to the north east of the modern village another possible street is located 120m to the north west of the road running parallel to it. Although the parchmarks and cropmarks are fragmentary, they are sufficient to suggest that there may be a core area of *Sorviodunum* with a planned, regular grid. Much of the crucial area is under grass and would be easily accessible for geophysical investigations that could confirm this and other details. The air photographs also show other rectangular-shaped areas of parching close to the edge of the Portway. These have average dimensions of approximately 10m x 7.5m, and it is tempting to interpret them as the floors of Roman structures. Their location close to the Portway is in keeping with the structures observed by excavation (*WANHM*, 65, 208). At one point (Fig. 2.7, b) part of a stone structure can be seen to front directly onto the south-east edge of the Portway. On the basis of excavation and the air photographs the core area of the settlement would appear to extend for a distance of approximately 500m to the north east from the River Avon. Beyond this point the side-ditches of the Portway are clearly visible suggesting that occupation onto the road frontage is less dense. If the width of the area over which Roman debris was recorded during observation of the pipeline (see above) is added to the extent of remains along the Portway, we have a potential area of at least 10ha (25 acres) for the settlement at Stratford-sub-Castle.

Closer to Old Sarum a small area of cropmarks set at right angles to the line of the Portway may indicate further Roman activity (Fig. 2.7, c), although the documented medieval suburbs of Old Sarum are known to have extended into this area and a post-Roman origin is possible. The further complex of cropmarks to the south of c is not aligned on the Portway and their origin and date is unknown. Again a post-Roman date seems most likely.

Although detailed information is frustratingly meagre, the status and function of *Sorviodunum* needs to be addressed. The settlement is sited at a junction of a number of important Roman roads in the provincial network. To the north it is linked to *Cunetio* and *Durocornovium*, both of which have substantial buildings that are best interpreted as *mansiones*. To the south west, at the crossing of the River Stour, lies the recently discovered settlement at Crab Farm, Shapwick, near Badbury hillfort in Dorset. This settlement is most probably the *Vindocladia* of the Antonine Itinerary and has been the focus of detailed study in recent years (Papworth 1997). Recent excavations here have shown that an earthen defensive circuit here is likely to be of 2nd-century AD date and it has been proposed that it was the site of a *mansio* (ibid.).

The presence of a *mansio*, or *mutatio*, at *Sorviodunum* should be seriously considered. The possibility of a regular street grid invites comparisons with *Durocornovium* and *Cunetio* and the distance of *Sorviodunum* from the latter and from *Vindocladia* (33km and 36km respectively) would be appropriate. Although proof of such a structure is lacking, the finds of Roman building materials at Stratford-sub-Castle show that structures of some size and pretension are certainly present. If this assertion should prove to be correct then, like *Cunetio* and *Durocornovium*, *Sorviodunum* may also have been a *pagus* centre acting as a local market and administrative centre.

There are no records of any features that could be considered as elements of a defensive system at *Sorviodunum*, although an earthen circuit might reasonably be expected if the site did indeed act as a local centre. There are two ditches visible as cropmarks on air photographs (Fig. 2.7, d and e) that would repay investigation to ascertain their character and date. One, d, is almost parallel to the Portway and 80m north west of it, the other, e, crosses its line at right angles. Whether these ditches actually met and form part of a full circuit can only be established by geophysics or excavation. However their location, close to the core area where most of the Roman structural material has been recovered and adjacent to the crossing of the River Avon, is of note.

Much of the detailed history of Roman *Sorviodunum* is unclear, but ironically it is one of the few immediately post-Roman places in Wiltshire that features in the historical record. The Anglo-Saxon Chronicle entry for 552 records that Cynric defeated the Britons at *Searobyrg*, the Anglo-Saxon name for Old Sarum (Gelling 1988, 54-5). This would imply that there was still a sub-Roman population and authority in the Salisbury area in the mid 6th century AD. By this date it is tempting to suggest that the hillfort of Old Sarum had been reoccupied as a regional centre and stronghold in much the same fashion as South Cadbury or Cadbury Congresbury in Somerset (Alcock 1995; Rahtz *et al.* 1992). Bruce

Eagles, in a brilliant and highly stimulating paper (1994, 13-32; see also Eagles this volume) has drawn attention to a number of early Germanic cemeteries in the Salisbury area, and suggests that it may be possible to recognise a sub-Roman enclave centred on *Sorviodunum*, possibly dependent on Germanic, or more likely, Frankish military assistance.

Sorviodunum offers enormous potential for further research.

White Walls/Easton Grey

This site is located on the Fosse Way roughly mid-way between Bath (*Aquæ Sulis*) and Cirencester (*Corinium*) at the point where the Roman road crosses the Sherston branch of the River Avon (Figs 2.8 and 2.9). The first detailed record of the site was provided by Colt Hoare (Hoare 1821, 100-1), although Collinson, writing *c.* 1790, recorded the discovery of coins, a tessellated pavement and foundations. Colt Hoare also described and published a detailed survey of the area with a plan showing the extent of the surviving earthworks (*ibid.*, fig. opposite p. 94, reproduced here as Fig. 2.8). The Roman name for the settlement is lost although Colt Hoare mistakenly identified the site as the *Mutuantonis* of the Ravenna Cosmography (*ibid.*, 100), now known to be erroneous (Rivet and Smith 1979, 185-215, 476-7). The site has never been methodically investigated and the description here is based on antiquarian accounts, records of stray finds, and on air photographic plots and an earthwork survey undertaken by the author (Fig. 2.9).

Traces of the settlement extend for almost 1km along the Fosse Way on either side of the River Avon, and traces of Roman settlement can be seen over an area of 9ha (22

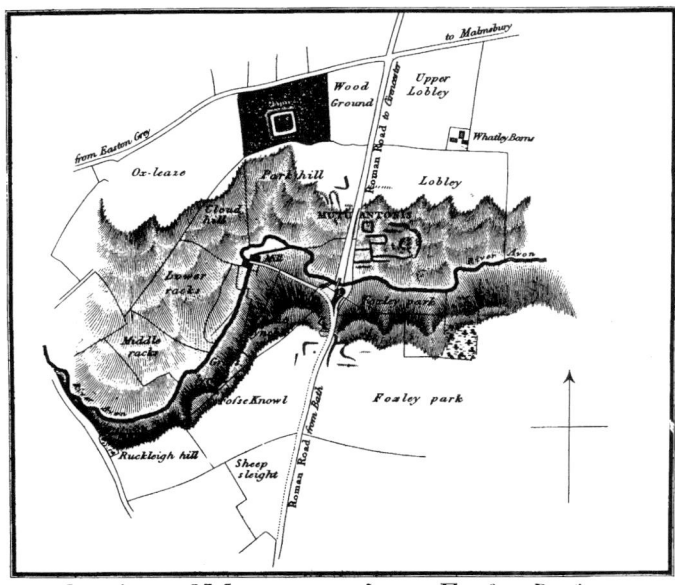

Station of **Mutuantonis** . *Foxley Park* &c.

Fig. 2.8 White Walls/Easton Grey, plan published by Sir Richard Colt-Hoare showing extent of visible surface features (Hoare 1821)

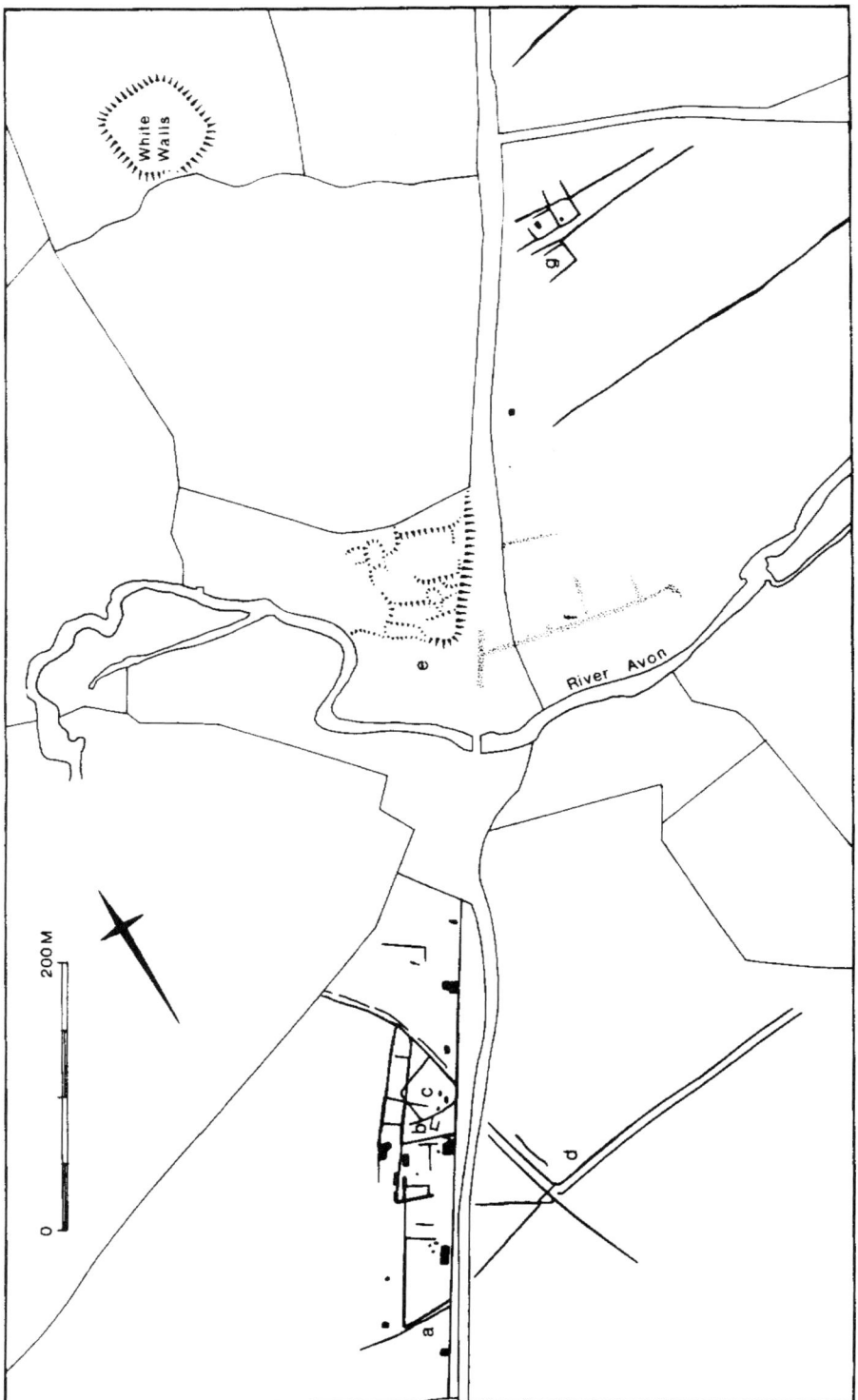

Fig. 2.9 White Walls/Easton Grey, plan showing features visible on air photographs and surviving earthworks, cf. Fig 2.8; source author

acres). Five hundred metres north of the point where the Fosse Way crosses the River Avon is an earthwork enclosure, known as Whitewalls, in Whitewalls Wood. Sometimes, erroneously, it has been described as a moat but the form of the earthwork and the area enclosed (0.4ha) is much more in keeping with other sites of a late prehistoric or Roman date in the area (Ian Powlesland, pers. comm.).

The course of the Fosse Way survives as a 'green lane' and descends the steep north-facing scarp to the River Avon in a series of dog-leg turns defined by a terraceway. The means by which the road crossed the River Avon is unclear. The river is fordable at this point and some traces of a possible stone surface are visible in the south bank. The modern bridge is on the line of the Roman road and, on the north side of the river, is adjacent to a substantial earthen ramp of unknown date that may mark the site of an earlier, possibly Roman, bridge abutment (*WANHM*, 46, 270).

Stray finds from the site include coins ranging from *denarii* of Julius Cæsar and Mark Antony to late 4th-century issues (Grinsell 1957, 68; Smith 1987, 291). First to 4th-century pottery, including a mortarium signed by DOINVS, a potter who worked near Brockley Hill in Hertfordshire in the late 1st century (Castle 1972), has also been found, as well as glass and metalwork (Grinsell 1957). Two pieces of sculpture, one now lost, the other in Wiltshire Heritage Museum, are also known (Cunliffe and Fulford 1982). The surviving piece is part of a female head, less than life size, with unusual headgear comprising a close-fitting cap and carved in a native style (*ibid.*, 37, no. 136, pl. 35; Fig. 8.10). The second piece, now missing, comprises a relief surmounted by a pediment with three standing male figures, probably suppliants, approaching a seated figure, possibly a *Genius* of Mars. Within the pediment is an inscription reading CIVILIS FEGIT (*ibid*, 34, no. 120, pl. 31).

The air photographs of the White Walls/Easton Grey area suggest that the landscape was already highly ordered before the construction of the Fosse Way. In the vicinity of the settlement a series of ditched boundaries are visible on a north-south and east-west alignment (Fig. 2.9). North of the River Avon this system can be seen to extend for a distance of at least 2.5km. The enclosure in Whitewalls Wood and other enclosed sites in the area also share this alignment. Thus it would appear that the Fosse Way was imposed on a landscape with apparent disregard for the existing layout. The boundary alignment, however, appears to have been retained in the Roman period. At the southern end of the site the limits of the settlement clearly respect one of these boundary features and share its alignment (Fig. 2.9, a).

The cropmarks of the settlement south of the River Avon show a classic roadside configuration with a series of properties, defined by ditches, parallel to the line of the Fosse Way. Cropmarks indicating areas of settlement are confined to the western side of the Fosse Way and a number of rectilinear 'block-marks' abutting the west side-ditch of the Roman road are most likely marking the location of structures. These appear to be set within ditched compounds and at one point (Fig. 2.9, b) part of a stone building can be seen. Immediately adjacent to this, at c, a small trapezoidal enclosure is integral with one of the earlier boundaries mentioned above and may be part of a pre-Roman settlement. On the east side of the Fosse Way the cropmarks are of ditches on the pre-road alignment and include a double-ditched feature, probably a track (Fig. 2.9, d) that makes a 90° turn and can be seen to link with the trapezoidal enclosure (Fig. 2.9, c). The plan of the site published by Colt Hoare – generally a reliable source (Fig. 2.8) – shows earthworks on the east side of the Fosse Way, and it is possible that settlement did extend across to this side of the road although nothing is now visible on the available air cover.

The main focus of the settlement appears to be on the north side of the River Avon. Colt Hoare shows extensive earthworks in the field called 'Lobley' (Fig. 2.8) and further earthworks (not shown by Colt Hoare) survive immediately west of the Fosse Way to the north of the river crossing (Fig. 2.9, e). Here, a series of terraces, set at right angles to the Fosse Way, contain the well-preserved remains of platforms that have produced finds of Romano-British pottery and pennant sandstone roof tiles (fieldwork by the author 1998). To the north of this, in the field called Park Hill on the plan of 1820 (Fig. 2.8), extensive spreads of Roman pottery are visible for a distance of up to 100m to the west of the Fosse Way. East of the Roman road, the air photographs show a possible metalled side street running parallel to the River Avon for a distance of 150m on the same alignment as the pre-Fosse Way boundaries (Fig. 2.9, f). This may be related to the settlement or indicate a minor route heading towards Malmesbury along the river valley. A further possible metalled street or lane is visible a further 75m to the north. These cropmarks are in the same area where Colt Hoare indicated extensive earthworks, including a square enclosure (Fig. 2.8). Beyond this there are a series of regularly spaced linear features on the pre-Fosse Way alignment. Associated with one of these is a further group of cropmarks suggestive of a settlement complex (Fig. 2.9, g).

The complete absence of excavation at White Walls/Easton Grey makes interpretation of the site difficult although it is clear that occupation spans the entire Roman period and the identification of a probable pre-Roman road landscape also demonstrates how little we still know of this part of the county in the later prehistoric period. South of the River Avon the pattern appears to be one of ribbon development along the Fosse Way. On the north side of the river the surviving earthworks and the hints of metalled streets or lanes east of the Fosse Way suggest a more extensive settlement. The sculptural fragments and antiquarian accounts of a tessellated pavement strongly suggest that the settlement contained buildings of some substance. The location of the settlement at a river crossing in a steep side valley is very similar to Nettleton, with its associated major religious complex, lying only 12km to the south west (see below).

Evidence for the decline of the site and its eventual abandonment is obscure. Post-Roman activity in the region is represented by an early Christian centre at nearby Malmesbury (Campbell 1987) and the discovery of a series of timber structures, including 'halls' and a possible church, at Foxley, only 2km to the east of Easton Grey. The latter are probably of 6th or 7th century AD date (Hinchliffe 1986) and raise intriguing questions concerning the post-Roman succession in the region (*cf.* Eagles 1994, 13-32; this volume).

Silbury Hill

Silbury Hill is internationally known as one of the most prominent and impressive prehistoric monuments in the Avebury region (Fig. 2.10). Work in recent years has now demonstrated that the mound, the adjacent Swallow Head spring (source of the River Kennet) and its immediate environs were also the focus of activity in the Roman period (Corney 1997b; Powell *et al.* 1996).

It had already been apparent that the great prehistoric mound had been used by engineers as a major survey point for the construction of the Roman road running west from *Cunetio* towards *Aquæ Sulis* (Margary 53). The presence of a Roman-period settlement around Silbury Hill had been known since the 19th century and numerous finds of pottery, coins (mainly of 3rd and 4th-century date) and building debris have been recorded (Grinsell 1957, 35-6; Wilkinson 1869). Brooke had excavated Roman 'wells' around the base of the mound (Brooke 1910; Brooke and Cunnington 1896) and Atkinson's 1968-9 excavation into Silbury Hill also recorded extensive late Roman deposits in the upper fill of the prehistoric quarry ditch (Whittle 1997). A single male inhumation, associated with hobnails and late-Roman pottery was discovered adjacent to the Winterbourne in 1964 (Evans 1966). There are no significant finds of Late Iron Age material from the area of the Roman settlement and, on current evidence, the site appears to be post-conquest in origin.

The first evidence of substantial Roman structures came only in 1993 with the construction of a pipeline to the east of Silbury Hill (Powell *et al.* 1996), followed shortly after by the recognition of a complex series of cropmarks on air photographs (Corney 1997b). The available evidence now suggests that the settlement covered at least 22ha (54 acres), probably on two axes; one aligned east–west along the main Roman road (Margary 53) and another aligned north–south between a stream, the Winterbourne, and the west-facing slope of Waden Hill. Along the latter axis at least nine stone structures are now known (Fig. 2.10, 1-5, recorded by excavation and a-i, recorded on air photographs). The air photographic transcription shows a regular layout to the settlement, with buildings set within a series of rectilinear ditched compounds arranged either side of road heading north along the Winterbourne valley (Fig. 2.10, x-x). West of the road property boundaries run down to the banks of the Winterbourne whilst on the east of the road the compound containing buildings d-f is significantly larger than the others, possibly reflecting a difference in function or status.

The stone structures recorded during the construction of the 1993 pipeline (Fig. 2.10, 1-5; Powell *et al.* 1996, 31-4) were of a substantial nature, although given the circumstances of the excavation no complete plan was recovered. Most of the walls had been robbed in antiquity although enough survived to demonstrate the use of chalk blocks, flint nodules, sandstone and local sarsen in their construction. The foundations were laid into trenches varying in depth from 0.35m to 0.9m and ranging from 0.73m to 1.4m in width, and a number of the buildings had been terraced into the lower slope of Waden Hill. Building 1, nearest to the presumed line of Margary 53, was the earliest structure, possibly of 2nd-century date. Although the dating evidence from the other buildings is meagre, they appear to be later Roman and so settlement may have expanded northwards during the Roman period. Overall, the datable finds from the settlement indicate that occupation continued in the early 5th century AD (*ibid.*, 56). Charred plant remains suggest that agriculture formed part of the economic base of the settlement with spelt wheat dominating (*ibid.*, 53).

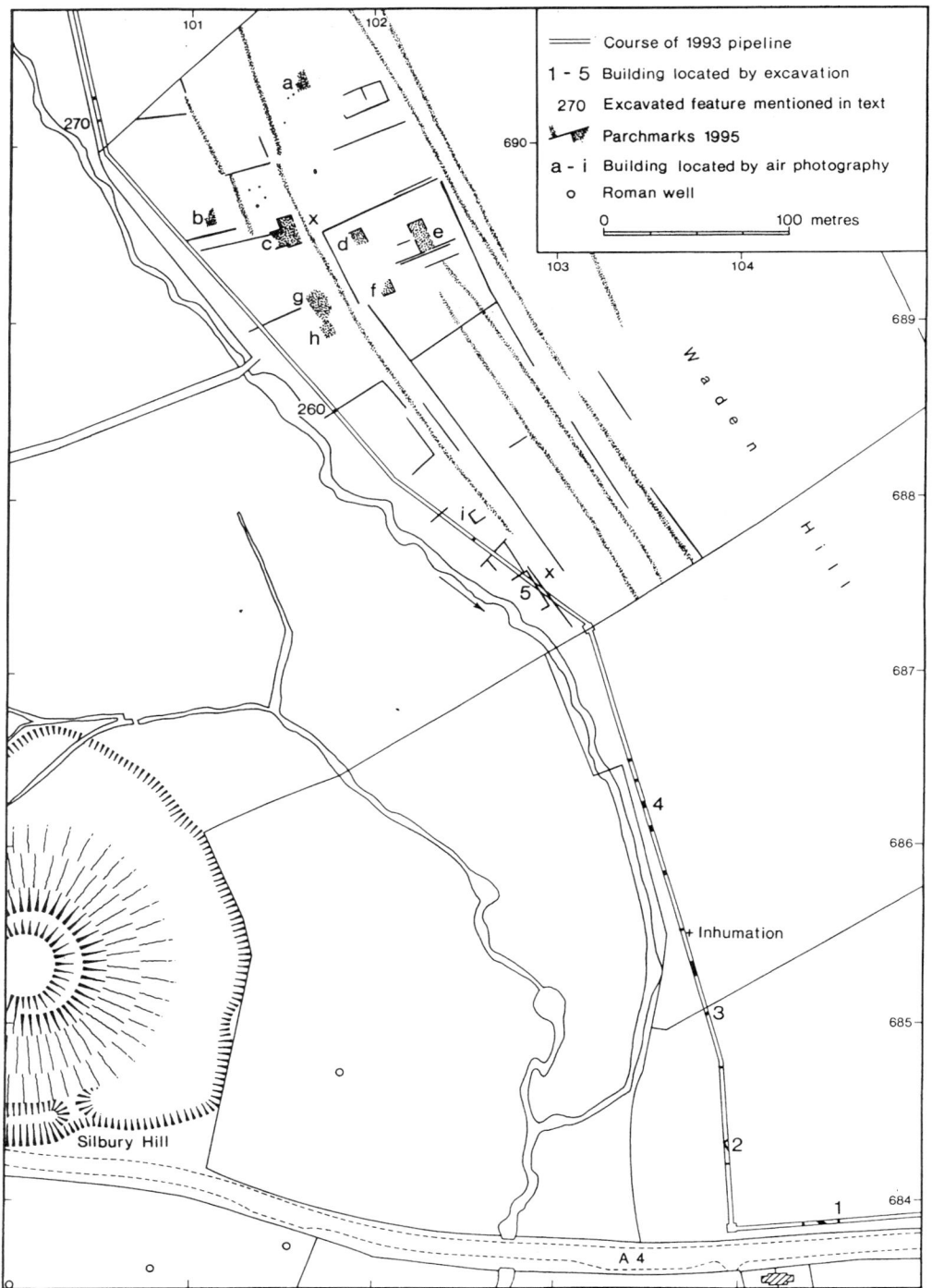

Fig. 2.10 The settlement adjacent to Silbury Hill, plan compiled from air photographs and antiquarian accounts; source author

The character of that part of the settlement sited along the main east–west road (Margary 53) is still unknown due to the lack of excavation or clear crop-marks.

The known area of the settlement (22ha) and the substantial nature of the recorded structures strongly points to a settlement of some substance that falls within the 'small town' category as defined by Burnham and Wacher (1990, 15-32). Located midway (12km in each direction) between *Cunetio* and *Verlucio*, the site could have had a local administrative function and, possibly, have been the site for a *mansio* (Black 1995). There are however other factors that may hint at a more complex situation that may include a ritual focus of activity (Robinson this volume).

The setting of the settlement, adjacent to a major prehistoric monument and the source of the River Kennet, is of considerable potential interest. Attention has been drawn recently to the correlation between the location of a number of Romano-British religious sites, 'votive' deposits, and prehistoric ritual monuments (Dark 1993; Williams 1997). Although no structure that could be interpreted as a temple or shrine is known from the settlement, there are a series of 'wells' around the base of Silbury Hill that require discussion. A total of four are known, forming an arc around the outer edge of the south-eastern quadrant of the quarry ditch of Silbury Hill (Fig. 2.10). Their location, close to the source of the River Kennet in an area prone to flooding, seems somewhat curious. One, excavated by Brooke (1910), had been deliberately backfilled and 'sealed' by massive undressed sarsen blocks. Is it possible that these 'wells' are in fact shafts of a type well-known in association with later Iron Age and Romano-British ritual and religious practices (Ross 1968). Is there a ring of such 'shafts' around the prehistoric monument? In terms of location, that part of the settlement sited on the lower slopes of Waden Hill provides a magnificent view of the prehistoric mound and the Swallow Head springs. The question can only be resolved by further fieldwork, but if a ritual function were to be established then the whole nature of the Silbury Hill settlement and the local Romano-British attitude towards the Avebury area will need to be reviewed.

Sandy Lane (Verlucio)

Located approximately midway between *Cunetio* and *Aquæ Sulis* on Roman road Margary 53 (Fig. 2.1) the roadside settlement of *Verlucio* is one of the most intriguing yet enigmatic Roman nucleated settlements in Wiltshire. It lies within the modern parishes of Bromham, Calne Without, and Heddington, and has a remarkable number of villas and other substantial buildings in its hinterland (Fig. 2.1). Convincingly identified as the *Verlucio* of the Antonine Itinerary (Rivet and Smith 1979, 494-5), the site has seen little modern, methodical archaeological work and has suffered severe damage by illicit treasure hunters. Evidence of antiquarian investigation of the site is surprisingly sparse. Stukeley records the discovery of Roman material including a coin hoard (1724, 128-31) in Heddington parish. Colt Hoare gives a brief description of the general location and mentions finds of coins, pottery and glass (Hoare 1821, 83-5). Uncharacteristically, he did not investigate the site personally, preferring to rely on accounts provided by his surveyor, Philip Crocker, and 'Brother Antiquarian' the Reverend Skinner of Camerton, Somerset (*ibid.*, 76). A substantial quantity of coins has been recorded from the site in recent years and spans the whole Roman period (Moorhead this volume).

In recent years fieldwork has been undertaken by Chippenham College but very little has yet appeared in print. However it has been established that there was a substantial earthwork defended enclosure on the site and that this was bisected by the Roman road (the late A. Clark, pers. comm.). Part of this enclosure still survives as an earthwork within woodland and has been sectioned by the Chippenham College researchers. A Roman date seems certain, but full details of the excavation and the sequence are still awaited (*WANHM*, 82, 178). The surviving earthwork is remarkably well-preserved and on the north side appears to have traces of a possible robber trench. The remainder of the circuit can still be traced as a very faint feature across the adjacent fields and has been subject to a geophysical survey (unpublished) by A. Clark, supplemented by fieldwalking (*WANHM*, 87, 156). The enclosure is rectangular in plan and encompasses an area of approximately 3ha – 7.4 acres (A. Clark, pers. comm.). The presence of a defended circuit underscores the local importance of *Verlucio* and may indicate the presence of a *mansio*. The area enclosed compares favourably with other defended sites in southern Britain where *mansiones* have been postulated such as Crab Farm, Shapwick in Dorset, 3ha, 7.4 acres (Papworth 1997, 354), and Neatham in Hampshire, 2.5ha, 6.2 acres (Millett and Graham 1986).

Greater understanding of this site is frustratingly difficult. The recent landuse history over the central area of the settlement, primarily market gardening utilising the locally fertile soils, does not produce cropmarks susceptible to conventional aerial reconnaissance methods. The large number of villas and other settlements in the vicinity would point to *Verlucio* being a potential local market centre at the very least.

Nettleton Scrubb

The roadside settlement and religious complex at Nettleton Scrubb (or Shrub) is located on the Fosse Way where it crosses a stream, the Broadmead brook, some 17km to the north east of *Aquæ Sulis* and 12km to the south west of Easton Grey/White Walls (Fig. 2.11). The Roman name for the site is unknown. Set within an attractive steep-sided valley, adjacent to the brook and springs, the settlement area is restricted on the north and west by steep natural escarpments that have been enhanced in places by quarrying, probably of Roman date. Only recognised as a Roman settlement in about 1911 with the discovery of part of a relief depicting Diana with a seated hound (Fig. 6.7; Cunliffe and Fulford 1982, 27), the settlement has been extensively excavated. The excavations, begun by W. C. Priestley in 1938 and continued by W. J. Wedlake from 1956 until 1971 (Wedlake 1982), revealed a large number of buildings, including a religious complex featuring a temple of octagonal form dedicated to Apollo Cunomaglos. The excavations established that occupation covers a minimum area of 6.5ha (16 acres) although it is clear that other substantial structures and areas of activity remain to be identified. Despite the extensive excavations by Wedlake, the detailed archaeological sequence is difficult to assess and many key questions remain unanswered. The scale and nature of the buildings recorded, strongly suggest that the site should be regarded as a 'small town' with a specialised religious and industrial function (Burnham and Wacher 1990, 40-1). The plan recovered by Wedlake (Fig. 2.11) shows an irregular layout of minor streets and tracks with numerous stone structures on a variety of alignments. The Broadmead brook appears to have been partially canalised, and a watermill, possibly of Roman date, was located to the east of the Fosse Way. The complexity of the site and the confused nature of the excavation record have been clearly summarised by Burnham and Wacher (1990, 188-92). For the purposes of this paper discussion will address only a number of key issues.

The origins of the settlement remain obscure. Two 'Dobunnic' coins are recorded (Wedlake 1982, 112) but these alone are insufficient to indicate pre-conquest settlement. Of the published brooches, five are made of iron and of a form current during the early to middle 1st century AD (*ibid.*, 120). The published pottery contains little that can be convincingly argued as being necessarily pre-conquest in date, the Gallo-Belgic types and copies of the same could all be post-AD 43 products. One short length of ditch, cut by early Roman ditches (see below) may, on stratigraphic grounds, be of pre-conquest origin and produced one of the recorded 'Dobunnic' coins. There is clearly early Roman activity at the site. Coins (including a number of Claudian 'copies'), brooches and pottery (including imported glazed and colour-coated fine wares) all demonstrate substantial pre-Flavian occupation on the southern fringe of the later settlement although the character of the remains is unclear. The profile of the pre-Flavian material has much in common with assemblages from Claudio-Neronian military sites. Wedlake excavated part of a triple-ditched complex which he postulated was a Claudio-Neronian enclosure of triangular form (even though the ditches contained coins ranging from Claudius to Trajan). He proposed that this was contemporary with the construction of the Fosse Way. However the published plan is largely conjectural and has no close military or civilian parallels in southern Britain. On current evidence there seems to have been no convincing strategic or tactical need for an early military base in this area and the question whether there was initially a fort remains unresolved. Given that Wedlake (1982, 5, 99) suggested the Fosse Way follows the course of the modern road in this area, an association between his postulated enclosure and the Fosse Way construction would appear to be highly unlikely. However, if the original Fosse Way passed further to the west, along the line of the excavated road running along the floor of the Wick Valley, then the enclosure (if indeed it is one) may be associated with an early Roman-period civil settlement.

The Roman settlement at Nettleton clearly attracted considerable investment although the detailed chronology is uncertain. Of the excavated stone structures, the octagonal temple (Wedlake's buildings 5 and 6) adjacent to the Broadmead brook, and buildings 7 and 11-13 stand out as being of some architectural merit. The temple has a complex structural sequence that continues into the early post-Roman period. It is sited on a low bluff at the foot of a steep escarpment opposite a spring and looks along the valley of the Broadmead brook.

The date of the first temple is uncertain. The excavator placed the initial construction in the late 1st century but, as Burnham and Wacher have pointed out (1990, 190), a hoard of coins ending with issues of Marcus Aurelius buried within the building may suggest a late 2nd-century date. Unfortunately the precise stratigraphic details of the hoard are not clear. Subsequently, probably in the early 3rd century, the temple received a massive octagonal

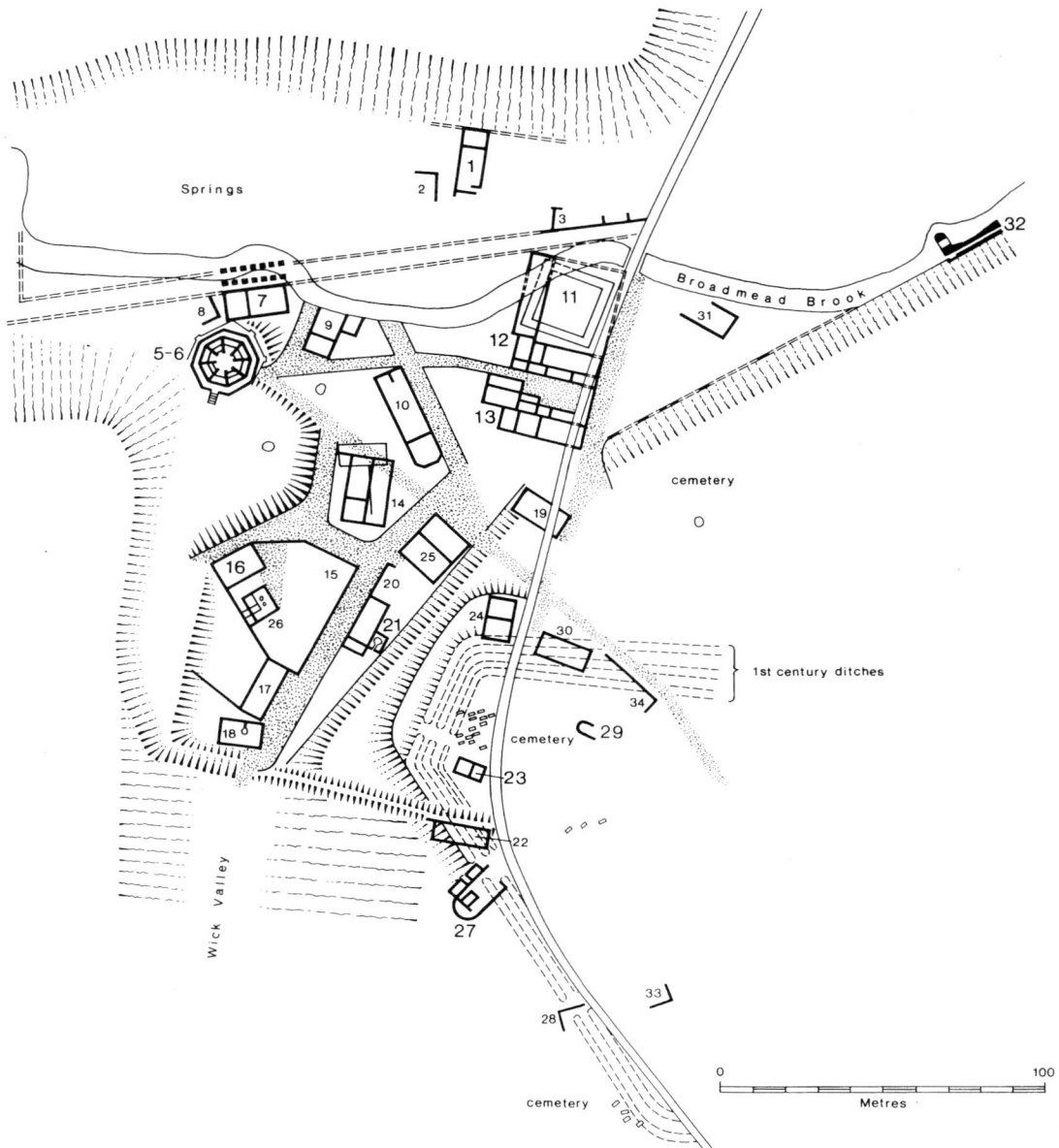

Fig. 2.11 Nettleton Scrubb, numbers refer to buildings discussed in the text (after Wedlake 1982 and Burnham and Wacher 1990, with amendments)

podium in rusticated masonry. Following a fire, the temple was rebuilt with internal walls creating eight chambers of trapezoidal form radiating from a central chamber. The building underwent further alterations during the 4th century and, at one point, the excavator suggested a possible conversion to Christian use although there is no convincing evidence for this (Wedlake 1982, 63). By the 5th century the temple appears to have ceased use as a religious building and may have been converted to a more mundane use, possibly a farmhouse. The date of abandonment is unknown, but occupation may extend into the early post-Roman period.

The closest parallel in western Britain for the temple plan at Nettleton is at Pagan's Hill, Chew Stoke in Somerset (Rahtz 1951; Rahtz and Watts 1991). This is clearly of later Roman date, most likely late 3rd or early 4th century. At Henley Wood, a Romano-Celtic temple of the more common double-square form, where the artefact sequence included a large amount of 1st-century material, the excavator favoured a late 2nd-century date for construction of the first stone building (Watts and Leach 1996, 142-3).

Building 7 at Nettleton, immediately to the north east of the temple, may have originally spanned the Broadmead Brook. It was of rectangular plan and of massive construction with a north-facing arcaded façade. The carved stonework associated with this structure shows that it was architecturally well-appointed (Wedlake 1982, 14) and included handsome stone roof-finials (*ibid.*, pl. xxxiiia). Probably dating to the late 2nd or early 3rd century, the function of the building remains unknown and the suggestion by Burnham and Wacher (1990, 191) that it was used for ritual bathing associated with the healing attributes of Apollo, whilst attractive, remains speculative.

To the east of the temple and occupying the west frontage of the Fosse Way is a large courtyard building complex (buildings 11-13) with building 11 being an earlier structure replaced by 12 and 13. The complex has the appearance of a hostelry, with accommodation around the courtyard of building 12. To the south of 12, across a rectangular courtyard with access to the temple, lay building 13. If the complex was indeed a hostelry or similar, then building 13 could be interpreted as stabling and a related service facility. The location of these buildings, directly on the main frontage of the Fosse Way, coupled with the provision of an access directly to the octagonal temple, would suggest that the postulated hostelry was closely related to the religious complex. By the 4th century AD the southern part of this complex, building 13, was given over to bronze smithing.

Evidence for an intensification of specialised metalworking during the 4th century AD is seen at a number of areas within the settlement. A number of buildings are associated with such activities. Buildings 16 and 27 were used for iron smelting and building 21 contained a furnace and five moulds for the manufacture of pewter vessels. The excavator saw the move to industrial manufacturing as signalling a decline in the importance of the religious focus within the settlement, but the two activities need not be mutually exclusive. Recent excavations at Bath have produced a pewter mould fragment from a site immediately adjacent to the temple precinct (R. Bell, pers. comm.).

Agricultural activity is represented by a watermill (building 32) and a well-constructed double-flue type 'dryer' set within the western end of building 27. The meagre dating evidence from the latter points to a 4th-century date. Very few watermills are known from Roman Britain (Spain 1984) and the discovery of an example at Nettleton is of especial interest. Located at the assumed eastern edge of the settlement, the excavated remains comprised a stone-lined leat and the housing for a wheel approximately 2.5m in diameter. Dating evidence is sparse but the style of the masonry suggested to the excavator that it might have been contemporary with the octagonal podium for the temple (Wedlake 1982, 95).

Nettleton is one of the few nucleated settlements in Wiltshire to have produced evidence for cemeteries (Foster this volume). The principle burial area located by Wedlake is on the south-east side of the settlement adjacent to the presumed course of the Fosse Way. The majority of the burials from this location are east–west inhumations, many in wooden coffins, largely devoid of grave goods and assumed to be late-Roman in date – although the possibility of an early post-Roman date should not be discounted. One building, 29, a small rectangular structure with an apse at its western end, is interpreted as a mausoleum. Another building, 23, was thought to be a cemetery 'chapel' (*ibid.*, 90). A 1st to 2nd-century cremation cemetery was partially investigated on the slopes between the Fosse Way and the watermill site.

On the north side of the Broadmead brook, Priestley investigated the area where the relief of Diana was found *c.* 1911-2 (see above; Wedlake 1982, 54). This revealed a rectangular building, 1, the north end of which was set against a substantial wall in rusticated masonry that retains a steep natural scarp. The relief of Diana appears to have been associated with the rusticated wall and therefore probably pre-dated building 1. The interpretation of this building as a temple (*ibid.*) seems doubtful and there are clearly other structures awaiting investigation on the north side of the stream.

The full nature and character of the settlement at Nettleton is not easy to understand. It clearly acted as a local cult centre with a principal dedication to Apollo Cunomaglos, although other deities are present (Robinson this volume). The relief of Diana has already been mentioned and statuettes of cockerels (*ibid.*, pl. xxxi) also point to an association with Mercury. The possible hostel, buildings 11-13, lacks any evidence of a bath-suite. A separate bathhouse, a common element of a religious centre, must still await discovery. The full extent of the settlement is unknown and the site is in clear need of further investigation. A full geophysical survey would doubtless be of considerable interest. Although the excavations have left many questions unanswered, they have demonstrated the diversity and apparent wealth of the site. The monumental building techniques such as the use of rusticated masonry and the canalisation of the Broadmead brook imply considerable local wealth and pretensions. The 4th-century industrial activity and the watermill also demonstrate a strong economic function. The ultimate fate of the settlement is obscure but the observations made by Wedlake would suggest that occupation may have continued into the post-Roman period.

The Ham (Westbury Ironworks)

The last site to be considered here is one for which we have no plans, no excavation records and no idea of its character or extent. During the years 1877-1882 a very large collection of Romano-British material was salvaged from ore extraction diggings belonging to the Westbury Iron Company at The Ham in Heywood parish, close to Westbury railway station. The range of material recovered – both in date and character – suggests a settlement of some duration and substance (Cunnington 1910, 464).

Colt Hoare (Hoare 1812, 53) noted a report of building foundations and a tesselated pavement at 'Compton's Plot', and of British and Roman antiquities in a common field called The Ham. The material discovered during the extraction of iron-ore covers the entire Romano-British period and includes a number of bronze vessels, leatherwork and a stone pewter-mould (Cunnington, *ibid.*). At least one well is recorded, the fill of which contained four human skulls, one horse skull and a cattle skull (*ibid.*, 465). These items could hint at a function more akin to a 'ritual' shaft rather than a well and may imply some religious activity.

In the absence of any plan or detailed record of the contexts of the 19th-century discoveries, the nature of this site remains enigmatic. Despite this lack of detail the finds, plus the proximity to substantial deposits of iron-ore, could indicate an industrial settlement. Elsewhere in Britain there are other settlements based on specialised industrial activities that are considered as 'small towns'. These range from large defended sites such as Irchester or Water Newton (Burnham and Wacher 1990, 142, 81) to lesser sites such as Camerton and Cowbridge (*ibid.*, 292, 296). Records of Roman period settlement in this part of Wiltshire have been slim, but in recent years a number of new sites have been recognised. A villa complex has been identified at Storridge Farm, 1km to the north west of The Ham (Wilts SMR) and another extensive settlement is known at Wellhead, 1.5km to the south east (Rogers and Roddham 1991). It is tempting to suggest that The Ham should be considered as a potential 'lost' small town serving as both an industrial and local market centre.

Conclusions

This rapid survey has shown the wide range in form and function of known or potential urban and nucleated settlements in Wiltshire. Although there are no major urban centres of *civitas* status in the county, the range and character of the sites discussed in this paper clearly demonstrate that the research potential is great. The nature and quality of the available evidence is highly variable and in some cases this can cause problems for comparisons and interpretation. Greater use of geophysics and detailed re-appraisal of existing assemblages must be a priority before further major excavations are contemplated. In addition greater understanding of settlement environs is needed to allow an appreciation of potential functions and economies. Long term management strategies are urgently required for those sites still under regular cultivation. This is especially true for *Cunetio*, White Walls and *Verlucio*. This paper is offered in the hope that it will lead to renewed interest in this aspect of Romano-British Wiltshire.

References

Alcock, L., 1995, *Cadbury Castle, Somerset: The Early Medieval Archaeology*, Cardiff

Allen, T. G., Darvill, T. C., Green, L. S., and Jones, M. U., 1993, *Excavations at Roughground Farm, Lechlade, Gloucestershire: a Prehistoric and Roman Landscape*, Oxford

Anderson, A. S., and Wacher, J. S., 1980, 'Excavations at Wanborough, Wiltshire: an interim report', *Britannia*, 11, 115-26

Annable, F. K., 1966, 'A late first-century well at *Cunetio*', *WANHM*, 61, 9-24

_____ , 1976, 'A bronze military apron mount from *Cunetio*', *WANHM*, 69, 176-9

_____ , 1980, 'A coffined burial of Roman date from *Cunetio*', *WANHM*, 72/3, 187-91

Besly, E., and Bland, R., 1983, *The Cunetio Treasure: Roman Coinage of the Third Century AD*, London

Black, E. W., 1995, *Cursus Publicus: The Infrastructure of Government in Roman Britain,* BAR Brit Ser, 241, Oxford

Borthwick, A., and Chandler, J., 1984, *Our Chequered Past,* Trowbridge

Bowen, H. C., 1990, *The Archaeology of Bokerley Dyke,* London

Brooke, J. W.,1910, 'The excavation of a Roman well near Silbury Hill, October 1908', *WANHM,* 36, 373-5

Brooke, J. W., and Cunnington, B. H., 1896, 'Excavation of a Roman well near Silbury Hill, July and October 1896', *WANHM,* 29, 166-71

Burnham, B., and Wacher, J., 1990, *The Small Towns of Roman Britain,* London

Bushe-Fox, J. P., 1926, *First Report on the Excavation of the Roman Fort at Richborough, Kent,* London

Campbell, J., 1987, 'The debt of the early English Church to Ireland', in P. Ní Chatháin and M. Richter (eds), *Irland und die Christenheit: Bibelstudien und Mission,* Stuttgart

Castle, S. A., 1972, 'A kiln of the potter Doinus', *Archaeol Journ,* 129, 69-88.

Clark, A. J., 1990, *Seeing Beneath the Soil,* London

Coe, D., Jenkins, V., and Richards, J., 1991, 'Cleveland Farm, Ashton Keynes: second interim report; investigations May-August, 1989', *WANHM,* 84, 40-50

Corney, M., 1989, 'Multiple ditch systems and Late Iron Age settlement in central Wessex', in M. Bowden, D. Mackay, and P. Topping (eds), *From Cornwall to Caithness,* Oxford, 111-28

———— , 1997a, 'The origins and development of the Romano-British small town at *Cunetio*, Mildenhall, Wiltshire', *Britannia,* 28, 337-50

———— , 1997b, 'New evidence for the Roman settlement by Silbury Hill', *WANHM,* 90, 139-41

Corney, M., and Griffiths, N., forthcoming, 'Late Roman belt-fittings: function, date and status'

Cunliffe, B. W., 1991, *Iron Age Communities in Britain,* 3rd edn, London

———— , (ed), 2000, *Danebury Environs Programme: The Prehistory of a Wessex Landscape,* Vols 1 and 2, Oxford

Cunliffe, B. W., and Fulford, M. G., 1982, *Corpus Signorum Imperii Romani: Corpus of Sculpture from the Roman World. Great Britain Volume I Fascicule 2: Bath and the rest of Wessex,* Oxford

Cunnington, M. E., 1910, 'Notes on the Roman antiquities in the Westbury collection at the Museum, Devizes', *WANHM,* 36, 464-77

Dark, K. R., 1993, 'Roman-period activity at prehistoric ritual monuments in Britain and in the Armorican peninsula', in E. Scott (ed.), *Theoretical Roman Archaeology: First Conference Proceedings,* Aldershot, 133-46

Eagles, B. N. E., 1994, 'The archaeological evidence for settlement in the fifth to seventh centuries AD', in M. Aston and C. Lewis (eds), *The Medieval Landscape of Wessex,* Oxford, 13-32

Entwistle, R., Fulford, M. G., and Raymond, F., 1994, *Salisbury Plain Project, 1993-4, Interim Report,* Reading

Evans, J., 1966, 'A Romano-British interment in the bank of the Winterbourne, near Avebury', *WANHM,* 61, 97-8

Fowler, P. J., 2000, *Landscape Plotted and Pieced: Landscape History and Local Archaeology in Fyfield and Overton, Wiltshire,* London

Frere, S. S., 1967, *Britannia: A History of Roman Britain,* London

Frere, S. S., and St Joseph, J. K., 1983, *Roman Britain from the Air,* Cambridge

Gaffney, V., and Tingle, M., 1989, *The Maddle Farm Project: an Integrated Survey of Prehistoric and Roman Landscapes on the Berkshire Downs,* BAR Brit Ser, 200, Oxford

Gelling, M., 1988, *Signposts to the Past. Place-names and the History of England,* 2nd edn, Chichester

Griffiths, N., 1982, 'Early Roman military metalwork from Wiltshire', *WANHM,* 77, 49-59

Grinsell, L. V., 1957, 'Archaeological gazetteer', *VCH, Wiltshire, Volume I, Part 1,* London, 21-279

Hampton, J. N., and Palmer, R. 1977, 'The implications of air photography for archaeology', *Archaeol Journ*, 134, 157-93

Hinchliffe, J., 1986, 'An early medieval settlement at Cowage Farm, Foxley, near Malmesbury', *Archaeol Journ*, 143, 240-59

Hoare, R. C., 1812, *The Ancient History of Wiltshire, Volume I*, London

_____ , 1821, *The Ancient History of Wiltshire, Volume II, The Roman Aera*, London

Hodder, I., 1974, 'The distribution of Savernake Ware', *WANHM*, 69, 84-97

Leech, R., 1977, *The Upper Thames Valley in Gloucestershire and Wiltshire: An Archaeological Survey of the River Gravels*, Gloucester

Millett, M., and Graham, D., 1986, *Excavations on the Romano-British Small Town at Neatham, Hampshire 1969-1979*, Winchester

Montgomerie, D. H., 1948, 'Old Sarum', *Archaeol Journ*, 104, 129-43

Morse, R., and Richards, J., 1989, *Cleveland Farm, Ashton Keynes, First Interim Report*, Trust for Wessex Archaeology

Musty, J. W. G., 1959, 'A pipe-line near Old Sarum: prehistoric, Roman and medieval finds including two twelfth century lime kilns', *WANHM*, 57, 179-91

Musty, J. W. G., and Rahtz, P. A., 1964, 'The suburbs of Old Sarum', *WANHM*, 59, 130-54

Ordnance Survey, 1978, *Map of Roman Britain*, 4th edn, Southampton

Palmer, R., 1984, *Danebury: an Air Photographic Interpretation of its Environs*, London

Papworth, M., 1997, 'The Romano-British settlement at Shapwick, Dorset', *Britannia*, 28, 354-8

Phillips, B., and Walters, B., 1977, 'A *mansio* at Lower Wanborough, Wiltshire', *Britannia*, 8, 223-7

Powell, A. B., Allen, M. J., and Barnes, I., 1996, *Archaeology in the Avebury Area, Wiltshire: Recent Discoveries Along the Line of the Kennet Valley Foul Sewer Pipeline, 1993*, Salisbury

Rahtz, P. A., 1951, 'The Roman temple at Pagans Hill, Chew Stoke, N. Somerset', *Proc Somerset Archaeol Nat Hist Soc*, 96, 112-42

Rahtz, P. A., and Watts, L., 1991, 'Pagans Hill revisited', *Archaeol Journ*, 146, 322-71

Rahtz, P. A., *et al.*, 1992, *Cadbury Congresbury 1968-73. A Late/Post-Roman Hilltop Settlement in Somerset*, BAR Brit Ser, 223, Oxford

Richardson, K. M., 1951, 'The excavation of Iron Age villages on Boscombe Down West', *WANHM*, 54, 123-68

Rivet, A. L. F., 1970, 'The British section of the Antonine itinerary', *Britannia*, 1, 34-82

Rivet, A. L. F., and Smith, C., 1979, *The Place-names of Roman Britain*, London

Robinson, P. R., 1977, 'A local Iron Age coinage in silver and perhaps gold in Wiltshire', *Brit Numis Journ*, 47, 5-20

_____ , 1993, 'Iron Age coins from Cunetio and Mildenhall', *WANHM*, 86, 147-9

_____ , forthcoming, 'The Iron Age coins', in M. Corney (forthcoming), *A Guide Catalogue to the Iron Age Collections in Devizes Museum*

Rodwell, W., and Rowley, T., (eds), 1975, *Small Towns of Roman Britain*, BAR Brit Ser, 15, Oxford

Rogers, B., and Roddham, D., 1991, 'The excavations at Wellhead, Westbury, 1959-66', *WANHM*, 84, 51-60

Ross, A., 1968, *Pagan Celtic Britain*, London

Selwood, L., 1984, 'Tribal boundaries viewed from the perspective of numismatic evidence', in B. Cunliffe and D. Miles (eds) *Aspects of the Iron Age in Central Southern Britain*, Oxford, 191-204.

Smith, R. F., 1987, *Roadside Settlements in Lowland Roman Britain*. BAR Brit Ser, 157, Oxford

Soames, C., 1878, 'Coins found near Marlborough', *WANHM*, 17, 84-8

Spain, R. J., 1984, 'Romano-British watermills', *Archaeol Cantiana*, 100, 101-28

St Joseph, J. K. S., 1953, 'Air reconnaissance of Southern Britain', *Journ Roman Stud,* 43, 81-97

Stone, J. F. S., and Algar, D. J., 1955, 'Sorviodunum', *WANHM,* 56, 102-26

Stukeley, W., 1776, *Itinerarium Curiosum,* facsimile edn 1989, Farnborough

Swan, V., 1975, 'Oare reconsidered and the origins of Savernake Ware in Wiltshire', *Britannia,* 6, 36-61

Trow, S., 1988, 'Excavations at Ditches Hillfort, North Cerney, Gloucestershire, 1982-3', *Trans Bristol Glos Archaeol Soc,* 106, 19-85

Van Arsdell, R. D., 1994, *The Coinage of the Dobunni: Money Supply and Coin Circulation in Dobunnic Territory. With a Gazetteer of Findspots by Philip de Jersey,* Studies in Celtic Coinage no. 1, OUCA Monograph, 38, Oxford

Wacher, J. S., 1969, *Excavations at Brough-on-Humber 1958-1961,* Soc Antiq Res Rep, 25, London
_____ , 1975, 'Wanborough', in Rodwell and Rowley 1975, 233-6

Watts, L., and Leach, P., 1996, *Henley Wood, Temples and Cemetery Excavations 1962-69 by the late Ernest Greenfield and others,* CBA Res Rep, 99, York

Wedlake, W. J., 1982, *The Excavation of the Shrine of Apollo at Nettleton, Wiltshire, 1956-1971,* Soc Antiq Res Rep, 40, London

Whittle, A., 1997, *Sacred Mound, Holy Rings. Silbury Hill and the West Kennet Palisaded Enclosures: A Later Neolithic Complex in North Wiltshire,* Oxford

Wilkinson, J., 1869, 'A report of diggings made in Silbury Hill and in the ground adjoining', *WANHM,* 9, 113-18

Williams, H. M., 1997, 'The ancient monument in Romano-British ritual practices', in C. Forcey, J. Hawthorne, and R. Witcher (eds), *Procs Seventh Theoretical Roman Archaeol Conference Nottingham 1997,* Oxford, 71-86

Wilson, D. R., 1974, 'Romano-British villas from the air', *Britannia,* 5, 251-61
_____ , 1975, 'The 'small towns' of Roman Britain from the air', in Rodwell and Rowley 1975, 9-49

3 THE ROMAN ARMY IN WILTSHIRE

by Nick Griffiths

Introduction

Unlike the areas covered by other modern counties in the south west, there are no definitely known conquest-period forts within Wiltshire (Fig. 3.1). This paper suggests that, despite this, the presence of Roman military forces can be demonstrated, and suggestions made as to their *modus operandi*. In his detailed work on the invasion, Webster (1980) produced a series of maps showing the road networks, and identifying known and possible fort sites; in many cases forts are presumed to have been the origin of later towns and other settlements. However, not every fort would have generated a *vicus*, a civil settlement, sufficiently prosperous to survive the removal of the military establishment. The pattern created by the maps is one of close garrisoning across much of the south, with forts some 20-25 miles apart (about a day's march). While this hypothesis looks good on paper, it does present a number of difficulties. It is a plan best suited to the static defence of a frontier, not the requirements of an army on campaign. Such a rigid system takes little account of varied local conditions and attitudes, in as far as they can be known. Given the steady movement of the army westward, an inordinate amount of manpower would have been tied up in constructing and dismantling, not to mention manning, so many forts.

It is more likely that the system employed was similar to that used by Caesar in Gaul, where the army occupied temporary camps through the campaigning season, then largely withdrew into *hibernae* for the winter months, leaving garrisons in newly conquered and secure territory. The *hibernae*, housing the headquarters and much, if not all, of the legion, would probably also have accommodated some auxiliary units. Once Roman rule had been extended for some distance, a new *hiberna* would be established, but the older base would be retained for possible further use. As the advance continued, the need for troops would have meant that garrisons would only be left where there was risk of further trouble; once newly conquered communities had settled down, much of the military presence would have been withdrawn.

During the Roman period as a whole, the paper will argue that the presence of the army can be seen in many aspects of civilian life, and that this can be demonstrated by the

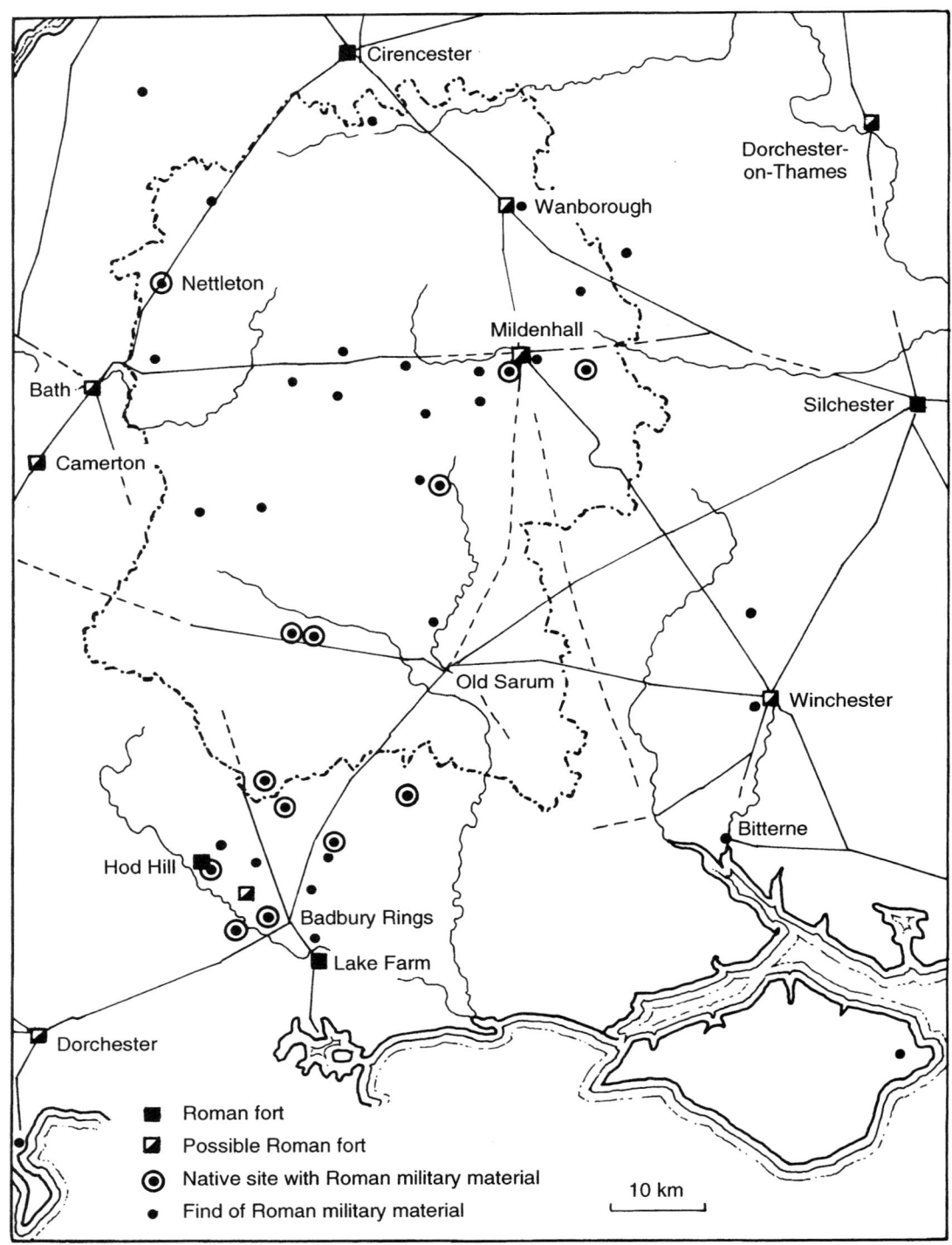

Fig. 3.1 Wiltshire and surrounding areas: 1st-century military activity

findspots of military metalwork in the county. A particular focus is on the later 4th-century material.

The conquest

Suetonius (*Vespasian,* 4) says of Vespasian's campaigns '......he fought thirty battles, subjugated two warlike tribes and captured more than twenty *oppida*, beside the Isle of Wight...'. The twenty-plus *oppida* have long been recognised as the hillforts of the Durotriges of Dorset, although the second 'warlike tribe' remains uncertain. Assuming that *Legio II Augusta* wintered at Silchester (with perhaps a detachment at Chichester with auxiliaries), then, once the Hampshire area was secure, the spring of AD 44 would have seen an advance into the south west, the lands of the Durotriges. Margary's (1955) route 4 perhaps represents the line of this thrust; beyond Old Sarum it swings southwards to Badbury Rings, before turning more westerly towards Maiden Castle and Dorchester. The first Durotrigian territory entered by the legion would have been Cranborne Chase, at the north-eastern extremity of Dorset, and home of a group identified by Corney as a 'sub-Durotrigan political entity' (Corney 1991). This was an area of few hillforts but numerous small settlements and 'banjo' enclosures. Such evidence as there is suggests that many of these settlements passed into the Roman era with little disruption, suggesting a rapid acceptance of Roman rule. Such a transition may be seen on more than 25 sites in the area (M. Green, pers. comm).

Two sites in particular, Rotherley, Wiltshire, and Woodcutts, Dorset, both excavated by General Pitt-Rivers in 1884-5, may give an indication of how the take-over took place. Neither site revealed any sign of destruction, and occupation carried on without interruption. At Rotherley, some five miles west of the Roman road, a number of finds reveal the presence of the Roman army: a bronze scabbard-mount (Fig. 3.5, 27) and four iron ballista-bolt heads (Fig. 3.6, 30-33). One of the bolt heads (Fig. 3.6, 31) was found in the filling of the Main Circle Ditch and Webster (1980, 145) suggested that a large hut may have been the target for a *ballista,* the Roman artillery weapon. A second bolt head (Fig. 3.6, 32) was found in 'surface trenching' over the ditch.

These bolt heads, attached to a short, flighted wooden shaft, could be fired over a range of perhaps 200 yards, far out-reaching native weapons. The ballista could be carried on a cart (or was perhaps mounted on a cart as shown on Trajan's column); each *centuria* (company) of the legion – perhaps sixty at this period – had at least one such machine, operated by a crew of two. Although they were mostly used for the bombardment of fortifications, they could be used in the field against opposing forces. The presence of four bolt heads at Rotherley, and one from Woodcutts ('filling of the Main Ditch', Pitt-Rivers 1887, pl. xxix, 22) might suggest that the Roman policy was one of bringing the natives to a state of surrender by a 'firepower demonstration'; only if they failed to respond would an assault be necessary. Settlements could thus be brought under Roman control with minimal risk and for the expenditure of a few ballista bolts.

The scabbard mount from Rotherley may represent a loss during the subsequent military presence, certainly a detachment must have been put in to disarm the residents.

Such an inevitable, if short-term, presence would also explain two further finds from Woodcutts. The first, an iron axe, was possibly a military loss, although a common tool on Roman sites of all types (Pitt-Rivers, 1887, 81, pl. xxvi, 2), while the second, fragments of a Central Gaulish lead-glazed pottery cup, is almost certainly an indication of the army's presence, such wares being supplied to the Rhineland (and later to Britain) from Augustan times to *c.* AD 70 for use by the troops (Greene 1971, 163f; 1979, 139f). This interpretation of the evidence from Rotherley and Woodcutts suggests a scenario in which the legion worked systematically across Cranborne Chase, accepting the surrender of many, if not all, of the largely undefended communities. It is likely that as word spread, few of the settlements would have required a show of Roman power!

The evidence for the use of artillery also raises other points, as the bolts are of varying types. When nos 29 and 30 were republished (Griffiths 1983, 57, nos 18, 19), it was suggested that their blunt, pyramidal heads were more akin to those of medieval cross-bow quarrels. However, quarrel-heads are usually less well-formed, the 'pyramid' often having rounded lower corners. Indeed the ballista-bolt from Fishbourne (Cunliffe 1971, 134, no. 49) is actually more likely to be a medieval quarrel-head! Roman ballista-bolts generally have longer, more slender heads (Brailsford 1962, pl. vi, B117, B118, B181), but parallels for the blunter form can be found from late Republican and Tiberian sites in Gaul (Feugère 1994, 10). Perhaps the legion was using 'old stock' – it is worth remembering that *Legio II Augusta* had been based at Strasbourg, and had perhaps less chance to use its artillery than its counterparts on the northern Rhine, *Legio XIV* and *Legio XX*. Both of them may have been involved in Gaius' abortive German 'expedition' and his 'invasion' of Britain, with the firing of artillery against the ocean (Suetonius, *Gaius,* 46). The weapon from Woodcutts and the third bolt from Rotherley (Fig. 3.6, 32) represent a different form entirely. Crudely made, with flat blades and roughly formed folded sockets, they were identified as ballista-bolts at Maiden Castle (Wheeler 1943, 281, fig. 93, nos 4-13) and Hod Hill (Brailsford 1962, pl. vi, B86); indeed the bolt embedded in the vertebra of a defender of Maiden Castle is of this type (Wheeler 1943, pl. lviiia). Possibly a large number of bolts had been expended in the initial months of the invasion, leading to a shortage, and the legion's armourers were forced to improvise. Figure 3.6, 33, the fourth from Rotherley, is an unusual weapon, with a leaf-shaped blade, similar to many Roman spearheads but with a flattened triangular cross-section. The socket is folded in the manner described above, and with a shaft diameter of only 7mm, the head must have been intended to fit an arrow or ballista-bolt shaft.

The evidence suggests a fairly smooth transition to Roman rule in north-east Dorset, and this may have been repeated in south Wiltshire. Hamshill Ditches, on the Groveley Ridge, has a pair of 'banjo' enclosures associated with multiple ditches, and it may represent the northern margin of the suggested 'sub-Durotrigian' area centred on Gussage Hill (Corney 1991). Finds show an apparently continuous occupation from the Late Iron Age down to the 4th century AD, with a substantial Roman development immediately east of the 'banjo' enclosures. The Roman road from Winchester to the Mendip Hills passes along the Groveley Ridge, and as lead was being exported from the Charterhouse mines by AD 49, it is clear that the road was laid out early in the Roman period. The Groveley

Ridge was clearly well-populated in the Late Iron Age, and Roman military equipment is known from at least two sites, Stockton Earthworks and Bilbury Rings. Two pieces of equipment, probably both from horse harness, are known at Stockton (Figs 3.3, 7; 3.4, 11), but, unfortunately, the Bilbury material has not been published and its whereabouts is currently unknown, though cavalry pieces appear to have been present (Webster 1980, 148-9, although that illustrated comes from Stockton, not Bilbury Rings).

The emphasis on horse harness might be coincidental, but, as the catalogue of pieces shows, of some 42 objects of military type and likely 1st-century date from Wiltshire, 21 are definite or probable horse-harness pieces, 11 are items appropriate to any military unit whilst only 10 are likely to be infantry items. Thus cavalry equipment is present in a ratio of 2:1 to infantry pieces.

Since much of Wiltshire is open downland and was almost certainly so by the Late Iron Age, it would have been ideal 'cavalry country'. Breeze (1993) has shown how cavalry regiments on frontiers in the 2nd century were often stationed where the terrain beyond the frontier was level and open, so that their speed and mobility could be exploited to the full when countering any threat. On campaign, it would make sense to employ a greater proportion of cavalry or mounted troops where the landscape favoured their deployment. In fact, the chalk downlands of Dorset are more dissected by river valleys, and more wooded, than their Wiltshire counterparts. The open landscape of Salisbury Plain extends into Hampshire and Berkshire, and, whilst some tracts of forest existed, it would have been possible for cavalry to range widely across the chalk downs from Silchester westwards. A stray find of a bridle-piece from the Berkshire Downs can be seen in this context (Fig. 3.8, A). If this was indeed the deployment of Vespasian's army, with the legion directed to an area where its siege skills would be needed and with less hostile areas dealt with by the auxiliary regiments, in particular the cavalry, then the absence of a close network of forts is easily explained. For, if a Roman garrison could be placed within a native settlement in fairly hostile country, as one was at Hod Hill, then troops could certainly be billeted at settlements in neutral or pro-Roman areas for a short period.

Of the 42 pieces of Roman military equipment mentioned above, 17 pieces in fact come from Late Iron Age sites, including 11 horse-harness items. The sites include Chisbury Camp, Casterley Camp and Oliver's Camp, all hillforts, Stockton Earthworks and Rotherley, defended settlements, and the shrine at Nettleton Scrubb (where no convincing evidence for a fort has been published). As the map (Fig. 3.1) shows, many of these sites are on or near Roman roads. A smaller number of pieces come from sites of Roman origin, notably at Wanborough and Mildenhall, though both lie close to native settlements, at Liddington and Forest Hill Farm respectively. Wanborough has produced several items of harness equipment and an axe-guard, and a fort might have existed under the later small town of *Durocornovium*. Excavation suggests that the earliest road was built in the Neronian period, although this does not preclude an earlier cleared route. Indeed, with its direct road from Silchester, it might be suggested that this was the outpost in Dobunnic territory established in the first months of the invasion according to Dio Cassius (LX, 20).

Corney (1997; this volume) has discussed the origins of the Roman town of *Cunetio*, at Mildenhall. A well excavated in the earthwork enclosure at Folly Farm in the 1880s produced a probable harness mount. Although only a sketch survives, it is clearly a standard type of cavalry mount (Fig. 3.4, 12). A terminal from a similar set of harness equipment came from a well sealed by the construction of *Cunetio's* late walls. (Fig. 3.4, 13). The well also contained Claudio-Neronian samian, copies of Gallo-Belgic wares and Savernake pottery (see Timby this volume), and Corney thinks it may represent the clearance associated with the demolition of a fort. The earthen enclosure seen on air photographs does not seem to be military, and any 1st-century fort is likely to be buried beneath the later town; but an initial military occupation of the Forest Hill enclosure is a distinct possibility.

Another local site which clearly attracted the attention of the Romans was the hillfort of Chisbury Camp, 5 miles south-east of *Cunetio*. Material recovered by a metal detector from the area to the west of the hillfort, includes two pendants, three junction-clips and a loop with stud, all horse harness (Figs. 3.3, 2, 4; 3.4, 14-16). An iron axe of Roman type was apparently also found, along with Republican *denarii* and those of Augustus and Tiberius, and an *aureus* of Augustus was found inside the earthworks.

Whilst there is no evidence for Roman defences as at Hod Hill, a simple palisade fence might have been thought adequate to limit the army's area in a friendly environment. Without large scale excavation such features would be almost impossible to detect. Initially the troops would be *sub pellibus* – under canvas, or rather, leather, tents. Wooden buildings might be expected for winter occupation. This hypothesis does, perhaps, reduce the need to look for Roman forts!

A similar situation to that of Mildenhall occurs at Old Sarum, *Sorviodunum*, north of Salisbury, where the hillfort is the focus of four Roman roads and two probable native trackways (Fig. 3.1; Corney this volume). A probable Roman masonry building has been noted inside the hillfort (*RCHME* 1980, 11) but this is hardly likely to be of military origin. The construction of the central motte with its castle and the cathedral by the Normans has probably buried any trace there might have been of early Roman military occupation within the hillfort. The Roman settlement lay down by the river to the south west, under modern Stratford-sub-Castle where Roman material has been found, but nothing military, although an air photograph shows a partial rectangular feature east of the likely river crossing. However, it would be unwise to call this a fort without excavation – a similar feature at Shapwick in Dorset proved to be 2nd century when excavated.

Branigan (1974) postulated an advance up the Avon valley and adduces as evidence three spearheads and an arrowhead from Salisbury Plain. Iron spearheads are difficult to date and whilst the Wilsford and Bulford Down spearheads are similar to the parallel cited, they also find parallels amongst Iron Age and Anglo-Saxon types (Swanton 1973, 46ff, Group C). The Bulford Down spearhead with its angular blade is almost certainly Saxon (*ibid.*, Group E2). The arrowhead (Fig. 3.6, 29) is a recognisable Roman type, but it is noticeably larger than the normal military examples, and may represent a civilian hunting weapon – Romano-British hunting spearheads are similar to many of the smaller military spearheads. Even if these spearheads (and the arrowhead) were of military origin, they need not represent any particular line of advance. The hypothesis suggested here of cavalry patrols across much of Wiltshire would involve the accidental loss of some weapons in the same way that horse-trappings were lost.

Apart from the horse-harness pieces from across the county, some of the other items are worthy of comment. A fine penannular brooch (Fig. 3.7, 41) of Fowler type B1, paralleled at Hod Hill, Ham Hill and a number of other early military sites, was found on Huish Hill near a small earthwork. Fowler (1960, 166-7) suggested that this type may have belonged to Spanish auxiliaries in the Roman army. At least one Spanish regiment is attested in the invasion force. M. Stlaccius Coranus was prefect of an *ala Hispanorum*, following a tribunate in *Legio II Augusta*, both posts held 'in Britannia' under Claudius or Nero. The transfer suggests that the *ala* was within the legion's area of command. It may have been the *ala I Hispanorum Vettonum c.R.*, known in the south west and Wales later in the 1st century (*RIB*, 159, Bath; *RIB*, 403, Brecon Gaer). Indeed, the unit's title of 'c[ivium] R[omanorum]', 'Roman citizens' (a reward to the whole *ala* for some outstanding action), may have been won under Claudius (Maxfield 1981, 251). Coranus' memorial (*CIL*, VI, 3539, near Rome) records the award of a *corona muralis*, the crown traditionally given to the first man over the wall of an enemy town. Although by the 1st century AD these decorations had become largely symbolic and were awarded according to rank (Maxfield 1981, 63ff), the 'mural crown' might have been seen as appropriate for a man who may have distinguished himself in the legion's Dorset campaigns. Since his career ends with his prefecture, he probably died while serving in Britain.

A fragment of a military saucepan from the Avon valley is probably a casual loss (Fig. 3.7, 38), typical of the equipment used by all soldiers. The iron spearhead from Oliver's Camp (Fig. 3.6, 28) deserves mention. The unusual shape, with rounded expansions at the lower end of the blade, is paralleled at a number of sites, e.g. Greta Bridge (Casey and Hoffman 1998, 135-6). These objects have been identified as the decorative heads of the 'staffs-of-office' carried by *beneficiarii*, soldiers attached to senior officers as aides. However, surviving examples and sculpture suggest that such spearheads were more ornate. An alternative is that these smaller spearheads were the heads of auxiliary standards. A surviving metal standard-head, almost certainly legionary, is a larger, more elegantly shaped silver version of the same shape from Caerleon (Boon 1972, 68). A number of tombstone reliefs show smaller spearpoints on auxiliary standards. Almost certainly silvered or gilded, each cohort or *ala* would have had several such standards, and the *vexillum* of a detachment was also topped by a spearpoint.

By the end of AD 45, if not earlier, the Roman army had probably completed the 'conquest' of Wiltshire. To the west, troops may already have reached the Severn Estuary. Further south, progress was perhaps not so rapid, with the need to pacify the Durotriges. Whatever the early successes, as at Hod Hill, the need to assault Maiden Castle shows that resistance and consequent fighting could be expected further west.

Field (1992) discusses in detail the evidence for the Roman army's activities in Dorset, but one thing is clear – if Waddon Hill was established in AD 47-8, then progress had been, understandably, slower than further north. In fact, it may be possible to see this reflected in the road system. The road from Chichester (and the associated store-base at Fishbourne) can be seen to run north, then north-westwards to Silchester (Margary 1955, route 155). The road from Hamworthy, where early pottery suggests a port (Webster and Dudley 1965, 104), leads to Lake Farm and then bears north-westwards towards Bath (routes 44, 46, 52). Further west the same arrangement is repeated, with a likely port at Radipole, near Weymouth. A road northwards to Dorchester, where there may have been a fort (or a store-base?), then bears north-westwards to Ilchester (routes 48 and 47). The three roads can be seen to run in a more or less parallel fashion. Another road from Chichester runs westward towards Bitterne before turning north-west to Winchester, and on to Mildenhall. However this route lacks the directness of the other roads and may be a later development (routes 421, 420 and 43). Recent fieldwork suggests that a road originally ran north-westwards from the head of Southampton Water. It may have started at Nursling, where a Roman settlement existed on the tidal reaches of the River Test, at the head of Southampton Water. The route can be traced as minor roads and lanes, largely between Mottisfont and Quarley in Hampshire, and then again as road alignments to the north of Ludgershall, where it enters Wiltshire and appears to be heading for Mildenhall. Its route through Savernake Forest is unknown, but at some point it may have intersected the road (route 44) from Old Sarum to Mildenhall.

When this probable road is added to the previously mentioned routes, it will be seen that they present a repeated pattern, clearly designed to provide seaborne supplies to the army, via ports and nearby store-bases. The north-westwards alignment of the system not only confirms that to the north, i.e. Wiltshire, the advance was proceeding faster than in Dorset, but also implies that the system had been planned before the army had come to grips with the Durotriges, again suggesting accurate knowledge of the likely situation ahead. Additionally it is worth noting that the central pair of these roads, which did not link *civitas* centres, survive only in piecemeal fashion. Once their initial military function was over, they presumably became minor roads of local importance only.

Whilst military action carried on against the Durotriges, the troops stationed in Wiltshire were probably reduced to a minimum, an *ala* perhaps divided into detachments at several centres – Old Sarum and Mildenhall (and possibly Wanborough) might have been sufficient. Cavalry patrols, linking up with the half *ala* at Hod Hill (and presumably other units in the adjoining legionary command to the north) could have kept the area under control. At some point, extra detachments would need to be placed further west. Military equipment is now known from Bath (J. Bircher, pers. comm.) and may indicate a fort to the north of the later city.

With a pacified population, the time would be right for the exploitation of natural resources, and the best known example in the south west is probably the lead mines of Charterhouse-on-Mendip, Somerset. In Wiltshire, the iron deposits at Westbury may well have attracted the army's attention. The large collection of Roman material in Wiltshire Heritage Museum (Devizes) found in the years 1877-82, includes two examples, and fragments of a third, of the bronze *trulleus,* the military saucepan or mess-tin (Fig. 3.7, 35-7). No other military material is present in the collection, although early pottery, including *terra nigra*, and early brooch types are represented (Cunnington and Goddard 1934, 175ff, pl. lvii, 1). Similarly, studies of the Oare and Savernake pottery industry concluded that the native potters may have received a great boost from military orders in much the same way that the Roman army in Dorset adopted the local Black-Burnished ware (Timby this volume). Savernake wares occur at a number of sites with evidence of a military presence:

Rodborough Common, Gloucestershire, a possible Roman fort; Bath; Ham Hill, Somerset; Sea Mills, near Bristol; and Kingscote, Gloucestershire. Obtaining local supplies would have removed the need to transport pottery from the continent.

Two military buckles from Ashton Keynes (Fig. 3.5, 22-3) may be connected with the tile and brick kilns at nearby Minety. Their production included some pottery, and the kilns were supplying Cirencester by the end of the 1st century (McWhirr 1981, 111-13). There may have been some early military involvement, again perhaps with pottery production. An industry that may have owed its origins to the Roman army was the quarrying of Bath stone. The fine oolitic limestone ('freestone') lies up to 50 feet below the surface of the plateau above Box, and is exposed on the hillside (Barron 1976, 42-4). That the stone was rapidly exploited is shown by its use for the gravestone of M. Favonius Facilis at Colchester, most probably erected before his legion left in AD 49 (Phillips 1975, 102-5).

A further activity involving troops in a newly pacified area would be the construction of permanent roads to replace the roughly cleared tracks of the initial advance. Military surveyors and engineers would have been involved, most probably legionaries. The isolated fragment of *lorica segmentata* (Fig. 3.5, 26) found near Aldbourne probably indicates a legionary presence. The find spot is some 2-3 miles from Ermin Street, the construction of which was dated to the Neronian period at Wanborough (Anderson and Wacher 1980, 116-17), and legionary engineers may well have been billeted on nearby local settlements.

Finally, the supply of food for the army must have involved purchases from local farmers. Requisitioning probably took place but it should be remembered that the purpose of the army now was to pacify the country and facilitate its conversion to a profitable province of the Empire, not to destroy the existing systems. That things could, and did, go wrong is demonstrated by the Boudiccan revolt. Wholesale destruction and impoverishment was normally an act of retribution for rebellion, not a tool of initial conquest.

The civilian province

With the withdrawal of the legion and its auxiliaries from the south and west of Britain in the AD 70s, military administration was replaced by newly created *civitates* based on the native tribes, the Durotriges, Dobunni, Dumnonii and the Belgae. Much of the groundwork had been done by the army or at least under its supervision. A census of population and surveys of land holding and ownership were necessary preludes to taxation. The road network had been put in place, with army surveyors and engineers no doubt using conscripted local labour. The planning of the new towns and their facilities, such as the Dorchester aqueduct (Putnam 1984, 38ff) would have made much use of military architects.

The *civitas* was often the basis on which auxiliary units would be formed, for example cohorts of Batavi, Tungri and Nervii in addition to those bearing provincial titles, i.e. Germanorum, Gallorum etc. In the case of Britain, the tribal populations were perhaps too small, and the auxiliary cohorts raised were titled *Britannica* or *Britannorum* (Holder

1980, 20-1). The Romans may have felt that there would be less trouble if young men from different tribes were placed in mixed units. The only cohort to bear a British tribal name, *Cohors I Cornoviorum* is only attested in the late 4th century, although the use of *cohors* suggests an earlier foundation, perhaps the conversion of a tribal militia into a regular army regiment.

While there may have been many men from the 'Wiltshire' *civitates*, the Belgae, Dobunni, Durotriges and Atrebates, in the first series of British cohorts, it is the later 1st and 2nd-century inscriptions and discharge diplomas that give evidence of the men's origins in more detail. An anonymous BEL[GA], perhaps of the British *civitas*, is listed on the Domitianic(?) cenotaph at Adamclisi, Romania (*CIL*, III, 14214); his unit is uncertain but may have been *Cohors I Batavorum*. The list shows a mixture of nationalities, perhaps indicative of the great reorganisation of units following the Civil War of AD 68-9. Julius Vitalis, armourer of *Legio XX*, buried at Bath (*RIB*, 156) was '*natione Belgae*', but a British Belga would be unusual in a legion in the late 1st or 2nd century, and he more probably came from *Gallia Belgica*. Lucco, of the Dobunni, honourably discharged from *Cohors I Britannica* in January AD 105 (*CIL*, XVI, 49) was probably recruited *c.* AD 80. Longinus, of the Belgae was similarly discharged in July AD 110 (*CIL*, XVI, 163) and had probably enlisted *c.* AD 85. His unit, *Cohors I Brittonum* (the title used for new British units from the late 1st century) had received a rare battlefield award of Roman citizenship in August AD 106 (*CIL*, XVI, 160).

Discharged auxiliaries received Roman citizenship and added the Emperor's names to their own, creating the citizen's *tria nomina* or three names. Marcus Ulpius Lucco and Marcus Ulpius Longinus, as they now were, derived theirs from Marcus Ulpius Traianus (Trajan). They appear to have settled in the areas where they had served, at *Brigetio* on the Danube and *Porolissum* in Dacia, respectively. This was quite common. After 25 years most of their friends would be their fellow-soldiers, and although marriage was forbidden to serving soldiers, liaisons with local women were common, and at this period, the 'wives' and any children also received citizenship. Roxan (1989, 462-7) has suggested that, if they moved away, it tended to be to their wives' home areas, presumably where family and land might be an attraction. The veteran, with his status and savings, might well represent an important addition to a small rural community. Claudius Terentianus, an Egyptian veteran, discharged in the early 2nd century was described as 'an honourably discharged soldier' and 'a man of means...' (Lewis 1983, 22).

It is entirely possible that some discharged veterans from the army of Britain may have retired with wives from southern *civitates*. Certainly, women from the south are known in the north of Britain. Verecunda Rufilia of the Dobunni (*RIB*, 621) was buried at Templeborough fort, in Yorkshire. Her husband, Excingus, has a Celtic name and may also have been from the Dobunni, serving in *Cohors IV Gallorum*, or she may have been at Templeborough to be near some serving relative, a circumstance met not infrequently on Hadrian's Wall. A small square enclosure, seen on air photographs, to the north of Barbury Castle has a single *clavicula* entrance, with the gateway protected by a projecting curved ditch and bank. Such entrances are a feature of the marching camps of Agricola's army in his Scottish campaigns of the early 80s (Frere 1987, 211). It is tempting to speculate that the enclosure may have been a farmstead of one of Agricola's veterans, unable to break the defensive habits of his service life!

From the early 2nd century, the army took on a more defensive role with units often remaining at the same forts for many years. With this came a policy of local recruitment, with sons of veterans often following their fathers into the same regiment. With the army so far away, the numbers of volunteers from the southern *civitates* probably diminished considerably. Precisely how one enlisted in the army is unclear; documentary and literary sources suggest that a medical examination was probably a requirement whilst physical fitness was important (Vegetius, I, 6; Milner 1993, 6). A letter of introduction could be useful as an example from Vindolanda (Chesterholm) indicates (Tab.Vindol. II, 250; Bowman 1994, 124). This is particularly important since it makes reference to 'Annius Equester, centurion in charge of the region at Carlisle'. 'Centurions in charge of regions' are well-attested in Britain, at Sens in Gaul (*CIL*, XIII, 2958) and Brigetio on the Danube (*AE*, 1950.105); they are probably identifiable in Africa, Egypt and elsewhere. In Britain, Annius Equester is the earliest known example, late in the 1st century. Two are known at Ribchester where the post was combined with temporary command of the *numerus* of Sarmatian cavalry during the 3rd century. Both were probably centurions of *Legio VI Victrix*, although only one specified this (*RIB*, 583; 587; Richmond 1945, 15ff). G. Severius Emeritus, legion unspecified (but perhaps *Legio II Augusta*), restored a desecrated shrine at Bath, probably during the 3rd century. REG[ionarius] has been added to the inscription (*RIB*, 152), presumably to make clear his official status at Bath, and that he was not merely there for his health.

What were the functions of 'regional centurions'? Clearly at Ribchester military command was involved, but *regionarius* clearly implies geographical command over and above that of a normal *praepositus* or acting commander. T. Floridius Natalis (*RIB*, 587) at Ribchester is called *Praepositus N[umeri] et reg[ionis]*, clearly implying two separate responsibilities. In Africa, an inscription at Lambaesis, of AD 162 (*CIL*, VIII, 18065) lists, by name and seniority, all the centurions of *Legio III Augusta*. Surprisingly, two cohorts list eight and seven centurions respectively, rather than the usual six; the supernumeraries might well represent 'regional centurions' detached to other parts of the province, with or without acting command of an auxiliary unit. These centurions remained 'on the books' of their legions for administrative and pay purposes, but clearly relinquished command of their centuries; in modern British army terms, 'extra-regimentally employed'. Although the title seems to be used mostly in the western provinces, frequent references in the east to centurions shows that the system was Empire-wide. In Egypt, where the Romans took over a complex administration, there are a number of instances where centurions were called upon to undertake civilian tasks. However most of the references are in the form of appeals to various centurions, seeking assistance. Reports of assaults, burglaries, misdemeanours and complaints about the arrogant behaviour of tax collectors are typical.

Provincial governors had, in addition to their guard (*singulares*) drawn from the auxiliary troops, a number of *beneficiarii* or aides, employed for various duties, one of whom erected an altar at Winchester (*RIB*, 88), as well as *speculatores*, legionary 'military policemen' responsible for the arrest and delivery of those accused of major crimes and for carrying out executions. Both presumably operated from the governor's headquarters at London, at least until the Severan division of *Britannia*. One might expect the regional centurions to be based on the *civitas* capitals but the evidence does not support this – Carlisle, Ribchester and Bath suggest some other, perhaps geographical, arrangement. An office in a well-known place would be important, in order that petitioners might know where to send appeals. For the centurion at Bath, it is tempting to suggest that he may have been accommodated at the *principia*, the headquarters, named on an inscription from Combe Down (*RIB*, 179). From here his jurisdiction may have covered much of the *civitas Belgarum*, particularly since their own capital lay away in the east of the *civitas*.

Accepting that centurions and the soldiers under their command were clearly an everyday part of civilian life, can this be demonstrated by the archaeological material? There has been some debate about military metalwork found in towns and on other civilian sites (Bishop 1991, 21-7). Items lost by troops in transit can hardly explain the frequent discoveries of objects too late in date to be connected with the invasion and conquest periods. The construction of town defences might explain a few pieces, as military architects were probably involved. It is extremely unlikely that the army would have provided garrisons for towns even in the 4th century, and any locally organised 'town watch' would be hardly likely to have worn 'army-issue' equipment.

Military material of 2nd and 3rd-century types from Wiltshire comprises some 26 items (Figs 3.9, nos 43-55; 3.10, nos 56-66). Their distribution is shown on Figure 3.2. Apart from three scabbard fittings, all are pieces of belt furniture, mostly with parallels at contemporary forts in Britain, e.g. South Shields (Allason-Jones and Miket 1984), or in Germany (Oldenstein 1976). One clear explanation is that these are casual losses (and the majority could be dropped easily, without being missed!) by soldiers engaged in the policing work of the regional centurion and his men. Since the system is attested in Britain from the late 1st to the mid 3rd century at least, the amount of 'lost' equipment should occasion no surprise.

The nature of the material is also instructive, all items representing the belts and defensive weapons (swords and daggers) by which a soldier on duty would be recognised. Their civilian role would hardly require offensive weapons (javelins and spears) nor helmets and body armour, all of which presumably remained in store at their base whilst they were absent. The distribution of the Wiltshire material shows precisely what might be expected – the presence of soldiers on 'civilian duties' at every level of society in town, villa and rural settlement.

The 4th century

The pattern outlined above, of a small-scale military presence on a regional basis, probably continued down to the end of the 3rd century at least. In the latter years of the century, the army started to undergo a series of radical changes in both organisation and equipment in response to changing demands. New units, probably smaller than the nominally 500-strong *alae* and *cohortes*, had been raised from the early 2nd century, using the title *numerus* (literally 'a unit') for infantry and *numerus equitum*, later *cuneus* ('a wedge') for cavalry. *Numeri*

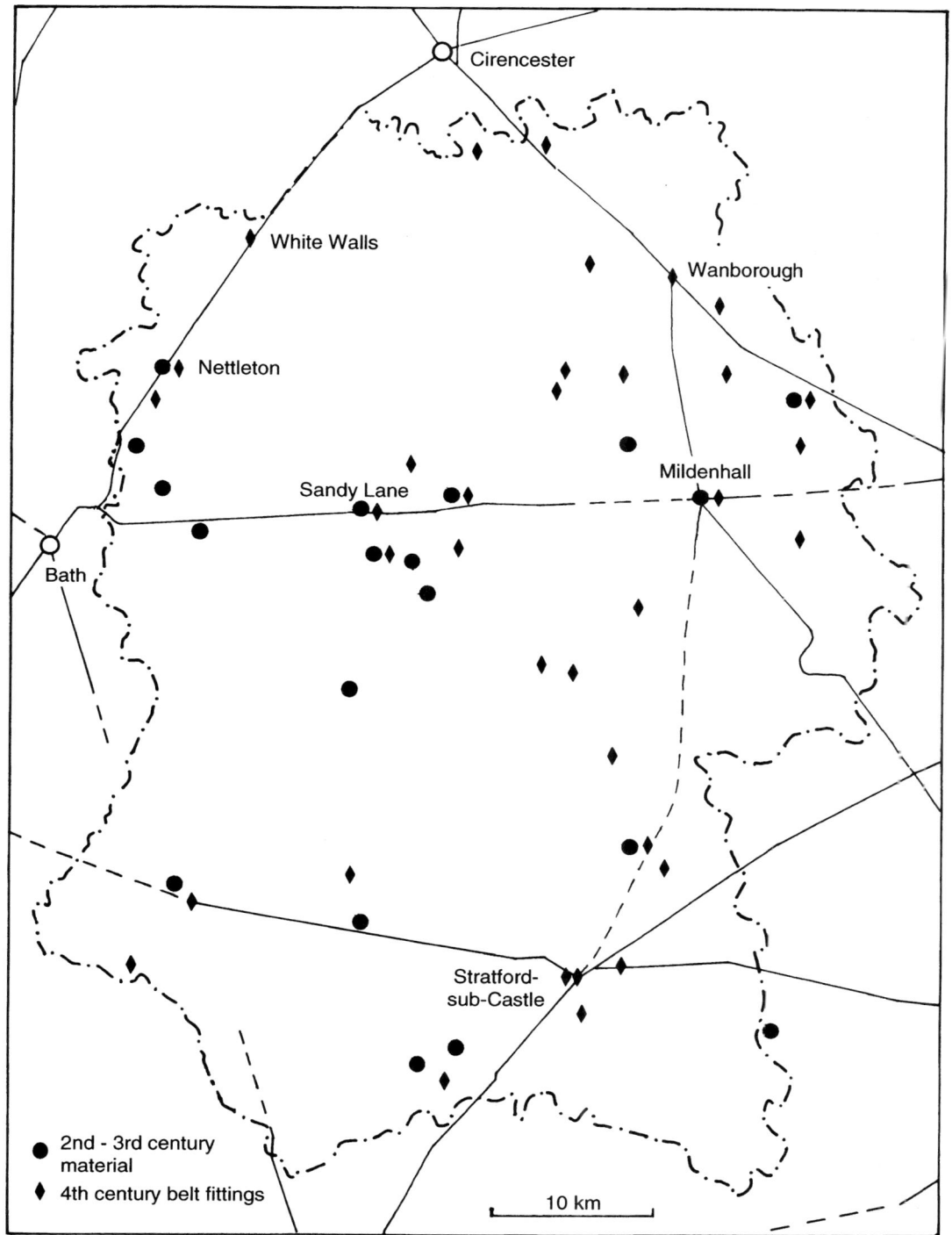

Fig. 3.2 Distribution of military material of 2nd to 4th-century date

Cirencester

White Walls

Wanborough

Nettleton

Mildenhall

Sandy Lane

Bath

Stratford-
sub-Castle

● 2nd - 3rd century
   material

♦ 4th century belt fittings

10 km

of Britons served along the German frontier, and Sarmatian cavalry from the areas across the Danube were sent to Britain (Richmond 1945, 15ff); a policy that echoed the 1st-century placing of auxiliary units, and one that may have been intended in part to re-invigorate the frontier armies, now settled and recruiting locally, by introducing a 'less-civilised' warrior element.

These new units proliferate in the 3rd century, and their smaller size may be behind the major changes that were to come, perhaps under Diocletian. In these reforms it appears that most army units were reduced in size. Many of these changes are evident from the probable 4th-century list of officials, the *Notitia Dignitatum*. Although figures are uncertain, it may be that the older legions were broken up to form 1000-strong (probably less in reality) regiments, with the older auxiliary units reduced to 150-200 men. The financial difficulties of the 3rd century may have brought about some of these reductions. Perhaps the greatest change was the creation of a two-tier army: the *limitanei* or frontier troops, usually commanded by *duces* or 'dukes', forming static garrisons with no duty but to guard the frontiers, the *limes*; and the *Comitatenses*, superior status, mobile field armies, commanded by a *comes* or 'count'. The latter were held in reserve behind the frontier, but able to move rapidly and in force to counter any intrusion from outside the Empire. Whether the manpower allowed for the continuation of the policing and other duties of the 'regional centurions' is unknown, but other systems may have replaced them.

In the 4th century, the distinctions between the civil service and the army became blurred. Civil officials were considered soldiers, and the wearing of a military belt as a mark of their status. The removal of the belt was a mark of dishonour. Ammianus Marcellinus, in a phrase that has been much referred to, describes the *'palatina'*, a palace official, as suffering this indignity, although the word would probably describe a palace-guard as well (*Ammianus Marcellinus*, XXII, 10, 5).

The military belts of the 4th century are well-known and have been much discussed, most notably in the early 1960s (Hawkes and Dunning 1961). These belts formed part of the great reform. They bore little resemblance to anything that had gone before, and large numbers of recent finds make it possible to suggest a different pattern of their usage, one that no longer sees them as closely connected with Germanic settlers, the view of Hawkes and Dunning (Corney and Griffiths forthcoming).

The earliest forms consist of cast bronze buckles, the loops formed of pairs of dolphins, usually hinged to oval or rectangular plates, the latter frequently openwork (Hawkes and Dunning 1961, type IIA). With these buckles go strap-ends of either 'amphora' or 'heart' shape, whilst the belt itself is often decorated with a number of 'propeller-shaped stiffeners'. Such stiffeners are shown on the belt of a cuirassed figure on the Arch of Constantine *c.* AD 330 (Bishop and Coulston 1993, 173). In Britain, these belts are present in graves at Winchester, dated to *c.* AD 350-370 (Clarke 1979, 264ff), and similar buckles and fittings are known across the western provinces, including Spain (Aurrecoechea 1996, 15) and Mauretania Tingitana (modern Morocco) (Boube 1960, 357).

Later graves at Winchester (Clarke 1974, 268ff) of *c.* AD 390-410 show a developed form of belt, much broader, where the buckles have zoomorphic decoration, though not dolphins. These belts (Hawkes and Dunning 1961, types IIIA, IVA) both have long straight stiffeners, and 'lancet'-shaped strap-ends. Type IIIA buckles have a simple loop and hinged plate whilst type IVA buckles have the loop and tongue set into a much larger rectangular plate. The distinction between types IIIA and IVA may have been one of rank, since their strap ends and associated fittings appear to be identical. Not surprisingly, given their late date, these types are represented by few examples, and must represent the last equipment to be sent to Britain, perhaps connected with Stilicho's restoration of the military situation *c.* AD 396. (Frere 1987, 225). In addition, a largely British series exists (Hawkes and Dunning 1961, types IA and IB) which appears to imitate the type IIA 'dolphin' buckles. Dateable examples suggest they first appeared in the 370s. They belong to narrow belts, rarely fitted with stiffeners, and with narrow strap-ends, the so-called 'Tortworth' type. These are slender versions of the 'lancet' type, although some imitate the earlier 'amphora' or 'heart'-shaped strap-ends. Their belts can only have been some 10-15mm wide.

Since much new information is available, it is clear that the origin of most, if not all, these buckles and their associated fittings is late Roman officialdom. Work in progress (Corney and Griffiths forthcoming) demonstrates that whether their usage was by the army or the 'civil service' they are found on all types of site, whether military or civilian, urban or rural (Fig. 3.2). It is clear from the documentary record that the army combined its military duties with 'civilian' tasks such as the collection of the *annona* or tax in kind, mostly grain for the use of the army. Corney (1997) has suggested that the massive stone defences of *Cunetio* should be seen as the creation of an administrative centre within the province of *Britannia Prima*. Papyri from Egypt attest to just such collection centres. Agathos, a military accountant, wrote to Abinnaeus that the Duke of the Thebaid had ordered the *annona* quotas of wheat and barley 'to be locked up in the camp' (Bell 1962, 73ff).

Nearer to Britain, the Gallic poet Ausonius refers to the storehouses of Gallia Belgica with the phrase *'non castris sed horreis Belgarum'* – 'not forts, but the granaries of the Belgae' (Branigan and Fowler 1976, 114, quoting Ausonius, *Mosella*, 456-7). In the light of these comments, it is clear that the presence of military or quasi-military officials at villas and other rural sites may have more to do with the supervised collection of the *annona* than with the defence of farms against surprise attacks. Even if the army of late-Roman Britain had sufficient manpower to spare soldiers for defensive duties in the south west, it would hardly have made military sense to place small groups in all the villas and settlements where belt fittings have been discovered. In the light of the 'new' finds, and the forthcoming corpus, a complete listing is included, though none of the pieces are illustrated here.

The presence of 'soldiers' at civilian sites in the late 4th century is only a continuation of earlier practices, since the army had always been responsible for policing and for much of the administration of the province. Whilst the army's initial involvement with Wiltshire may well have been short-lived and relatively small-scale, soldiers would have been a routine part of life, even when the military areas had moved far to the north. Thus while the army played many roles in 'Roman Wiltshire', it is true to say that they represented a major feature of life throughout the centuries of Roman rule.

Catalogue

In the following catalogue items are grouped chronologically as outlined in the text; within these groups the order is by type of object, rather than provenance. Those objects that were discussed in the present author's earlier paper (Griffiths 1983) are dealt with here in a more summary fashion; for fuller references the reader is referred to the earlier work, although in some cases, a revised dating is presented here. The references have been simplified to Griffiths no. 1, 2, 3 etc.

Objects dating from the initial military occupation (Figs. 3.3-3.7)

1. Crescentic pendant, bronze. A type well known from both surviving examples, e.g. Chichester (Down 1974, 52, fig. 5.5, no. 10), and tombstones, e.g. T. Flavius Bassus at Koln and Flavinus at Hexham (Anderson 1984, 59-60, 56). Of the various types of pendant, the crescent-shaped come in the most varieties and varying qualities, and appear throughout the 1st century and into the early 2nd, perhaps outlasting other types; Griffiths no. 2. Box, WHM, 53/1967.
2. 'Trifoliate' shaped pendant, bronze. Damaged, but retaining traces of silvering and niello inlay, probably the usual 'vine-tendril' pattern (*cf.* Richmond 1968, 41, fig. 31, no. 2). Finds from Britain suggest that this type was disappearing during the Flavian period, one of the latest perhaps being that from Y Gaer, Brecon, dated to the end of the 1st century (Wheeler 1926, 114, fig. 57, no. 2); Griffiths no. 5. Chisbury Camp, Great Bedwyn; in private possession.
3. 'Trifoliate' shaped pendant, bronze. Very worn but retaining a trace of decoration. Originally the design on both nos 2 and 3 would have resembled that on no. 4. From Alton Barnes; reported to WHM March 2000 (daybook 2186).
4. Phallic pendant, bronze, found with no. 2. A common type of pendant on sites of Claudian to Flavian date. The phallic motif was popular in the ancient world symbolizing, amongst other aspects, good fortune. Griffiths no. 6. From Chisbury Camp; WHM, 1989.222.
5. 'Winged' pendant, bronze. A fine example with transverse bar and grooved 'fantail' at the base. It retains much of its thin silver foil covering, through which the decoration was cut, and then filled with niello, forming a pattern of vine tendrils and bunches of grapes. This type is found in Britain and Germany, and, further afield, Syria and Morocco. Most date from the Claudian-Flavian period. Griffiths no. 13. From Edington, 1981; in private possession.
6. 'Winged' pendant, bronze. Although badly abraded, this is clearly similar to no. 5. There are faint traces of vine-tendril and niello decoration. Probably of Claudian or Neronian date. Anderson and Wacher 1980, 122-3, fig. 4, no. 1. From excavations at Wanborough 1976, SF 250; Swindon Museum and Art Gallery.
7. Pendant, bronze, with tinned or silvered surface. One knobbed terminal survives, and the leaf-shaped central feature may have ended in a further knob. While exact parallels are hard to find, a similar piece is known from Hod Hill (Brailsford 1962, 5, A137), and the object is perhaps a variant of the crescentic type. Griffiths no. 20. From Stockton Earthworks; Salisbury Museum.
8. Disc, bronze, with a stud on the rear and a hinge on one edge retaining part of the object that hung from it. This may be the back-plate from a composite *phalera*, the decorative mount from which pendants were hung. Griffiths no. 3. From Casterley Camp, near Upavon; WHM, 1994. 294.50.

Fig. 3.3 Cat. nos 1-7: bronze objects of 1st-century date; actual size

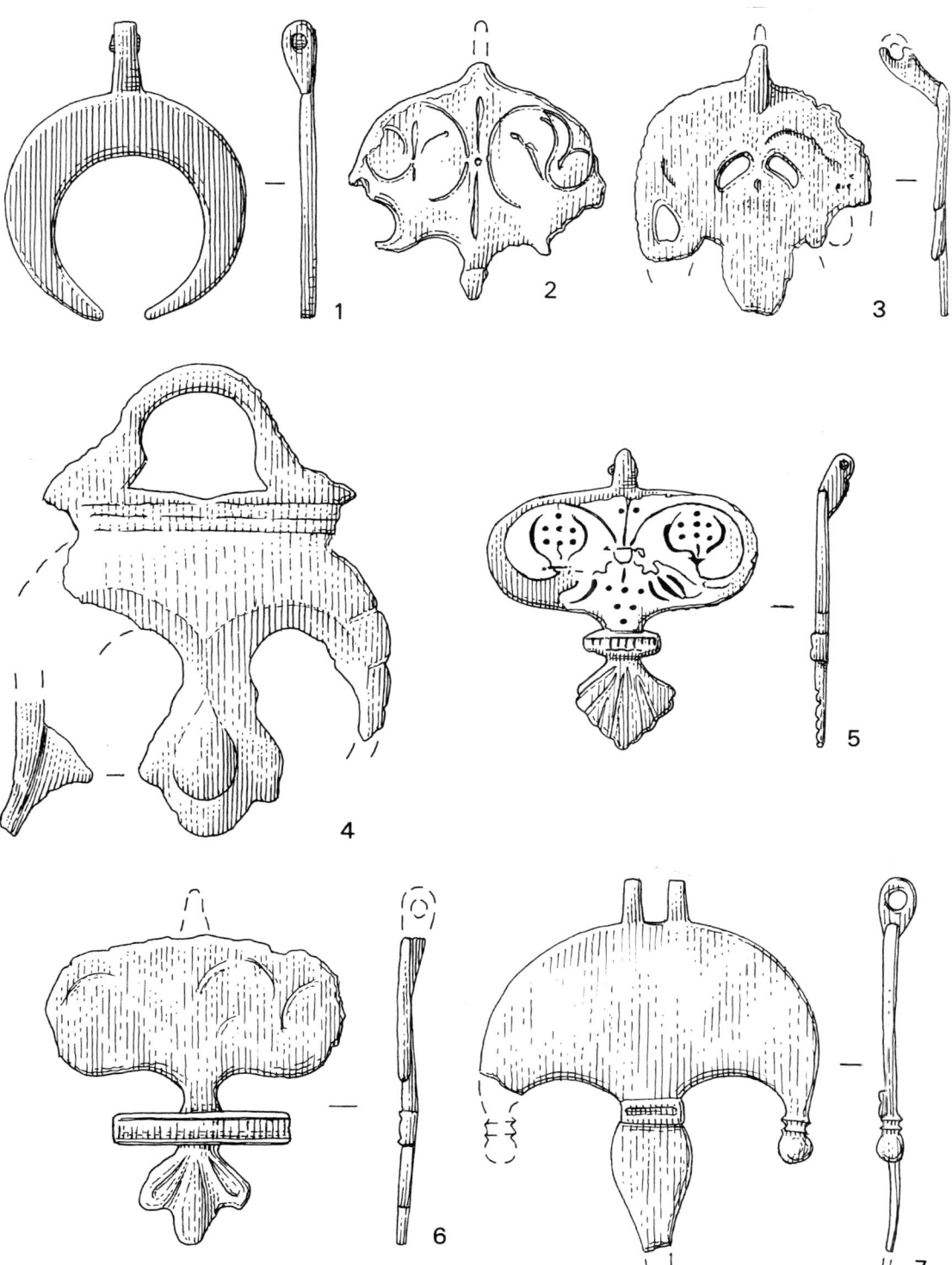

1

2

3

4

5

6

7

9. Mount, bronze, with hinged 'loop', with a ?silver inlay. Such objects fastened two harness-straps: a matching mount, on the other strap, had a T-shaped 'hook' which engaged in the 'key-hole' slot. An alternative identification, that of 'baldric-fastener', seems unnecessary; baldrics are lifted on and off, over the head, and do not require any fastening. The Doorwerth find of harness fittings shows that, decoratively, these objects form sets with the *phalerae* and pendants (Holwerda 1931). Around the middle of the 1st century, the hinged form was replaced by a simpler, single-piece loop. Swan 1970, 195-8; Griffiths no. 16. From Nettleton Scrubb; WHM, 5/57/280.

10. Strap-mount, bronze with niello decoration. Although no exact parallels have been found, its form and inlay are similar to well-known 1st-century types, cf. nos 11-13 (Jenkins 1985; Webster 1980, 152). Griffiths no. 15. From Manton Down, near Marlborough; WHM, Brooke Collection 52.

11. Strap-mount, bronze, probably originally with niello decoration and perhaps silvering (Annable 1974, 176, fig. 2, 2; Webster 1980, 149, where it is erroneously attributed to 'Bilbury Camp', Wylye). Griffiths no. 21. From Stockton Earthworks; Salisbury Museum.

12. Strap-mount, probably bronze, recorded in a sketch by the Revd Soames. It appears to have been a variant of no. 10, and may have retained traces of decoration (Annable 1976, 126f., fig. 1). Griffiths no. 10. From Forest Hill Farm, Mildenhall. Lost.

13. Strap-terminal, bronze, of the same general type as nos 10-11, but with a terminal knob; an exact parallel was found at Winchester. Annable 1974, 176, fig. 2, 1; Griffiths no. 9. From a mid 1st-century well at Mildenhall; WHM.

14-16. Harness hooks, bronze; three examples, varying slightly in decoration, mid 1st century. These hooks, riveted to the ends of harness straps, were clipped onto a ring, providing a flexible junction. Stylistically and decoratively, these differ from the strap-fittings (nos 8-12) and their associated hooks; the types represented here may represent harnesses not carrying *phalerae* and pendants. For double and triple junctions from Hod Hill, see Brailsford (1962, 2, A30, A31). The mouldings on nos 14 and 15 are very similar to the Hod Hill pieces. From Chisbury Camp; WHM 1999.23.3 (no. 14), 1999.23.2 (no. 16). Number 15 remains in private possession.

17. Ring and stud, bronze. Such objects are frequently associated with harness fittings and may have served as 'easy-release' strap fasteners, the stud being pushed through a narrow slot in the subsidiary strap, the ring perhaps being attached to hooks such as nos 13-15. There are traces of fine punched decoration around the circumference of the ring. Anderson and Wacher 1980, 122-3, fig. 4, no. 3. From excavations at Wanborough, 1976, SF 86. Swindon Museum and Art Gallery.

18. Ring and stud, bronze, with both incised and raised 'beaded' decoration. Since similar objects occur in Iron Age contexts, a Roman date is uncertain, but an unpublished, decorated example comes from Hod Hill. This piece was found in association with the harness hooks, nos 14-16. From Chisbury Camp; in private possession.

19. Bell, bronze, with an angular loop, similar to those on a number of bells from military sites, e.g. Fishbourne (Cunliffe 1971, 115, nos 106-8) and perhaps from horse-harness. Anderson and Wacher 1980, 122-3, fig. 4, no. 2. From excavations at Wanborough, 1976. Swindon Museum and Art Gallery.

20. Martingale or strap-distributor, bronze, with three circular loops and a decorative horse head. Punched dots perhaps indicate harness. Although dating is uncertain, examples are known from sites with military occupation. Griffiths no. 26. From Easton Grey; in private possession.

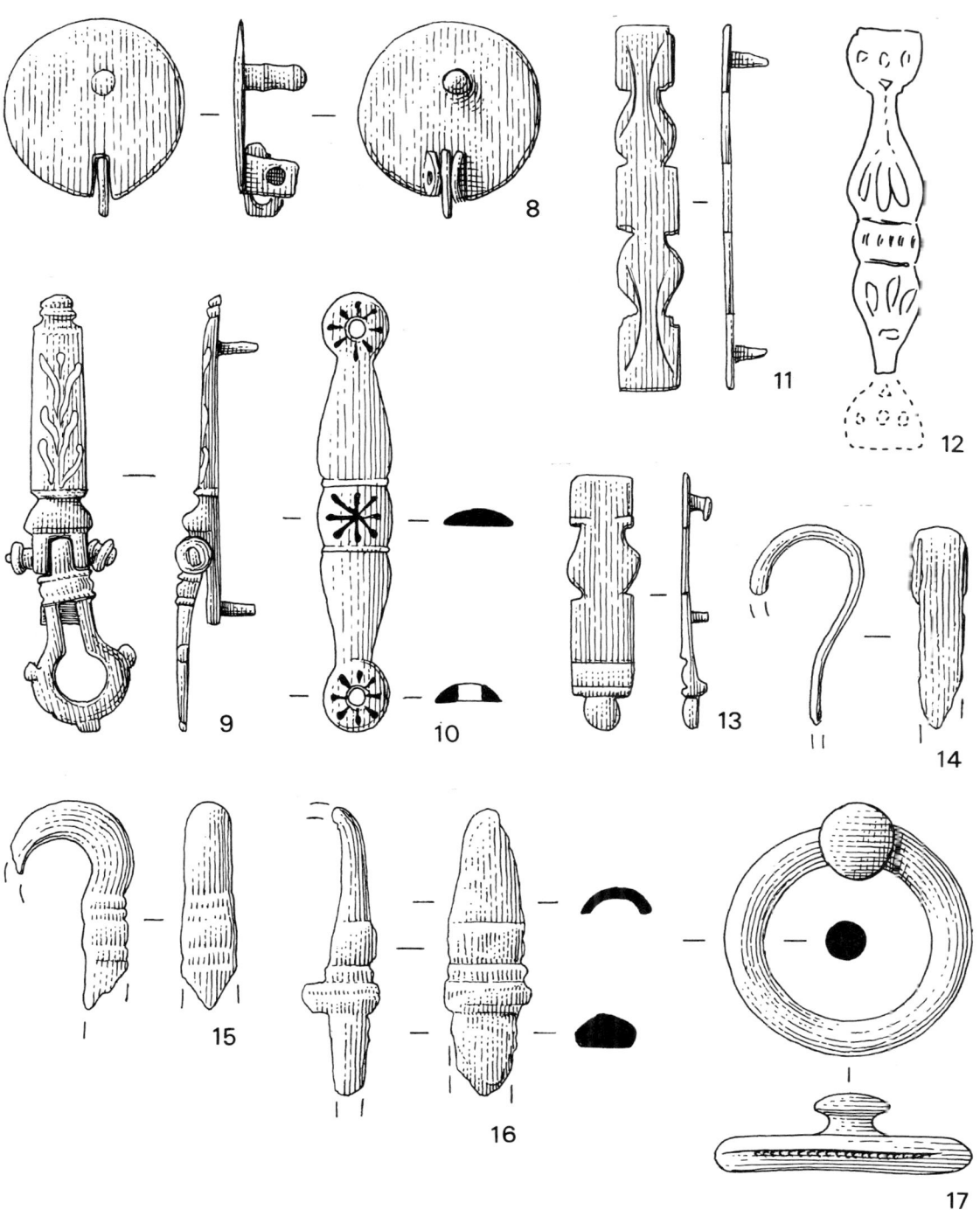

Fig. 3.4 Cat. nos 8-17: bronze objects of 1st-century date; actual size

21. Decorative mount, bronze. Leaf-shaped with rounded knobs at top and bottom, with the remains of a 'square loop' on the back. An oval harness mount in the Yorkshire Museum has a similar 'loop' but is probably of 2nd-century date or later (Webster 1971, 122-3, no. 91). The simpler leaf-shape of the piece in question suggests a possible 1st-century date; a similar object from Piddington, Northants, closely resembles 1st-century pendants (Friendship-Taylor and Friendship-Taylor 1989, 22-3, fig. 14, no. 3; Wacher and McWhirr 1982, 112ff, no. 115). From East Kennett; in private possession.

22. Buckle, of bronze, perhaps originally tinned but now heavily stained with iron. An elaborate example with both internal and external scrolls and a 'lily' form of tongue. Buckles of this type are well known from Britain, where they appear to be passing out of use during the 60s (Grew and Griffiths 1991; the closest parallels illustrated are nos 142 and 154, both from Hod Hill). This type of buckle most likely fastened an infantryman's belt, either legionary or auxiliary. From Ashton Keynes; in private possession.

23. Buckle, bronze; a fragment, of the same type as no. 21, but slightly smaller. From excavations at Ashton Keynes, SF 755.

24. Circular stud of bronze, with a notched edge and faint cruciform pattern. A type frequently found on 1st-century sites in Britain, and thought to have been fitted to the infantry 'apron', the group of straps that hung from the waist-belt. For the 'apron', see Bishop and Coulston (1993, 98-9). From Wanborough; Swindon Museum and Art Gallery

25. Stud, of bronze, of phallic form, with a single projecting pin on the rear. Although studs of a multitude of designs were used to decorate both personal belts and horse-harness throughout the Roman period, the phallic form finds its best parallels in the pendants of the 1st century (*cf.* no. 3). From Wanborough; WHM, 72.1966.1.

26. Hinged buckle of bronze, badly damaged. Enough remains to identify it as a buckle from a laminated armour ('*lorica segmentata*'), most likely a legionary's equipment. The hinge arrangement allowed some movement; these buckles were used to fasten the breast and back plates and also connected the upper and lower portions of the armour. They are present on the armours from Corbridge, of late 1st-century date, but the 2nd-century Newstead type has a sturdier bronze hook-and-eye arrangement (Robinson 1975, 174ff). From the Aldbourne area; WHM, 1994.320.

27. Scabbard-mount, bronze. Possibly a decorative band from the lower part of a scabbard. It is too narrow to have fitted the scabbard and also to have accommodated the suspension rings that were a feature of Roman scabbards. Pitt-Rivers, 1888, 131 and pl. ciii, no.10; Griffiths no. 17. From Rotherley; Salisbury Museum 3M 1A 41.

28. Spearhead of iron; the base of the blade expands into a 'circular' shape, and the piece was perhaps a standard head. From Roundway Down; WHM 1998.86.

29. Arrowhead, iron; the fluted triangular section and short tang were distinctive features of 1st and 2nd-century Roman arrowheads, although this one is rather large. Griffiths no. 4. Probably from Rushall Down; WHM no. 557 d.

30-33. Ballista-bolts of iron from Rotherley. No. 30, Salisbury Museum 3M 3A 4 (Pitt-Rivers 1888, 133-4, pl. civ, 12), Griffiths no. 18; no. 31 Salisbury Museum 3M 3A 11 (*ibid.*, 133-4, pl. civ, 13), Griffiths no. 19; no. 32 Salisbury Museum 3M 1A 36 (*ibid.*, 138, pl. cvi, 8); no. 33 Salisbury Museum 3M 2A 21 (*ibid.*, 136, pl. cv, 4).

34. Hooked-guard of bronze from an axe-sheath. A pair of such hooks were attached to a bronze and wood binding, which protected the cutting edge of the *dolabra* or military pick-axe. An early example was found at Hod Hill (Brailsford 1962, 5, A137). From Wanborough; now lost. *WANHM*, 41, 280, pl. i, no. 10; Griffiths no. 23.

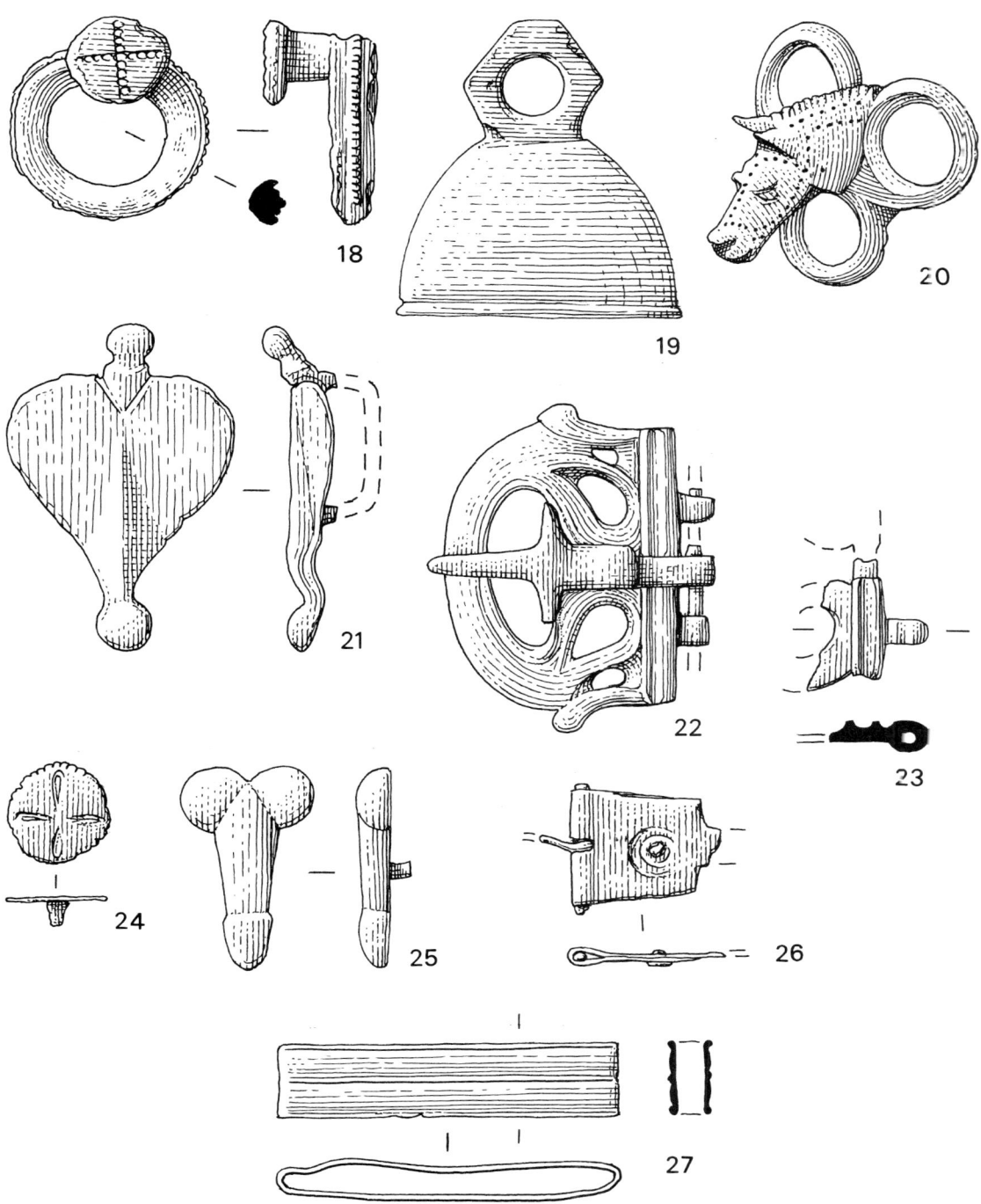

Fig. 3.5 Cat. nos 18-27: bronze objects of probable 1st-century date; actual size

35-37. Two skillets of bronze, with the corroded fragments of a third base and handle. These are the typical '*trulleus*' or military mess-tin/saucepan, frequently found on 1st-century sites, e.g. Hod Hill (Brailsford 1962, 4-5, A135). From Westbury Ironworks, 1877-1882; WHM 624, 625. Griffiths nos 24 and 25.

38. Skillet-handle fragment, bronze. Although very worn, this seems to be part of the ring-end of a skillet handle, as nos 35-37. From Upper Woodford; in private possession.

39. Eagle-head fitting of bronze; the upper part of a cylindrical socketed mount, from which sprang a bird's (?swan's) neck and head. These items are considered to be wagon fittings, perhaps finials to which reins could be tied. A number come from sites with military associations, e.g. two examples from Cirencester (Wacher and McWhirr, 1982, 111-12, fig. 37, nos 105-6). From Calstone Wellington; in private possession.

40. Masked loop of bronze, an unusual item. The masked loop is similar to a type of terret or rein-guide often found on military sites, but the grooved stud is unlike any example known to the author. The normal upper part would be a ring through which the reins would pass. Although this item has been included, its military connections remain rather tenuous. From Mother Anthony's Well; Bromham; WHM 1996.110.

41. Penannular brooch, bronze, of Fowler's type B1 (British Omega-brooches). From Wilcot; WHM 1979.35.

42. Knife-handle of bronze, with the remains of an iron blade. The handle has a rectangular open centre into which a biconical shaft has been riveted. There is a ring for suspension at the 'pommel', and a circular cut-out at the blade end, originally terminating in a diagonal edge. The form of the suspension ring with two internal projections resembles 1st-century buckle-loops, and it may be that the design was intended to appeal to soldiers. A more elaborate, but generally similar knife was found in the Roman fort at Nanstallon, Cornwall, occupied between *c.* AD 60 and *c.* AD 80 (Fox and Ravenhill 1972, 95, and fig. 19, no. 12). From Wiltshire, exact findspot unknown; WHM 1993.614.

Two further types of find are frequently cited as evidence of the army's presence: imitation Claudian coin issues and pre-Flavian fineware ceramics. For the sake of completeness, a listing of both is provided.

Imitation Claudian coins
These were produced, presumably under army control, to make up for a deficiency of 'official' bronze coinage (Kenyon 1987). Colchester was almost certainly one 'mint'. Whilst much of the production was perhaps intended to be army pay, too much should not be read into finds of these coins. No doubt supplemented by pre-Claudian issues, they represented the general small change of both soldiers and civilians down to the mid-60s, and would have circulated widely. Imitation Claudian coins are known to the author from the following Wiltshire sites: Wanborough (9 examples); Mildenhall (2); Wilcot (2); Aldbourne area (2); Westbury (Heywood) (1); ?North Wraxall (1); Fifield Bavant (1); Casterley Camp (1); Charlton Down (1); Liddington (1); Bromham (1); 'Wiltshire' (1).

Pre-Flavian finewares
A Central Gaulish lead-glazed pottery cup from Woodcutts, Dorset, was mentioned above. Greene (1979, 100) lists only Wanborough as a Wiltshire findspot, although ceramics were perhaps less likely to pass from soldiers to the natives than coins.

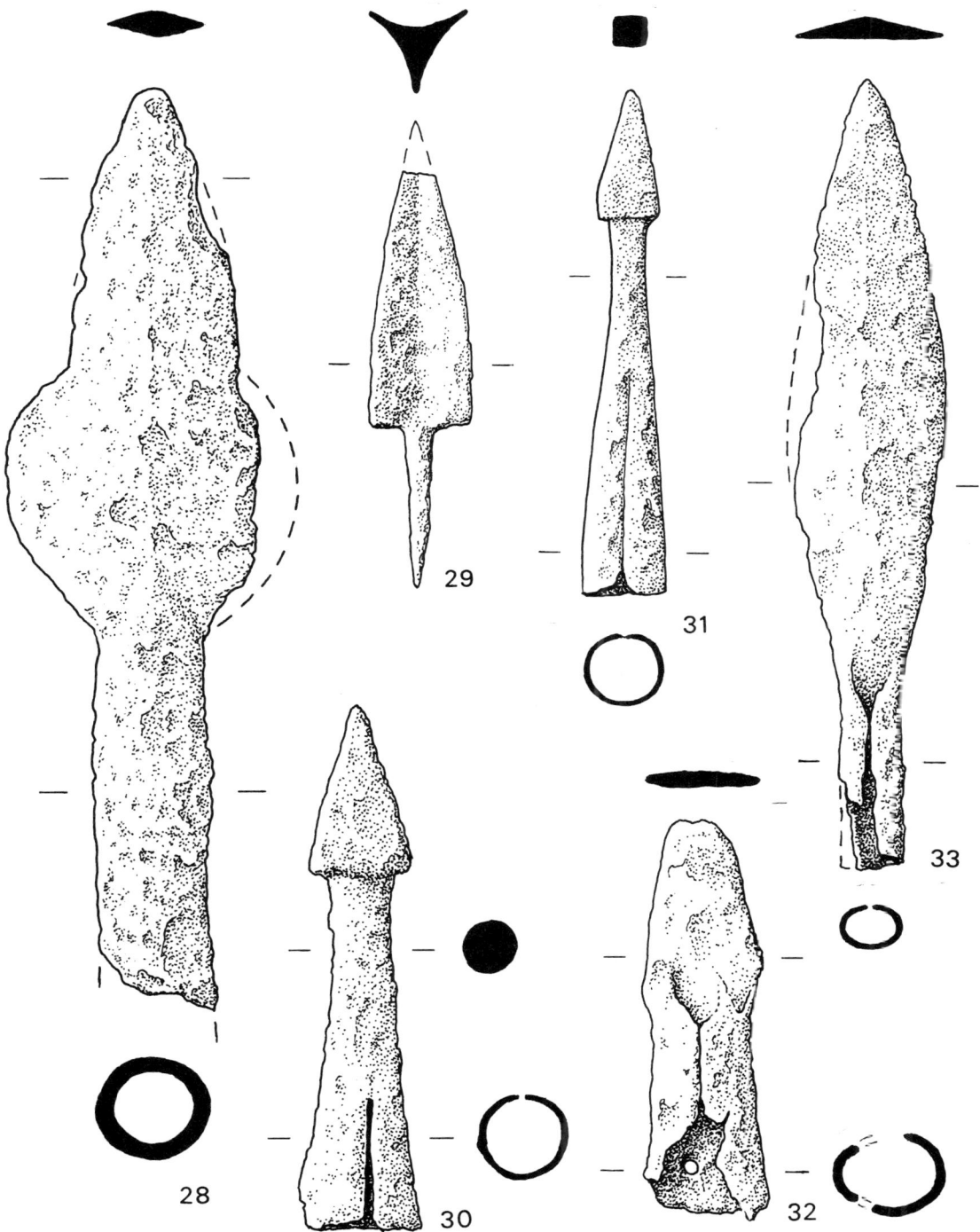

Fig. 3.6: Cat. nos 28-33: iron objects of probable 1st-century date; actual size

Purported military items

During the early 1970s a 'Roman helmet' and 'Roman armour' were said to have been found in the River Thames in North Wiltshire. Nothing can be found to substantiate these reports, and if anything was found it is likely to have been of a later date and misreported. In April 1979, the magazine *'Treasure Hunting'* contained a letter which mentioned 'a Roman sword and some coins' being found in the north Wiltshire Thames. The county SMR has no note of such a find, and it seems unlikely that the sword was correctly identified. A large collection of Roman military metalwork was reported in 1981, and initially a findspot in west Wiltshire was suggested (Griffiths 1983, 59). This material was eventually shown to have been found at Camerton, Somerset, and most of it was acquired by the British Museum (Jackson 1990).

A SELECTION OF FINDS OF 1ST-CENTURY DATE FROM ADJACENT COUNTIES (FIG. 3.8)

A Side-plate from bridle-bit, of bronze. Very similar to three plates from Hod Hill (Brailsford 1962, 2, A25-A27). From the Lambourn area, Berkshire; in private possession.

B Strap-terminal, bronze. As no. 12 from Mildenhall. Found at the Castle, Winchester; now lost.

C Knife-handle, bronze, *cf.* no. 41. This example is a very close parallel to that from Nanstallon. From Sutton Scotney, Hampshire; in private possession.

D Pendant, of 'leaf'-shape, bronze with niello decoration and traces of silvering. Although this object has few close parallels, its niello decoration uses motifs more commonly seen on 1st-century belt-plates (Webster and Dudley 1965, 192, no. 10; Grew and Griffiths 1991, 56ff). From Lancing Down, Sussex; Ashmolean Museum 1927.6436.

E Crescentic pendant, of bronze with fine punched decoration and a hole for a very small internal pendant. A very similar pendant was found at Gloucester (Green 1943, 28, pl. i, 17). A 1st-century type. From the Yeovil area, Somerset; in private possession.

F Mount with hinge for loop; bronze with traces of decoration. Whilst this piece was similar in function to no. 9, its form and decoration echo those of no. 11. Probably mid 1st-century. From Langport, Somerset; in private possession.

G Pendant of bronze, of unusually ornate form and with traces of silvering. Whilst the generally crescentic shape resembles various pendants, the elaborate scroll-work within the arc (and supporting a small circular pendant) are very unusual, as are the opposing scrolls on the outside of the crescent. However, there can be little doubt that this is a Roman object and belongs to the period *c.* AD 49 – *c.* AD 70 when Cirencester held a cavalry garrison (Paddock 1998, 305-7). From Cirencester, Gloucestershire; Corinium Museum A309/10.

Objects dating from the 2nd and 3rd centuries, found in Wiltshire (Figs. 3.9-3.10)

From the early 2nd to the late 3rd century, there is a great proliferation of small belt fittings, unlike most of the earlier material. While a number of types can be recognised, there is considerable variety within any one type, and exact parallels are often hard to find. One common feature is that the studs by which these objects were secured frequently have broad flat heads.

43. Buckle, of bronze; a common type, derived form the heavier pre-Flavian buckles though no longer hinged to the belt-plates. This example is more ornate than most, incorporating openwork scrolls. From Sandy Lane (*Verlucio*); WHM 1989.12.

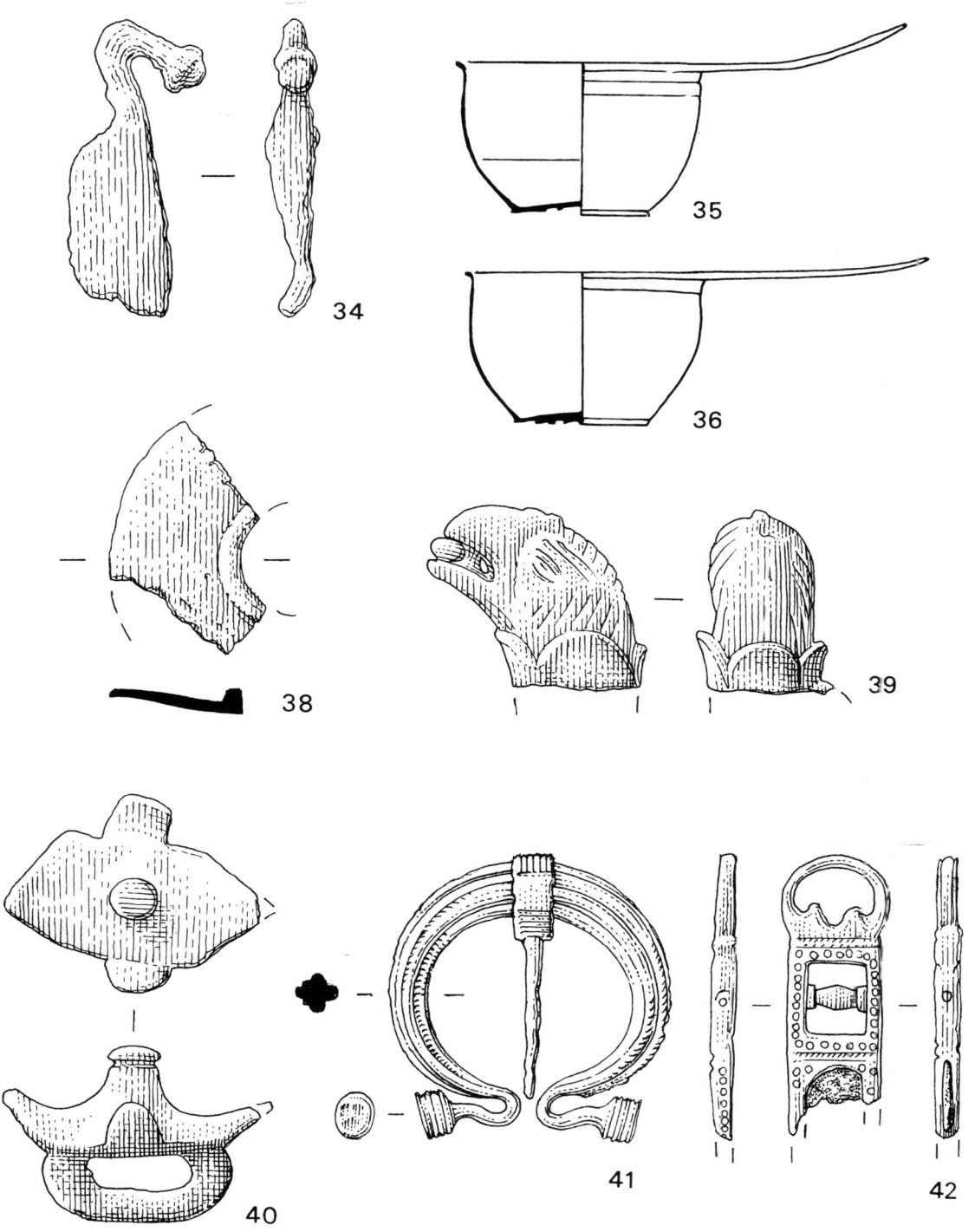

Fig. 3.7 Cat. nos 34-6, 38-42: bronze objects of probable 1st-century date; actual size except 35-6, 1:4

44. Belt-plate, bronze; a fragment of an openwork rectangular plate; as with no. 43, typical of the lighter (and cheaper to produce!) belt fittings of the 2nd century. Griffiths no. 7. From Colerne Park; WHM 11/56/258.

45. Small pendant of leaf-shape, bronze. Such pendants were perhaps used on the 'apron' hanging from the military belt, which seems to have lasted in use into the 2nd century (Bishop and Coulston 1993, 112, fig. 72). Two, possibly Antonine, examples were found in the Caerleon amphitheatre (Wheeler and Wheeler 1928, 169, pl. xxxiii, 1, nos 7 and 8). From the Aldbourne area; WHM 1989.91.

46. Small pendant of leaf-shape, bronze. Slightly larger than no. 45, but otherwise very similar. From Amesbury; Salisbury Museum 79/1989.

47. Small crescentic pendant, bronze, the loop broken. Such objects, with knobbed terminals, were perhaps used in the same way as nos 45-46 above. Examples from Germany date to the 2nd century, e.g. at Stockstadt (Oldenstein 1976, taf. 45, no. 445). Griffiths no. 8. From Mildenhall; WHM, Brooke Collection 63.

48. Small crescentic pendant, bronze with panels of blue and yellow enamel, and a damaged hole for the suspension of a very small pendant in the centre. Generally similar to no. 46, the enamel suggests an Antonine or later date (Bishop and Coulston 1993, 119). A very similar piece from Stockstadt (Germany) is suspended from a circular stud with the same decorative scheme (Oldenstein 1976, taf. 45, no. 449). From Devizes; in private possession.

49. Circular stud with attached crescent; bronze. The hollow-backed upper element has three small projections and the trace of a central pin. Although the complete object is hard to parallel, the knobbed crescent is so similar to nos 47 and 48 that a 2nd-century date seems likely. From Atworth Roman villa excavations, SF2990.

50. Openwork mount, bronze, with a pelta-shaped end, perhaps originally symmetrical, with two studs. A similar piece was found at Caerleon (Nash-Williams 1932, 83, fig. 33, no. 26), unfortunately unstratified. Griffiths no. 12. From Mildenhall; WHM, Brooke Collection, 69.

51. Mount, bronze; although difficult to parallel exactly, the form of the stud would suit a 2nd century or later date, and the shape of the mount is close to that of the internal shaft of no. 41. From Calstone Wellington; in private possession.

52. Pelta-shaped mount, bronze, one arm damaged, with two studs on the rear. A typical example of a motif, derived from the classical Greek shield borne by the Amazons. Common in the 2nd century, the pelta is frequently used in the framing of inscriptions (e.g. *RIB*, pl. xiv, xv, xvii). From Broad Chalke; in private possession.

53. Pelta-shaped mount, bronze, one arm missing; a variant of no. 52, with a single stud. Griffiths no. 11. From Mildenhall; WHM, 110.1981.D3, ex-Marlborough College Collection.

54. Pelta-shaped mount, bronze; a more elaborate version of nos 52 and 53, with the arms conjoined to the decorative upper part, forming a closed shape. Two worn studs are present on the rear. From Cold Kitchen Hill, Monkton Deverill; WHM 1214.

55. Pelta-shaped mount, bronze; a very small example, close in shape to no. 53, with a single pin on the rear. From Atworth Roman villa excavations, SF 4242.

56. Mount, bronze, with two studs on the rear. Four crescentic cut-outs produce the appearance of a pair of opposed pelta-shapes, to which are added two so-called 'vulvate' motifs, for which see no. 58. Although difficult to parallel, the combinations of motifs confirms its Roman attribution. From Bromham; in private possession.

57. Escutcheon-shaped mount, bronze; two large flat-headed studs on the rear. A type of mount which may be a simplified form of the pelta, and is well-represented on 2nd to 3rd-century sites, e.g. Niederbieber, Germany (Oldenstein 1976, taf. 57, nos 696-9); Richborough,

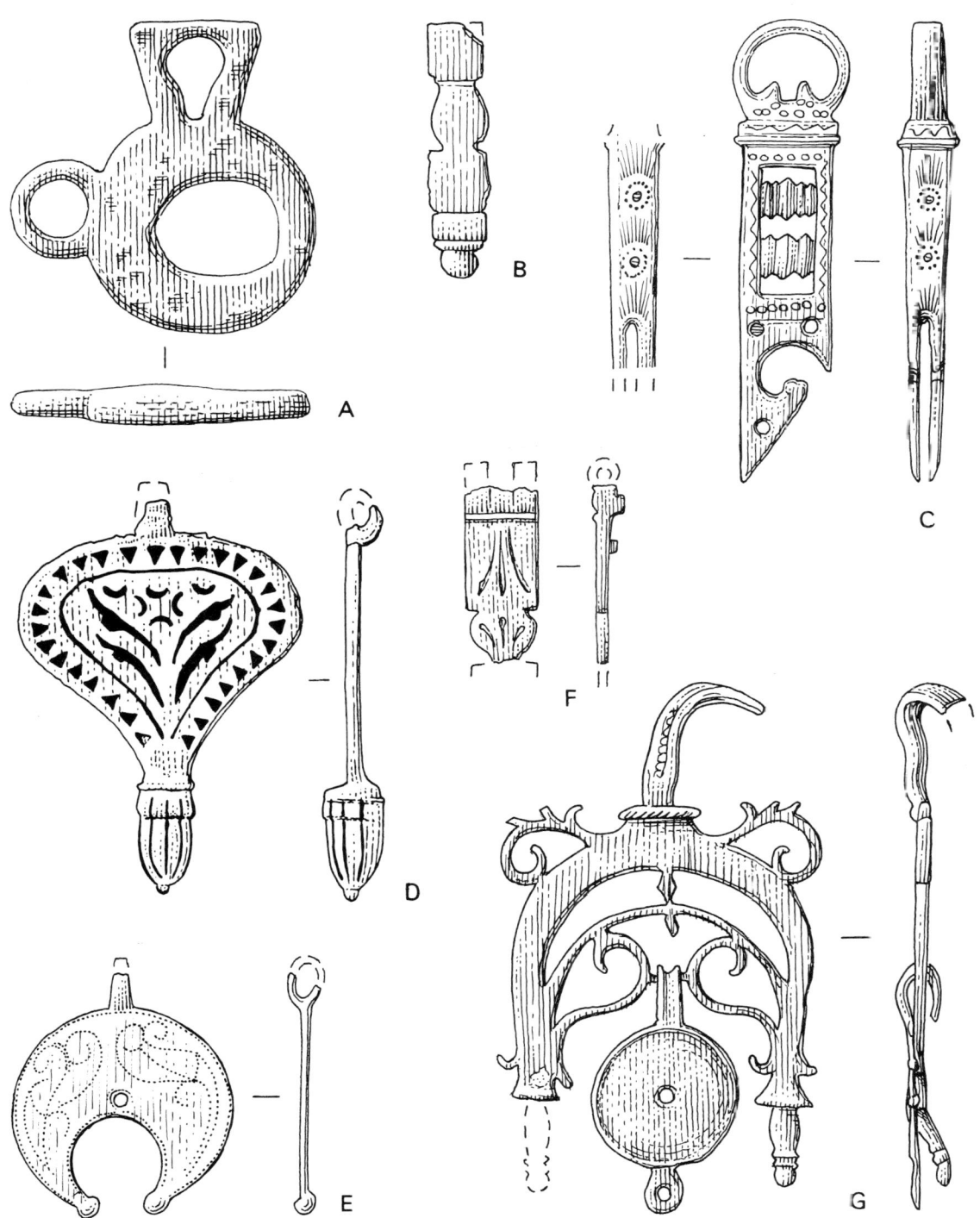

Fig. 3.8 Comparative bronze material from adjacent areas; actual size

unpublished, no. 3722; Lydney, Gloucestershire (Bathurst 1879, pl. xii, no. 10). From Box; WHM 1997. 65.

58. Sub-rectangular stud, bronze; of 'vulvate' form, with two studs on the rear. Similar studs, sometimes with a suspension loop for a small pendant on the lower edge, are now widely recognised finds on 2nd to 3rd-century sites, e.g. Brougham, Cumbria, SF 409 from burial 270 in the 3rd-century cremation cemetery; Saalburg, Germany (Oldenstein 1976, taf. 34, nos. 267 -70). Griffiths no. 14. From Erlestoke; WHM 36. 1982.1.

59. Circular mount, bronze; with two studs on the rear and a raised concentric ridge. This item, and the following two, are typical of the circular mounts that were commonly used to decorate leatherwork throughout the Roman period. However, the form of the studs suggests a 2nd or 3rd-century date. From Fifield Bavant; in private possession.

60. Circular mount, bronze; with two studs on the rear. From West Dean villa (but just in Hampshire); Salisbury Museum.

61. Circular mount, bronze; with damaged edge and a single stud on the rear. From Stockton Earthworks; Salisbury Museum.

62. Strap-junction (?), bronze. A rectangular plate, slotted to take a strap, from which projects a leaf-shape, with incised decoration. Behind the leaf is a single stud with an expanded head. An unusual object with no obvious parallels. However, the stud, and the similarity of the incised decoration to that on nos 45-6 (and on the terminal of no. 64) suggests a 2nd or 3rd-century date. The item may well have served to link two straps, one held by the stud, the other looped through the plate. From Mother Anthony's Well, Bromham; WHM for identification, Daybook 2090.11. The object remains in private possession.

63. Crescentic mount, bronze, with a single stud on the rear. Whilst there is some resemblance to crescentic pendants, the stud suggests a 2nd or 3rd-century date, and the object may be another of the myriad types of decorative mount seen at this period. Griffiths no. 22. From Stockton Earthworks; Salisbury Museum.

64. Leaf-shaped mount, bronze, with a single pin on the rear, expanding into a short bar, and a knobbed tip. Probably of 2nd or 3rd-century date. From Temple, near Marlborough; WHM, Brooke Collection 71.

65. Scabbard loop fragment, bronze; a sub-circular loop, originally the upper terminal of a scabbard loop such as no. 66. That this loop is not the terminal for no. 66 is shown by the difference in the metal of the two objects. For a complete example, see Webster (1971, p.120, fig.16, no. 82). From Atworth Roman villa excavations SF 3431.

66. Scabbard loop, bronze. A standard 2nd and 3rd-century type, fastened to the front of the scabbard and worn with a baldric. The expanded tip carries an incised X, seen on other examples. A number of scabbard loops of this type were found at Caerleon (Nash-Williams 1932, p. 43-4, fig. 36, nos 2-11), the majority dating to the 2nd century. Several of the Caerleon examples show the ribbed projection which may be missing here; an alternative would be an oval or circular loop, *cf.* no. 65. Griffiths no. 1. From Atworth Roman villa excavations, SF 2195.

67. Scabbard fitting (?), ivory. A slotted sub-rectangular plate of ivory with a transverse perforation and two damaged, curved, cut-outs. Whilst this object bears a superficial resemblance to a known series of ivory scabbard-chapes (seven examples, from Caerleon, dated between *c.* AD 120-300; Nash-Williams, 1932, p. 53ff, nos 1-6, 8), no exact parallel can be found. From Nettleton Scrubb (Wedlake, 1984, 145f. and pl. xxiiib). Not illustrated here.

68. A circular bronze stud with traces of millefiore ornament of a type sometimes associated with the army has been noted amongst the objects from Atworth Roman villa (J. Bircher, pers comm). WHM, not illustrated.

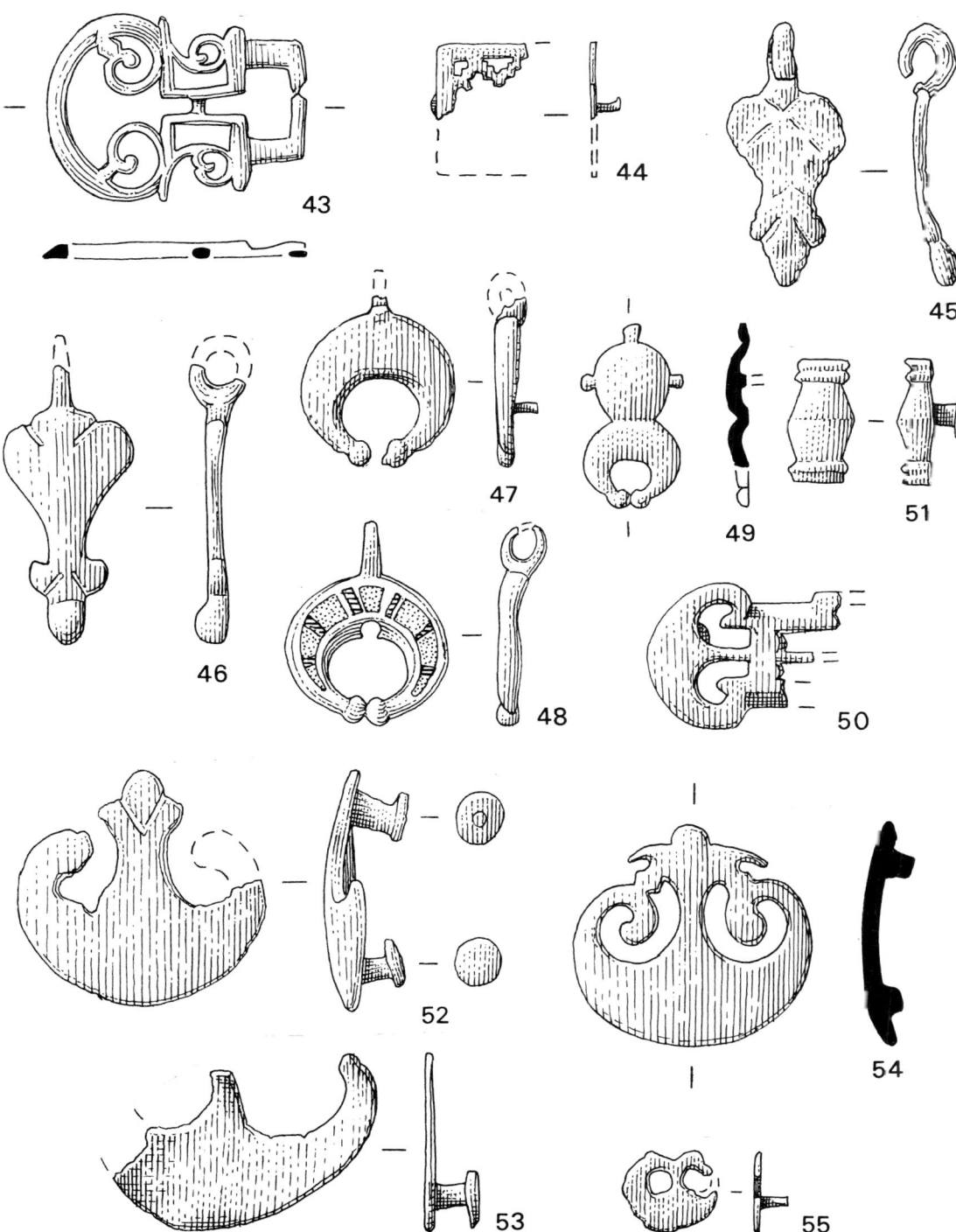

Fig. 3.9 Cat. nos 43-55: bronze objects of 2nd to 3rd-century date; actual size

Fourth-century belt-fittings

As noted above, a major survey of 4th-century metalwork is in progress, and accordingly a simple list of Wiltshire provenances is offered here. Whilst the typology is basically that of Hawkes and Dunning (1961), it has been extended to include strap-ends and the other related items that made up these complex belt-suites. The material has been divided, here, into the officially produced equipment (with parallels across the Western Empire), and the largely British series.

a) Buckles (and associated fittings) of types II (mid to late 4th century), III and IV (late 4th to early 5th centuries) and related plain buckles: Amesbury, Ashton Keynes, Barbury Castle, Baydon, Bowerchalke, Broad Hinton, Bromham, Calne, Calstone Wellington, Codford, Ford, Great Bedwyn, Mere, Mildenhall, Netheravon, Nettleton, North Wraxall, Old Sarum, Pewsey, Stratford-sub-Castle, Wanborough, Widdington.

b) Buckles of types IA and IB; 'Tortworth' strap-ends and associated fittings (late 4th to early 5th centuries): Aldbourne, Ashton Keynes, Bishops Cannings, Boscombe Down, Bowerchalke, Easton Grey, Great Bedwyn, Harnham, Latton, Monkton Deverill, Netheravon, Pewsey, Ramsbury, Rushall Down, Sandy Lane, Swindon, Upper Upham, Wanborough, Winterbourne Bassett.

Acknowledgements

I am grateful to the following, both for making objects available for study, and for giving permission to publish them: Julian Adams, Brian Cavill, Andrew Deathe (Salisbury Museum), Arthur MacGregor (Ashmolean Museum), Andrew Mitchell, Dr John Paddock (Corinium Museum), Brian Read, and Dr Paul Robinson (Wiltshire Heritage Museum) whom I also wish to thank for much help and advice. I am indebted to Jane Bircher and Mark Corney for discussing the metalwork with me and for much assistance and encouragement. Richard Dace and John Smith kindly commented on the text. I am most grateful to Polly March who not only turned manuscript into typescript, but in the process improved both spelling and syntax immeasurably! Lastly, but by no means least, I should like to express my gratitude to Ken Annable for his early encouragement of my interest in this aspect of Wiltshire's history.

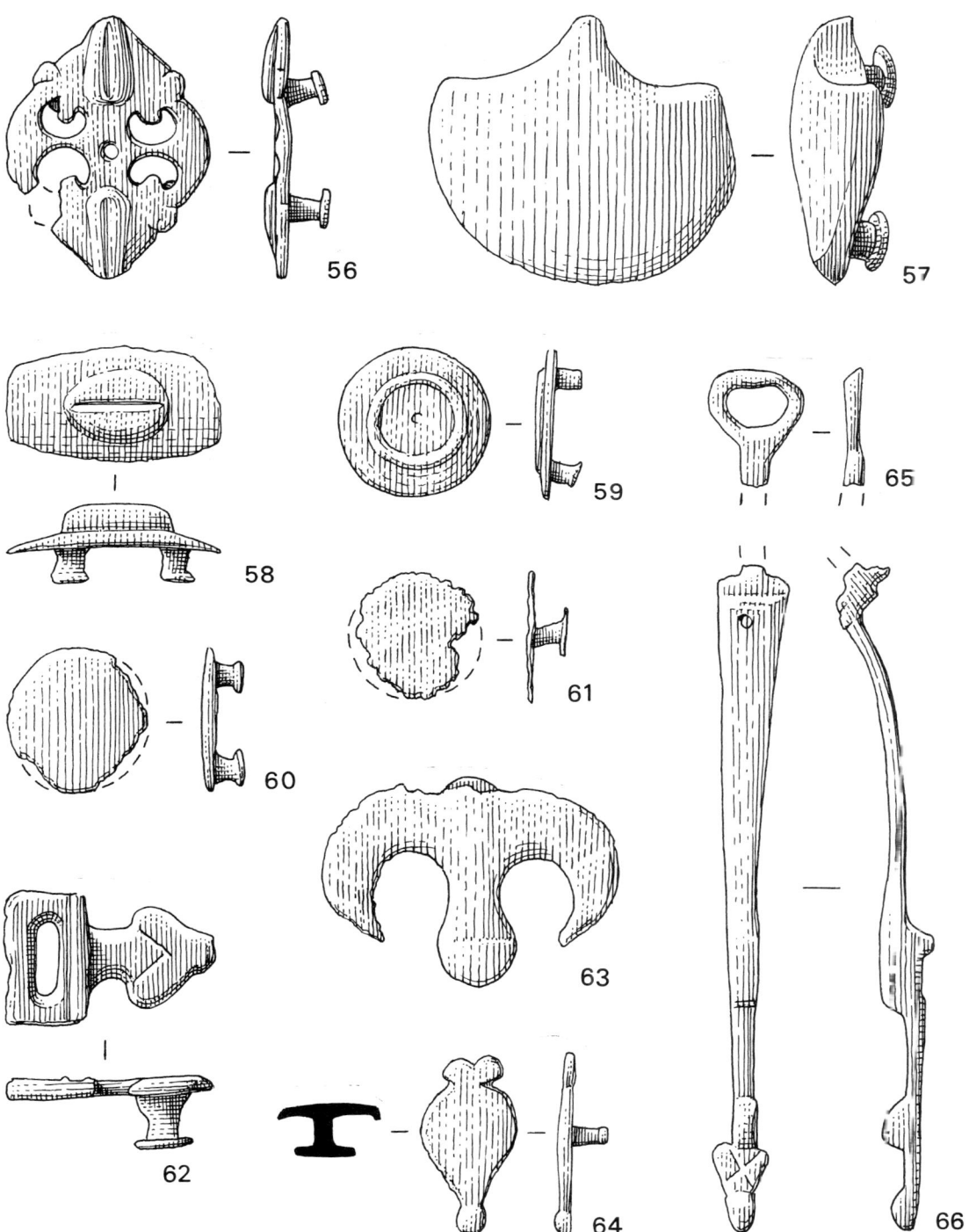

Fig. 3.10 Cat. nos 56-66: bronze objects of 2nd to 3rd-century date; actual size

References

Allason-Jones, L., and Miket, R., 1984, *The Catalogue of Small Finds from South Shields Fort*, Newcastle upon Tyne

Anderson, A. S., 1984, *Roman Military Tombstones*, Princes Risborough

Anderson, A. S., and Wacher, J. S., 1980, 'Excavations at Wanborough, Wiltshire', *Britannia*, 2, 115-26

Annable, F. K., 1974, 'A bronze military apron mount from Cunetio', *WANHM*, 69, 176-9

_____ , 1976, 'A bronze military mount from Folly Farm', *WANHM*, 70/71, 126-7

Aurrecoechea, J., 1996, 'Chip-carved fittings in Late Roman Hispania', *Arma*, 8, 15-9

Barron, R. S., 1976, *The Geology of Wiltshire*, Bradford on Avon

Bathurst, W. H., 1879, *Roman Antiquities at Lydney Park, Glos*, London

Bell, H. I., 1962, *The Abinnaeus Archive*, Oxford

Bishop, M. C., 1991, 'Soldiers and military equipment in the towns of Roman Britain', in V. Maxfield and M. Dobson, *Roman Frontier Studies*, Exeter, 21-7

Bishop, M. C., and Coulston, J. C. N., 1993, *Roman Military Equipment*, London

Boon, G. C., 1972, *Isca*, Cardiff

Boube, J., 1960, 'Fibules et garnitures de ceinture d'époque Romaine tardive' *Bull d'Archéologie Marocaine*, 4, 319-79

Bowman, A. K., 1994, *Life and Letters on the Roman Frontier*, London

Brailsford, J. W., 1962, *Hod Hill, I: Antiquities from Hod Hill in the Durden Collection*, London

Branigan, K., 1974, 'Vespasian and the South-west', *Proc Dorset Nat Hist Archaeol Soc*, 95, 50-7

Branigan, K., and Fowler, P. J., 1976, *The Roman West Country*, Newton Abbot

Breeze, D. J., 1993, 'Cavalry on frontiers: Hadrian to Honorius', in D. F. Clark (ed.), *The Later Roman Empire Today*, London, 19-35

Casey, P. J., and Hoffmann, B., 1998, 'Rescue excavations at Greta Bridge', *Britannia*, 29, 3-83

CIL, Corpus Inscriptionum Latinarum (1863-), Berlin

Clarke, G., 1979, *The Roman Cemetery at Lankhills*, Winchester Studies, 3, Oxford

Corney, M., 1991, 'The Late Bronze Age and Iron Age', in J. Barrett, R. Bradley, and M. Green, *Landscape, Monuments and Society : the Prehistory of Cranborne Chase*, Cambridge, 227-42

_____ , 1997, 'The origins and development of the 'small town' of *Cunetio*, Mildenhall, Wiltshire', *Britannia*, 28, 337-50

Corney, M., and Griffiths, N., (forthcoming), Late Roman belt-fittings: function, date and status

Cunliffe, B. W., 1971, *Excavations at Fishbourne 1961-9, II, The Finds*, London

_____ , 1973, 'The period of Romanization', *VCH, Wiltshire*, 439-52, Oxford

Cunnington, M. E., and Goddard, E. H., 1934, *Catalogue of the Antiquities in the Museum at Devizes*, part II, Devizes

Down, A., 1974, *Chichester Excavations, II*, Chichester

Feugère, M., 1994, 'L'équipement militaire d'époque republicaine en Gaule', *Journ Roman Military Equipment Studies*, 4, 3-23

Field, N. H., 1992, *Dorset and the Second Legion*, Tiverton

Fowler, E., 1960, 'The origins and development of the penannular brooch in Europe', *Procs Prehist Soc*, 26, 149-77

Fox, A., and Ravenhill, W., 1972, 'The Roman fort at Nanstallon, Cornwall', *Britannia* 3, 56-111

Frere, S. S., 1987, *Britannia*, 3rd edn, London

Friendship-Taylor, R.M., and Friendship-Taylor, D.E., 1989, *Iron Age and Roman Piddington*, Hackleton

Green, C., 1943, 'Glevum and the Second Legion', *Journ Roman Studies*, 23, 15-28

Greene, K. T., 1971, 'An unusual Roman glazed vessel from Woodcuts in Cranborne Chase, *Procs Dorset Nat Hist and Archaeol Soc*, 93, 163-6

_____, 1979, *Report on the Excavations at Usk, 1965-76: The Pre-Flavian Finewares*, Cardiff

Grew, F., and Griffiths, N., 1991, 'The pre-Flavian military belt: the evidence from Britain', *Archaeologia*, 109, 47-84

Griffiths, N., 1983, 'Early Roman military metalwork from Wiltshire', *WANHM*, 77, 49-59

Hawkes, S. C., and Dunning, G. C., 1961, 'Soldiers and settlers in Britain, fourth to fifth century', *Med Archaeol*, 5, 1-70

Holder, P., 1980, *The Auxilia from Augustus to Trajan*, BAR Brit Ser, 70, Oxford

Holwerda, J. H., 1931, 'Een vondst uit den Rijn bij Doorwerth', *Oudheid Mededeelingen*, 12, 1-26

Jackson, R., 1990, *Camerton: Late Iron Age and Early Roman Metalwork*, London

Jenkins, I., 1985, 'A group of silvered horse-trappings from Xanten (*Castra Vetera*)', *Britannia*, 16, 141-64

Kenyon, R., 1987, 'The Claudian coinage' in N. Crummy, *The Coins from Excavations in Colchester, 1971-9*, Colchester, 24-41

Lewis, N., 1983, *Life in Egypt under Roman rule*, Oxford

Margary, I. D., 1955, *Roman Roads in Britain*, London

Maxfield, V. A., 1981, *The Military Decorations of the Roman Army*, London

McWhirr, A. D., 1981, *Roman Gloucestershire*, Gloucester

Milner, N. P., 1993, *Vegetius: Epitome of Military Science*, Liverpool

Nash-Williams, V. E., 1932, 'Report on the excavations carried out in the Prysg Field, 1927-9, pt. II: the finds', *Archaeologia Cambrensis*, 87, 48-104

Oldenstein, J., 1976, 'Zur Ausrüstung römischer Auxiliareinheiten', *Bericht der Römisch-Germanischen Kommission*, 57, 49-284

Paddock, J. M., 1998, 'The military equipment', in N. Holbrook (ed.), *Cirencester: The Roman Town Defences, Public Buildings and Shops*, Cirencester, 305-7

Phillips, E. J., 1975, 'The gravestone of M. Favonius Facilis at Colchester', *Britannia*, 6, 102-5

Pitt-Rivers, A. H. L. F., 1887, *Excavations in Cranborne Chase, I*, privately printed

Pitt-Rivers, A. H. L. F., 1888, *Excavations in Cranborne Chase, II*, privately printed

Putnam, B., 1984, *Roman Dorset*, Wimborne

RCHME, 1980, *City of Salisbury, I*, London

RIB, The Roman Inscriptions of Britain, I. Inscriptions on Stone (1965), II. Instrumentum Domesticum (1990-1995), Oxford

Richmond, I. A., 1945, The Sarmatae, *Bremetennacum Veteranorum* and the *Regio Bremetenacensis*, *Journ Roman Studies*, 35, 15-29

_____, 1968, *Hod Hill, II : Excavations Carried Out Between 1951 and 1958*, London

Robinson, H. R., 1975, *The Armour of Imperial Rome*, London

Roxan, M., 1989, 'Women on the frontiers', in *Roman Frontier Studies*, Procs 15th International Congress of Roman Frontier Studies, Exeter

Swan, V., 1970, 'An unpublished early Roman bronze from Nettleton, Wiltshire', *WANHM*, 65, 195-8

Swanton, M. J., 1973, *The Spearheads of the Anglo-Saxon Settlements*, London

Wacher, J. S., and McWhirr, A. D., 1982, *Early Roman Occupation at Cirencester*, Cirencester

Webster, G., 1971, 'A hoard of Roman military Equipment from Fremington Hagg', in R. Butler (ed), *Soldier and Civilian in Roman Yorkshire*, 107-25

_____ , 1980, *The Roman Invasion of Britain*, London

Webster, G., and Dudley, D. R., 1965, *The Roman Conquest of Britain*, London

Wedlake, W. J., 1982, *The Excavation of the Shrine of Apollo at Nettleton, Wiltshire, 1956-71*, Soc Ant Res Rep, 40, London

Wheeler, R. E. M., 1926, *The Roman Fort near Brecon*, London

_____ , 1943, *Maiden Castle, Dorset*, Soc Ant Res Rep, 12, London

Wheeler, R. E. M., and Wheeler, T. V., 1928, 'The Roman amphitheatre at Caerleon, Monmouthshire', *Archaeologia*, 78, 111-218

4 A REAPPRAISAL OF SAVERNAKE WARE

by Jane Timby

Introduction

It is now some 38 years since the discovery and excavation of Roman pottery kilns in the Savernake Forest by Ken Annable and colleagues (Annable 1962) and more than 20 years since the last seminal works on both the origins of the industry by Vivien Swan (1975) and the distribution of its products by Ian Hodder (1974). I am grateful for the opportunity to air some thoughts on the Savernake industry in the light of recent finds. This is by no means a totally comprehensive review of the industry or update on earlier work. It is a reappraisal made possible through the study, by the author, of numerous assemblages containing this ware, mainly in the Gloucestershire and Oxfordshire areas.

Background

Although earlier fieldwork had hinted at the presence of a Roman pottery production site in Savernake Forest, Wiltshire (Watson 1921), the first positive evidence was demonstrated through fieldwork and subsequent limited excavation by Annable in 1957-8. As a result of his investigations two kilns were located and excavated close to Bitham Pond, near Column Ride in the Forest. Subsequently five other kilns were discovered in the same area but these have not been fully published (Annable 1959, 235; Anon. 1960, 396; 1961, 34-5, 244-5; Luckett 1970). The kilns are located some 0.8km west of the Roman road linking Old Sarum with *Cunetio* (Mildenhall) and approximately 0.8km east of the road from Winchester to *Cunetio*. *Cunetio*, the nearest major Roman settlement, lies about 1.25km north of the kilns.

The Column Ride kilns are just part of a much more widespread industry for which evidence of production has been found at Milton, Pewsey (Broomsgrove Farm: Cunnington 1893); Great Bedwyn (Tottenham House Deer Park: Anon. 1965, 135); Oare, immediately north of Martinsell hillfort (Cunnington 1909); just outside the west rampart of Martinsell hillfort, Pewsey (Swan 1975, 39); and Wilcot (Withy Copse: Swan 1984) (Fig. 4.1). Swan (1975, 39) also notes other concentrations of Romano-British pottery including kiln debris in ploughed ground south-east of the Oare site.

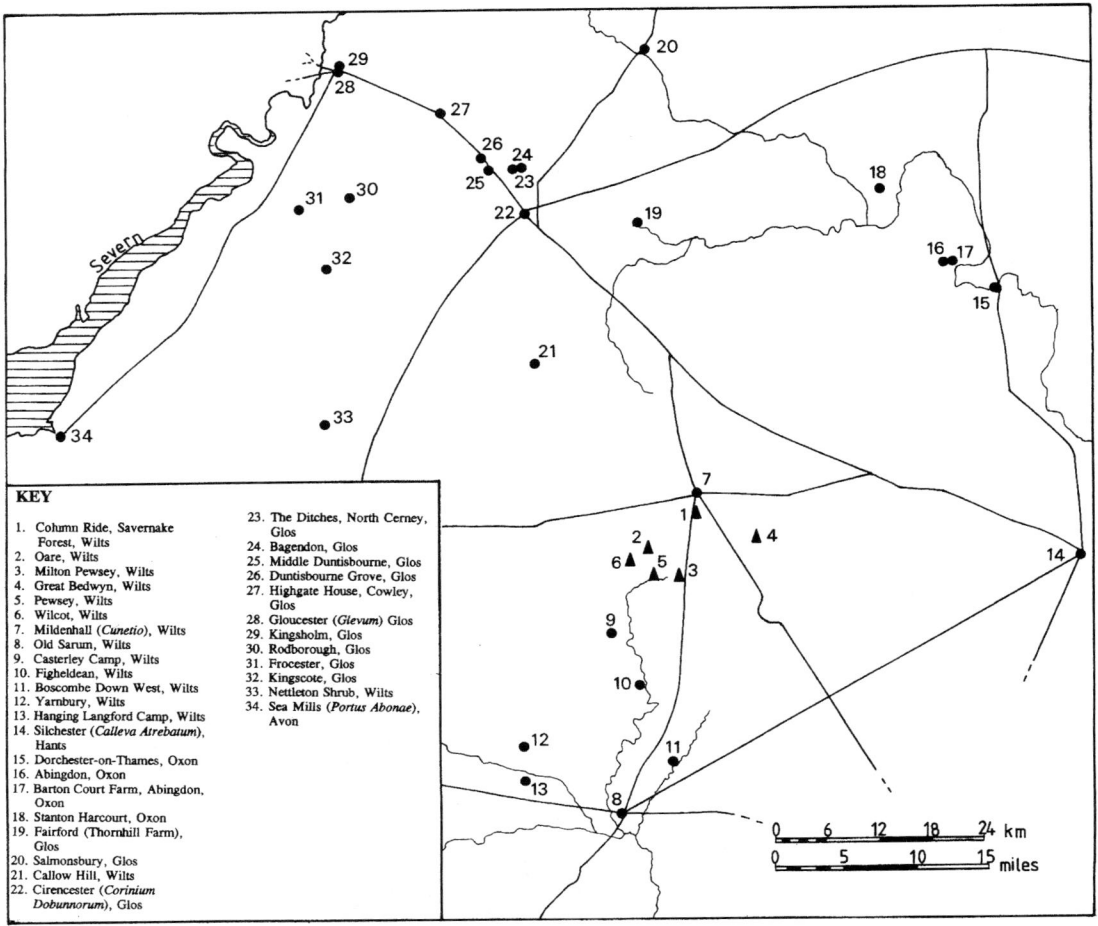

KEY

1. Column Ride, Savernake Forest, Wilts
2. Oare, Wilts
3. Milton Pewsey, Wilts
4. Great Bedwyn, Wilts
5. Pewsey, Wilts
6. Wilcot, Wilts
7. Mildenhall (*Cunetio*), Wilts
8. Old Sarum, Wilts
9. Casterley Camp, Wilts
10. Figheldean, Wilts
11. Boscombe Down West, Wilts
12. Yarnbury, Wilts
13. Hanging Langford Camp, Wilts
14. Silchester (*Calleva Atrebatum*), Hants
15. Dorchester-on-Thames, Oxon
16. Abingdon, Oxon
17. Barton Court Farm, Abingdon, Oxon
18. Stanton Harcourt, Oxon
19. Fairford (Thornhill Farm), Glos
20. Salmonsbury, Glos
21. Callow Hill, Wilts
22. Cirencester (*Corinium Dobunnorum*), Glos

23. The Ditches, North Cerney, Glos
24. Bagendon, Glos
25. Middle Duntisbourne, Glos
26. Duntisbourne Grove, Glos
27. Highgate House, Cowley, Glos
28. Gloucester (*Glevum*) Glos
29. Kingsholm, Glos
30. Rodborough, Glos
31. Frocester, Glos
32. Kingscote, Glos
33. Nettleton Shrub, Wilts
34. Sea Mills (*Portus Abonae*), Avon

Fig. 4.1 Distribution of sites mentioned in the text

Although no positive evidence for an *in situ* kiln was identified at Oare, the presence of kiln furniture in what Mrs Cunnington originally described as a rubbish deposit alongside a group of ill-fired vessels has led to the site being reinterpreted as a pottery production centre (Swan 1975; 1984, 38-9).

The Savernake kilns

Of the two kilns excavated by Annable in Column Ride, one proved to be of horizontal-draught type, the other a normal up-draught type (Annable 1962). The other five kilns investigated were also probably horizontal-draught types (Anon. 1961, 34, 244-5). Numerous pieces of kiln furniture were recovered, some from one of the stokeholes, mainly comprising flat, circular plates of baked clay containing coarse vegetation (?grass/straw). The plates have a diameter of around 255mm and a thickness of 15-25mm. Amongst the material at the Wiltshire Heritage Museum, Devizes, is a conical clay pedestal which may have been used to support the kiln floor (Fig. 4.2).

The product

FABRIC

Savernake ware is quite a distinctive grey colour with a lumpy feel. The vessel surfaces are usually pale to dark blue-grey with a paler light-grey to off-white core. Occasionally vessels are part oxidised or show irregular patchy coloration from uneven firing. The paste contains distinctive inclusions of grey or white sub-angular grog accompanied by variable quantities of white angular flint fragments and iron. Within the general category there are quite a few variants, particularly in the degree of sandiness of the fabric which may signify different kilns or the exploitation of different clay deposits. Rigby (1982, 153-4), for example, identified six variants amongst the early assemblages from Cirencester. In broad terms there are coarse wares, mainly used for the large handmade jars (Fig. 4.3, 1-4) and, more rarely, tripod bowls (Fig. 4.3, 5), and finer wares, still containing grey grog, used for wheelmade flagons, jars, bowls (Fig. 4.3, 6), platters (Fig. 4.3, 7-8) and beakers. The local geology comprises Tertiary clays overlying a chalk subsoil. The Broomsgrove kiln lies on Upper Greensand.

Fig. 4.2 Restored kiln furniture recovered from the Savernake kilns, width 200mm, ht. 114mm; WHM.

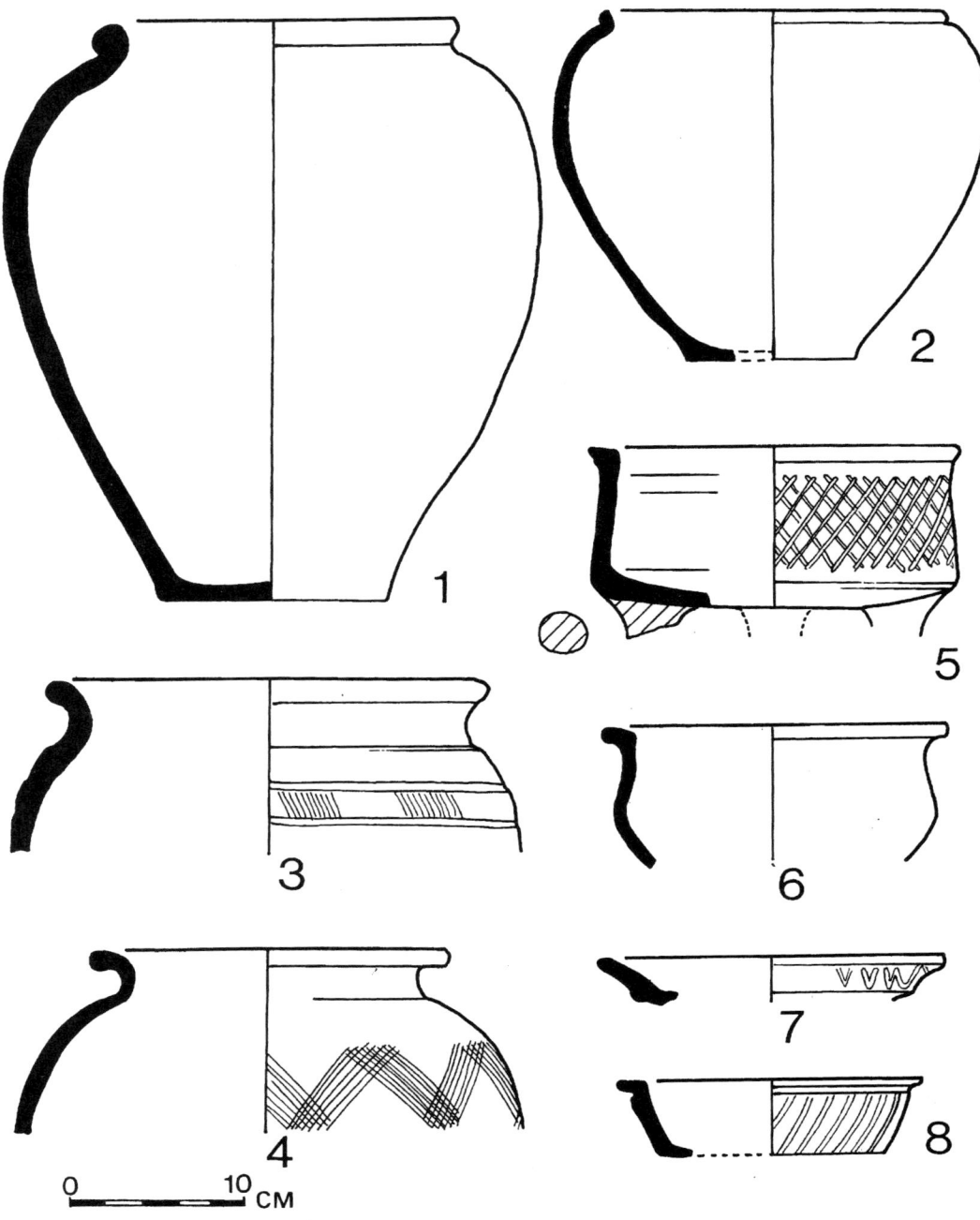

Fig. 4.3 A selection of Savernake vessels: numbers 1-2, Bagendon (after Fell 1961); numbers 3, 5, Kingscote (after Timby 1998); numbers 4, 6, Cirencester (after Rigby 1982); and numbers 7-8, Column Ride, Savernake (after Annable 1962); scale 1:4

Thin-section analysis by Hodder (1974) showed the matrix to contain largely quartz, grog and iron-ore. Although a textural analysis was also carried out by Hodder, the sample selected was small and evidence from subsequent work has highlighted the pitfalls in such work (*cf.* Darvill and Timby 1982).

The general similarity of the fabrics suggests a common source for the ware, although it is possible that there may be clones from other kilns, especially amongst material from the Oxfordshire sites. In addition there is a more soapy, dark-coloured grog-tempered ware used almost exclusively for storage jars which appears across Oxfordshire in the later 1st to 3rd centuries. This ware is likely to have a source somewhere in the Oxford area and may have been a more local replacement for the storage jar element of the Savernake industry which seems to have fallen out of production sometime in the 2nd century. Storage jars in Severn Valley ware fulfilled a similar role to the north west in Gloucestershire.

FORMS

The pottery recovered from the kiln excavations shows quite a diverse range of products including a variety of jars, platters, dishes, beakers, lids and ring-necked flagons (Annable 1962, fig. 5). The Oare deposit republished by Swan (1975, appendix 1, figs. 1-5) contained examples of collared flagons in the finer wheelmade variant of the fabric, butt beakers and platters imitating Gallo-Belgic forms including the footring, and carinated bowls – all new forms in the late Iron Age repertoire but interestingly all represented amongst the imported finewares found with the deposit. The most frequent types in the Oare group were bead-rim bowls or jars in both the finer and coarser variant of the fabric. Domed lids and necked jars and bowls and storage jars were also well represented. The Broomsgrove kiln(s) appear to have been mainly producing large jars (Cunnington 1893, 294).

Away from the kilns, particularly outside Wiltshire, Savernake ware is primarily known as jars, notably large handmade storage jars, wheelmade necked jars, beaded rim jars and less commonly lids. The assemblage of Savernake ware from the early military levels at Cirencester, one of the closer major Roman settlements to the production centre, is similarly overwhelmingly dominated by jars, both necked and beaded rim varieties, with a small proportion of other wares such as flagon (Rigby 1982, fig. 53.119), flat-rim hemispherical bowls (*ibid.*, fig. 56.233-4; 61.383) and lids (*ibid.*, figs. 52.83 and 56.235). Other forms such as a tripod bowl from Kingscote, Gloucestershire, are rare (Timby 1998, fig. 109.2).

Decoration was frequently employed on the shoulders of large jars, mainly as burnished-line chevrons or wavy-lines. The butt beaker from Oare has rouletted zig-zag directly copying a continental style. Burnishing was also frequently employed, especially on the rim and shoulder area of vessels.

Distribution

Savernake ware has an extensive distribution across Wiltshire, Gloucestershire, Avon and Oxfordshire. A study undertaken by Hodder (1974) to examine the relationship between the production centre and its market area lists 83 sites in Wiltshire where Savernake ware had been recorded. An additional 22 sites outside Wiltshire are listed, taking the extent of distribution across Berkshire, Gloucestershire, Hampshire and Somerset (*ibid.*, appendix). It is not the purpose of this paper to update Hodder's gazetteer in detail, but suffice it to say that the distribution has considerably filled in and can now be extended up into Oxfordshire. Most sites in Gloucestershire occupied in the second half of the 1st century AD, or earlier, have yielded sherds of Savernake ware, for example, Bagendon, Cirencester, Salmonsbury, Fairford (Thornhill Farm), Frocester, Kingsholm and Dymock amongst others. In Oxfordshire, Savernake ware is present at Barton Court Farm, near Abingdon (Miles 1986), Abingdon (material in Oxfordshire County Museum Service store), Stanton Harcourt (Ashmolean Museum), Callow Hill (Ashmolean Museum) and Dorchester-on-Thames (e.g. Frere 1962, fig. 12.24). Savernake ware was also getting as far afield as Silchester but in extremely small quantities suggesting that this was perhaps the very limit of its market area. By the same token, the relatively small percentage of wares from sites in the Gloucester area suggests this marked the westward range. Large storage jars in the more local Severn Valley wares, and Malvernian vessels, probably fulfilled a major part of the market in the Gloucester area.

Chronology

The pottery recovered from the Savernake Forest kiln site was dated by the excavator to the closing years of the 1st century AD. In support of this a coin of Domitian (*c.* AD 79) came from the stokehole of kiln 2 (Annable 1962, 155). The range of forms illustrated would not contradict a date in the last quarter of the 1st century AD. The copies of imported Roman forms such as the platters are very devolved.

Swan (1975), in her review of the industry, concluded that the Oare deposit dated to the mid 1st century AD and as such probably represented one of the earliest phases in the production of Savernake ware. The vessels from Oare present an admixture of local indigenous types alongside copies of Roman forms such as the platters, flagons and beakers. She also (*ibid.*, 45) suggested the presence of immigrant potters moving across from the Hertfordshire-Essex area attracted by a military market, perhaps joined by local potters. It would appear from the repertoire of forms recovered that the potters, whatever their pedigree, were perhaps trying to cater for both the local native population and a military market based at *Cunetio* and *Corinium* (Cirencester) amongst others during the second half of the 1st century AD. There are no known examples of the production of this range of Roman forms in Britain prior to the conquest, although a certain degree of familiarity with the new vessels (platters, flagons, butt beakers), might be expected in some areas, particularly the south east and along the south coast. Post-conquest, pre-Flavian production of butt beakers has been hinted at in the Abingdon area and in Chichester, but the vessels are of a much higher quality compared with the Savernake wares. It may be significant that few of the 'new' wares appear to have been marketed outside the core production area, perhaps emphasising the likelihood that *Cunetio* formed the main market for this more diverse range of wares.

Recent work on the origins of the site of *Cunetio* points to the presence of an early military base here (Burnham and Wacher 1990, 148; Corney 1997; Corney this volume).

Excavation of a well sealed by the town wall (Annable 1966, fig. 1) produced a 1st-century AD assemblage containing a significant quantity of Savernake ware throughout the sequence. Samian from the fill was dated *c.* AD 50-60. The well contained very few artefacts other than pottery and it was noted that there were several joining sherds distributed vertically though the fill. Of note amongst the other pottery from the well were imitations of moulded platters (*ibid.*, fig. 3.36; fig. 4, 55-6), fineware butt beakers (*ibid.* figs. 3, 21 and 4, 22, 61-2, 66) and flagons (fig. 4, 65). All these pieces would support a pre-Flavian date. The butt beakers range in colour from cream to pale orange with a grey core. Although these particular sherds have not been examined by the author, the descriptions would fit material excavated from a possible military kiln in Chichester (Down 1978, 204ff) dated to the immediate post-conquest period. Dating of the well at *Cunetio* proved problematical to Annable as it was believed that the Savernake ware had to date from the end of the 1st century on the basis of comparable material from the available kiln excavations. It was concluded that the samian probably represented curated material and that on the basis of the coarseware the well was filled in around AD 100. It has now been suggested, more reasonably, that the well was military in origin and backfilled as a single operation in connection with the abandonment of the fort in the early AD 60s (Swan 1975, 44). The copies of the moulded platters and the presence of the butt beakers and flagon would support a Neronian date. A similar operation took place in Cirencester with the dumping of probable stores in the defensive ditch of the Leaholme fort, probably in the later Neronian period. Here the deposit included a number of unused samian vessels (Hartley and Dickinson 1982, 133ff), various imports, amphorae, mortaria, butt beaker, flagon and Savernake wares (*cf.* Rigby 1982, figs 57-61).

There is a high density of Savernake wares in the locality of the kilns as so clearly shown by Hodder (1974, fig. 5). Potential early associations of Savernake ware in Wiltshire may be found at Casterley Camp (Cunnington and Cunnington 1913), Knap Hill (Hodder 1974, 67), Hanging Langford Camp (*ibid.*) and Yarnbury (Cunnington 1933).

Although limited in number it is perhaps fortunate that most of the non-military assemblages in the Wiltshire/Gloucestershire region that have produced 1st-century imported finewares have also yielded Savernake ware. In Wiltshire the most significant of these are the Oare deposit itself, Casterley Camp and Boscombe Down West; in Gloucestershire such sites include Bagendon, The Ditches (North Cerney) and two satellite sites outside the Bagendon dyke complex at Middle Duntisbourne and Duntisbourne Grove. All these sites appear to have pre-conquest origins.

Mrs Cunnington originally dated the Oare deposit to between the 1st century BC and the early 1st century AD based on the presence of imports. Swan has subsequently discarded this date in favour of one around the middle of the 1st century AD (Swan 1975, 40). The imports are varied and comprise Gallo-Belgic wares, North, Central, and South Gaulish products. Amongst the Gallo-Belgic products is a *terra rubra* (TR1C) platter stamped by the potter Attissus probably operating in the Rheims area in the later Augustan period, a girth beaker (TR3) and a *terra nigra* (TN) platter. The butt and ovoid beakers, of which there are at least four (Swan 1975, fig. 5, 55-9) would appear to be products of North and possibly Central Gaul. The painted bowl (Swan 1975, fig 5.57) is a Roanne or Roanne type manufactured in Central Gaul. The group is a curious one in terms of its composition and origins, and could suggest a personal table service rather than evidence of trade. The only other find of a Roanne-type bowl in Britain comes from Ower in the Poole Harbour area, unfortunately redeposited in a late horizon (Timby 1987, fig. 41.33). The five sherds of samian, all from South Gaul, would appear to fall mainly into the Claudio-Neronian period.

Casterley Camp, an early Iron Age defended site within which lies a later rectilinear double-ditched enclosure apparently associated with other irregular ditched enclosures, has also produced imported continental finewares (Cunnington and Cunnington 1913, pls. v-vi) associated with Savernake ware from the later occupation. The finewares include various butt beakers including one with fine notched zig-zag rouletting and a red painted interior, a TR3 girth beaker with combed decoration, a TR platter base stamped ATTISSVS and a creamware collared flagon.

Excavations at Boscombe Down West (Richardson 1951) produced a diverse assemblage spanning the Early to Late Iron Age/early Roman period. The settlement appears to have started as an open settlement dating to the earlier Iron Age succeeded by a later circular bivallate enclosure. The latest material from the inner enclosure ditch includes numerous beaded rim jars and carinated bowls with tooled decoration, along with Savernake ware jars, imported butt beakers and copies of TN plates.

Substantial quantities of Savernake ware were found at Bagendon (Clifford 1961) and both beaded rim and everted thickened rim storage vessels can be recognised from the published report (Fell 1961, figs 54, 56-7). Vessels were recovered from Period IA and IIA features originally dated by Mrs Clifford to the first and second quarters of the 1st century AD respectively. A published Period IA group shows Savernake type jars (fig. 59, 15-17) associated with Gallo-Belgic imports, notably TN platters, a *Camulodunum* (Cam) type 5 stamped CANICOS, Cam 8 and Cam 13/14 (fig. 59.1-3), a Cam 113 buff ware butt beaker (fig. 59.7) and possibly a TR pedestal beaker (fig. 59.6). The dating of Bagendon still remains a subject of debate in terms of trying to reconcile the different dates arrived at from different classes of material.

The relatively recent excavations at The Ditches, North Cerney (Trow 1988), also yielded vessels of Savernake ware (*ibid.*, Group E, TF 11), mainly as globular or pear-shaped storage jars with rolled or beaded rims and occasionally platters. Some of these vessels were found in assemblages containing imported finewares. Of particular note are three groups, all from the inner enclosure ditch, which are worth describing in greater detail. The first group of pottery is that from B17. This has at least one Savernake jar (fig. 32.11) associated with a TR2 cup Cam 56A of Tiberio-Claudian date, TN platters Cam 13/14 and 7, Cam 113 butt beakers, Arretine Loeschcke type 2 of Augustan-Tiberian date and at least four vessels of South Gaulish samian of Tiberio-Claudian date. Other finds from the same deposit include four brooches (Mackreth 1988, nos 9, 10, 14 and 26) not closely datable. The second group, D100, has a Savernake storage jar (Trow 1988, fig. 35.93) associated with Claudian South Gaulish wares, two Dobunnic coins (Sellwood 1988, 43) and a pre-conquest 'Aucissa' type brooch (Mackreth 1988, no. 16). The third group, from D187, has a cordoned necked Savernake jar (Trow 1988, fig. 37.125) alongside a TN platter Cam 14, whiteware flagon and Cam 113 beaker all dated to the immediate post-conquest/pre-Flavian period, two vessels of Claudian South Gaulish samian and three brooches possibly pre-conquest in origin (Mackreth 1988, nos. 17, 18, 20).

Recent excavations along the A417 have located further occupation in the Bagendon area although beyond the dyke systems. Of particular note are the sites at Middle Duntisbourne and Duntisbourne Grove which have both produced pottery assemblages containing imported finewares which appear contemporary with those from Bagendon and The Ditches (Timby 1999).

At Middle Duntisbourne the bulk of the assemblage, 80.5% by count, came from twelve associated ditches. The pottery from these was dominated by sherds of early Severn Valley ware (42% by count) in both handmade and wheelmade forms, and Savernake ware jars (18.5%). Malvernian limestone-tempered wares were also quite well represented accounting for 12.5%. This complex of ditches also produced the bulk of the imported wares. These included Arretine, TR, TN, fine whiteware and a possible Central Gaulish beaker. The site at Duntisbourne Grove, perhaps originating slightly earlier but abandoned around the same time, produced sherds of Savernake ware, early or proto-Severn Valley ware with imported vessels of TN, TR, Gaulish flagon, white ware butt beaker and amphora.

Sherds of Savernake ware have also been recovered from the settlement at Thornhill Farm, Fairford, which spans the Middle Iron Age through to the mid 2nd century AD (Timby in prep). Here the earliest occurrence of Savernake ware appears to be in ceramic phase 3 dated AD 1 to 50 but becomes more common in ceramic phase 4 where it occurs almost exclusively as large handmade storage jars with beaded, thickened finger-depressed or everted rims, wheelmade jars and rarely as lids. There are no exotic continental imports from the site which appears to be a typical rural native settlement possibly connected with horse rearing.

Looking further afield, at Dorchester-on-Thames a beaded rim jar in Savernake ware associated with a TR beaker and other coarsewares was recovered from layer (59), sealed below the west rampart of the fort (Frere 1964, fig. 12.24). Further unpublished examples of Savernake ware also came from the site (Ashmolean Museum). In summing up his excavations at Dorchester, Frere (*ibid.*, 128-9) concluded that the site might have begun as a pre-Roman Belgic settlement although an alternative scenario of a *de novo* native settlement alongside the putative Claudian fort was also suggested.

Dating evidence for the end of the Savernake industry is difficult to establish at present. It is a marked component of assemblages from Cirencester in the early 2nd century but was clearly being challenged by Dorset Black-Burnished ware. There is a dramatic fall-off after the mid 2nd century. Storage jars tend to be longer-lived elements in pottery assemblages and it is not uncommon to find Savernake wares in later 2nd to 3rd century assemblages but this is more likely to be a reflection of survival rather than ongoing manufacture.

Conclusions

In her review of the Savernake industry, Swan (1975) focused on the incidence of the ware on post-conquest military sites, for example, *Cunetio*, *Corinium*, Rodborough and Nettleton Scrubb. She considered that the forms produced by the Savernake potters were not typical of the region, containing a number of 'Belgic' traits more characteristic of the Hertfordshire/ Essex area. It was concluded that the Savernake potters were supplying the Roman army and that the presence of a military market attracted potters from the Essex/Hertfordshire region perhaps joined by more locally based potters. Some of these ideas can now be challenged and perhaps modified in the light of recent discoveries and further research.

Although many Iron Age sites are known throughout the county of Wiltshire very few have been investigated archaeologically, most of them by the Cunningtons and others some time ago. Our knowledge of the social and economic background in the later Iron Age, and details of the pottery assemblages for this area, still remain very sketchy. Most of the settlements appear to show a continuity of occupation over considerable periods of time. A later Iron Age assemblage recovered from Figheldean in the Avon Valley from Iron Age and Romano-British enclosures (Graham and Newman 1993) includes Atrebatic style handmade rim jars, high-shouldered bowls, and necked jars in grog and sandy fabrics which seem to reflect the Late Iron Age (LIA) traditions in the area. Continental imports, including TR and flagons, were also penetrating this area (Mepham 1993, 27). In form Savernake ware appears to be a direct continuation of local indigenous traditions for which it is not necessary to seek inspiration from 'Belgic' areas away to the east. Bead-rim jars are not exclusively related to the Hertfordshire/Essex 'Belgic' traditions as intimated by Swan (1975, 45). It is an interesting feature that, although the sample of investigated sites dating to this period is small, nearly all have produced evidence of pre or early-Roman imports or imitations.

The appearance of Savernake ware on sites further afield, particularly those with no recognised military component, from at least the mid 1st century AD, requires further explanation. It is unlikely that an industry originating around the mid 1st century AD could have achieved such a widespread distribution of products so quickly, especially when the vessels are found in rubbish deposits presupposing a previous period of use before discard.

Savernake ware appears to occur on a large number of sites established in the pre-Roman period throughout Gloucestershire, for example Frocester, below the Kingsholm fort, at Bagendon, The Ditches (North Cerney) and Thornhill Farm (Fairford), to mention a few. Although none of these sites can provide unequivocal dating for the pottery, its widespread circulation and the dominance of LIA forms might suggest production was already underway prior to any Roman intervention. This should perhaps not accord too much surprise if the origin of other coarseware pottery industries in the western region is considered. Back in 1968 Peacock published his work on the Malvern pottery industry showing the existence of specialist potters operating from the mid to later Iron Age whose products achieved a wide distribution over Herefordshire, Worcestershire and peripheral counties. Since that work was undertaken, Malvernian ware has been found on many sites in Gloucestershire, for example, Kingsholm, Frocester, Highgate House (Cowley), Thornhill Farm (Fairford) and Salmonsbury hillfort, demonstrating an extensive market area. The industry continues into the Roman period and eventually adopts the wheel although probably not until the 3rd century AD. The Severn Valley industry also appears to have its origins in the later Iron Age (Timby 1990) as does the Dorset Black-Burnished industry (*cf.* Williams 1977, 168ff). The development of organised pottery production in the later Iron Age may simply be an intensification of earlier production systems where specialised fine or decorated wares were being traded over quite wide areas (*cf.* Morris 1996). The presence of imported Roman finewares across the area covered by Gloucestershire, Wiltshire and Dorset, and the widespread distribution of tribal coinages away from their tribal territories (*cf.* van Arsdell 1994 for distribution of Dobunnic coinages suggesting movement along the Jurassic Way and various river routes, in particular the Severn, Kennet and Thames corridors), illustrate the operation of complex systems of exchange. A correlation of the pottery distributions against other traded goods such as shale, salt, coinage and other metalwork would be a fruitful way forward for future studies.

There is no question that the arrival of the Roman army acted as a stimulus for experimentation with new forms and technology, including the use of permanent kilns and the potters wheel. Their presence undoubtedly gave a boost to the industry as seen in the presence of Savernake ware on various early military sites in the area extending out as far as Sea Mills, Avon. The military sites appear to display a greater diversity of forms in contrast to the native sites away from the production centres, where the standard large handmade jars are the norm. On balance it is suggested that Savernake ware first appears in the ceramic record some time in the second quarter of the 1st century. The industry continues well into the 2nd century AD with a significantly higher proportion of wheelmade wares being produced towards the latter part of the 1st century AD.

It is clear that further work on the Savernake industry is long overdue. Further study of the associations of material on consumption sites both from new excavations and from a reappraisal of the assemblages from older excavations residing in museums would perhaps put our understanding of the origins and growth of the industry on a better footing.

Acknowledgements

I am grateful to Professor Tim Darvill and Dr Paul Tyers for reading and commenting on a draft of this paper and to Dr Paul Robinson of the Wiltshire Heritage Museum for encouraging me to discuss the subject.

References

Annable, F. K., 1959, 'Excavation and field-work in Wiltshire: Column Ride, Savernake Forest', *WANHM*, 57, no. 207, 235

_____ , 1962, 'A Romano-British pottery in Savernake Forest, kilns 1-2', *WANHM*, 58, 142-55

_____ , 1966, 'A late first-century well at Cunetio', *WANHM*, 61, 9-24

Anon. 1960, 'Excavation and field-work in Wiltshire 1959: Column Ride, Savernake Forest', *WANHM*, 57, no. 208, 396

_____ , 1961, 'Excavation and field-work in Wiltshire 1960: Column Ride, Savernake Forest', *WANHM*, 58, no. 209, 34-5

_____ , 1965, 'Excavation and fieldwork in Wiltshire, 1964', *WANHM*, 60, 132-9

Burnham, B. C., and Wacher, J., 1990, *The Small Towns of Roman Britain*, London

Clifford, E. M., 1961, *Bagendon, a Dobunnic Oppidum*, Cambridge

Cunnington, B. H., 1893, 'Notes on the discovery of Romano-British kilns and pottery at Broomsgrove, Milton, Pewsey', *WANHM,* 27, 294-301

Cunnington, B. H. and Cunnington, M. E., 1913, 'Casterley Camp', *WANHM,* 38, no. 119, 53-105

Cunnington, M. E., 1909, 'Notes on a late Celtic rubbish heap near Oare', *WANHM,* 36, 125-39

_____ , 1933, 'Excavation in Yarnbury Camp, 1932', *WANHM,* 46, no. 158, 198-213

Darvill, T. C. and Timby, J. R., 1982, 'Textural analysis: a review of potentials and limitations', in I. Freestone, C. Johns, and T. Potter (eds), *Current Research in Ceramics: Thin-Section Studies,* British Mus. Occas. Paper, 32, 73-87

Down, A., 1978, *Excavations at Chichester, Vol III,* Chichester

Fell, C., 1961, 'The coarse pottery of Bagendon', in Clifford 1961, 212-67

Frere, S. S., 1964, 'Excavations at Dorchester, 1962', *Archaeol Journ,* 119, 114-49

Graham, A., and Newman, C., 1993, 'Recent excavations of Iron Age and Romano-British enclosures in the Avon valley, Wiltshire', *WANHM,* 86, 8-57

Hartley, B. R., and Dickinson, B., 1982, 'The samian', in Wacher and McWhirr 1982, 119-52

Hodder, I., 1974, 'The distribution of Savernake ware', *WANHM,* 69, 67-84

Luckett, L., 1970, 'The Savernake kilns', *WANHM,* 65, 200-1

Mackreth, D. F., 1988, 'The brooches', in Trow 1988, 43-51

Mepham, L. N., 1993, 'The pottery', in Graham and Newman 1993, 25-34

Miles, D., 1986, *Archaeology at Barton Court Farm, Abingdon, Oxon,* CBA Res Rep, 50, London

Morris, E. L., 1996, 'Iron Age artefact production and exchange', in T. Champion and J. Collis (eds) *The Iron Age in Britain and Ireland: Recent Trends,* Sheffield, 41-66

Peacock, D. P. S., 1968, 'Romano-British pottery production in the Malvern district of Worcestershire', *Trans Worcs Archaeol Soc,* 1, 15-28

Richardson, K. M., 1951, 'Excavations on Boscombe Down West', *WANHM,* 54, no. 195, 123-68

Rigby, V., 1982, 'The pottery', in Wacher and McWhirr 1982, 118-98

Sellwood, L., 1988, 'The British coins', in Trow 1988, 40-1

Swan V. G., 1975, 'Oare reconsidered and the origins of Savernake ware in Wiltshire', *Britannia,* 6, 36-61

_____ , 1984, *The Pottery Kilns of Roman Britain,* RCHME supp ser 5, London

Timby, J. R., 1987, 'First century imports and native finewares', in N. Sunter and P. Woodward, *Romano-British Industries in Purbeck,* Dorset Nat Hist Archaeol Soc monograph, 6, 73-9

_____ , 1990, 'Severn Valley wares: a reassessment', *Britannia,* 21, 243-51

_____ , 1998, *Excavations at Kingscote and Wycomb, Gloucestershire,* Cotswold Archaeol Trust, Cirencester

_____ , 1999, 'Later prehistoric and Roman pottery', in A. Mudd, R. Williams, and A. Lupton, *Excavations alongside Roman Ermin Street, Gloucestershire and Wiltshire; the Archaeology of the A419/ 417 Swindon to Gloucester Road Scheme. Vol 2,* Oxford Archaeol Unit, 320-65

_____ , in prep., The pottery from Thornhill Farm, Glos.

Trow, S. D,. 1988, 'Excavations at Ditches hillfort, North Cerney, Gloucestershire, 1982-3', *Trans Bristol Gloucestershire Archaeol Soc,* 106, 19-85

Van Arsdell, R. D., 1994, *The Coinage of the Dobunni,* OUCA monograph, 8

Wacher. J., and McWhirr, A., 1982, *Early Roman Occupation at Cirencester, Cirencester Excavation I,* Cirencester

Watson, A. J., 1921, 'Roman pottery site in Savernake Forest', *WANHM,* 41, 425

Williams, D. F., 1977, 'The Romano-British Black-burnished industry: an essay on characterization by heavy mineral analysis', in D. Peacock (ed.) *Pottery and Commerce. Characterization and Trade in Roman and Later Ceramics,* London, 163-220

5 ROMAN COIN FINDS FROM WILTSHIRE

by T. Sam N. Moorhead

Introduction

I first started to study Roman coins from Wiltshire at the then Devizes Museum (now Wiltshire Heritage Museum) in the early 1980s when Ken Annable was curator. As a result of working as a student intern at the museum in 1982, I was able to begin a study of Roman coin finds from the county which covers both hoards and site-finds. In 1957, when Ken was at the forefront of Romano-British studies in Wiltshire, Christopher Hawkes noted that about 20,000 Roman coins from the county had received academic attention (1957). Over 40 years later, that figure can be multiplied by at least a factor of five, largely due to the controversial activity of metal-detecting and the finding of some very large coin hoards, like the *Cunetio* treasure which totalled nearly 55,000 coins (Besly and Bland 1983).

This article stems from research for an M. Phil. thesis awarded in 2001 (at the Institute of Archaeology, London; Moorhead 2001) which covered *all* types of Roman coin finds from Wiltshire. The focus of this paper, however, is on site-finds: single or stray coins found in excavation, whilst field-walking or with the aid of a metal detector. Hoards (groups of coins buried together) will only be considered when they have a direct bearing on evidence provided by site assemblages. While Wiltshire hoards have generally received detailed attention in the pages of *WANHM* and other archaeological and numismatic journals, excavation, field-walking and, more recently, detector finds have often escaped publication. In the 1970s, Cathy King, at the Ashmolean Museum, catalogued six major assemblages, and Paul Robinson has continued to catalogue material and bring new groups to the author's attention. To these two the author is deeply indebted for permission to use their unpublished material. He is also most grateful to numerous archaeologists and detectorists who have made previously unrecorded material available for cataloguing. Also of great benefit has been the author's access to the manuscript for the just-published *Romano-British Coin Hoards* by the late A. S. Robertson (Robertson 2000).

Because the author has catalogued a further 19 groups of coins from various sites, and has gained extra information from earlier and often overlooked published sources and notebooks, it does seem that a synthesis is now desirable. A total of 44 groups of coins from as many as 39 different sites are considered – the *Gazetteer* explains the sometimes complex nature of these assemblages. This puts at our disposal 10,552 coins which can be used for statistical analysis.

Some of the assemblages have certain provenances and have been catalogued to a high standard. Some coins have dubious provenances and others are not recorded with any great precision. There are numerous permutations for reliability ratings, and the author makes this clear in the *Gazetteer* which follows – it is strongly advised that statistics are not merely taken from the tables without consulting the *Gazetteer* to gain a view on the reliability of the material. However, this survey does provide an overview that should assist numismatists, archaeologists and historians, and the author would welcome any new information that this work might provoke.

Unlike the Norfolk coins (Davies and Gregory 1991) the Wiltshire groups cannot be assigned to a meaningful tribal region or *civitas* in Roman Britain. In many ways, one can argue that the study of Roman coins within a single modern county is a bogus exercise. Maud Cunnington's answer to this charge was to draw on material elsewhere in the country to illuminate the situation in Wiltshire (Cunnington 1949, xi). The same approach will be adopted here, and, in addition, Wiltshire will be used as a springboard to inquire about phenomena that seem to affect a wider region beyond this county. Most important, however, is that a corpus of material is presented here which others will be able to draw upon for their own research. The sites noted in the *Gazetteer* are shown in Fig. 5.1 and the coin totals by Reece's (1973) periods are shown in Table 1.

Commentary

When discussing the significance of these Wiltshire site-finds, one needs to consider the different types of site, changes over time, and relationships with other regions in the province of *Britannia*. The author will adopt a chronological approach, covering the different groups of sites within this framework.

Iron Age to AD 260 (Reece's Periods 1-12; Reece 1973)

Fifteen of the sites have British Iron Age coins in the assemblages (Ashton Keynes, Wanborough, Easton Grey, Nettleton, Box, *Verlucio*, Calstone, Urchfont, *Cunetio*, Littlecote, Charlton Down, Westbury, Cold Kitchen Hill, Heytesbury, Butterfield Down and Rotherley) which attests to continuity of occupation and/or continued use of Iron Age coins in the early Roman period. The author knows of several Republican *denarii* from Wiltshire sites, notably three from Wanborough and two from *Verlucio*. There is also the interesting find of two Carthaginian bronze pieces from Castle Combe/North Wraxall and a coin of Juba I of Numidia or Juba II of Mauretania from Ashton Keynes. The circulation of Republican and pre-Claudian coins in Wiltshire in the early Roman period is also attested by four important hoards from Warminster (to 7/6 BC; *Coin Hoards of Roman Britain* - henceforward *CHRB* - 10, 30), Membury (to AD 37; *CHRB* 9, 11-19; *CHRB* 10, 34), Little Bedwyn/

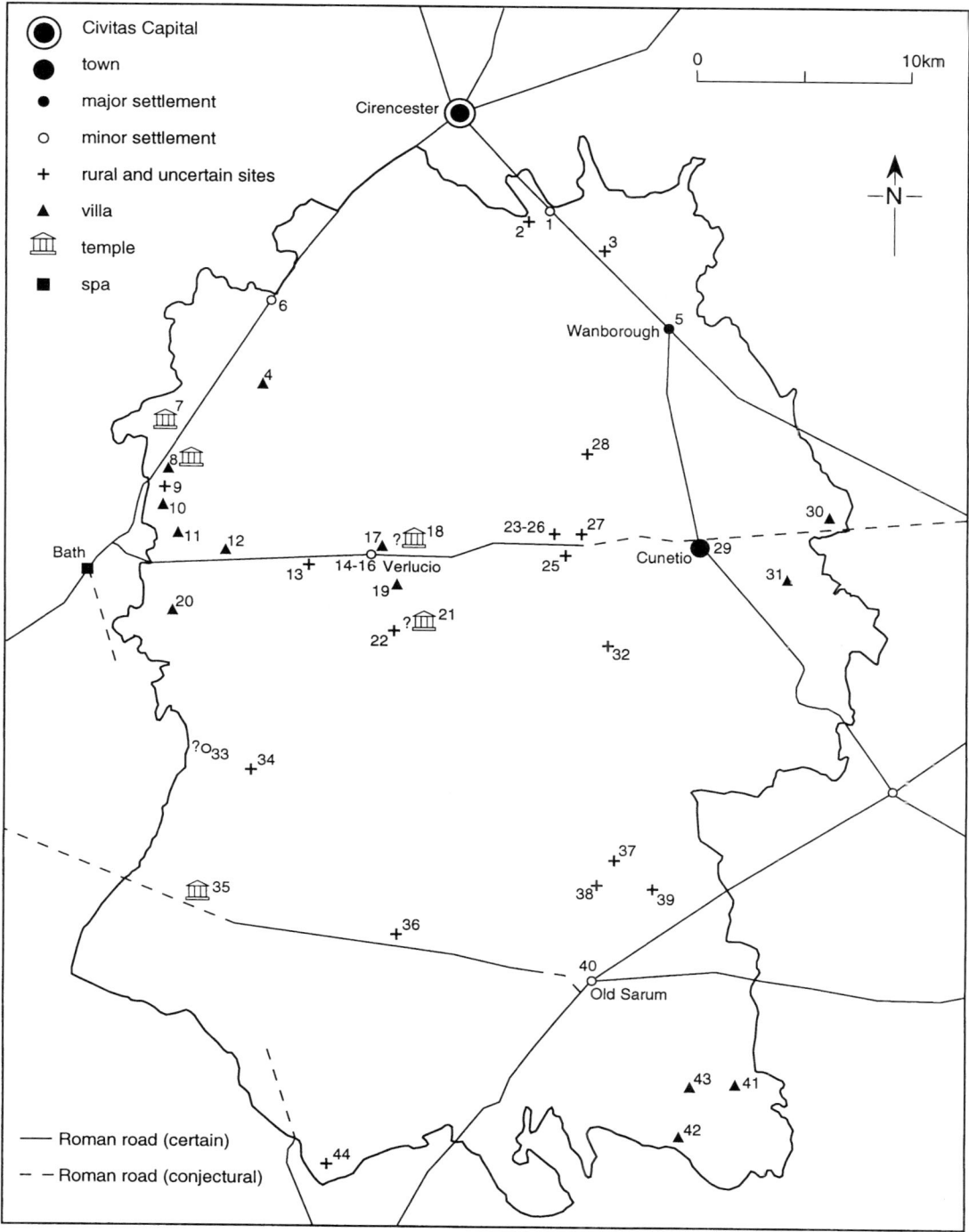

Fig. 5.1 Distribution of coin finds: for sites see Gazetteer

Chisbury Camp (to AD 37; Robinson 1997b, 30) and Savernake (to ?AD 37; *British Numismatic Journal*, 45, 1-11).

That Roman coinage was adopted at an early date in the county is shown by the large number of base metal coin imitations that are so common in southern Britain. A total of 46 or more are known from Wiltshire sites which are copies of 6 imperial figures: Augustus, Agrippa, Tiberius, Claudius, Antonia and Nero.

A glance at the Wiltshire and Britain bar-chart (Fig. 5.2) shows that, in the period up to AD 260, Wiltshire sites tend to have fewer proportion of coins than the national average. There are probably two reasons for this. First, there was not a lengthy military presence in the region. Forts or military installations are surmised at Littlecote, *Cunetio* and Wanborough, and the author suggests on coin-finds that *Verlucio* and Westbury might be added to this list. However, like Cirencester, they would not have outlived the Flavian period. Secondly, Wiltshire has no major Roman towns, Cirencester being just over the northern border in Gloucestershire, and Bath just to the west in Somerset. Urban sites, like military ones, tend to have a larger proportion of early coins.

Site	1	2	3	4	5	6	7	8	9	10	11	12	13	14	15	16	17	18	19	20	21	Site TOTAL
1†				P			P			P			8	8	P		17	2	6			N/A
2†		6					25					357						649				1037
3	-	-	-	-	-	1	-	-	-	1	-	-	3	8	2	4	7	4	2	-	-	32
4	-	-	-	-	-	1	1	1	-	-	2	1	15	7	2	2	19	6	34	-	1	92
5	10	20	15	44	28	14	18	20	5	11	5	5	284	202	38	79	539	184	376	13	314	2224
6	1	-	-	4	3	1	8	3	1	-	3	1	106	53	10	20	92	16	44	1	7	374
7	3	14	4	13	4	10	9	14	2	11	6	12	150	111	12	34	448	220	507	4	202	1790
8	2	1	-	1	-	-	-	-	-	-	-	-	18	5*	-	1	28	15	104	2	7	184
9	-	-	-	1	-	-	-	-	-	-	-	1*	1	-	-	-	2	-	11	-	1*	17
10	-	1	1	3	-	1	2	-	-	-	-	-	9	10	1	3	30	15	42	1	13	132
11	1	-	-	1	-	-	-	-	-	2	-	-	2	1	1	1*	1*	1*	1	-	-	12
12	-	-	-	1	-	-	1	1	-	1	-	-	25	24	8	22	73	19	20	-	-	195
13	-	-	-	-	-	1	-	-	-	1	-	-	10	11	-	1	13	5	8	-	-	50
14	3	6	-	8	3	4	9	2	3	7	5	3	158	111	24	33	190	85	189	3	12	858
15	-	-	-	-	-	-	2	-	-	-	1	-	32	42	9	40	207	45	61	2	8*	449
16†	3	6	-	8	3	4	11	2	3	7	6	3	190	153	33	73	397	130	250	5	20	1307
17	-	-	-	-	-	-	-	-	-	-	-	-	3	-	-	-	3	7	-	-	-	13
18	1	-	-	-	-	-	1	1	-	1	-	1	12	4	2	2	49	12	45	1	3	135
19	-	-	1	1	3	1	3	-	-	2	-	1	34	42	7	37	302	31	79	4	4	552
20	-	-	-	1	-	-	-	-	-	1	1	-	2	2	1	-	3	1	7	-	1	20
21	15	2	2	25.5	5.5	7	5	1	3	2	-	-	25	19	6	16	65	29	131	3	10*	372
22	-	-	-	-	1	-	-	1	-	-	-	-	3	2	-	-	-	2	1	-	2	12
23	-	-	-	-	-	-	-	-	-	-	-	-	-	4	-	1	20	14	53	1	1	94
24	-	-	-	-	1	-	-	-	-	-	-	-	1	2	-	2	7	4	4	-	15*	36
25	4	-	4	7	4	4	5	4	-	3	2	3	1	2	1	-	-	-	1	-	0	45
26†	4	-	4	7	5	4	5	4	-	3	2	3	2	8	1	3	27	18	58	1	16	175
27	-	-	-	-	-	-	1	1	-	1	-	-	2	11	1	7	38	15	39	4*	14	133
28	-	-	-	-	1	-	2	-	-	1	-	-	19	24	4	12	59	11	69	-	5	207
29	6	2	-	-	1	1	-	2	2	2	-	1	225	53	7	13	358	59	109	5	25	871
30	1	1	1	2	6	5	6	7	1	1	3	-	43	43	2	4*	30*	16	3*	3*	11	189
31	-	-	-	-	-	1	-	-	-	1	-	-	6	-	-	6	29	4	9	1	2	59
32†	1	1	-	2	-	1	-	-	-	-	-	-	21*	5	-	-	29	-	28	-	1*	89
33	3	2	-	3	4	2	3	-	-	2	-	5	69	27	5	4	18	9	9	1	4	170
34†	P	-	-	P	P	-	P	-	-	P	-	P	P	P	-	P	P	P	P	-	-	n/a
35	3	-	-	2	2	-	4	3	1	7	1	1	26	31	11	11	53	2	7	-	-	165
36	-	-	-	-	-	-	-	-	-	-	-	-	22	9	1	11	127	25	40	-	2	237
37	-	-	-	-	-	-	-	-	-	-	-	-	-	1	-	-	4	-	1	-	2	8
38	-	1	1	1	-	-	1	-	-	-	-	-	3	1	-	-	4	4	3	-	1	20
39	2	-	-	-	-	-	2	-	2	3	-	-	54	63	7	29	128	37	288	13	64	692
40	-	-	-	1	2	1	1	-	-	3	1	-	3	5	2	5	8	4	4	2	1	43
41†							P		P				P	P	P	P	P	P				n/a
42	-	-	-	-	-	-	1	-	-	-	-	-	5*	5*	2	2	1	-	-	-	-	16
43	-	-	-	-	-	-	-	-	-	-	-	-	13	21	-	2*	4*	-	1	-	-	41
44	2	-	-	-	2	3*	2*	1	-	-	-	-	3	-	-	-	-	-	-	-	-	13
Wiltshire Period Totals	57	50	29	119.5	70.5	58	86	63	20	63	30	35	1387	956	166	404	2959	901	2302	64	732	10552

Table 1 Number of coins for each site by the Periods defined by Reece (1973); for per mills totals see Moorhead (2001, 105-9); * = uncertain totals, P = present, † = excluded from Period totals

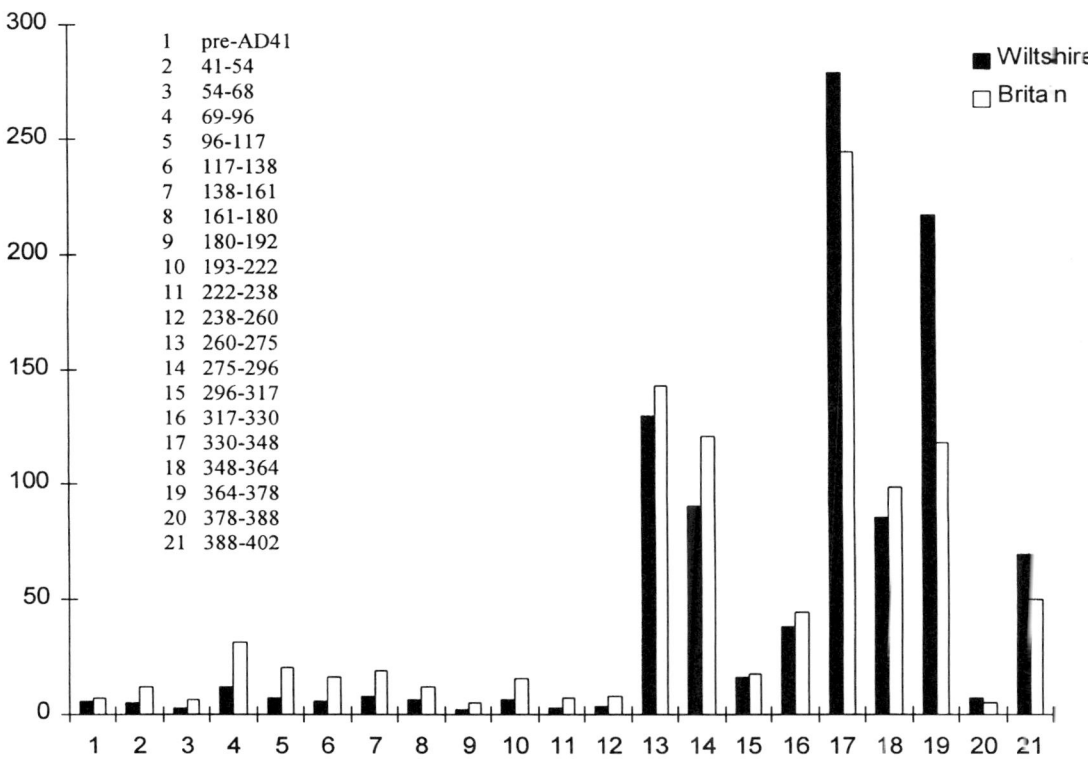

1	pre-AD41
2	41-54
3	54-68
4	69-96
5	96-117
6	117-138
7	138-161
8	161-180
9	180-192
10	193-222
11	222-238
12	238-260
13	260-275
14	275-296
15	296-317
16	317-330
17	330-348
18	348-364
19	364-378
20	378-388
21	388-402

*Fig. 5.2 Bar-chart comparing Wiltshire site finds with those from Britain as a whole (*per mills*) by Period*

Wiltshire sites with a higher proportion of early coins tend to be the small towns and major settlements like Wanborough, Easton Grey, *Verlucio*, and Westbury. The first three of these sites grew up on major roads and the last probably around an iron-works. These would have been the first sites to be heavily Romanized and the coin records come as no surprise.

However, there are other interesting assemblages. The probable temple site at Urchfont has a significant number of 1st and 2nd-century base metal coins which might be individual votive offerings, as found in the sacred spring at Bath (Walker 1983), or a foundation hoard buried when the structure was built. There was also early activity at the other temple sites of Cold Kitchen Hill and Nettleton. 'Kennet', the site to the south of Silbury Hill, has a problematical coin record, but even if Joshua Brooke's records are only partially reliable, it does seem to have been an important settlement from early in the Roman period. Littlecote obviously flourished as a native settlement after its probable military origins, later developing into an important villa.

Other villa and rural sites often have a small smattering of pre-AD 260 coins, but they are not very plentiful and this does support Walker's view that the use of coinage was not particularly widespread in the province before AD 260 (Walker 1988, 305).

AD 260-330 (Periods 13-16)

Figure 5.2 shows that across Britain there was a major increase in coin-loss in the period from AD 260 to 296. This reflects an increasing number of debased coins in circulation as a result of serious inflation. It is also argued that it was only now that the average Romano-Briton could be fully part of the money economy because there was a plentiful supply of low denomination coins (Walker 1988, 305-6). The sheer volume of this coinage is aptly reflected by almost 55,000 examples in the *Cunetio* treasure which is still the largest coin hoard from Roman Britain (Besly and Bland 1983).

This relative increase in coin-loss is reflected on Wiltshire sites, being most pronounced at the major settlements of Easton Grey, *Cunetio* and Westbury, the villas at Littlecote, Downton and East Grimstead, and the temple at Cold Kitchen Hill. This is partly explained by the fact that, with the exception of *Cunetio*, these sites do not have such a high proportion of later 4th-century coins. The higher proportion of AD 260-296 coins to AD 330-402 coins shown by these sites is generally a characteristic of urban sites (Reece 1987, 93, fig. 9.8). Most of the other Wiltshire sites, however, have an increase in coins for the period AD 260-296 which is *below* the national average, reflecting how Wiltshire generally has a rural coin loss profile.

It is interesting to note that in south Wiltshire, the rural settlement at Rotherley has no coins post-dating the 270s. It is the only Wiltshire site known to the author for which no 4th-century coins have been recorded.

The decline in numbers of site-finds for the period AD 296 to 330 throughout the province is mirrored by Witshire sites.

AD 330-364 (Periods 17-18)

It is in the period AD 330-348 that Wiltshire starts to show a higher coin-loss in comparison with the national average (280.5 *per mills* – per thousands - as opposed to 245.45 *per mills*: Fig. 5.2). Several sites peak in this period: the major settlements at Wanborough, *Verlucio* and *Cunetio*; the villas at Atworth, Mother Anthony's Well and Castle Copse; the temple site at Cold Kitchen Hill and possible temple site at Calstone; the Romano-British village at Stockton and the rural site at Lacock. Other sites have a significant proportion of coins and one can argue for a flourishing rural economy in Wiltshire at this time. The decrease in coin loss in Period 18 (AD 348-364) in Wiltshire follows the national trend, although Wiltshire has a slightly lower proportion.

AD 364-378 (Period 19)

From the time that the author started working on Wiltshire site-finds in the early 1980s, it became apparent that bronze coins from the period AD 364-78 were often very common in assemblages (Tables 2 and 3). This is clearly seen when the bar-chart data for British and Wiltshire finds are compared – Wiltshire has 218.2 *per mills* as opposed to the national average of 118 *per mills* (Fig. 5.2). This phenomenon has been the subject of earlier discussions (Moorhead 1997a, 48-9; 1998b, 406).

Table 2   *British sites in rank order according to Period 19 (AD 364-378) coins* (per mills)

Site	per mills	total coins	site type	reference (and see *Gazetteer*)
1 Colerne Mounds	647.06	17	?religious	
2 Castle Combe	571.42	182	villa and/or temple site	
3 Silbury Ditch	563.83	94	?religious	
4 Butterfield Down	416.18	692	rural settlement	
5 Great Witcombe (Glos.)	390.25	64	villa	
6 Lowbury Hill (Oxon.)	377.5	800	temple site	Davies 1985
7 Fisons Ways (Norfolk)	377	106	temple site	Davies & Gregory 1991, 100
8 Stanton Park	369.56	92	villa	
9 Chedworth (Glos.)	361.64	318	villa	Reece 1991, no. 91
10 Urchfont	352.15	372	?temple site/ rural settlement	
11 Bradford-on-Avon	350	20	villa	
12 Pagan's Hill (Som.)	345	200	temple site	Boon 1951; 1955/6
13 Broad Hinton	333.3	207	unspecified rural site	
14 Calstone		135	?temple	
15 Trevelgue (Corn.)	328.36	67	unspecified rural site	Reece 1991, no. 79
16 Euridge	318.18	132	villa	
17 Charlton Down	314.6	89	rural settlement	
18 Kingscote I (Glos.)	304.18	526	unspecified rural site	Reece 1991, no. 66
19 Overton Down	293.23	133	rural settlement	
20 Nettleton	283.24	1790	temple site	
21 Hockwold 1 (Norf.)	275	160	temple site	Davies & Gregory 1991, 99-100
22 Lympne (Kent)	c. 270	c. 370	unspecified site near fort	unpub
23 Hockwold 2 (Norf.)	264	264	temple site	
24 Shakenoak (Oxon.)	257.35	544	villa	Reece 1991, no. 99
25 Sapperton (Lincs.)	257.05	319	unspecified rural site	Reece 1991, no. 76
26 Great Casterton (Rut.)	253.89	193	villa	Corder 1950; 1954; 1961
27 Lydney 1 (Glos.)	247.81	6219	temple site	Reece 1991, no. 137
28 Chelmsford (Essex)	244.57	184	temple site	Reece 1991, no. 132
29 Gt Walsingham (Norf.)	242	885	temple site	Davies & Gregory 1991, 100
30 Gatcombe 1 (Glos.)	233.84	526	enigmatic rural site	Reece 1991, no. 101
31 Lydney 2 (Glos.)	231.31	856	temple site	Reece 1991, no. 138
32 Dorn (Glos.)	229.73	74	unspecified rural site	Reece 1991, no. 86
33 Woodcock Hall (Norf.)	227	2532	fort and settlement	Davies & Gregory 1991, 100
34 *Verlucio*	220.28	858	minor settlement	
35 Alchester 68 (Oxon.)	219.7	132	small town	Reece 1991, no. 62
36 Winterton (Lincs.)	210.53	95	villa	Reece 1991, no. 98
37 Rudston (Yorks.)	206.35	63	villa	Reece 1991, no. 108
38 Ilchester (Soms.)	206.35	126	town	Reece 1991, no. 33
39 Gloucester 3	205.88	102	town	Reece 1991, no. 15
40 Gatcombe 2 (Glos.)	205.67	141	enigmatic rural site	Reece 1991, no. 100
41 Caernarvon (Caern.)	196.7	971	fort	Bradford & Goodchild 1939
42 Frilford (Oxon.)	196.08	153	temple	Reece 1991, no. 121

Other Wiltshire sites above the British Mean of 118 (Reece 1995, 183)

Wanborough	169.06	2224	major settlement	
Stockton	168.77	237	rural settlement	
Lacock	160	50	unspecified rural site	
Mother Anthony's Well	159.02	327	?villa	
Castle Copse	152.54	182	villa	
Stonehenge	150	20	?religious site	
Bowood/Calne	135.86	449	?mostly from *Verlucio*	
Cunetio	125.14	871	town	
Durrington	125	8	unspecified rural site	

91

Coins from this period provide the highest totals for thirteen sites: Stanton Park 34 coins/369.57 *per mills*; Nettleton 507/283.24; the problematic assemblage/hoard from Castle Combe/North Wraxall 104/571.42; Colerne 11/647.06; Euridge 42/318.18; Calstone 45/333.34; Bradford-on-Avon 7/350; Urchfont 131/352.15; Silbury Ditch 53/563.83; Overton Down 39/293.23; Broad Hinton 69/333.3; Charlton Down 28/314.6; Butterfield Down *c.* 288/416.8. Another nine sites have totals over the national mean of 118 *per mills* (Reece 1995, 183): Wanborough 376/169.06; Lacock 8/160; *Verlucio* 189/220.28; Bowood/Calne 61/135.86; Mother Anthony's Well 79/143.12; *Cunetio* 109/125.14; Castle Copse 9/152.54; Stockton 40/168.77; Stonehenge 3/150. Although fourteen Wiltshire assemblages are below the national mean for this period, they are generally small and/or problematical groups.

When compared against sites covered in Reece's 1991 corpus (Reece 1991) and sites in other sources, it is clear that this high number of Valentinianic coins is consistent with a wider pattern of coin-loss in the West Country (Fig. 5.3). Of the 35 assemblages with over 200 *per mills* for coins of the period AD 364-78, 13 are from Wiltshire, 12 from neighbouring counties, 5 from Norfolk and the remainder from Lincolnshire, Yorkshire, Essex and Kent.

Table 3   *Coin hoards with over 100 Valentinianic bronze coins of Period 19 (AD 364-378)*

	Terminal date	Total Aes	Coins AD 364-78	Reference
Wiltshire				
Nettleton (1960)	378-3	131	128	Wedlake 1982, 115-17
Bishops Cannings	395-402	5,837	1,128	*CHRB* X, 426-462
*Castle Combe	?388-402	*c.* 300	?100+	See *Gazetteer* no. 8
Somerset				
Cheddar (Gough's Old Cave)	Gratian	376	281	*NC* 1957, 231-7
Wrington	378-3	1,283	1,158	*CHRB* IX, 345-55
Shapwick	388	1,116	994	*NC* 1939, 128-42
Wiveliscombe	388	1,128	828	*NC* 1946, 163-5
Gloucestershire				
Gloucester	378-3	647	602	*Britannia*, 3, 339, 341
*Lydney	Gratian	up to 4994	*c.* 1296	Wheeler & Wheeler 1932
Buckinghamshire				
Aylesbury	378	452	422	Robertson 2000, no. 1455
Hampshire				
Holybourne/Alton	378	117	117	*CH* III, 68, no. 213

* Calculated as site-finds but possibly dispersed hoards

Before attempting to explain this phenomenon, it is important to consider the incidence of hoards containing a large number of Valentinianic bronze coins. Table 3 shows hoards with a large number (100+) of these coins. There are other smaller hoards with Valentinianic coins from all over the province, but none of them contain more than 100 Valentinianic coins, and most have less than 30 (Robertson 2000). These hoards mirror the evidence of the site finds, with the only outliers being hoards in Buckinghamshire and Hampshire. Interestingly, the largest single find of 5,837 pieces comes from the recently found Bishops Cannings hoard in Wiltshire (Guest *et al.* 1997). Therefore, the picture portrayed by the site-finds seems to be supported by hoard evidence.

There is no simple explanation for this phenomenon and a number of factors need to be considered. First, it is noteworthy that at least 13 of the site-find assemblages in Table 2 come from temple sites. Davies has already noted the high incidence of Valentinianic coins at some temple sites (Davies 1985, 8; Davies and Gregory 1991, 75). There is not the space to show the full findings, but the author's analysis of 25 temple, or possible temple, site assemblages from Roman Britain shows that 11 out of 23 have over 200 *per mills* for Period 19, and that 5 others are over the national mean of 118 *per mills*. It is tempting to suggest that these coin records reflect a vigorous renewal of religious activity at pagan sites after the shortlived pagan revival of Julian the Apostate (AD 360-363). Valentinianic bronze coins were the first common pieces of their kind to circulate prolifically after Julian's reforms, and these finds might attest to continued pagan practices in rural regions.

However, five temples do have significantly fewer Valentinianic coins, including Cold Kitchen Hill in Wiltshire, Henley Wood (Reece 1991, no. 130) and Bath Spring (Walker 1988) in Somerset, and Crownthorpe and *Venta* in Norfolk (Davies and Gregory 1991, 100). It should be mentioned that with the exception of Chelmsford (Reece 1991, no. 132), all the sites with a large number of Valentinianic coins lie in the regions already identified as being rich in Valentinianic coins. Therefore, coin loss at the temple sites could merely be a reflection of the circulating currency rather than of any particular religious or votive activity, but it is possible that one can become caught up in a circular argument. However, it would be interesting to explain why there are four temples with low totals in regions where Valentinianic coins are common; it might just be that the pagan revival did not affect these temples so strongly, or merely that local circumstances or ritual practices were different.

A second factor that should be borne in mind is that many of these assemblages of coins from Wiltshire and Norfolk, and the single Kent group, have been found with the aid of metal detectors. These sites are rural ones and are beginning to tilt the balance away from the military and urban-based emphasis of coin records over the years – they represent over half of Richard Reece's sites (Reece 1991). There is no doubt that high proportions of Valentinianic coins tend to be found on rural or temple sites. As detectorists find more coins on rural sites, so this phenomenon might be found in other parts of the country. Given that the only detector finds to be published in any quantity so far are from Wiltshire and Norfolk, it might just be that these counties are setting a trend for others to follow.

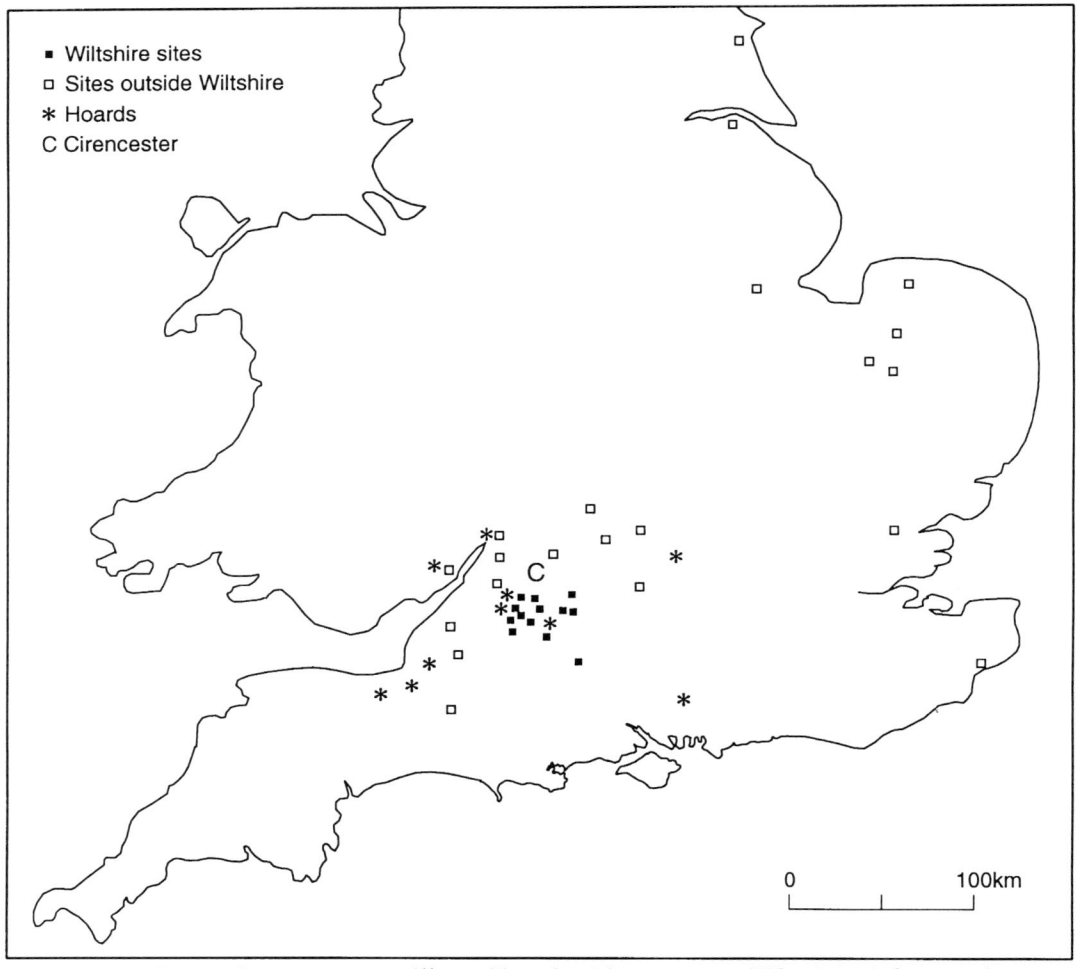

Fig. 5.3 Sites with over 200 per mills *and hoards with 100 or more Valentinianic bronze coins from Period 19 (AD 364-378)*

Thirdly, it is now clear that the West Country, focused on Cirencester, was becoming increasingly wealthy. In fact, Cirencester's coin record is more rural in character, suggesting greater than average prosperity for an urban site in the 4th century (Reece 1985, 94). It should come as no surprise that surrounding major settlements like Wanborough, villas like Euridge, and temple sites like Nettleton reflect this prosperity. Farming was undoubtedly the major source of wealth with villas in north Wiltshire and Romano-British villages, like Stockton and Butterfield Down in south Wiltshire, probably being major suppliers of agricultural produce for the towns and the *annona militaris*. It has been suggested by Bryn Walters (1994; this volume) that some of the grain sent to the Rhineland in the 4th century (Ammianus 18, 2, 3; Julian, 279D-280A) originated in Wiltshire. If there was an increase in the number of barges under Julian in AD 359, can one suggest that output in places like the West Country increased to satisfy this extra demand? Might this be a possible explanation for the high proportions of Valentinianic bronze coins in the region? This hypothesis would need to be tested by an investigation of the nature of agricultural activity in Norfolk at this time.

A fourth factor that needs exploring is the possible importance of the Mendips as a major source of silver in the late-Roman period. The Mendips are an important focal point for late Roman silver hoards in Britain (Archer 1979, 30, fig. 1; Guest 1997, 417, fig. 1). These hoards might further underline the wealth of the region as a whole. Indeed, this might be a prosaic reason for the presence of so many bronze coins in the region, their having been issued in order to attract gold and silver back to the authorities in the form of taxes. This might be supported by the evidence from the Bishops Cannings hoard which had 1 gold, 1569 silver and 5837 bronze pieces (Guest *et al.* 1997). It is interesting to note, however, that such hoards of silver coins are not common in Norfolk, although one cannot overlook the enormous Hoxne hoard and other hoards found over the border in Suffolk (Guest 1997, 471, fig. 1). A publication of Suffolk site-finds comparable to this paper for Wiltshire would clearly answer many questions.

Walters has argued that Cirencester, capital of *Britannia Prima*, was probably the major centre of late-Roman Britain (Walters 1994). Certainly, the city does seem to have had the richest hinterland, and the coin-finds support this argument. He has even suggested that there was political unrest and even sedition here during the so-called Great Barbarian Conspiracy of AD 367. Corney has outlined a possible scenario for the building of stone circuits in the second half of the 4th century at *Cunetio*, Kenchester and Alcester, important minor towns in *Britannia Prima* (Corney 1997, 349). It is possible that these walls were built in the Valentinianic period, possibly as a result of Count Theodosius' visit, which could explain the increased number of bronze coins in the region. Furthermore, Callu argues that bronze coins were used to finance the military at this time, especially on frontier projects (1980, 105-6). Corney suggests that these towns might have been centres for not just the *annona militaris* but also some of the comitatensian troops in the province (*ibid.*, 349).

AD 378-402 (Periods 20-1) and later

Much of what has been said above also applies to the final period of coin loss that we will consider. Before looking at the last two periods in detail, it is worth mentioning that there is a distinctly lower proportion of coins from the second half of the 4th century at three south Wiltshire villa sites: West Dean, Downton and East Grimstead. This contrasts somewhat with the more northerly half of the county, but on initial analysis does seem to be consistent with several nearby Hampshire and Dorset sites like Rockbourne and Winchester (Reece 1991, sites 20-2 and 97) and Iwerne and Woodcuts (Hawkes 1947; Pitt-Rivers 1881-5). The author will publish a fuller study in due course.

The period AD 378-388 has few coins from throughout Britain, and Wiltshire is just above the average. Overall, Wiltshire is better represented in the period AD 388-402 with 69.4 *per mills* as opposed to the national average of 50.25 *per mills*. Theodosian coins are found at nearly all the sites with valid samples, the notable exceptions being the villa at Atworth and the temple at Cold Kitchen Hill. It is worth stating that the first two groups of coins (321 identifiable) that the author catalogued from Mother Anthony's Well had no coins post-dating 378; it was only in the last group (225 coins identifiable) that 8 such coins were found, a warning that absence of evidence is not always evidence of absence!

Sites with a proportion of coins for the period AD 388-402 over the British mean of 50.25 are wide-ranging: Eastcroft (166.66 *per mills*), Wanborough (141.19), Nettleton (112.85), Overton Down (105.263), Euridge (98.48), Silbury (all sites: 91.42), Littlecote (58.2) and Butterfield Down (92.49). Other sites in neighbouring counties also have a strong representation in this period, 12 of the top 16 sites in Reece's corpus coming from the West Country (Reece 1991): the major towns of Cirencester, Dorchester and Caerwent; the minor towns of Alchester, Ilchester, Dorchester-on-Thames; the major settlements of Somerton, Camerton, Dorn; the villa at Dewlish; and temple sites at Jordan Hill and Brean Down. Looking at the region as a whole, it does seem that coin-use was more prevalent at the major centres, although this does not seem to be the case in Wiltshire. It might have been the case, however, that coin-usage declined in rural regions before it did so in more urbanised settlements.

How long these coins continued to circulate is still open to much debate, but Peter Guest suggests that they could have been in use until as late as AD 420 (Guest 1997, 415). Given the large number of silver and bronze hoards from the West Country from this period, it can be argued that coin-use continued well into the 5th century. Certainly there are several hoards which contain clipped silver *siliquae,* the Bishops Cannings hoard being the most important (Guest *et al.* 1997). In the report for this hoard it was suggested that the clipping of silver coins started in the last quarter of the 4th century and continued into the 5th century. As yet, the author knows of no clipped *siliquae* which are definitely site-finds, although the odd unclipped piece does turn up occasionally. Is it possible, therefore, that clipping was taking place when coins were beginning to circulate mainly in large hoards rather than as small change? It should be mentioned that the only clipped gold *solidus* from Britain was found at Melksham (Burnett 1992, 148-9).

The Chisbury hoard of worn late bronze coins (Burnett 1983, 145) appears to belong in Guest's Group 3 (Guest 1997, 423-4) which he argues is the last phase of bronze coin use in the province. Most of these hoards are from eastern England, but the Chisbury hoard does suggest coin-use in Wiltshire until the very end of coin-use in the province, some time in the early 5th century AD.

Summary

In what can only be an abridged account, it can be seen that Roman coins circulated in Wiltshire from the 1st to 5th centuries AD. Wiltshire's overall coin loss profile is typical for a rural region which had only brief military occupation and no major towns. However, a study of the 4th-century coin finds has shown that Wiltshire sites as a whole have a much larger proportion of Valentinianic coins than the national average. This is a phenomenon which requires further research, but it seems to point to a wider trend in the West Country amongst sites which surround Cirencester. When sites in northern Wiltshire were generally flourishing in the second half of the 4th century, it looks as if others in the south were not, and this south Wiltshire decline is paralleled across the border in Dorset and Hampshire.

Although my tutor, Richard Reece, often warns one of reading too much into the analysis of site-finds, is it possible that this study of Roman coins from Wiltshire has uncovered some trends which might help us better understand the history of this county?

Statistical tables

The statistics are presented in several ways. Table 1 shows the identifiable coins from each site listed according to the 21 periods now commonly used for analysing Romano-British coin-finds (Reece 1973, 228; 1987, 73). Totals that are not absolutely certain are denoted with an asterisk. Some sites have insufficient records and P denotes that there were coins present from that particular period. Sites excluded from overall statistical analysis are marked with a dagger. The *per mills* totals are available elsewhere (Moorhead 2001, 105-9). These enable quick comparison between different groups. This method is explained and used in Reece (1991), a work which provides much comparative material for the sites in this article. The bar-chart (Fig. 5.2) shows all the Roman coins from Wiltshire (*per mills*) by period, and all the Roman coins from Britain (*per mills*) by period (see Reece 1995, 183).

Gazetteer

The sites are listed geographically from north to south Wiltshire (Fig. 5.1). WHM = Wiltshire Heritage Museum (Devizes), where many coins and relevant documents are held. The unpublished reports mentioned are held on file at Wiltshire Heritage Museum along with coin listings by Paul Robinson, C. E. King and the author. * denotes a period listing by the author.

1. Cricklade
   A significant Roman settlement, and a nearby villa. At present, the author has insufficient material to provide complete listings which can be used in statistical analysis. A. D. Passmore (*WANHM* 41,1920-2, 390) notes a quantity of coins found from Domitian to Constantine, but no totals are provided. King, in her unpublished Stockton and Easton Grey reports provides totals for some periods.
2. Ashton Keynes
   One north African, one Iron Age and 1035 Roman coins recovered in excavations and metal detector survey by Wessex Archaeology. They include a silver denarius of Juba I of Numidia (60-46 BC) or Juba II of Mauretania (25 BC-AD 23). Provisional report only with period listing by century (N. Wells, pers. comm.). Possibly similar to Butterfield Down (no. 39).
3. Blunsdon Ridge
   Excavations of a shrine and other buildings in 1997 uncovered 18 coins. A further 19 coins were found with a metal-detector. Coins catalogued by Moorhead (Phillips and

Walters 1997). Further excavation is required to determine the exact nature of this site – is it indeed a temple site, or, as the author believes, a shrine associated with a villa?

4. Stanton Park villa

Two groups of coins are available. 78 coins come from an excavation of a fox-earth near the villa (Wilcox 1977), catalogued by King; 14 coins from the villa excavation by Henslow (*WANHM* 41,1920-2, 215), collated by Robinson.

5. Wanborough (*Durocornovium*)

Four groups of coins are available from this minor town on Ermin Street between Cirencester and *Cunetio*, which probably started as a fort (Burnham and Wacher 1990, 160-4). i) and ii) The1966-76 excavations produced 763 and 904 coins (Reece 1991, 64, 65); iii) *Passmore Collection of 464 coins in WHM, of which nearly all come from Wanborough. Some are mentioned in Passmore's 'Archaeological Notebook' in WHM, iv) *93 coins in possession of Bryn Walters.

6. Easton Grey

Major settlement between Cirencester and Bath, often known as 'White Walls' (Cunnington 1930-2, 186). 374 coins, found with a detector, have been catalogued by King.

7. Nettleton

An important temple site and associated settlement, where the 1956-71 excavations uncovered 1790 coins (Reece 1991, 131; Wedlake 1982, 112-15).

8. Castle Combe/North Wraxall

*182 coins in WHM, labelled as being found at Castle Combe (1825) and North Wraxall villa (1859-60). The author believes that the majority come from the likely hoard at Castle Combe (Scrope 1860, 162, 248), but it is not possible to separate the two groups. A relief of a hunter spearing a stag was found with the Castle Combe coins (Scrope 1855, 136) suggesting the coins were votive offerings. 24-30 coins from the excavations at North Wraxall were listed in summary form by G. P. Scrope (1860, 161; 1862, 59-75), but cannot be used for statistical purposes.

9. Colerne mounds

17 coins from A. S. Mellor's excavation of this enigmatic site in 1953 (*WANHM* 55, 1954, 333-40). This sample is possibly too small to be valid, although Reece (pers. comm.) sets the validity limit at 12.

10. Euridge

Recent research by the WANHS Field Group suggests this is a villa site, but there could be a religious element. 132 surface finds, with possibility of contamination (Moorhead in Luckett, *WANHM* 93, 2000, 228-30).

11. Box

12 coins from various excavations and surface finds summarised by H. R. Hurst (*WANHM* 81, 1987, 44). Although known as a villa there are strong reasons for identifying this site as a religious one (*ibid.*, 29). The sample is too small to be valid.

12. Atworth

195 coins from this villa site catalogued by King (Reece 1991, 105).

13. Lacock
    *50 detector finds made by D'Arcy Hunt from an unspecified site that straddles the Roman road between *Verlucio* and Bath (as well as an indeterminate conglomerate of AE 4 coins which the author considers a hoard): i) Farthing collection of 12 coins, ii) King collection of 38 coins (plus conglomerate).

14. *Verlucio* (Sandy Lane)
    *Major settlement between *Cunetio* and Bath (Cunnington 1930-2, 180-1). R. Wilcox excavated a small part of the earth fortifications on the site in 1985 which seem to be no earlier than the 2nd century (Wilcox 1986). The site has also been subject to much field-walking and responsible detectorist activity. The results of a geophysical survey are awaited. Two groups of coins have been catalogued, to which one can probably add most of the Bowood (Calne) coins (see no. 15, below). Another collection of several hundred coins has been lost. i) D'Arcy Hunt collection of 840 coins found with a metal detector, ii) D. Bryant collection of 18 coins found on the surface.

15. Bowood (Calne)
    446 coins in a collection at Bowood House that probably came from local sites like *Verlucio* (no. 14) and Nuthills (no. 17). Listed by King (*WANHM* 72-3, 1977-8, 180-6) and Reece (1991, 55). The author has revised the totals, and believes no. 448 to be an intruder of Mediterranean origin.

16. *Verlucio* and Bowood/Calne
    The author provides combined statistics for groups 13 and 14.

17. Nuthills
    13 coins from this villa site have been catalogued by the Marquess of Lansdowne (*WANHM* 44, 1929, 55-6). This sample seems to be too small to be valid. Some of the Bowood (Calne) coins possibly came from Nuthills (see no. 15).

18. Calstone
    *135 coins found with a detector by T. Morris from three sites in Calstone, the main one being Black Furlong (see Cunnington 1930-2, 181). Finds of votive objects might suggest a religious site.

19. Mother Anthony's Well
    *546 coins found with detectors by Mr Early at this probable villa site, which might have a religious element as it is located by a spring. Three groups have been period listed/catalogued by the author. Also, 6 coins recorded in the WHM register.

20. Bradford-on-Avon
    20 coins from the excavation of this villa catalogued by Robinson (WHM) (see also Cunnington 1930-2, 177).

21. Urchfont
    *15 Iron Age and 357 coins, with bronze objects, found mostly by K. Palmer on a likely temple site next to a Romano-British settlement. Some coins found away from main concentration. Catalogued by Robinson and Moorhead (WHM).

22. Eastcroft Farm
    *Just west of Urchfont (no. 21) K. Palmer found 17 coins, of which 12 can be identified.

Although a small and dispersed sample, they should be recorded here. There was probably a small settlement in the area.

23-26. Silbury Hill area

There was a Roman settlement by the Neolithic mound, on both sides of the Roman and modern road. Three groups of coins have been recorded:

23. *94 coins from the ditch around Silbury Hill, excavated by R. Atkinson in 1969-70. They are possibly from a midden, or they might be votive (for context, see Whittle 1997, 22ff),

24. *36 coins from J. W. Brooke's excavations of wells near Silbury (*WANHM* 36, 1909-10, 373-5; 29, 1897, 166-71),

25. 45 coins from 'Kennet' listed by Brooke (*Marlborough College Nat Hist Soc* 37, 146ff; 38, 110ff; 39, 105ff; 41, 55ff). Brooke referred to the settlement at Silbury as Kennet, but his coin lists are not entirely reliable. He does state that there were very few 3rd and 4th-century coins which does suggest that his listing can be used with caution,

26. In Table 1, I have also provided totals and an analysis of the three groups combined which might provide an indication for a possible overall coin record.

27. Overton Down

133 coins from excavations directed by P. Fowler on this rural site (*WANHM* 62, 1967, 26-33; full listing in Penton 1987).

28. Broad Hinton

*207 surface finds from this unspecified site (see Cunnington 1930-2, 178). Passmore also found 4 coins here (Passmore 'Archaeological notebook', p. 94, in WHM).

29. *Cunetio* (Black Field; Mildenhall)

Many coins have been found at this major settlement on the Silchester to Bath road, fortified in the 4th century, recently discussed by Corney (1997).

i) Soames collection of 691 coins in WHM. Catalogue by King,

ii) *Author's 112 site-finds from 1970s in WHM. Possible chance of slight contamination,

iii) *63 detector finds in 1996, now in WHM,

iv) 6 (or more) Iron Age coins, 5 reported by Robinson (*WANHM* 86, 1993, 147-9) and one from author's finds (WHM *Iron Age Coin Register*)

v) Not included in the totals are coins recorded by Brooke (*Marlborough Coll Nat Hist Soc* 37, 1888, 146ff; 38, 1889, 110ff; 39, 1890, 105ff; 41, 1892, 55ff). He catalogues 25 1st to 3rd-century coins, and mentions finds of several hundred 3rd and 4th-century coins.

30. Littlecote

189 coins from the 1978-91 excavations (*WANHM* 85, 1992, 144-7). Preliminary listing kindly provided by B. Walters, by emperor, hence uncertainty about some period totals. Although generally regarded as a villa, this is a problematic site which probably started as a Roman military installation. It then became a native settlement before growing in to a major villa. Walters regards this site to have been a *collegium* in its final phase.

31. Castle Copse

59 coins from the 1983-6 excavations, catalogued by T. V. Buttrey (Hostetter and Howe 1997, 207-19).

32. Charlton Down

This rural settlement is incorrectly called Rushall Down in some sources (see Cunnington 1930-2, 182; Robinson 1997b, 141-3). Brooke ('Notebook' 2C, pp. 41-2, in WHM) gives details for almost 100 coins from the site, including 89 Iron Age and Roman coins. The information does not enable a thorough statistical breakdown, but the author has estimated *per mills* figures. Nearby, there has been the recent find from Rushall of five clipped *siliquae*. The four seen range from Julian to Arcadius/Honorius. They might be further site-finds or from a dispersed hoard, but Robinson believes that they are more likely to be site-finds (pers. comm.). They are not included in the statistics because they are not from Charlton Down, but they will be the subject of a short report by the author elsewhere.

33. Westbury Ironworks, Heywood

*Large settlement near Westbury, probably founded around an iron-works. This site appears to have been on the course of the putative road that ran south from Bath towards Cold Kitchen Hill. Most of the 170 coins were found in 1877-82 when there was digging for iron ore, and were noted by M. Cunnington (*WANHM* 36, 1909-10, 464-74). Also two Iron Age coins in the WHM *Iron Age Coin Register*.

34. Heytesbury

Hoare mentions a 'variety of Roman coins' from the Romano-British villages on Knook Down. They ranged from Vespasian to Gratian, with many Constantinian and some barbarous radiates (Hoare 1812, 83-6). There is insufficient information to create a complete listing.

35. Cold Kitchen Hill (Brixton Deverill)

*165 coins survive in WHM from this religious site from various sources:
i) 3 coins from Goddard's excavation (*WANHM* 27, 1893, 279-91),
ii) 180 coins from Nan Kivell's 1924 excavation (*WANHM* 43, 1927, 190-1; 44, 1929, 141),
iii) Baker bequest to Devizes Museum (1911).

36. Stockton Earthworks

237 coins are available from this Romano-British village (Cunnington 1930-2, 203):
i) 150 coins from Nan Kivell's work in the 1930s,
ii) 107 coins in Salisbury and South Wilts Museum from 1976 excavation. Catalogue by King,
iii) Hoare notes 'a series of coins from the first Claudius to Theodosius' and comments on how common they were. There is insufficient information to include these coins in the statistics (Hoare 1812, 106-8).

37. Durrington

8 coins from the 1970 excavations by G. J. Wainwright in the Neolithic henge monument (*WANHM* 66, 1971, 116) where there was a Romano-British village. There are insufficient coins for full statistical analysis.

38. Stonehenge

A selection of 20 coins from Stonehenge excavations which J. A. Davies felt could be published with confidence (Cleal *et al.* 1995, 431-2).

39. Butterfield Down

692 coins from the 1990-3 excavations of this large late-Roman village. Period totals

are estimated from the report on the coins by M. Corney (*WANHM* 89, 1996, 20).

40. Old Sarum (on or around *Sorviodunum*)

    43 coins from the region around this Roman settlement at crossroads of the Silchester to Dorchester and Winchester to Charterhouse roads reported on by J. Stone and D. Algar (*WANHM* 56, 1955-6, 119-26). One must beware linking these coins with the actual settlement at Old Sarum/Stratford-sub-Castle (Cunnington 1930-2, 203-4). This group can be used in statistical analysis only with great caution.

41. West Dean

    Indeterminate number of coins from this villa site mentioned by G. S. Master who only recorded the rulers represented (*WANHM* 22, 1885, 249).

42. Downton

    16 coins from P. Rahtz's 1953-7 excavations of this villa, catalogued by G. C. Boon (*WANHM* 58, 1961-3, 336).

43. East Grimstead

    41 coins found on Sumner's excavation of a Roman villa. Because H. Mattingly's coin report does not specify types for all the Constantinian coins, the totals for Periods 16 and 17 have been slightly estimated (Sumner 1924, 49-51).

44. Rotherley

    12 coins found in Pitt-Rivers' excavation of the native settlement north of Tollard Royal. The Period 13-14 totals are estimates and the two uncertain 2nd-century coins have been put in Periods 6 and 7 (Pitt-Rivers 1888, 188-9).

Acknowledgements

There are numerous people who the author must thank for their help during this research. Advice has been received from numerous numismatists: Andrew Burnett, Roger Bland, John Orna-Ornstein, Jonathan Williams, Richard Abdy, Peter Guest, Richard Hobbs, Robert Kenyon and John Casey. Several people have kindly provided new material and information: Bryn Walters, Mark Corney, Simon Esmonde Cleary, Alastair Whittle, Ron Wilcox, Andrew Fitzpatrick, Nicholas Wells, Judith Atkinson, Nicholas Ryan, Mick Stone, Paul Collins, Tony Spence, David Bryant, Norman Farthing, Clive and Paul King, Graham Palmer, Keith Palmer, Tony Morris, Mr Early, Mr Aldridge, and especially D'Arcy Hunt. Valuable assistance has been received from John Witherington and the late Tim Potter, and two librarians, Pamela Colman at Wiltshire Heritage Museum (Devizes), and Annette Calton in the Department of Coins and Medals in the British Museum. The author will always remain indebted to the work of the late Anne Robertson, and is deeply grateful to Cathy King for permission to use her unpublished material. Deepest gratitude is owed to Paul Robinson (and all the other staff at Wiltshire Heritage Museum, Devizes) and Richard Reece, both of whom have provided patient and invaluable assistance throughout the project. I must also acknowledge the support and encouragement that I received for my numismatic work from the late Christopher Blunt. Finally, I must acknowledge the support of my family and, most recently, my wife, Fiona.

References

Ammianus Marcellinus, *Histories*, published in English as: *The Later Roman Empire*, Harmordsworth, 1986

Archer, S., 1979, 'Late Roman gold and silver coin hoards in Britain: a gazetteer', in P. Casey (ed.) *The End of Roman Britain*, BAR Brit Ser, 71, Oxford, 29-64

Besly, E., and Bland, R., 1983, *The Cunetio Treasure*, London

Boon, G. C., 1951 and 1955/6, 'Coins from the temple well and other buildings at Pagans Hill/ Chew Stoke', *Procs Somerset Archaeol Nat Hist Soc*, 96, 127-35; 101/2, 33-7

Bradford, J. S. P., and Goodchild, R. G., 1939, 'Excavations at Frilford, Berkshire, 1937-8', *Oxoniensia*, 4, 1-70

Brooke, J. W., 1888, 'Finding of gold coins (British and Roman) since 1885', *MCNHSR*, 37, 146-50.

_____ , 1889, 'Coins near Beckhampton', *MCNHSR*, 38, 110-13

_____ , 1890, 'Roman remains', *MCNHSR*, 39, 105-13

_____ , 1892, 'Roman coins', *MCNHSR*, 41, 55-7

_____ , 1897, 'Excavations of a Roman well near Silbury Hill', *WANHM*, 29, 166-71

_____ , 1909-10, 'Excavation of a Roman well near Silbury Hill, October, 1908', *WANHM*, 36, 373-5

Burnett, A. M., 1983, 'A late Roman coin hoard from near Chisbury Camp', *WANHM*, 77, 145-6

_____ , 1992, 'A clipped solidus from Wiltshire', *WANHM*, 85, 148-9

Burnham, B., and Wacher, J., 1990, *The Small Towns of Roman Britain*, London

Callu, J. P., 1980, 'The distribution and the role of bronze coinage from A.D. 348 to 392', in C. King (ed.) *Imperial Revenue, Expenditure and Monetary Policy in the Fourth Century AD*, BAR Int Ser, 76, Oxford, 95-124

Cleal, R. M. J., Walker, K. E., and Montague, R. (eds), 1995, *Stonehenge in its Landscape*, London

Corder, P., 1950-61, *The Roman Town and Villa at Great Casterton, Rutland*, 3 vols., Nottingham

Corney, M., 1997, 'The origins and development of the 'small town' of *Cunetio*, Mildenhall, Wilts', *Britannia*, 28, 337-50

Crawford, M. H., 1974, *Roman Republican Coinage*, Cambridge

Cunnington, M. E., 1909-10, 'Notes on the Roman antiquities in the Westbury collection at the museum, Devizes', *WANHM*, 36, 464-77

_____ , 1930-2, 'Romano-British Wiltshire', *WANHM*, 45, 166-216

_____ , 1949, *An Introduction to the Archaeology of Wiltshire*, Devizes

Davies, J. A., 1985, 'The Roman coins from Lowbury Hill', *Oxoniensia*, 50, 1-15

Davies, J. A., and Gregory, A., 1991, 'Coinage from a *Civitas*: a survey of the Roman coins found in Norfolk and their contribution to the archaeology of the *Civitas Icenorum*', *Britannia*, 22, 65-101

Fowler, P. J., 1967, 'The Archaeology of Fyfield and Overton Downs, Wiltshire', *WANHM*, 62, 16-33

Goddard, E. H., 1893, 'Notes on the opening of a tumulus on Cold Kitchen Hill, 1893', *WANHM*, 27, 279-91

Guest, P., 1997, 'Hoards from the end of Roman Britain', *Coin Hoards of Roman Britain*, 10, 411-23

Guest, P., Bland, R., Orna-Ornstein, J., Robinson, P., 1997, 'Bishops Cannings (Blagan Hill), Wiltshire', *Coin Hoards of Roman Britain*, 10, 426-62

Hawkes, C. F. C., 1957a, 'Britons, Romans and Saxons round Salisbury and in Cranborne Chase', *Archaeol Journ*, 104, 27-81

_____, 1957b, Roman coins from Wiltshire, unpub mss at Devizes Museum

Hoare, R. C. 1812, *The Ancient History of South Wiltshire*, London

_____, 1831, *History of Modern Wiltshire, III, Warminster Hundred*, London

Hostetter, E., and Howe, T. N. (eds), 1997, *The Romano-British Villa at Castle Copse, Great Bedwyn*, Indiana

Hurst, H. R., 1987, 'Excavations at Box Roman villa, 1967-8', *WANHM*, 81, 19-51

Julian, 'Letter to the senate and people of Athens, AD 358-9', in J. Mann and R. Penman (eds), *Literary Sources Roman Britain*, LACTOR 11, 2nd edn, London, 1985

King, C. E., 1977-8, 'A group of 479 coins found near Bowood House, Wilts.', *WANHM*, 72-3, 180-6

Kivell, N., 1926, 'Objects found during excavations on the Romano-British site at Cold Kitchen Hill, Brixton Deverill, Wiltshire', *WANHM*, 43, 327-32

_____, 1929, 'Objects found during excavations at the Romano-British site at Cold Kitchen Hill, Brixton Deverill, Wiltshire', *WANHM*, 44, 138-142

Lansdowne, The Marquess of, 1929, 'A Roman villa at Nuthills, near Bowood', *WANHM*, 44, 49-59

Luckett, L., 2000, 'Investigation of a Roman villa site at Euridge Manor Farm', *WANHM*, 93, 219-32

Master, G. S., 1885, 'Collections for a history of West Dean', *WANHM*, 22, 239-317

Mellor, A. S., 1954, 'The Roman site in Colerne Park', *WANHM*, 55, 330-40

Moorhead, T. S. N., 1997a, 'A reappraisal of the Roman coins found in J. W. Brooke's excavation of a late Roman well at Cunetio (Mildenhall), 1912', *WANHM*, 90, 42-54

_____, 1997b, 'All Cannings, Wiltshire', *Coin Hoards of Roman Britain*, 10, 406-9

_____, 1997c, 'The Roman coins', in Phillips and Walters 1997, 27-35

_____, 2000, Coin report, in L. Luckett, 'Investigation of a Roman villa site at Euridge Manor Farm, Colerne', *WANHM*, 93, 228-30

_____, 2001, 'Roman coin finds from Wiltshire', unpub M Phil thesis, Univ. London

Passmore, A. D., 1920-2, 'Notes on Roman finds in North Wilts', *WANHM*, 41, 389-95

Penton, D., 1987, 'The coin report and catalogue for Overton Down XII', unpub MA Dissertation, Univ Durham

Phillips, B and Walters, B., 1997, *Blunsdon Ridge, 1997 (BR97), An Archaeological Evaluation*, Swindon

Pitt-Rivers, A. L. F., 1881-5, *Excavations in Cranborne Chase, Vol. I*, privately printed

_____, 1888, *Excavations in Cranborne Chase, Vol. II*, privately printed

Rahtz, P. A., 1961-3, 'A Roman villa at Downton', *WANHM*, 58, 303-41

Rawlings, M. and Fitzpatrick, A. P., 1996, 'Prehistoric sites and a Romano-British settlement at Butterfield Down, Amesbury', *WANHM*, 89, 1-43

Reece, R., 1973, 'Roman coinage in the Western Empire' *Britannia* 4, 227-51

_____, 1981, 'Coinage and currency in the third century', in A. King and M. Henig (eds) *The Roman West in the Third Century*, BAR Int Ser, 109, part i, 79-88

_____, 1987, *Coinage in Roman Britain*, London

_____, 1991, *Roman Coins from 140 Sites in Britain*, Cirencester

_____, 1995, 'Site-finds in Roman Britain', *Britannia* 26, 179-206

Robinson, P. R., 1993, 'Iron Age coins from Cunetio and Mildenhall', WANHM, 86, 147-9

_____, 1997a, 'A Roman inscription from Charlton Down', *WANHM*, 90, 141-3

_____, 1997b, 'Chisbury Camp and Northeastern Wiltshire in the Iron Age', in Hostetter and Howe 1997, 20-33

Robertson, A. S, 2000. *Romano-British Coin Hoards*, Royal Numismatic Soc Special Publication 20

Scrope, G. P., 1855, 'The manor and ancient barony of Castle Combe', *WANHM*, 2, 133-58

_____ , 1860, Notes on North Wraxall and Castle Combe in 'Proceedings', *Archaeological Journal*, 17, 160-2; 248

Stone, J., and Algar, D. J., 1955-6, 'Sorviodunum', *WANHM*, 56, 102-26

Sumner, H., 1924. *Excavations at East Grimstead Villa, Wiltshire*, London

Wainwright, G. J., 1971, 'The excavation of prehistoric and Romano-British settlements near Durrington Walls, Wiltshire, 1970', *WANHM*, 66, 76-128

Walker, D. R., 1988, *Roman Coins from the Sacred Spring at Bath*, Oxford

Walters, B., 1992, 'Littlecote Park Excavations, 1978-1991', *WANHM*, 85, 144-7

_____ , 1994, 'Wealth and influence in late Roman Wiltshire', unpub. conference paper

Wedlake, W. J., 1982, *The Shrine of Apollo at Nettleton, Wiltshire, 1956-1971*, London

Wheeler, R. E. M., and Wheeler, T. V., 1932, *Report on the Excavation of the Prehistoric, Roman and Post-Roman Site in Lydney Park, Gloucestershire*, London

Whittle, A.,1997, *Sacred Mound and Holy Rings*, Oxbow monograph 74, Oxford

Wilcox, R., 1977, 'An artificial fox-earth, Stanton Park, near Chippenham', *Post-Med Archaeol*, 2, 105-6

_____ , 1986, *Verlucio* fieldwork, March 1986, unpub mss

6   ART IN ROMAN WILTSHIRE

by Martin Henig

Introduction

The county of Wiltshire does not correspond to any known Roman administrative unit. Like Oxfordshire, for example (Henig and Booth 2000), it contains several small towns but no cantonal capital and this means that the richer inhabitants will in many instances have looked beyond what are now the county boundaries for their major markets as well as for the craftsmen and artists who embellished villas and other buildings. The north and north west of the county will have been part of the territory of the Dobunni, ruled from Cirencester, Gloucestershire, although the spa at Bath (just over the modern county boundary in Somerset) was another major centre of patronage, probably with quasi-urban functions; further south and to the west lay the Durotriges with their tribal capital at Dorchester, Dorset, and to the east the Belgae whose administrative centre lay at Winchester, Hampshire.

We cannot, therefore, expect an account of the Roman period in Wiltshire to be co-ordinated in the way that studies of Dorset, Gloucestershire, Hertfordshire or Sussex can be presented. There are, however, compensations for this lack of clear focus. Essentially a survey of the Roman period in Wiltshire whether dealing with art, pottery, religion or farming practice will be a representative sample of sufficient size to address the question of the impact of Roman ways on the largely rural communities of the province and the success of Romanisation in southern Britain. It thus provides an opportunity to look at art in Roman Britain from an angle rather different from the one I attempted in my book on the subject (Henig 1995).

It is convenient to arrange the major categories of material in a sequence which provides an almost chronological ordering. Figural work in bronze seems to cast most light on developments in the latest Iron Age and the period of Romanisation; the art of the Roman province from the late 1st century until the 3rd is best addressed through sculpture; while the majority of the mosaics are dated to the period of late antiquity. Several important examples of decorative metalwork are also assigned to the 4th century (or early 5th) and provide a starting point from which others may embark on the examination of the art of the next (Dark Age, 'Anglo-Saxon') phase. I am proud to have been invited to offer this paper to Ken Annable as a token of my regard for his work on the archaeology of the county, and more especially to pay tribute to his interest in Roman Britain.

The smith and classical iconography

Mediterranean influences were present in Britain during the Iron Age and anthropoid masks and figurines are recorded from various sites in southern Britain. A comparatively simple example is the escutcheon in the form of a female bust with lentoid eyes, from Heywood (Westbury Ironworks site), now in the Wiltshire Heritage Museum (Cunnington and Goddard 1934, 177, no. 616, pl. lv, 8). It was originally attached to the body of a bowl. An altogether exceptional item which combines classical with native iconography is the Marlborough bucket or vat, one of the great treasures of the Wiltshire Heritage Museum and indeed of early Celtic art in Britain, probably made in the middle of the 1st century AD (Fox 1958, 68-70). It is ornamented with confronted animals as well as with masks *en repoussé* (Fig. 6.1). Pairs of confronted youthful masks (*ibid.*, pl. 34 c, d) are certainly derived from a well-known Roman motif (e.g. the gem, Henig 1978, no. 526). Equally telling are the facing masks (*ibid.*, pl. 36 b, c) with hair of Julio-Claudian appearance, silvered eyes and empty pupils, probably once filled with glass. Close comparison in this case should be made with such items as the South Cadbury (Somerset) plaque, possibly itself a fragment of sheeting from a bucket, upon which a male mask is figured in *repoussé* technique; this too displays a coiffure influenced by the current Roman style (Alcock 1972, 167-8, pl. xii). There is also a facing head on a plaque from a late Roman context at the temple site at Nettleton in our county, though its actual date of manufacture is not known. It was dedicated to Apollo by Decimius, who was surely a Celt, as was the designer of this striking but stylised image (Toynbee 1982, 143-5, no. 1 and frontispiece). Nettleton is only a few miles from Bath and it is not impossible that the head owes something to the form of the famous male gorgon which is carved in the centre of the pediment of the Temple of Sulis Minerva (Cunliffe and Fulford 1982, 11, nos 32-7). Finally there is a very small head with patterned hair modelled in relief upon the lid of a little casket found at the native village at Rotherley in Cranborne Chase (Pitt Rivers 1888, 130-1, pl. ciii, fig. 6), now in Salisbury Museum and perhaps the most striking of the 'Celtic' heads from the county in its physiognomy (Fig. 6.2).

All these masks exemplify continuity of tradition which is also apparent in full-length images. The Rotherley casket is itself cast in two parts in the form of a goose, with distinctive inset eyes, once filled with glass. Similar eyes are to be seen in several late Iron Age figurines like the little boar from Duncliffe Hill, Motcombe, just over the Dorset border from South Wiltshire (Henig and Keen 1984). I have taken the surviving part of the Southbroom (Devizes) cache of figurines, 8 out of 19 recorded all in the British Museum (Boon 1973), as marking the decisive emergence of a Romano-British tradition. Pre-conquest figurines are fairly widely distributed in south-west Britain (Henig 1996b) but amongst the Southbroom bronzes we can see Romano-British versions of deities such as Mars, Mercury, Vulcan and Minerva, as well as attempts at portraying non-Roman concepts of the divine, amongst them a figure with two ram-headed serpents, possibly Cernunnos (Fig. 6.3). There is a high degree of stylisation here, both in the stiff folds of clothing and in the simplified physiognomies. In several instances the eyes are represented by simple borings, originally surely filled with glass. The cache was associated with 3rd-century coins but, as with the Nettleton plaque, an earlier date is probable – here much

Fig. 6.1 Restoration of the excavated elements of a 1st-century AD bucket, from Marlborough, ht. 594mm, diam. 680mm; WHM

earlier, probably mid 1st-century AD. Other (lost) figurines in the deposit were thoroughly classical and might even have been imports from across the channel. Amongst them were representations of Vulcan, Venus and a Genius, all of which are incidentally significant in assessing the Romanisation of art in the county. It is tempting to see these objects as having been cleared from display in the temple and thrown into a *favissa*, or temple repository. With regard to the further development of this Iron Age tradition, a portrayal of Vulcan from North Bradley is now in the Wiltshire Heritage Museum (Henig 1991); it is closely related in style to the figurines in the British Museum but iconographically perhaps nearer to the classical prototype. Apart from the Southbroom figurines, a further bronze in the British Museum is said to have been found in Wiltshire, although, alas, its findspot within this large county is not recorded. It depicts the pony-goddess Epona seated between

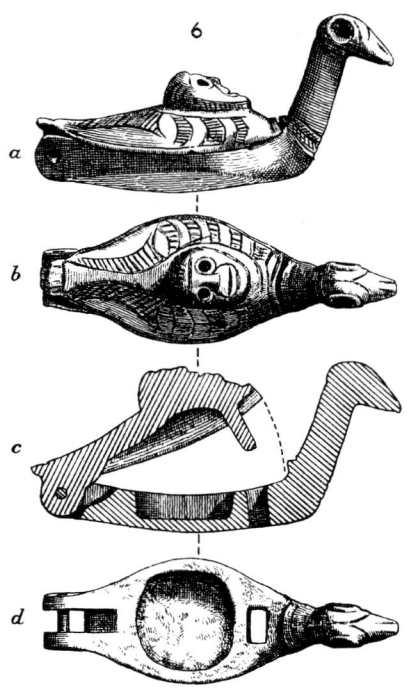

Fig. 6.2 Casket in the shape of a goose, with 'Celtic' head on lid, from Rotherley (Pitt-Rivers 1888, pl. ciii, fig. 6), length 52mm, ht. 26mm; Salisbury and South Wilts Museum

two foals (Alcock 1963, 119-21, pl. xix c; Mackintosh 1995, 36, pl. 4). Here, patterned clothing and rather stylised physiognomy and hair suggest Romano-British or, more probably, Gallo-Roman workmanship: the veneration of this goddess was centred in eastern Gaul and, apart from this bronze, she is not attested in the south west while in Britain generally evidence for her worship is rare (Mackintosh 1995, 30-1).

Another fascinating work, this time in relief, and certainly produced by a British smith, is the well-known plaque from Charlton Down, Lavington, depicting Minerva writing upon a shield (Toynbee 1962, 176-7, no. 124, pl. 146). Her mask-like features recall the art of the Nettleton head (above) and this plaque may similarly have been a votive dedicated

Fig. 6.3 Bronze figurine of Hercules/Cernunnos, one of a group from Southbroom, Devizes, ht. 108mm; British Museum

110

within a temple (Fig. 6.4). The curving lines of the folds of the goddess's mantle provide a very effective pattern and I enthusiastically endorse Graham Webster's judgement that this is a case where 'the Celts imparted new life and vigour in the process of copying' (Webster 1986, 43). It is surely one of the most interesting and attractive figural bronzes from Roman Britain.

Fig. 6.4 Bronze plaque depicting Minerva, from Charlton Down, Lavington, ht. 130mm; WHM

The Iron Age tradition was equally applied to animal art and is well exemplified by the Marlborough bucket menagerie, the Motcombe boar and the Rotherley goose, all mentioned above. It appears in the early Roman period on three intriguing but lost figurines from the Southbroom hoard, a three-horned bull, a horse and particularly a lion-like creature which could depict the same ferocious monster as the creature represented by a figurine of a man-devouring wolf-lion from Oxfordshire, probably from Woodeaton (Alcock 1963, 121-3, pl. xix d; Henig 1984, 65, ill. 22; Henig and Booth 2000, 124, ill. 5.8). A figure of a bird which originally surmounted a sceptre or tipstaff, excavated at Butterfield Down, Amesbury (Henig 1996a, 21, fig. 13), is likewise comparable to figurines from Ramsden (Henig and Chambers 1984; Henig and Booth 2000, 125, ill. 5.9) and Woodeaton (Bagnall Smith 1995, 181) in that county, by virtue of its simplified plumage with the pinions indicated by means of vigorous grooving. It may be asked whether such images reflect the Roman practice of augury or whether more native ideas were involved. There is less doubt about the cockerel candle-holder from Nettleton (Toynbee 1982, 143, no. 10). This bird with its prominent crown and ornamental, hatched plumage is presumably the familiar of Mercury; not only was the head and neck of a terracotta cockerel found at Nettleton but a limestone relief of Mercury with his female consort, sometimes known as Rosmerta, was recovered here (Fig. 8.5; Cunliffe and Fulford 1982, 33, no. 117).

It is not possible to tell whether any of the bronzes of more classical appearance from Wiltshire sites were made in Britain or whether they were all imported. Local manufacture cannot be ruled out but even in the cases where such items were certainly imported they indicate the forces of Romanisation at work in the villas and small towns of the region. One of the finest of these is the lost statuette of Venus from Mildenhall (*Cunetio*) which stood 150mm in height; it is illustrated by Colt Hoare who writes that it 'is not devoid of elegance in proportion and design; she appears to have held a speculum in her hand' (Hoare 1821, 72 and ill. shown here as Fig. 6.5). The image of a nude Venus holding a mirror and arranging her hair is one of the variants of the type of Hellenistic Aphrodite widespread in the Empire. The figure seems to have been close in size and workmanship to the Gunskirchen Venus (Fleischer 1967, 69, no. 75, pl. 40-1) though in that case right and left are reversed. Venus who looked after gardens as well as love was popular everywhere and thus often found in *lararia* (see Petronius, *Satyricon* XV, 29), but is it merely chance that so many other examples are recorded from Wiltshire? These are

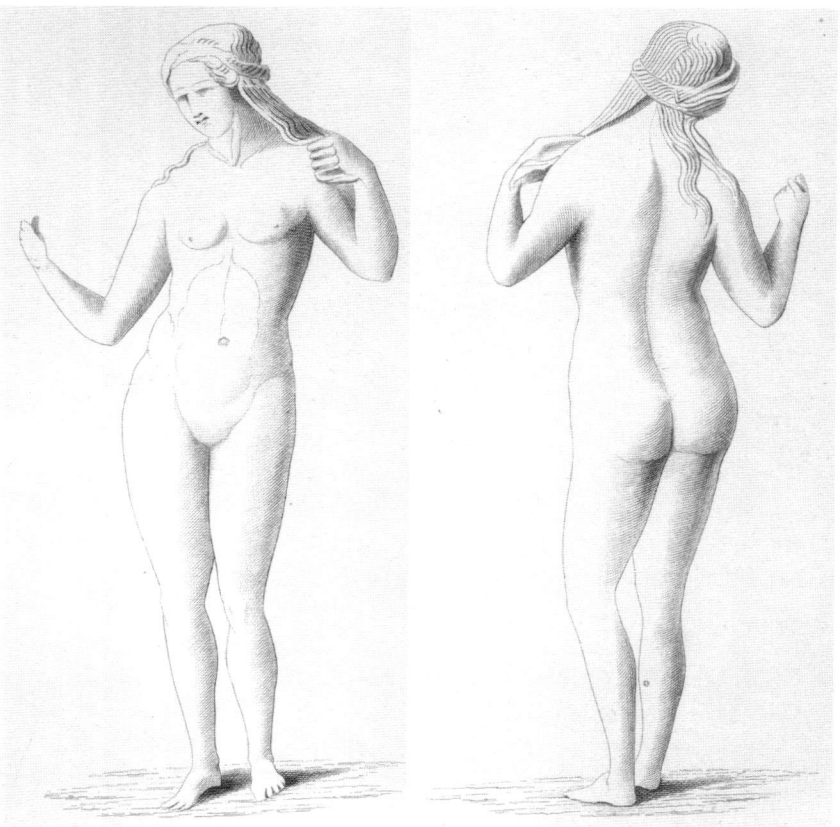

Fig. 6.5 Bronze figurine of Venus, from Folly Farm, Mildenhall (Hoare 1821), ht. 150mm

mainly in bronze but include a small statue in stone from Rudge Farm, Froxfield (Cunliffe and Fulford 1982, 30, no. 111), where a small bronze head of the goddess, with silver eyes, came to light a few years ago (G. Webster, pers. comm.). Other records include an excellent classical Venus figurine from the Southbroom cache (Boon 1973, 267, taf. 58, fig.1), and two from Wilcot, one of them of the *Anadyomene* type and the other an abraded head (Henig 1994).

A figurine of a Genius from the Southbroom cache and a Fortuna from Duncliffe Hill, Motcombe, just in Dorset (Henig and Keen 1984), both represent concepts which can also be found in stone reliefs (see below). Second-century classicism is represented by an appliqué from Westbury in the form of a bust of Hercules (Henig 1999a). Fine as it is, even more accomplished is another appliqué depicting the bust of a youth which was found at Littlecote (Walters and Henig 1988). It represents the art of Hadrian's time at its most refined and may, indeed, portray the Emperor's deceased favourite Antinous regarded here as Bacchus Zagreus – 'Bacchus reborn' (Fig. 6.6). Another, far more ordinary, appliqué representing Bacchus was found with it. We do not know whether they were at the villa from the beginning or introduced when the remarkable triconch hall, which seems to have served the dual purpose of dining hall and Orphic cult chapel, was inaugurated around AD 360.

Fig. 6.6 Bronze appliqué bust of a youth - perhaps Bacchus/Antinous, from Littlecote, ht. 116mm

Sculpture in Roman Wiltshire

Wiltshire has not yielded the large quantity of sculpture recorded from Gloucestershire but much of what has been found is iconographically of high interest. Most of it comes from the northern fringes of the county and belongs to the Cotswold tradition of oolitic limestone-carving. Indeed in many instances connections can be established with Gloucestershire sculpture both with regard to style and iconography. Stone-carving seems only to have begun with the Roman conquest, but quite soon native-born sculptors were giving physical expression to religious ideas. Amongst the more ordinary sculptures there are several close parallels in style and iconography. One such is the signed work of a man called Civilis, found at Easton Grey and depicting a mother goddess and three male figures, perhaps votaries but more probably subordinate godlings (*RIB* 99; Cunliffe and Fulford 1982, 34, no. 120). The subject is the same as that on two Gloucestershire reliefs from Cirencester and two from Daglingworth (Henig 1993, 34-5, nos 101-3; Henig 1998). Civilis is the only sculptor known to us by name from Wiltshire, though several local artists signed carvings from elsewhere in the Cotswold region, notably Sulinus at Bath and Cirencester (*RIB* 105, 151) and Searigillus at Uley (Woodward and Leach 1993, 94-6). A relief of a mother-goddess from Colerne Park was, however, dedicated by someone with a native name whether or not he also made it; the inscription here may read Ing[enuius] Fabill[is] (Cunliffe and Fulford 1982, 34, no. 121) and the *mater* has the same arrangement of clothing, portrayed in a similar manner to that on a relief from Cirencester, excavated beyond the Bath Gate (Henig 1993, 40-1, no. 121). A female head in Stroud Museum, evidently found at North Wraxall in Wiltshire (Henig 1993, 51 no. 147) is very like that of a *mater* from Cirencester (Henig 1993, 40, no. 120), and I now believe it too represents a *mater*.

Another votive relief, this time figuring Mercury and his female consort who holds a water-jar and is conventionally identified with 'Rosmerta', the name by which his wife was known on inscriptions from Gaul, comes from Nettleton (Toynbee 1982, 137, no. 4; Cunliffe and Fulford 1982, 33, no. 117, pl. 31). It is matched by a relief of the same deities from nearby Bath (Cunliffe and Fulford 1982, 11, no. 39, pl. 11).These simple works, while in no way matching the quality of the best of the Gloucester carvings of Mercury and 'Rosmerta' from the *colonia* of Gloucester (Henig 1993, 26, no. 78, pl. 22), demonstrate the community of culture across the region.

Far more distinguished than the Nettleton Mercury and Rosmerta as a work of art is the well-known block from a large monument or altar from the same site which shows Diana (Toynbee 1982, 136-7, no. 3; Cunliffe and Fulford 1982, 27, no. 100); upon this stone the goddess is accompanied by a hound which looks up at its mistress. It is unfortunate in both instances that what remains is so fragmentary. A much smaller relief which shows Diana slaying a deer comes from Castle Combe and is now in the Ashmolean (Fig. 6.7; Cunliffe and Fulford 1982, no. 99). This is a classical type which goes back to the end of the 5th century BC, the date of a Greek marble relief in Cassel (Kahil 1984, 653, no. 397). The Diana from Nettleton is paralleled by a block of the same size and with a relief of even higher quality from Box (Cunliffe and Fulford 1982, 34, no. 122), which must have

Fig. 6.7 Votive relief in oolitic limestone of Diana, from Castle Combe, ht. 350mm; Ashmolean Museum

come from a large monument such as a gateway or a mausoleum (Fig. 6.8). It portrays a hunter-god holding a boar and a hare, the result of a successful hunt; his patterned clothing, especially the frilled overfold of his jerkin, demonstrates masterly handling of limestone carving. This is by far the most beautiful of the representations of the Cotswold Hunter god who is widely attested through Gloucestershire and by three images from London (compare Henig 1993, 37-8, nos 110-14; see Boon 1989; Merrifield 1996) and who may be identical with that Apollo Cunomaglos – the 'hound prince' – venerated at Nettleton (Toynbee 1982, 135-6, no. 1).

Sophistication in the understanding of classicism is shown in other reliefs from Wiltshire. Fortuna is typically represented by a standing woman with steering-oar and rudder, and a wheel by her side. The best example of the type from the entire province is in north Wiltshire, built into the inner west wall of St Mary's church, Marlborough (Cunliffe and Fulford 1982, no. 102). There is, however, a statue of a seated Fortuna from Cirencester with which it can be compared with regard to style (Henig 1993, 11, no. 24). Two votive reliefs of far more native style, which show belted female figures, probably also represent Fortuna. The Wiltshire examples come from Nettleton (Toynbee 1982, 138-9, no. 6; Cunliffe

Fig. 6.8 Oolitic limestone relief of a hunter god, from Box, ht. 350mm, width 400mm; WHM

and Fulford 1982, 33, no. 118) and from Mildenhall (*Cunetio*) (Cunliffe and Fulford 1982, 33-4, no. 119); they can be compared with others from Cirencester (Henig 1993, 13, no. 29) and Kingscote (Henig 1993, 13, no. 30) in Gloucestershire. Simple as they are, these also provide good evidence for a common 'Cotswold' cultural area.

The well-known image of a togate Genius set into the south wall of Tockenham church (Cunliffe and Fulford 1982, no. 104) is another successful translation into British stone of a thoroughly Roman type; he is veiled and togate as he pours a libation over an altar around which a serpent is curled, the snake being the attribute of Genius (Fig. 6.9). Close comparison can be made to reliefs from Gloucestershire and Oxfordshire, especially to one now in Chedworth manor (Toynbee 1978; Henig 1993, 13-16, nos 32-41) and it is, once again, likely that the sculptor was a Cotswold man.

Two images in the round are also noteworthy. The first, a Venus with hair arranged in a chignon but with free locks cascading over the shoulders, comes from Rudge Farm, Froxfield (Cunliffe and Fulford 1982, no. 111) and has already been mentioned; it shows deftness in presenting a nude torso. By contrast the figure of Mercury from Wanborough is enveloped in a *paenula* which reaches the ground and is treated as a rich pattern of folds, comparable with the drapery of the Nettleton Diana (Cunliffe and Fulford 1982, no. 108, *cf.* no. 100), or indeed Minerva's mantle upon the bronze plaque from Lavington discussed above.

Garden sculpture is very rare in Roman Britain but a superb spout in the form of a fish with large convex eyes and well-defined scales came to light in recent excavations at Tockenham (Fig. 6.10; Henig 1997, 35-6). Each of the features encountered can be matched in other Cotswold sculpture, the eyes in the figures upon the Cirencester Jupiter-column

(Henig 1993, 8-9, no. 18) and the scales upon a fragmentary figure of a scaly monster from the same city (Henig 1993, 57, no. 170) but this is a highly original work of art in its own right. Did it come from an ornamental pool or a spring, or from a bath suite?

Fig. 6.9 Oolitic limestone relief of a Genius, set into the south wall of Tockenham church, ht. 830mm

Beyond the area where limestone was freely available, the tally of sculpture from the county is as pitiful as it is from several neighbouring shires (Berkshire, Hampshire and Dorset). Only three items deserve comment. A female head from Winterslow near the Winchester–Old Sarum road was apparently carved from greensand (Cunliffe and Fulford 1982, 25, no. 94). The pear-shaped head has lentoid eyes with well-defined lids, wedge-shaped nose and slit mouth. The diadem or ridge of hair above her brows could represent a Middle Empire hair style but looks to me rather like the coiffure of the Aust Venus-figurine (see Cunliffe 1978, 155, and pl. 22b; reassessed and redated by Henig 1996b, 131-3). It certainly shows little sign of an emergent Romano-British tradition. The relief of a genius carved from chalk from Rushall Down (Cunliffe and Fulford 1982, 28, no. 103), a very simple facing figure, enveloped in a knee-length garment, also has the simple Iron-Age type physiognomy of wedge-shaped nose and lentoid eyes. Roman influence is once again minimal.

Fig. 6.10 Water spout in oolitic limestone in the form of a fish, from the Roman villa at Tockenham, length 650mm, width at head 290mm

One piece that does stand out by virtue of the attractive, patterned carving of the hair is the herm of a clean-shaven man carved out of Chilmark limestone found built into the wall of a cottage at Sutton Mandeville (Cunliffe and Fulford 1982, 25, no. 95). The origins of the hair-style must be sought in Julio-Claudian portraiture. But is it Roman? It looks far more like an insular Renaissance attempt to produce a 'Caesar' as a garden ornament. A good, local context would be Sir Matthew Arundell's work at Old Wardour Castle around 1570: a building which preserves a certain amount of classical sculptural detailing even in its ruined state (Girouard 1983, 78-81).

Mosaics in Wiltshire

Romano-British sculpture is hard to date and no example from Wiltshire, any more than from neighbouring counties, can be assigned to the late Roman period though it is possible that some of the works mentioned above were used in the same milieu as the mosaics, most of which can be assigned to the 4th century. The research of Dr David Smith (1984) has resulted in the recognition of six schools in Roman Britain, though scholars are coming to see that the situation was probably rather more complex and we should perhaps think of a larger number of independent workshops within regional traditions. Not surprisingly, in view of what has been written above about the Cotswold affinities of so much of the Wiltshire sculpture, many of the mosaics in the north of the county belong to the Corinian (Cotswold) tradition. Box (Hurst *et al.*, 1987) near Bath at the southern limit of the Cotswolds, had mosaics from the 2nd century but most of what remains, one of the largest collections of mosaics from Britain, date to the 4th century and can be assigned to mosaicists from the region. Some features such as the *peltae* in Room 1 can be compared to floors at Lydney which David Smith interpreted as Durno-Corinian, having features of both Dorchester and Cirencester mosaics. We probably need to think of far more separate workshops employing the same basic traditions, and Bath has recently been suggested as a major centre of mosaic work (Beeson and Henig 1997). Who exercised patronage here is another question. Did the complex at Box operate as a large villa-complex like the villa of Dominus Iulius depicted on a mosaic from Carthage or was it a centre of a temple estate, like the courtyard building at Lydney Park or perhaps even the so-called 'villa' at Chedworth?

Another complex where several mosaics have been found, some of them figured, lay further south at Pit Meads near Warminster. One panel depicted a female figure, 'graceful and elegant; and the drapery expressed in a very easy and flowing manner. The colours and shades are thrown in very beautifully, so as to have the effect of a good painting. The *tessellae* used in the formation of the figure are very small and some of them minutely so, particularly the black in which the outline of the figure is delineated.' (*Gentleman's Magazine*, 57 (1787), 221 and pl; cited by Colt Hoare 1821, 114). The subject may have been a muse. Below her in another compartment 'the figure of the hare is in its natural colours, light brown and white; and most admirably and naturally expressed' (*ibid.*). Another mosaic with a figural theme within a circle surrounded by a square may have been an Orpheus mosaic. A mosaic from the Rudge villa showing a satyr and maenad with an overturned cantharus (Hoare 1821, 121) is another Corinian mosaic, matched by the Bacchic figures from the Chedworth triclinium.

A mosaic from Bromham depicting a marine scene does not survive but the engraving in Colt Hoare (1821, 123) suggests analogies with mosaics at Bath (Clews 1996) and Cirencester (Toynbee 1962, 197, no. 182, pl. 213) both in subject matter and composition. It may tentatively be ascribed to the Corinian tradition, perhaps laid by a Bath studio in the early 4th century (I here take issue with Smith 1984, 370 who attributes the Bromham and Bath floors to the Durnovarian school).

Less can be said of the mosaic from Calne not far away which seems to have shown Mars, not a subject previously attested for the Corinian school though the subject of a mosaic at Fullerton, Wherwell, Hampshire not too far to the east of our county (Smith 1977, 117-18, no. 8, pl. 6. xvia), and perhaps to be associated with the Central Southern tradition. By contrast, the Downton Mosaic (Smith 1963, 334-6), now in Salisbury, is nearly complete and in my opinion should certainly be attributed to the Central Southern group and, perhaps, to a Winchester mosaic workshop (Fig. 6.11). It comes from the main reception room of a small villa and depicts a cantharus with dolphin handles within a pair

Fig. 6.11 Mosaic with a design incorporating a cantharus and dolphins, from the Roman villa at Downton, ht. 3.14m; Salisbury and South Wilts Museum

of interlocking squares set in an octagon. In detail the motif is without parallel but the general configuration of the pattern is fairly well matched by a geometric mosaic from the villa at Chilgrove, West Sussex (Smith 1979, 109-10, pl. 1 and 7) and in its setting within the house by the mosaic with a star motif from Sparsholt, Hampshire (Neal 1981, 98, no. 71).

An exceptional floor within the area is the mosaic from Cherhill near Calne, dating from *c.* AD 350 (Johnson 1985), as it is without doubt an eastern outlier of the south-western (Durnovarian) tradition (Fig. 6.12). What remained to be lifted and displayed in Devizes is a fragment from a hunting scene showing a hound which could have come from the Frampton or the Hinton St Mary (Neal 1981, 87-8, no. 61) pavements.

The famous but totally anomalous Orpheus floor at Littlecote which indeed figures Orpheus with his dog/fox surrounded by figures representing the seasons and beasts reflecting Bacchus' transformations when he fled from the titans, conflates him with Apollo and Bacchus. Its esoteric programme has been explained by Bryn Walters (1984) to my satisfaction, though others have been less convinced. The unusual iconography is way beyond the usual perceptions of the local gentry and suggests a special order. As with some of the geometric Box mosaics, the tradition represented is one which draws on Cirencester as one might expect in the north of the county but like other late mosaics shows strong influence from Dorchester.

Fig. 6.12 'Hunting dog' mosaic, from the Roman villa at Cherhill, width 1.35m; WHM

Art and life in Late Roman Wiltshire

The mosaics come in some instances from large complexes (like Box and Pit Meads) while others are from modest farms like Downton (see Cunliffe in *VCH* 1973 for villas). The Pit Meads hare and the hound on the Cherhill mosaic both make reference to the popularity of hunting amongst the provincial gentry also attested by the sculptures from Castle Combe and Box. The Froxfield (Rudge Farm) and Littlecote mosaics are alike concerned with Bacchus and are reminders of that other popular activity, feasting, which at Littlecote almost certainly had an added religious frisson. A mosaic uncovered at Colerne in 1838 seems to have shown a chariot-race, so far a rarity in Roman Britain, representing no doubt the uncertain turns of life rather than actual participation in the sport (Rainey 1973, 56). The remains evidently figured a four-horse team with a charioteer called either Servius or Severus (*RIB* 2448.10). Evidence for classical culture is provided by the Pit Meads muse, the Bacchic scene at Froxfield, the Calne Mars and above all by the complex iconography at Littlecote which apart from invoking Apollo and Bacchus depicts Orpheus surrounded by figures of Venus, Leda (= Nemesis), Demeter and Persephone (Walters 1984, 436). It may be significant that no mosaic nor, to my knowledge, any other work of art from the county provides evidence for Christianity. The gentry here seems to have remained defiantly pagan, as in Gloucestershire and in contrast, so it would appear, to the situation in Dorset.

A number of small finds add to our knowledge of the refinement of life in this aristocratic milieu. A recently discovered cache of silver from the villa (or possibly sanctuary) site at Blunsdon Ridge near Swindon includes a fluted bowl of the sort used for hand-washing at table, and hints at the elaborate ceremony in the lives passed by members of the aristocracy (B. Walters pers. comm.). At a lower level of life a *ministerium* consisting of twelve pewter vessels from Manton, near Marlborough, including a plate with an attractive centrepiece of two interlaced lozenges (Cunnington and Goddard 1934, 169-71) also hints at elegant dining and shows the same taste for abstraction found on other contemporary pewter as well as on 4th-century silver, like the niello dish in the Mildenhall (Suffolk) Treasure in the British Museum.

The marriage contract which bound together members of the leading families is represented by an onyx cameo (once set in a ring) and two rings. The little cameo found on the site of the villa at North Wraxall some 25 years ago was presented by its finder, an 8-year-old girl, to the Ashmolean Museum, Oxford (Fig. 6.13; Henig 1973; 1978, 289 no. App. 30). It depicts in relief a pair of clasped hands, one of which wears a bracelet, and it was clearly a betrothal or marriage gift. In confirmation it is inscribed in Greek, above with the word EYTYXΩC (εὐτύχως), 'with good fortune' and below OMONOIA (ὁμόνοια), 'harmony' (*RIB* 2423.11). Greek was used as the language of love rather as French is now. The cameo was probably cut in the later 3rd century. Two betrothal rings of the same date, with clasped hands in relief on the bezel, have been found in Wiltshire. There is a gold example from the Littlecote villa (Walters 1985) and another of silver set with a gold plate in a hoard of coins probably dating down to the early 4th century from Grovely Wood north-west of Wilton (Henig 1978, no. 776; Johns 1996, 63, fig. 3.24).

Another mixed hoard containing a few items of jewellery and nearly seven and a half thousand coins was found in 1992 at Bishop Cannings near Devizes (Bland and Orna-Ornstein 1997). The jewellery here included an ovoid silver brooch with a zig-zag surround, set with a plain cornelian. This is a more precious example of a common 3rd-century type of disc-brooch, set with a glass jewel and often gilded. Examples have been found at Cold Kitchen Hill and at Nettleton (Wedlake 1982, 148 and fig. 63, 5). The use of plain stones in brooches and other jewellery was a sign of increasing interest in the luxury arts as signs of status in the Late Roman world (see Henig 1981).

Fig. 6.13 Cameo inscribed in Greek 'EΥTΥXΩC' (with good fortune) and 'OMONOIA' (harmony), from the Roman villa at North Wraxall, length 42mm, ht. 29mm; Ashmolean Museum

The end of the Roman period is marked by several items which would be regarded as important wherever they were found. A gold belt-buckle has recently come to light near Corsham and has been acquired by the Wiltshire Heritage Museum (P. Robinson, pers. comm.). This is a type of very high-status object only previously represented in Britain by the example from the Thetford Treasure (Johns and Potter 1983, 23-4, 78-9, 81 col. pl. 1). That was dedicated to the god Faunus but others, represented, for example, in the Ténès treasure, Algeria (Heurgon 1958, 31-2, pl. III, 1 and 2), were insignia of important officials or soldiers. Another object which comes near this high-status category is a silver ring from Roundway Down which bears, engraved on its square bezel, an imperial bust and the Greek legend NIKH, 'Victory' (Fig. 6.14). This may attest the campaigns of the Emperor Valentinian's general, Count Theodosius, to counter the so called Barbarian Conspiracy of AD 367, very probably, in part at least, a more widespread rising of disgruntled provincials. The ring, at any rate, was probably made in the eastern, Greek-speaking, part of the Roman empire.

Four other silver rings of the same late Roman form are known from Wiltshire. Three were found together in 1843 with a late Roman (5th-century) coin hoard at Amesbury (Fig. 6.15; Henig 1978, 281, nos 801-3, pl. lix; 1995, 172, ill. 101; Johns 1996, 54, fig. 3.13) and the fourth is a loose find from Corsham discovered in 1997 (Fig. 6.16; Henig 1999b). The rings demonstrate a major change in artistic style, almost a return to the characteristic aesthetics of the late Iron Age with which this paper began. One of the Amesbury rings depicts a crouching deer within a beaded outline, a second a griffin with an enlarged, circular eye, and the third, four helmeted heads disposed around a swastika design. All three rings have shoulders decorated with abstract pattern. Of the Corsham ring only the

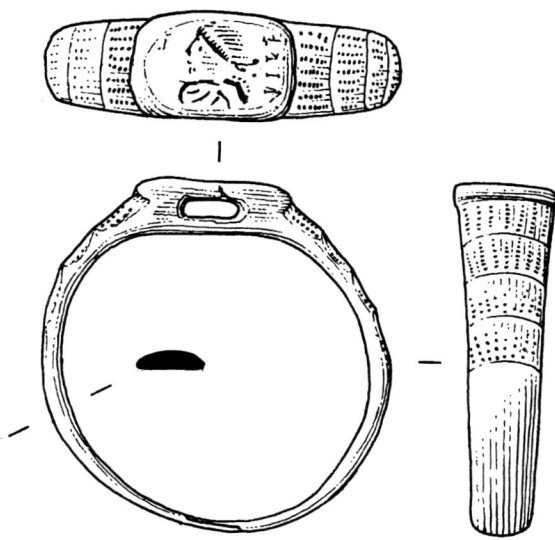

Fig. 6.14 Silver ring inscribed in Greek 'NIKE' (Victory), from Roundway Down, diam. 23mm

bezel remains, possibly showing two birds and a branch. The style of the devices is analogous to that of the 5th-century quoit-brooches, best known from such items as the betrothal or marriage-brooch from Sarre, Kent, and the belt set from Mucking, Essex (see Henig 1995, 170-3). It is most likely that they were made and worn in the period after *c.* 409 when the central empire had lost its direct political control of Britain.

Fig. 6.15 Group of three silver finger rings, from Amesbury, diam. of each 25mm; British Museum

Fig. 6.16 Rectangular silver bezel from a finger ring, from Gastard, Corsham, width 12mm, ht. 9mm; WHM

In earlier prehistoric times Wiltshire was regarded as being on a cross-roads. The Roman period may not exactly offer a Wessex Culture, and indeed there are no major towns within its boundaries, while such large settlements as there are (for example Wanborough, Mildenhall and *Sorviodunum*) have not been sufficiently explored and in any case do not at present offer much to the art historian. But civilisation was never far away, and whether villa-owners looked to Cirencester or Bath, Winchester or Dorchester, they could obtain fine sculpture, mosaics and jewellery. Sometimes links were with distant places. Rudge Farm (Froxfield) is, after all, best known for an enamelled bronze cup bearing a stylised representation of Hadrian's Wall of which it was a souvenir (Henig 1995, 72-3, ill. 41; RIB 2415.53). Other items, such as the bust of Antinous/Bacchus from Littlecote or the North Wraxall cameo lead us to the Greek-speaking culture of the east Mediterranean. Even in a purely local context, Wiltshire has much to offer, including the best group of bronzes from which to understand how native, Celtic art became Romanised; there is also a select and often high quality selection of Cotswold sculpture. If we begin with the Marlborough bucket and end with the Amesbury rings our exploration of Roman art in Wiltshire can hardly be described as a survey of merely parochial interest.

References

Alcock, J. P., 1963, 'Three bronze figurines in the British Museum', *Antiq Journ*, 43, 118-23

Alcock, L., 1972, *By South Cadbury is that Camelot. The Excavation of Cadbury Castle 1966-1970*, London

Bagnall Smith. J., 1995, 'Interim report on the votive material from Romano-Celtic Temple sites in Oxfordshire', *Oxoniensia*, 60, 177-203

Beeson, A., and Henig, M., 1997, 'Orpheus and the Newton St Loe mosaic pavement in Bristol City Museum', in L. Keen (ed.), *Almost the Richest City. Bristol in the Middle Ages*, British Archaeol Assn Conf Transactions, 19, Bristol, 1-8

Bird, J., Hassall, M., and Sheldon, H. (eds), 1996, *Interpreting Roman London. Papers in Memory of Hugh Chapman*, Oxbow Monograph 58, Oxford

Bland, R., and Orna-Ornstein, J., 1997, *Coin Hoards from Roman Britain*, 10, London

Boon, G. C., 1973 'Genius and lar in Celtic Britain', *Jahr RGZM*, 20, 265-9

_____ , 1989, 'A Roman sculpture rehabilitated: the Pagans Hill dog', *Britannia*, 20, 201-17

Clews, S., 1996, 'A Sea Beasts mosaic from Aquae Sulis', *Mosaic*, 23, 10-11

Cunliffe, B, 1978, *Iron Age Communities in Britain*, 2nd edn, London

Cunliffe, B. W., and Fulford, M. G., 1982, *Corpus Signorum Imperii Romani. Great Britain. I.2. Bath and the rest of Wessex*, British Academy, Oxford

Cunnington, M. E., and Goddard, E. H., 1934, *Catalogue of the Antiquities in the Museum of the Wiltshire Archaeological and Natural History Society II*, Devizes

Farioli Campanati, R., 1984, *Terzo Colloquio Internazionale Sul Mosaico Antico*, Ravenna

Fleischer, R., 1967, *Die Römischen Bronzen aus Österreich*, Mainz

Fox, C., 1958, *Pattern and Purpose. A Survey of Early Celtic Art in Britain*, Cardiff

Girouard, M., 1983, *Robert Smythson and the Elizabethan Country House*, 2nd edn, New Haven and London

Henig, M., 1973, 'An inscribed cameo from North Wraxall, Wiltshire', *Antiq Journ*, 53, 76-7

_____ , 1978, *A Corpus of Roman Engraved Gemstones from British Sites*, BAR Brit Ser, 8, 2nd edn, Oxford

_____ , 1981, 'Continuity and change in the design of Roman jewellery', in A. King and M. Henig (eds), *The Roman West in the Third Century*, BAR Int Ser, 109, Oxford

_____ , 1984, *Religion in Roman Britain*, London

_____ , 1991, 'A bronze Vulcan from North Bradley', *WANHM*, 84,120-2

_____ , 1993, *Corpus Signorum Imperii Romani. Great Britain I. 7. The Cotswold Region*, British Academy, Oxford

_____ , 1994, 'Two Roman figurines from Wilcot', *WANHM*, 87,142-3

_____ , 1995, *The Art of Roman Britain*, London

_____ , 1996a, 'Sceptrehead', in Rawlings and Fitzpatrick 1996, 21

_____ . 1996b, 'The bronze figurine', in L. Watts and P. Leach (eds), *Henley Wood, Temples and Cemetery Excavations 1962-69*, CBA, London

_____ , 1997, 'The sculpture', in P. Harding and C. Lewis, 'Archaeological investigations at Tockenham', *WANHM*, 90, 26-41

_____ , 1998, 'A relief of a *Mater* and three *Genii* from Stratton, Gloucestershire, *Trans Bristol and Gloucs Archaeol Soc*, 116, 186-9

_____ , 1999a, 'A bronze appliqué mount from Westbury', *WANHM*, 92, 123-4

_____ , 1999b, 'A silver ring-bezel from Gastard, Corsham', *WANHM*, 92, 125-6

Henig, M., and Booth, P., 2000, *Roman Oxfordshire*, Stroud

Henig, M., and Chambers, R. A., 1984, 'Two Romano-British bronze birds from Oxfordshire', *Oxoniensia*, 49, 19-21

Henig, M., and Keen, L., 1984, 'Figurines from Duncliffe Hill, Motcombe, Dorset', *Proc. Dorset Nat.Hist. and Arch.Soc.*, 106, 147-8

Heurgon, J., 1958, *Le Trésor de Ténès*, Paris

Hoare, R. C., 1821, *The Ancient History of Wiltshire, Volume II, The Roman Aera*, London

Hurst, H. R., Dartnall, D. L., and Fisher, C., 1987, 'Excavations at Box Roman villa, 1967-8', *WANHM*, 81, 19-51

Johns, C., 1996, *The Jewellery of Roman Britain. Celtic and Classical Traditions*, London

Johns, C., and Potter, T., 1983, *The Thetford Treasure. Roman Jewellery and Silver,* British Museum, London

Johnson, P., 1985, 'The hunting dog mosaic of Cherhill, Wiltshire', *Mosaic*, 12, 14-15

Kahil, L., 1984, 'Artemis', in *Lexicon Iconographicum Mythologiae Classicae, I*, 618-753

Mackintosh, M., 1995, *The Divine Rider in the Art of the Western Roman Empire*, BAR Int Ser 607, Oxford

Merrifield, R., 1996, 'The London hunter-god and his significance in the history of Londinium', in Bird *et al.* 1996, 105-13

Neal, D. S., 1981, *Roman Mosaics in Britain*, Britannia Monograph no. 1, London

Pitt Rivers, A. H. L. F., 1888, *Excavations in Cranborne Chase, II*, privately printed

Rainey, A., 1973, *Mosaics in Roman Britain*, Newton Abbot

Rawlings, M., and Fitzpatrick, A. P., 1996, 'Prehistoric sites and a Romano-British settlement at Butterfield Down, Amesbury', *WANHM*, 89, 1-43

RIB, The Roman Inscriptions of Britain, I. Inscriptions on Stone (1965), II. Instrumentum Domesticum (1990-1995), Oxford

Smith, D. J., 1963, 'The mosaic in room 1', in P. Rahtz, 'A Roman villa at Downton, Wiltshire', *WANHM*, 58, 334-6

_____ ,1977, 'Mythological figures and scenes in Romano-British mosaics', in J. Munby and M. Henig, *Roman Life and Art in Britain. A Celebration in Honour of the Eightieth Birthday of Jocelyn Toynbee*, BAR Brit Ser, 41, Oxford, 105-93

_____ , 1979, 'The mosaics of Chilgrove', in A. Down (ed.), *Chichester Excavations IV. The Roman Villas at Chilgrove and Upmarden*, Chichester, 109-10, pl. 1 and 7

_____ , 1984, 'Roman mosaics in Britain: a synthesis', in Farioli Campanati 1984, 357-80

Toynbee, J. M. C., 1962, *Art in Roman Britain*, London

_____ , 1978, 'Two Romano-British Genii', *Britannia*, 9, 329-30

_____ , 1982, 'The inscribed altars; statuary; terracottas; intaglios; and special bronze objects', in Wedlake 1982, 135-43

VCH 1973, *Victoria County History of Wiltshire, I, Pt 2*, London

Walters, B., 1984, 'The "Orpheus" mosaic in Littlecote Park, England', in Farioli Campanati 1984, 433-42

_____ , 1985, 'A gold ring from Littlecote Park', *Britannia*, 16, 247-8

Walters, B., and Henig, M., 1988, 'Two busts from Littlecote', *Britannia*, 19, 407-10

Webster, G., 1986, *The British Celts and their Gods under Rome*, London

Wedlake, W. J., 1982, *The Excavation of the Shrine of Apollo at Nettleton. Wiltshire, 1956-71*, Rep Res Comm Soc Antiqs, 40, London

Woodward, A., and Leach, P., 1993, *The Uley shrines. Excavation of a Ritual Complex on West Hill, Uley, Gloucestershire:1977-9*, English Heritage Archaeol Rep, 17, London

7 A PERSPECTIVE ON THE SOCIAL ORDER OF ROMAN VILLAS IN WILTSHIRE

by Bryn Walters

On purely archaeological grounds the modern boundaries of a single county do not recommend themselves as the limits for an archaeological survey; they can, indeed, only be tolerated on the grounds of a certain convenience that is practical rather than suited to the subject (Cunnington 1933)

During the post-war years, even within the limitations imposed on his unfailing services to the Wiltshire Archaeological and Natural History Society, and the care of its museum and archive, Ken Annable unquestionably laid the modern foundations of Roman archaeology in the county.

Maud Cunnington's opening words in her *Introduction to the Archaeology of Wiltshire* also embody the restrictions that a county curator must bear, yet Ken's contribution in the field developed the realisation that Wiltshire's hills and valleys contained a vast resource which future exploration would reveal. His work on the Savernake potteries created the genesis, and more important, the datum-point from which the spreading Roman pottery industry in the county area would be calculated. The minor explorations which were shared with the late Tony Clark at Mildenhall in the 1950s were masterly strokes of economic excavation technique, putting down trenches where the maximum information might be extracted. It is the results of these explorations which to this day represent a major contribution in research into the later antiquity of Roman Wiltshire.

The following paper is an appraisal of the distribution and, in some cases, the functions of Roman villas in the Wiltshire area. The villa has for generations been seen as the epitome of *Romanitas* over the Britons. Recent research has shown these distinctive communities to have had, in many cases, a continuity which many of the larger Roman settlements and small towns failed to achieve. Many of our Roman towns, especially in the east of the province, gradually decayed and were increasingly abandoned from the late 3rd century. In the west of Britain, however, several towns prospered under the late empire whilst the villas expanded. In many cases villas were the foundation for settlements which were to develop in the early medieval period.

The Roman villa is no longer seen solely as a comfortable country residence but as a centre of rural industry, managed by an elite branch of society. Strident attempts have been made by a number of researchers, most notably Professor Shimon Applebaum (1975), to reconstruct theoretically an economic pattern and ratio of production for a villa estate: a task which, in the writer's opinion, it is logistically futile to pursue. This is not simply because we have no comparable measure on which to base such a hypothesis, but because insufficient data survive in the archaeological context (Britain was quite different from Columella's 1st-century Italy). We cannot know which fields produced what crops and when, nor do we know the limits of any single villa estate. The bones which survive in the faunal archive from a villa excavation can only be representative of the species and are unlikely to reflect the actual numbers of animals raised and slaughtered in a single season.

When examined comparatively, the villas present a variety of guises with a diversity of functions. They may also be seen to reflect the system, not only of agricultural production, but also of the autocracy by which the province of Britannia was governed. At varying social degrees, including political officials, we should be able to find a broad distribution of this autocratic society reflected in the quality and style of certain of the more prosperous villa houses; alongside these, lesser villa establishments may well represent subservient tenants or bailiffs controlling divisions of large land holdings. Other villa-type sites could have been economic or commercial centres, partially controlled by the provincial Procurator or, later in the 4th century, by the *rationales vicarii,* while others appear to suggest religious elements.

The modern boundaries of the county of Wiltshire encompass former territories from three tribal cantons: the Dobunni to the north, the Belgae to the south and south west and the Atrebates to the east. This implies administration directed from three separate cantonal capitals: *Corinium Dobunnorvm* (Cirencester), *Venta Belgarum* (Winchester) and *Calleva Atrebatum* (Silchester). Consequently there may have been a variation in the type and quality of villas the more distant they were from their respective capital.

In the late 1950s, around the time Ken Annable commenced his investigations at Mildenhall, the number of known or suspected villas in the county was not that extensive. Details of these were published in the gazetteer produced by the late Leslie Grinsell for the *Victoria County History of Wiltshire* (Grinsell 1957). Even in the later treatise on Roman Wiltshire compiled for part two of that volume, the county was generally regarded as something of a rural backwater (Cunliffe 1973). Subsequent field research has however shown that the picture is far more extensive and certainly much more colourful. Certainly in the north of the county, and across the Marlborough Downs especially (Fig. 7.1), lies one of the densest concentrations of villas in Britain, including some of the most extensive and palatial villas yet discovered.

The villa system would have relied on marketing and centres for the transit of produce. It is generally considered that small towns provided a source for direct local marketing of

---

Sites numbered on Fig. 7.1: 1 Aldbourne Gorse, 2 North Farm, 3 Stock Lane, 4 Upper Upham, 5 Avebury, 6 Baydon, 7 Forty Farm, 8 Starveall Farm, 9 Russley Park, 9a Botley Copse, 10 Rowde Field (Mother Anthony's Well), 11 Cherhill, 12 Badbury, 13 Plough Inn, 14 South Farm, 15 Cuffs Corner, 16 Harrow Farm (Rudge II), 17 Rudge, 18 Fyfield, 19 Castle Copse, 20 Tottenham Park, 21 Basset Down, 22 Forest Hill, 23 Poulton Down, 24 Southend, 25 Barton Down, 26 Littlecote, 27 Callas Hill, 28 Sugar Hill, 29 West Overton, 30 Barbury Down

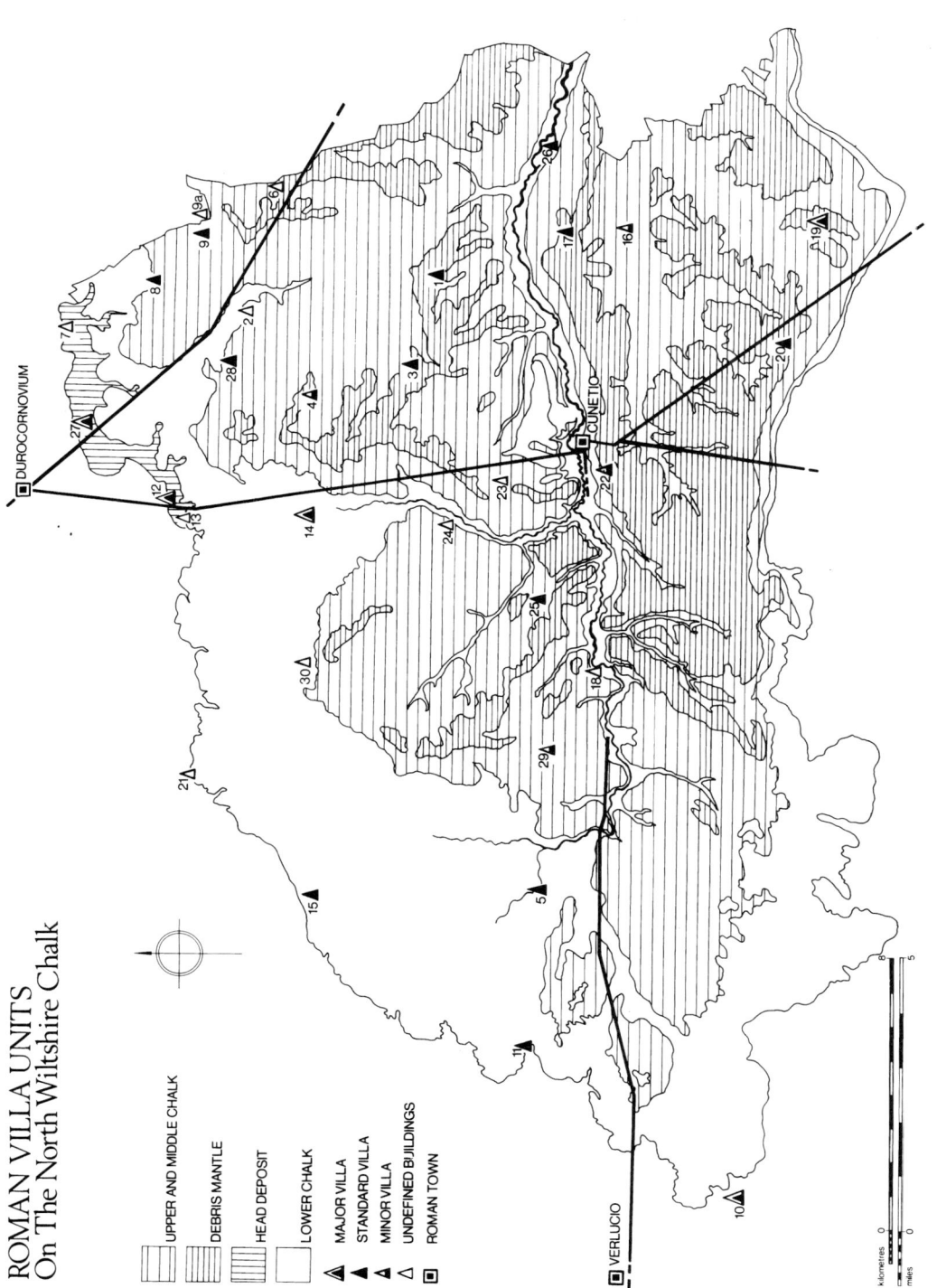

ROMAN VILLA UNITS
On The North Wiltshire Chalk

UPPER AND MIDDLE CHALK

DEBRIS MANTLE

HEAD DEPOSIT

LOWER CHALK

MAJOR VILLA

STANDARD VILLA

MINOR VILLA

UNDEFINED BUILDINGS

ROMAN TOWN

Fig. 7.1 Distribution of villa-type sites in the north Wiltshire Downs

Fig. 7.2 Mansio *and baths,* Durocornovium, *view south; photo Bryn Walters*

villa produce, but the functions of these smaller urban foci are likely to have been far more significant, containing administrative offices for procuratorial officers levying a tax in kind, in the manner of the *annona*. The north Wiltshire area contains three probable centres of this type: Lower Wanborough (*Durocornovium*), Sandy Lane (*Verlucio*) and, more significant, Mildenhall (*Cunetio*). Each of these sites acted as a nucleus to a group of villas. At *Durocornovium* an undoubted government lodging house, a *mansio* (Fig. 7.2), has been identified (Phillips and Walters 1977), with another possible example at the centre of *Cunetio* (Corney 1997; this volume). But just how reliant on the villas were the minor towns? It may be significant that most of the minor towns appear to have been abandoned at around the same time as the eclipse of the villas themselves.

During the late Roman period, it is clear that agriculture in south-west Britain was producing a variety of crops, of which wheat and barley were the most significant in the province's economy. The soil types of the Wiltshire hills and the many valleys were well-suited to a varied mixture of crops and livestock on a single estate. The faunal material that has been examined from the downland villas at Littlecote, Draycot and Great Bedwyn indicates that cattle, sheep and pigs were reared. The high chalk downland grasses were ideal for the sheep which were required for the much-sought-after British woollen products levied in Diocletian's price edicts at the end of the 3rd century. The wetter valley pastures were more suitable for cattle. The heavier clay soils or plateau gravel deposits sustained areas of coppice or woodland necessary for fuel, building materials and hunting. Nevertheless, grain must have been the most significant product and would have been more tightly controlled by the imperial administration. When we consider how Julian, as Caesar in Gaul in AD 359, trebled the number of ships to carry British grain to his armies on the Rhine, we realise the importance this export product had become to the administration of the Western Empire (Salway 1981, 359-60).

Perhaps we are now in a position to ask how research on the Wiltshire villas has helped us in reinterpreting the Romano-British countryside. Are we now at a stage where we can reconsider who the villa owners were? Indeed, were all their holdings economic units and what role did they play in the political stability of the province? The social status of an individual villa is difficult to interpret from the archaeological record. Were particular villas freehold, or tenanted as part of much larger estates? Were single complexes dual or multi-partite, housing more than one family (Smith 1997)? Were particular villas government-controlled administrative centres? Would a single villa estate hold two or more complexes of buildings within its boundary? Did any villa serve the functions of a religious community? The varying sizes and styles of villa buildings in the Wiltshire area might well reflect one or more of these categories.

At least one villa in the north of the county, at Castle Copse, Great Bedwyn near Marlborough, is an establishment laid out on a palatial scale; unquestionably it is among the largest villas known in Britain. If it was the rural retreat of a government official, it is quite likely that other farming villas would have lain within the confines of its estate. Within two miles of Castle Copse there are a number of other Roman buildings which may represent smaller tenanted villas, subservient to the great *domus* at Castle Copse (Hostetter and Howe 1997).

Near Swindon, two other very extensive complexes have been partially examined, one during its destruction by the M4 motorway at Badbury (Walters 1981) and the other more recently at Draycot Foliat as part of a research evaluation (Walters 1996a; 1997). Both of these sites are known to have covered a large area and incorporated more than one residential unit. At Badbury, at least four larger residential buildings were recorded (Fig. 7.3). Spread over some five acres (2ha), three of the buildings produced evidence of tessellated and mosaic floors, hypocausts, decorated walls and two bath suites, yet no evidence was found to suggest agricultural activity. This site lies immediately adjacent to the road between *Cunetio* (Mildenhall) and *Durocornovium* (Lower Wanborough), the major route between the cantonal capitals of *Venta Belgarum* (Winchester) and *Corinium Dobunnorum* (Cirencester). Significantly, the site was bisected by the Liden Brook which flowed northwards for two miles to the suggested procuratorial collection centre at Lower Wanborough, implying the possibility of water-borne transportation. What then was the function, social or otherwise, of the Badbury complex? Could it have been the administrative residence of a procuratorial officer, or a multi-partite villa, housing four separate families with farming interests in the surrounding hinterland? Tragically, owing to its destruction, we are unlikely ever to be able to answer these questions.

On the other hand, the Draycot Foliat complex remains virtually unscathed by the progress of the 20th century. Lying two miles to the south of Badbury and adjacent to the same Roman road, this site holds great potential for understanding at least a part of the economic process behind the villa system in western *Britannia*. Here a number of large and detached stone-built structures have been identified over an area of up to 12 acres (5ha) but their functions remain unclear (Fig. 7.4). These buildings may have been associated with a navigable stream, the River Og, apparently canalized on the eastern edge of the complex, 600 feet (190m) above sea level. Some of the structures identified to date may

BADBURY ROMAN VILLA
Conjectured Plan

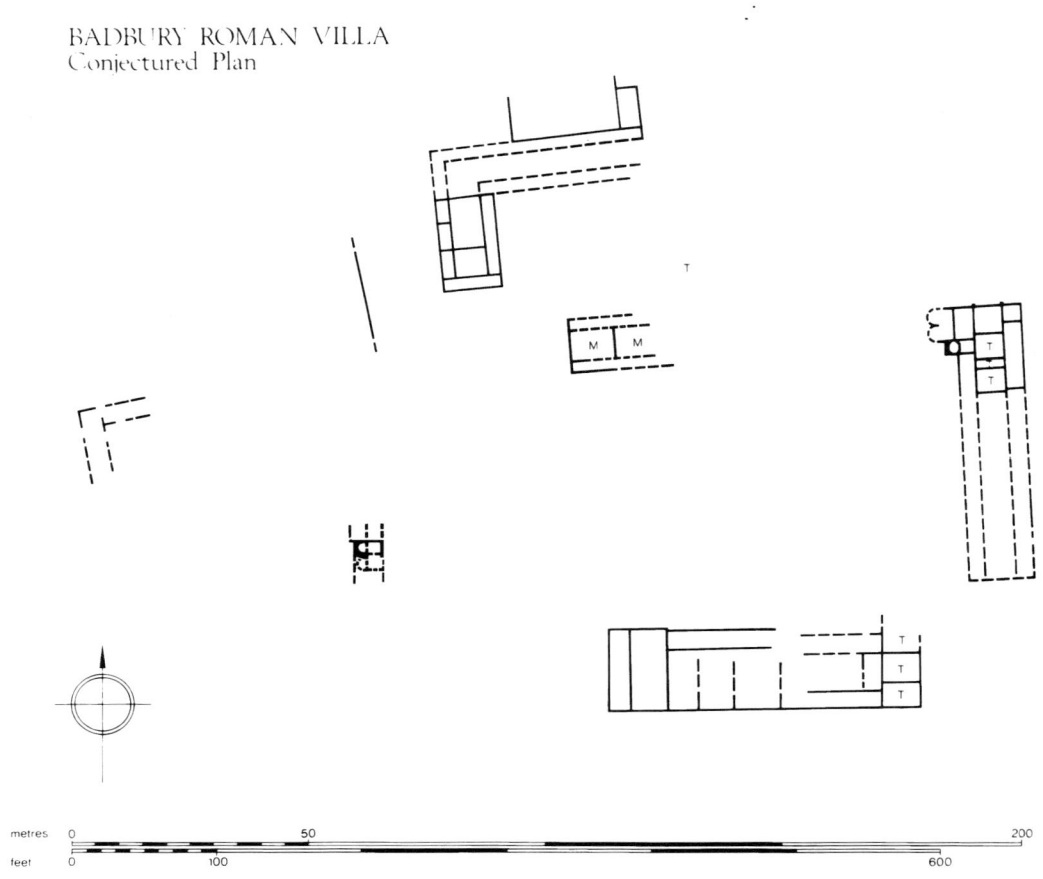

| metres | 0 | | 50 | | 200 |
| feet | 0 | 100 | | | 600 |

Fig. 7.3 Badbury Roman villa as planned 1969-71

be granaries, intimating a produce collection centre and transit point for a Procurator's tax office at *Cunetio*, five miles to the south and towards which the River Og flows. The suggestion has much to commend it. Among the structures on this site are two wing-fronted houses, approximately 300m apart and both facing south-east, the most favoured aspect for Roman rural houses. The more southerly of the two lies within its own embanked enclosure, which has an axial entrance opposite the house. The northern has been the subject of an evaluation excavation which identified a 3rd-century wing-fronted house that had been demolished by the middle of the 4th century and replaced by a temple-like building (Fig. 7.5, a, b, c). Aerial reconnaissance of this dwelling also implies a possible ornamental avenue or pergolas aligned on its central axis, leading down to the river frontage. The complete plan of the site looks remarkably like two (or more) separate villa houses situated side by side, separated by a small shallow combe containing a stream leading into the main course of the Og. But is this likely? Similar 'twin-villa' sites seem a rare phenomenon. Undoubtedly this site holds great promise for future research.

Fig. 7.4 South Farm, Draycot Foliat: Building S II, view north, photo Bryn Walters

On the higher chalk, south and east of Draycot are a number of significant and undoubted agricultural villa units. At least four lie within the Aldbourne parish boundary along with adjacent communal settlements. At Upper Upham a substantial baths complex was located earlier this century, surely forming part of the villa which had been central to the well-preserved field systems in the area.

The fine villa at Aldbourne Gorse survived with extensive structural remains concealed by undergrowth until the mid 1960s when advancing agricultural expansion rendered considerable damage to its buildings and well-preserved earthworks. Located on sloping clay soil, its buildings once enjoyed a fine vista across the Kennet valley to the south. The multiple inner earthworks, though now much slighted, can still be seen under the right conditions from the air and must once have protected livestock, most likely sheep (Fig. 7.6). The production of wool could have been the primary economic basis for this villa. The whole complex is confined within a much larger outer embankment which, no doubt, provided a semi-protective winter enclosure for livestock. The writer's own minor excavations on this site indicated a wealthy establishment. Its southern range of buildings had mosaics, fine wall paintings and baths, all closely confined within an embanked and ditched inner earthwork attached to the stock enclosures referred to above. Two other villas are also likely in the Aldbourne area, at Stock Lane and North Farm. A strikingly similar site to Aldbourne Gorse, with well-defined earthwork enclosures, lies north of Marlborough on Barton Down. Although long regarded as a 'settlement of the Britons', material evidence which includes painted plaster, fragments of Pennant sandstone roofing tiles and tesserae would imply a substantial villa complex, probably reliant on wool production as a major component in its economic structure.

North of Aldbourne, two large villa sites existed at Bishopstone (Phillips 1981) and Russley Down. At the latter, aerial photographs have revealed an extensive series of ploughed-out field embankments and trackways radiating from the central villa enclosure, which closely resemble the embankments at Aldbourne Gorse (Fig. 7.7). Although ploughed for centuries, the site is covered with debris indicative of former well-appointed structures. Interestingly, it is also adjacent to the dual-vallate enclosure at Botley Copse which may have been the more industrialised part of the estate, as it

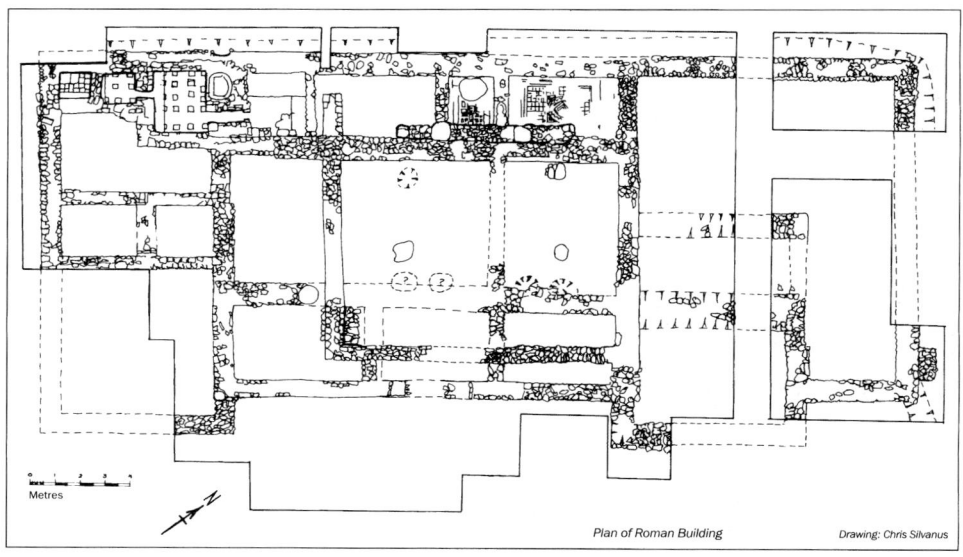

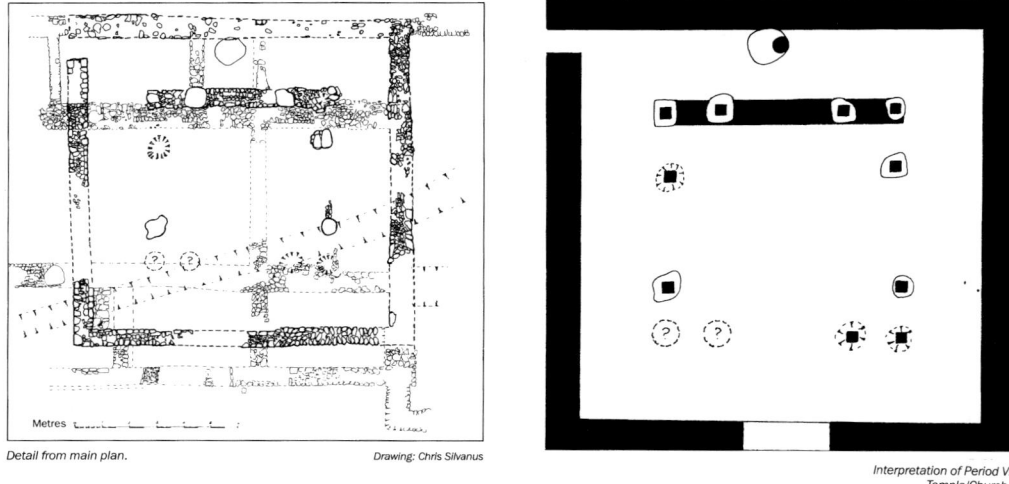

Fig. 7.5 South Farm, Draycot Foliat: a) winged house, b) detail Period IV foundation, c) interpretation of Period VI temple/church

has produced an iron carding comb used in wool production as well as the ubiquitous 'corn drier' (Rhodes 1950).

These enigmatic 'corn driers' are one of the most common discoveries on rural sites, the lesser settlements as well as the villas. Extensive experimentation has been conducted on these peculiarly British constructions by Dr Peter Reynolds (Reynolds and Langley 1979). His argument convincingly holds that the quantity of grain produced each year from a single farm was far too great for these structures to have been capable of processing each season. Also, turning grain on a heated floor merely returns the moisture

Fig. 7.6 Aldbourne Gorse: villa earthworks, view north; photo Bryn Walters

driven to the upper layers back to the bottom again, thereby defeating the object. More significant, where charred grains have been recovered from these structures during excavation, they are almost always shown to have reached the point of germination; too late for the production of flour but just right for the fermentation process required in malting beer. Consequently, these furnaces were probably not for drying grain for bread-making but a major factor in the production of beer, the staple drink of the indigenous rural population. Fine examples of malting furnaces have been found at the villa at Atworth and more recently at Draycot Foliat near Swindon, whilst at Littlecote, a sequence of furnaces was accompanied by oak-lined fermentation vats (Figs 7.8 and 7.9; Walters and Phillips 1982). These furnaces are regularly found on villa sites in Britain and quite frequently on other rural settlements where they can occur in pairs or larger groups as at Catsgore in Somerset (Leech 1976). Villas invariably produce a single example at any one period, reflecting the smaller number of inhabitants requiring liquid refreshment. It is now time to refrain from categorising these structures as 'corn driers' and substitute the more appropriate term 'malting furnace'. Grain required for bread making was most probably air-dried in sheaves stacked where they were cut in the field.

To the south of the Kennet near Ramsbury is the courtyard complex at Rudge (Fig. 7.10), famous for its small bronze bowl depicting forts on Hadrian's Wall, found in a well in the 18th century. The plan of the villa is not dissimilar to that of its near-neighbour at Littlecote, 1½ miles to the north-east. Though now seriously damaged by deep ploughing, the Rudge villa was most probably at the centre of a considerable estate, which incorporated a satellite villa a mile to the south (Fig. 7.11). This lesser villa was confined within its own dual-vallate enclosure with an agricultural building laid out to one side in a manner strikingly similar to the larger Rudge villa to the north. It also maintained a malting furnace in its south-east corner, identified when a new pipe line was laid along the valley in 1979.

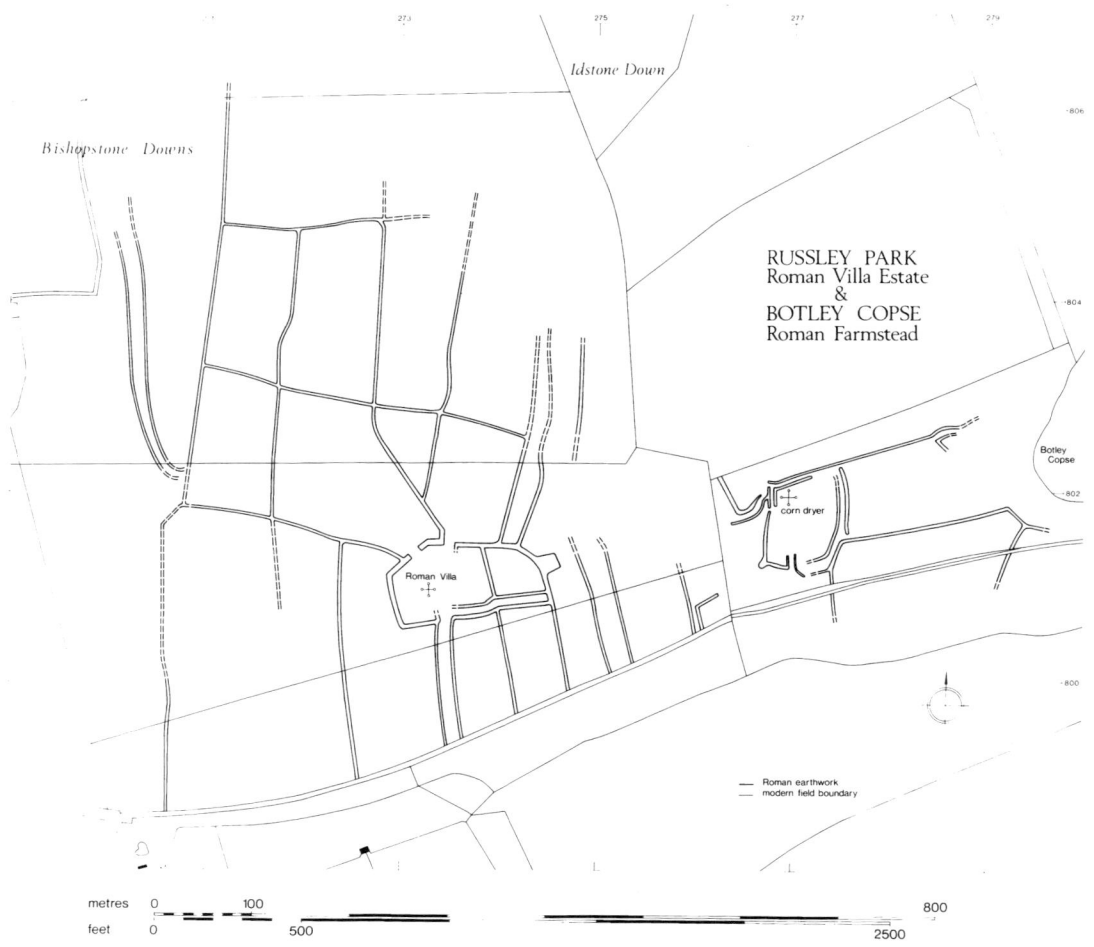

Fig. 7.7 Russley Down, villa enclosures and field system

There survives, in the archives of Alnwick Castle in Northumberland, a letter describing the discovery of the two Rudge villas in the 18th century, in which it appears that, lying overgrown in a small coppice, the walls of the larger villa still stood over a metre in height above the inner floor levels and at least one hypocaust remained intact and hollow beneath its mosaic floor. This hypocaust would appear to have been of a most unusual construction, as the correspondent refers to the supports being of hollow *tubuli* rather than the conventional stacks of *pilae* usually used for this purpose. Again, tragically, the site is now just a flat field covered with building debris.

The well known Littlecote villa certainly operated as a farming community for at least the first two and a half centuries of its existence, before it succumbed to a social transformation in the 4th century (Figs. 7.12 and 7.13), when the villa is thought to have become a rural retreat or *collegium* for a quasi-religious fraternity devoted to the cults of Bacchus (Walters 1984). This is not an implausible proposal, when one considers the

Fig. 7.8 Littlecote villa: malting furnace; photo Bryn Walters

Fig 7.9 Littlecote villa: fermentation tank; photo Bryn Walters

nature of the cults of the indigenous rural population. During aerial reconnaissance in the ploughing season, when the soils are exposed, it is still possible to discern ploughed-out banks of ancient fields over the downland slopes immediately south of the villa, and a series of ancient field embankments still survives in woodland only half a mile to the south east (Walters and Phillips 1980). It would appear that cereal production once formed part of the economy at Littlecote. The grain appears to have been transported on shallow draught barges down stream on the River Kennet to a collection point en-route to the Thames. Evidence for this was seen in small water-filled dykes, cut at right angles to the river, at the eastern end of the riverside building in the first half of the 2nd century (Fig. 7.14). These features could easily have accommodated narrow barges during loading or off-loading of produce. Littlecote has therefore produced indisputable evidence for the utilization of water transport directly on to the River Kennet, upon the banks of which the villa had been, no doubt, initially constructed for that very purpose.

The River Kennet is a vital component in understanding the distribution of produce and the economic functions of the villas on the high Marlborough Downs, as at least a

Fig. 7.10 Parch marks of Rudge villa; photo Bryn Walters

Fig. 7.11 Parch marks of Rudge II villa; photo Bryn Walters

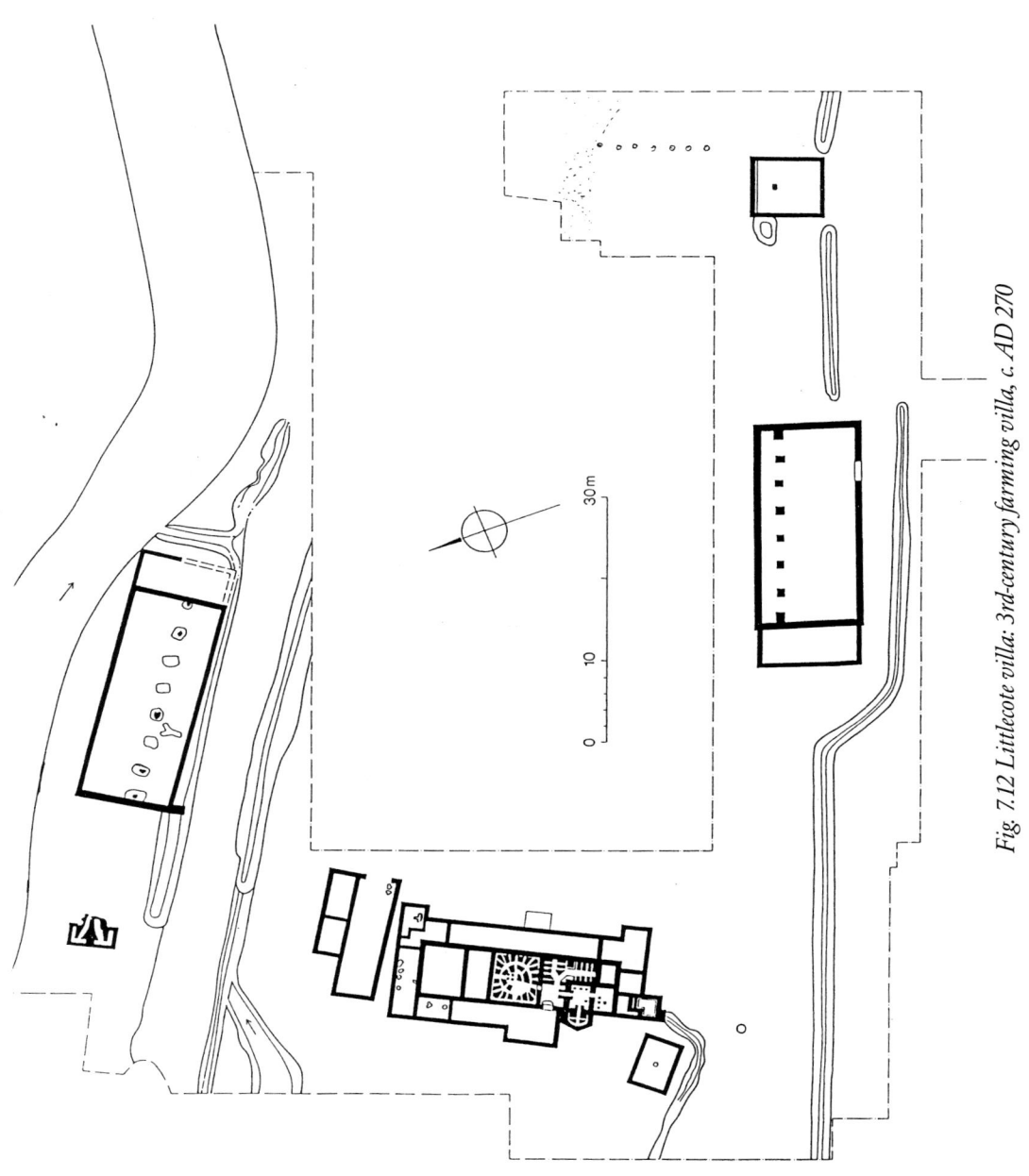

Fig. 7.12 Littlecote villa: 3rd-century farming villa, c. AD 270

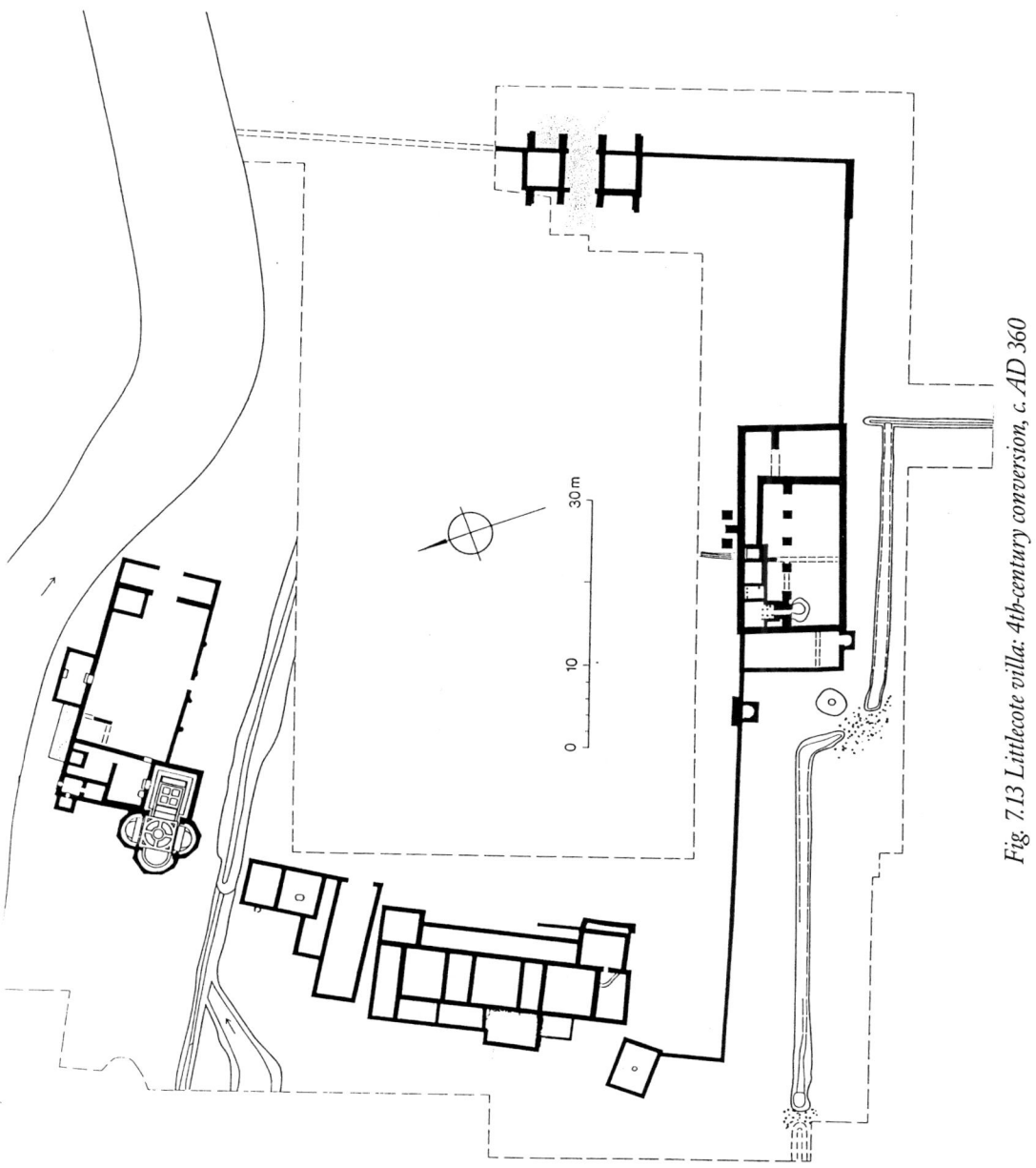

Fig. 7.13 Littlecote villa: 4th-century conversion, c. AD 360

Fig. 7.14 Littlecote villa: boat channels cut from River Kennet; photo Bryn Walters

dozen villas so far located have reasonable access to the main river, or one of its minor tributaries. Even the villa at Avebury Trusloe straddles the upper spring line of the Kennet and the little-understood site at Fyfield lies, like Littlecote, immediately adjacent to the river. Again, at Cherhill, on the extreme western edge of the chalk downs, where all that is known of the villa is its once gracious suite of mosaic-floored chambers, a small perpetual stream flows at the base of the slope, only 100m from the site of the house (Johnson and Walters 1988).

It used to be considered that villas developed adjacent to major roads in order to facilitate the transport of goods, but we must be more circumspect with this observation. If all the rural produce of the fields at harvest or collection time were to descend on to the roads, serious congestion would have occurred, a problem that a military controlled government is unlikely to have permitted. In his West Country survey of villa distribution, Branigan pointed out that only 17% of villas lay within 500m of a major road, with only half the known sites being within 2km of a road (Branigan 1977, 25-6). Land produce and indeed large industrial output such as tiles, pottery and stone are far more likely to have been transported, however indirectly, by water. Streams and rivers were probably maintained by the villa estates as a form of vital communication to the transit centres. The hinterland of known villa sites should be examined for minor streams which could have been utilised as small canals leading towards larger river systems. In similar vein, small streams and rivers in appropriate topographical areas could be a factor in helping to locate as yet unidentified sites.

Accessibility to water is unquestionably a significant factor in understanding the distribution of produce. Where a known villa or 'substantial building' is located adjacent to, or very close to, a river or stream, it is safe to assume that it was located on that site for reasons connected with the transport of produce down stream. At Bradford on Avon a villa was recently identified near the river and at Norton Bavant the villa lies hard by the banks of the Wylye. South from the Vale of Pewsey through to Salisbury, a scatter of villas lies along the valley of the River Avon at Manningford Bruce (Johnson and Walters 1988), Enford, Netheravon, Amesbury and Downton. East of Salisbury, the well-known sites at East Grimstead and West Dean are similarly situated and there must be many more awaiting discovery.

All the villas and the satellite settlements due west of *Cunetio* could have taken advantage of gentle streams flowing into the Kennet itself. *Cunetio* was most likely sited for that very purpose, in order to facilitate the gathering of taxable produce with the major advantage of a navigable river which ultimately flowed into the Thames and on to *Londinium.* To date, within a nine mile radius of *Cunetio,* one may safely estimate on the

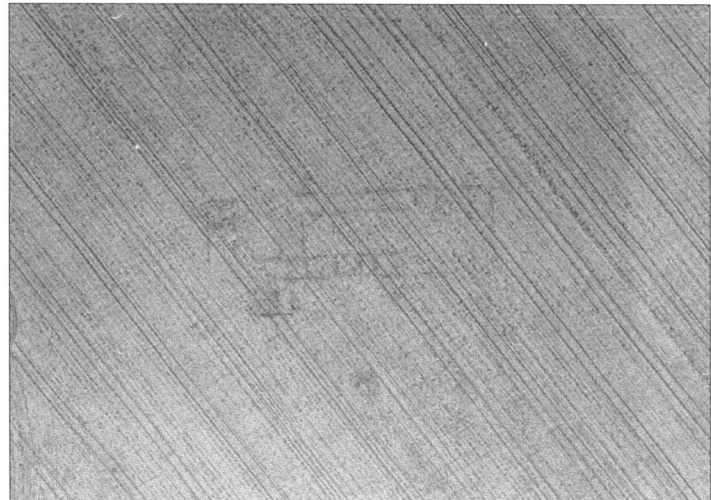

Fig. 7.15 Folly Farm villa, Mildenhall, in spring barley, photo Bryn Walters

available evidence that up to 35 villa sites, such as that at Folly Farm, Mildenhall (Fig. 7.15), have been identified.

The argument that a large imperial estate had control of what is now Salisbury Plain and Cranborne Chase has been deliberated upon for half a century (Hawkes 1947). This theory was based on the paucity of villas in the area compared with the number of recognisable native-type settlements. The passage of time, however, is slowly eroding this hypothesis as more substantial rural houses, with associated villa enclosures, are being recognised across these areas. Some have been identified through geophysical survey in the very native settlement enclosures used by Hawkes to support his argument. A large courtyard villa has recently been found just over the county border at Minchington on Cranborne Chase (Esmonde Cleary 1998; C Sparey-Green, pers. comm.), with another identified at South Warnborough within a large rectangular enclosure (Corney 1996).

A rurally-based industry might also result in a well-appointed residential unit for its proprietor which could justifiably be classified as a villa. The extensive pottery manufacturing areas which have been identified in the West Swindon area have also produced evidence of substantial buildings at Toothill and Westlea which may have been the rural homes of master potters. Unfortunately these sites were mostly destroyed without full investigation during the rapid expansion programme of the modern town. The major tilery at Minety has also provided evidence of a villa-type building utilizing tiles and tessellated flooring approximately 400m north-west of the principal industrial area (M. Stone, pers. comm.). At Westbury, distinctive material and finds found over many years are suggestive of a wealthy establishment probably associated with the Roman iron workings there. Alas, this site may also now be destroyed by local quarrying.

The north Wiltshire villas are distributed west and north of the chalk downs with a major concentration around Sandy Lane and Bromham. Two of the Bromham villas are certainly major sites, though their true social status still remains a mystery. With their neighbours at Bowood, Studley, Sandy Lane and Heddington they were evenly distributed around the small enclosed township of *Verlucio*. It is hoped that research in the near future will indicate that this urban site played a very significant role during the 4th and 5th centuries. Around the Swindon area, focused undoubtedly on *Durocornovium*, up to ten villa-like sites can be postulated, including the extensive villas at Stanton Fitzwarren and Hannington Wick (Fig. 7.16).

To the west of this area, lying on the Corallian Ridge near Lyneham, is an isolated villa at Tockenham, the subject of a Channel 4 television programme in 1995 (Harding and Lewis 1997). A sequence of substantial ditched enclosures, revealed by geophysical survey, appeared to surround a series of structures which undoubtedly formed a farming establishment. The site was extensively quarried for its stone in early medieval times, and the all-too-limited period of *Time Team* fieldwork was unable to elucidate fully the structural sequence or the changing status of the villa over the centuries. Nonetheless, the results obtained, along with the writer's own work on the site, imply an interesting history for this outlying villa. In the opinion of the writer, it is clear that farming activity was drastically reduced or even terminated in the mid-to-late 4th century and the site converted to an alternative function. Unusual structural alterations were in evidence and the enclosure ditches had been infilled and sealed with rubble by the mid 4th century. The site could once boast a very fine late mosaic of considerable proportion in its detached apsidal chamber. Perhaps this isolated villa had been selected for a transformation not that dissimilar to Littlecote's. It is particularly interesting to note that, in his translation of the Saxon Charters, Birch identified Tockenham with '*Weoland*', adding that in Old English *weoh* means 'heathen temple' or 'sacred precinct' (Birch 1885-1893).

This point leads us on to a most intriguing area of assumed villas further to the west and adjacent to the Fosse Way, where significantly rich establishments might testify to a different social and economic order, as we are now in the vicinity of important religious establishments at Bath and Nettleton Scrubb. The inter-visible sites at Box, Colerne and Euridge need to be very carefully re-assessed. Box is most unsuitably located for a farming villa, hanging literally on the edge of a precipitous cliff with a prolific spring rising from

Fig. 7.16 Hannington Wick: west range of courtyard complex: photo Bryn Walters

beneath its buildings. The known plan of the building at Colerne does not suggest a farmhouse. The evidence of material finds recovered from Euridge Farm incorporates considerable coinage of the later Empire and a figured relief of Hercules, implying that at some time in the 4th century, here also may have been a functional conversion from a farming villa to a ritual centre, within sight of the great *temenos* of Sulis Minerva at Bath.

Religious observances, and belief in the nature deities especially, would have been a major aspect of the lives of the Romano-British, at all levels of society, and it should not be assumed that all such practices took place in the easily identifiable Romano-Celtic temples. As has been suggested for the late phases at Littlecote and Tockenham, *collegia* may have existed more numerously in the proximity of major religious centres like Bath and Nettleton Scrubb. One may therefore suggest such a function for the sites at Box, Colerne and, possibly, Euridge. It is already well-recognised that pagan tradition survived well into the late Roman period in Britain (Henig 1984, 217-28) – and major temples flourished in the West Country during the 4th century at Lydney and Uley in Gloucestershire, and at Woodeaton and Frilford in Oxfordshire. Nettleton Scrubb in Wiltshire witnessed a revival in the reign of Valentinian I. These represent but a small sample of the considerable evidence for pagan practice in the late Roman West Country.

In the foregoing, an attempt has been made to illustrate the alternative functions and developments that could have taken place at some of the villas across the county, presenting, albeit only briefly, a renewed approach to the interpretation of villas in general across Britain. We can no longer assume that the remains of a comfortable Romano-British country residence with adjacent extra-mural structures is simply a farming establishment. Such agrarian activities would have been the primary purpose for the majority of villas, but when sufficient archaeological evidence can be extracted from the ground and logically interpreted in a historical context, certain sites suggest a more diverse and complex function by the late Roman period.

Architectural elements need to be brought in as additional evidence for the interpretation of a villa. The plan and layout of rooms or individual buildings needs methodical comparison with continental examples to help elucidate the social function and status of an individual site. For example, the astonishingly Byzantine-styled triconch at Littlecote, supported by further evidence extracted from the extensive excavation of that site, argues most convincingly for an unusual social transformation following the elimination of farming activities there in the 4th century. At Badbury and Draycot Foliat, the disposition of the individual buildings, lying adjacent to a major road with ample evidence for alternative water-borne transport, implies an element of procuratorial administration.

At Castle Copse, the villa is enigmatically linked with the Bedwyn dyke system and consequently with the sub-Roman defences at Chisbury Castle. Their probable contemporaneity with Wansdyke suggests a longevity not previously considered possible for a rural villa (Walters 1998). Unquestionably, the production of grain would have dominated the area of Roman Wiltshire. The huge field systems managed from such sites as Russley would have supplied the increasing demand for supplies to defend the Western Empire, especially along its Germanic frontier in the 4th century. Julian, when Caesar of the Western Empire, recognised the significance of the produce of Britain which guaranteed supplies to his forces along the Rhine and which, indirectly, helped to secure him the Empire in AD 360. But it is later in that volatile decade that a major event occurred which may have played a significant part in the history of late Roman Wiltshire.

In the summer of AD 367, Valentinian I was preparing for a major offensive against the Alamanns when he received news of serious problems in Britain. According to Tomlin's assessment of this event (Tomlin 1974), the Emperor deflected his advance towards the Rhine and headed instead in completely the opposite direction to Amiens, the most important town on the road to Boulogne: *the port of embarkation to Britain.* At Amiens he fell gravely ill and despatched two of his most senior officers, Severus and Jovinus, in rapid succession to Britain to assess the situation and put it to rights if possible. This episode is known as the Barbarian Conspiracy of 367, an event about which scholars have commented on many occasions, quoting the events related by Ammianus Marcellinus. Whatever the facts behind this drama, it undoubtedly created a serious disruption to the shipment of supplies demanded by Valentinian's campaign against the Alamanns. Without guaranteed grain the Emperor could not advance, and for that reason he deflected the Roman army towards the Channel, and Britain in particular, in order to re-establish supplies to the mainland.

Valentinian was a firm and masterful ruler, and yet he granted toleration to all religions, pagan and Christian alike. His predecessor Julian had bestowed considerable favours on those who restored 'the old religions' which had been savagely put down by his predecessor Constantius II. Under Valentinian the Christian Church began to recover the strength which had been seriously curtailed during Julian's brief apostasy, and from which some scholars maintain it never really recovered (Frend 1992). Nonetheless, these restored rights granted to the Christian bishops may have been conceived as a threat by and to the wealthy pagan landowners in Britain, who feared a renewed suppression of their beliefs. They may, as a consequence, have been less willing to provide the extra grain demanded over and above that passed through the *annona*, to prosper an Emperor who tolerated Christianity and was well-known for being contemptuous of the aristocracy, no doubt even those of British extraction.

By AD 369 the troubles in Britain had been suppressed by Count Theodosius, but in the heart of Wiltshire at *Cunetio* we have the most formidable example of a Valentinianic fortress so far identified in Britain. Here, as postulated above, a major tax and corn supply depot was already in operation on the Kennet (see also Corney 1997). The surveys and excavations undertaken by Ken Annable and Tony Clark in the 1950s firmly established the massive walls and bastions to be of a single-phase construction, most probably post-AD 367 (Annable 1957). Was *Cunetio* so strongly developed to protect the rich farms of north Wiltshire? Or was it, as the writer firmly believes, a military imposition, intended to control the landowning pagans by force and secure the produce from the rich villa estates of *Britannia Prima*, and the area of Wiltshire in particular, for the Emperor.

In the late Empire, Wiltshire was part of the greater area of *Britannia Superior* and was subject to its overall economic and political climate. There is little doubt that a rich and powerful elite society dominated the West Country in the 4th century, many of whom were almost certainly of the 'old persuasion', if the number of non-Christian religious sites can be cited as evidence. The imperial administration based in Trier was reliant on the productivity of Britain, which was in the hands of the province's lesser nobility. Should any disruption have befallen the flow of produce it would undoubtedly have resulted in a crisis and such a situation would automatically have resulted in a dramatic response from the highest authority. It was the embryonic excavations at Mildenhall undertaken in the late 1950s that revealed the first vital evidence leading to a clearer interpretation of the villa-based economies of late Roman Wiltshire. But even more significant, they led to a more logical understanding of the long-misunderstood conspiracy of AD 367.

Only a very small number of Wiltshire's villas have undergone any detailed excavation over the past 50 years, only Littlecote having had the benefit of a reasonably extensive examination. It is therefore still not possible to form a clear perspective of the villas as a specific economic entity. Each site undoubtedly presents an economic pattern and social structure which differs from its neighbours. Consequently we may never be able to fix a rigid model of the villa system of the county, or for the rest of Britain either. What is beginning to emerge, however, is the individuality of each villa. This may be expressed in three possible ways: through distinctive architectural elements (Walters 1996b), social status or economic structure. Perhaps somewhere here we may find the keys towards an understanding of these particularly 'classical' imprints on the landscape of Britain.

Acknowledgements

The author wishes to thank Grahame Soffe for his comments and suggestions on an earlier draft of this article; Chris Silvanus for Fig. 7.5 and Luigi Thompson for Figs 7.3, 7.7, 7.12 and 7.13.

References

Annable, F. K., 1957, 'Black Field, Mildenhall', *WANHM*, 57, 233-4

Applebaum, S., 1975, 'Observations on the economy of the villa at Bignor', *Britannia*, 6, 118-32

Birch, W., de G., 1885-93, *Cartularium Saxonicum*, 3 vols, London

Branigan, K., 1977, *The Roman Villa in South-West England*, Bradford-on-Avon

Corney, M., 1996, 'Roman Britain in 1995', *Britannia*, 27, 437

_____, 1997, 'The origins and development of the small town of *Cunetio*, Mildenhall, Wiltshire', *Britannia*, 28, 337-50

Cunliffe, B., 1973, 'The period of Romanization', in *The Victoria County History of Wiltshire, Vol. 1 (ii)*, 439-67

Cunnington, M., 1933, *An Introduction to the Archaeology of Wiltshire from the Earliest Times to the Pagan Saxons*, Devizes

Esmonde Cleary, A. S., 1998, Roman Britain in 1997: sites explored, *Britannia*, 29, 423-4

Frend, W. H. C., 1992, 'Pagans, Christians, and the Barbarian Conspiracy of AD 367 in Roman Britain', *Britannia*, 23, 121-31

Grinsell, L. V., 1957, 'General gazetteer', in *The Victoria County History of Wiltshire, Vol. 1 (i)*, 21-131

Harding, P. A., and Lewis, C., 1997, 'Archaeological investigations at Tockenham 1994', *WANHM*, 90, 26-41

Hawkes, C., 1947, 'Britons, Romans and Saxons round Salisbury and Cranborne Chase', *Archaeol Journ*, 104, 27-81

Henig, M., 1984, *Religion in Roman Britain*, London

Hostetter, E., and Howe, T. N., 1997, *The Romano-British Villa at Castle Copse, Great Bedwyn*, Indiana University

Johnson, P., and Walters, B., 1988, 'Exploratory excavations of Roman buildings at Cherhill and Manningford Bruce', *WANHM*, 82, 77-91

Leech, R. H., 1976, 'Larger agricultural establishments in the West Country', in K. Branigan and P. Fowler, *The Roman West Country*, Newton Abbot, 142-61

Phillips, B., 1981, 'Starveall Farm, Romano-British villa', *WANHM*, 74/75, 40-55

Phillips, B., and Walters, B., 1977, 'A *mansio* at Lower Wanborough, Wiltshire', *Britannia*, 8, 223-7

Reynolds, P. J., and Langley, J. K., 1979, 'Romano-British corn-drying oven: an experiment', *Archaeol Journ*, 136, 27-42

Rhodes, P. P., 1950, 'The Celtic field system on the Berkshire Downs', *Oxoniensia*, 15, 1-28

Salway, P., 1981, *Roman Britain*, Oxford

Smith, J. T., 1997, *Roman Villas, A Study in Social Structure*, London

Tomlin, R., 1974, 'The date of the Barbarian Conspiracy', *Britannia*, 5, 303-9

Walters. B., 1981, 'Badbury Romano-British villa', in P. Fowler and B. Walters, 'Archaeology and the M4 Motorway, 1969-77', *WANHM*, 74/75, 91-110

_____, 1984, 'The Orpheus mosaic in Littlecote Park, England', in *Atti del III Colloquio Internazionale Sul Mosaico Antico*; Ravenna, 1980, Bologna

_____, 1996a, 'The D.A.R.T. project 1996-97', in *ARA, Bulletin Assoc Roman Archaeol*, 2, 13

_____, 1996b, 'Exotic structures in 4th-century Britain', in P. Johnson and I. Haynes (eds), *Architecture in Roman Britain*, CBA Res Rep, 94, 152-62

_____, 1997, 'The D.A.R.T. project 1996-97', in *ARA, Bulletin Assoc Roman Archaeol*, 4, 4-5

_____, 1998, 'The Romano-British villa at Castle Copse, transition and continuity', *Journ Roman Archaeol*, 11, 624-8

Walters, B., and Phillips, B., 1980, *Archaeological excavations in Littlecote Park: Interim Report 2*, Swindon

_____, 1982, *Archaeological excavations in Littlecote Park: Interim Report 3*, Swindon

8 RELIGION IN ROMAN WILTSHIRE

by Paul Robinson

The present day picture of religion in Wiltshire in Roman times is derived chiefly from the extensive, relatively recent excavations of two important religious sites – the complex at Nettleton on the Fosse Way (Wedlake 1982; Corney this volume) and the probable Orpheum, or shrine to Orpheus, which was attached to the villa at Littlecote in the late Roman period. There were certainly other religious sites in Wiltshire in Roman times which were of comparable if not greater importance. Some, such as an octagonal shrine near Marlborough, remain still unexcavated. Others have been either badly excavated or only partially investigated, with the result that their religious nature is only imperfectly understood or is in question. One example of this is the building at Box customarily described as a villa. Numerous discoveries of religious objects made on the site and listed by Hurst *et al.* (1987, 28) have led to the suggestion that it may rather be the guest house attached to a Roman temple (Webster 1983). Another building which may be suspected to have been religious in function is that lying to the south of Silbury Hill (Corney this volume). Wells from this building were excavated by Joshua Brooke and others in the late 19th and early 20th century. It was evidently an unusually important building (in provincial terms) as it had stone columns: as such it is only one of a handful from Wiltshire. Its religious nature may be suspected from the discovery of a miniature vessel and a group of metal rings on the site, which are similar to votive rings found at other Roman religious sites such as Uley temple in Gloucestershire. Possibly like Nettleton it was a roadside shrine and it is tempting to link it directly to the prehistoric earthwork at Silbury Hill.

Regrettably there are two important Roman religious sites in Wiltshire which have been virtually destroyed in modern times without being adequately recorded. A Roman temple complex at Cold Kitchen Hill appears clearly on present day aerial photographs. Between 1925 and 1927 it was extensively but poorly excavated (Nan Kivell 1925; 1926a; 1928) and the different features constituting the site were not identified or recorded by the excavator. Although careful re-investigation of the site would almost certainly distinguish them, it will no longer be possible to relate the exceptionally important and extensive collection of finds made, which include votive offerings of both Iron Age and Roman date, to the different features of the site, as the excavator did not keep records of where each find was made. The second site is – or rather was – that at Westbury Ironworks in Heywood which was almost totally destroyed in the 19th and 20th centuries in the course of the commercial quarrying of iron ore (Cunnington 1910). Very few records have been kept of the features exposed and probably a small proportion only of the finds made have been recorded and preserved. They include part of a pottery cult figurine in the form of a female deity (Fig. 8.1) and a hanging bowl decorated with escutcheons also in the form of a female deity, who is perhaps to be seen as horned or 'crowned' with a garland or wreath from the way the vessel has now been reconstructed (Fig. 8.2). In having important religious sites sadly destroyed in relatively recent times, it is doubtful if Wiltshire has fared any differently from most other counties in Britain. However, the recent discovery of a major Roman building at Blunsdon Ridge near Swindon which has initially been identified as a temple/Nympheum and the excavation of the grave of a possible priest at Nursteed illustrate how important new religious sites continue to be found which will certainly in the future greatly extend our knowledge (Walters and Phillips 1997).

Fig. 8.1 Ceramic cult figure of a female deity, from Westbury Ironworks, ht. 110mm; WHM

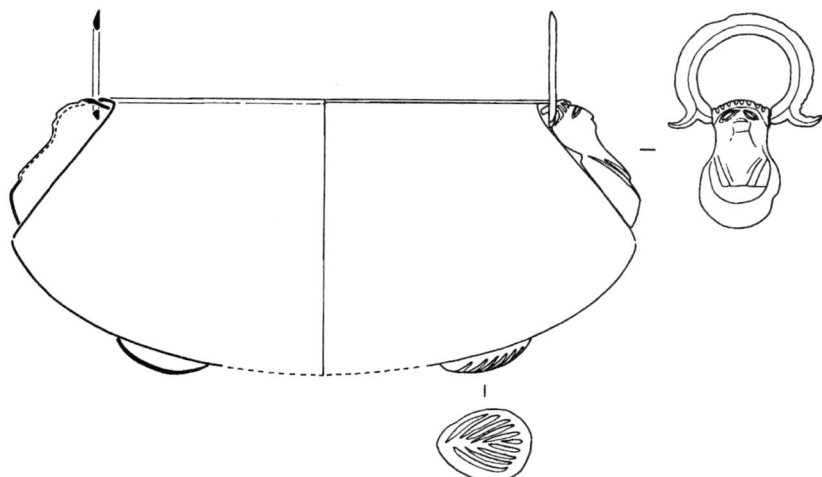

*Fig. 8.2 Bronze hanging bowl with escutcheons in the form of a female deity,
from Westbury Ironworks, width 235mm.; WHM*

Apart from excavated or partially investigated religious sites, our understanding of religion in Wiltshire in the Roman period comes from a variety of different sources. They include stray finds of religious sculpture, bronze or pipe clay figurines, priestly regalia and votive offerings, which include miniature representations of everyday objects. In many, perhaps even most cases we may suspect that these 'stray' finds in fact come from as yet unrecognised temples, shrines or other sacred places, while others are from domestic *lararia* or household shrines in town or country houses. Other evidence for religious thought or belief comes from essentially secular objects, such as jewellery which might be decorated with a religious motif. Thus two finger rings from Roundway Down and Potterne decorated with gemstones depicting Mercury and Mars respectively (Henig 1977/8; 1979/80), confirm the particular importance of these two gods in Wiltshire in Roman times in the same way as the silver finger ring from the shrine at Nettleton with an intaglio which depicts Apollo, who, it is believed, was the principal deity of the temple. There remains, of course, the difficulty that an item of jewellery may be decorated with a religious subject less for devotional reasons than to demonstrate how 'Romanised' or well-educated the wearer was, and to demonstrate his or her status. Together these varied sources combine to provide an overall picture of religious belief and practice in the county in Roman times.

The background to religion in Wiltshire in the Roman period must be sought in the evidence for religion in the county in the preceding Iron Age (*c.* 800 BC to AD 43). In itself this is a large and very poorly known subject. The Iron Age peoples in Wiltshire will have worshipped the universal deities found throughout the Celtic world of mainland Europe and the British Isles as well as the many individual spirits which were associated with local cults at natural features, such as lakes, rivers and springs; woods, groves or individual trees; and hills or valleys. Caesar equated the chief gods of the Celtic peoples in Gaul with the classical gods, Mercury, Mars, Apollo, Jupiter and Minerva and these may indeed have been the classical equivalents of the principal gods also worshipped in Wiltshire in the Iron Age as all were certainly important in the county in the Roman period.

Regrettably we have no knowledge of the names of the deities of the local Iron Age peoples. Cunomaglos, the hound prince, was the Celtic name of the deity venerated at Nettleton in Roman times and equated with Apollo, and it is fair to assume that he may also have been venerated in Wiltshire before the Roman conquest. Similarly other Celtic deities such as Cernunnos, Epona and Rosmerta also known from sculptures or figurines to have been venerated in Wiltshire in Roman times, may also have been worshipped in the Iron Age – although there is a possibility that some may have been introduced by continental Celts into the region after the Roman conquest.

In the absence of historical evidence for religion in Wiltshire in the Iron Age we must rely upon archaeological evidence including contemporary representations of deities found in the county. The Marlborough bucket is one of the outstanding examples of Celtic art and craftsmanship to have been found in Britain and, from the evidence of the relationship of its design to the designs of Celtic coins from Gaul, was probably made in the 1st century BC (Piggott *et al.* 1985; Fig. 6.1). The design of profile and facing male and female heads, strikingly executed in deep *repoussé* work, some with the white of the eye tinned to stand out and with holes in which (blue?) glass irises were once set, certainly represent deities, perhaps a pantheon of gods, accompanied by pairs of horses some of which are shown devouring the bodies or souls of the dead. Without attributes, however, their individual identities are lost to us. Other heads of Celtic deities appear on some Late Iron Age silver coins which are believed to have been struck in Wiltshire (Robinson 1977). On these a wheel is frequently shown in front of the god's face, which is plausibly to be seen as a solar symbol and an attribute of the god, who may then be a sky god (Fig. 8.3). Other unequivocal images of Iron Age date are rare. A bronze mount from near Marlborough depicts a schematised bearded and perhaps horned head. A roughly scratched figure of a man in a cloak perhaps wearing a baldric on a broken chalk disk from Cold Kitchen Hill may represent a god but could also be a worshipper or a secular figure (Fig. 8.4).

A small number of Iron Age religious sites have been identified in Wiltshire. The most important of these is certainly that at Cold Kitchen Hill where the number of Iron Age brooches found in the course of the excavations in 1925-27, should without doubt be seen as indicative of their being votive objects. They suggest either that the temple was in existence from the Middle Iron Age or that there was another religious structure on the site at that date. Finds made in the 19th century either on or close to the unexcavated octagonal temple near Marlborough suggest that that site also may have originated in the Late Iron Age. The small number of finds of Iron Age coins, or other items, at Nettleton, Westbury Ironworks and Box, however, seem more likely to have been deposited or lost after the Roman conquest and do not provide satisfactory evidence to show that these religious sites may have had their origin in the Iron Age.

The Iron Age settlement at Coombe Down on Salisbury Plain, recently excavated by Reading University, included features which certainly were religious in purpose, and it has been suggested that the Early Iron Age site also currently being investigated at Cherhill may have had a religious function (G. Swanton, pers. comm.). In contrast, none of the Iron Age hillforts which have been investigated in Wiltshire have provided evidence of religious structures of this period, although it has been suggested that the rectangular earthwork at Lidbury (Cunnington 1917) may have been religious in purpose – perhaps a *viereckschanze* (S. Piggott, pers. comm.). Recent excavations near Warminster have also identified religious or ritual features within the settlement which will greatly extend our understanding of religion in Wiltshire in the Iron Age.

Fig. 8.3 Design from a locally struck Late Iron Age coin depicting a god with a wheel emblem, from Cunetio, diam. 13mm; British Museum

The archaeological evidence for religion and worship at natural features will inevitably be slight. The hoard of iron and bronze weapons and bronze *phalerae* of Late Bronze Age and Early Iron Age date discovered in the River Avon near Melksham (Gingell 1979) is certainly a ritual deposit illustrated in particular by the symbolic damage inflicted on the objects. This, which one would not expect to find on casually lost or discarded items, suggests that the river may have been venerated at this point. A similar votive deposit is the hoard of Bronze Age and Iron Age objects including miniature cauldrons and bronze shields, the latter decorated with La Tène designs found at Netherhampton in the 1980s and concealed around 200 BC (Stead 1991).

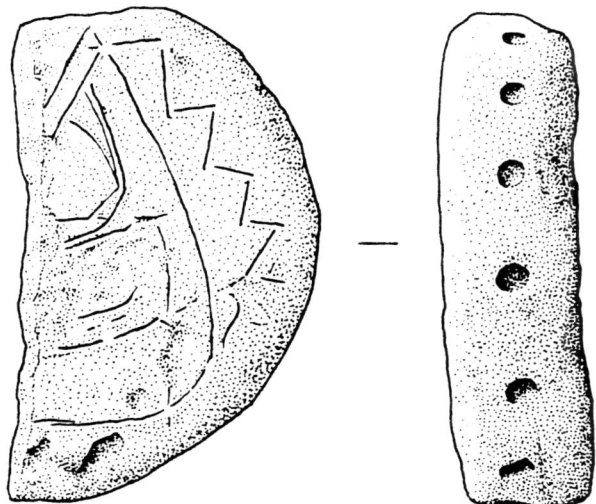

Fig. 8.4 Broken chalk disk with the incised figure of a man, perhaps a god or worshipper, from Cold Kitchen Hill, ht. 67mm; WHM

After the Roman conquest of Britain, no attempt was made to suppress the religion of the Iron Age peoples and to impose upon them worship of the Roman deities. Rather the status of the native gods was fully respected. In the course of the 'Romanisation' of the native peoples, the classical deities were absorbed by the British into their religion and

Fig. 8.5 Votive relief depicting the Celtic goddess Rosmerta accompanied by her consort, Mercury, ht. 288mm; WHM

equated as far as was possible with their Celtic deities. In this assimilation the native deities seem generally to have taken second place. This may be seen with the worship of Apollo Cunomaglos at Nettleton, where the name of the native god, the 'hound prince', appears to be treated in effect as an epithet or a cult title of the classical god, Apollo. A possible similar pairing is to be seen on an enigmatic and damaged inscription on lead from the Marlborough Downs where Mars is coupled with the incomplete name A[ ]unisea (Tomlin and Hassall 1999, 378-9). If this is not the name of the petitioner, it may be that of a local native god again used here as an epithet or cult title for Mars. Interestingly there are instances where the native deity has prevailed over the classical equivalent as with Sulis Minerva at Bath.

Apart from Apollo, Mars and Minerva, other classical deities which are known from inscriptions frequently to have been assimilated with native Celtic gods include Jupiter, Mercury, Venus, Vulcan and Hercules. All are depicted on sculpture or bronze or pipe clay figurines found in Wiltshire. In a few instances we may be reasonably certain that the deity represented was the classical deity *per se* – as with the bust of Hercules which appears as a mount from a domestic water heater from Westbury (Henig 1999). In the main, however, without an inscribed name we may not truly be certain whether a particular representation was intended to depict the classical god alone or the classical god assimilated with the native god. In an essentially rural area such as Wiltshire, we may suspect that in most instances the representations mainly depicted a native deity masked behind a classical one.

Some Celtic gods had no acceptable classical counterparts and their names and identities remained essentially unaffected by the process of Romanisation. Examples from Wiltshire include Epona, depicted with her attendant ponies on a bronze figurine now in the British Museum from, it is said, an unknown find spot in Wiltshire; Rosmerta, the 'good purveyor', was the consort or companion of a native god so firmly assimilated with Mercury that his native name is not used (Fig. 8.5); Cernunnos, possibly represented on one of the bronze figurines from the Southbroom deposit; and the three-horned bull also from Southbroom.

The hunter god depicted on a carved block from Box is depicted running and holding in each hand a hare and a boar (Fig. 6.8; Cunliffe and Fulford 1982, no. 122). He may be a version of the hunter god depicted elsewhere in the Cotswolds and may possibly be equated with the archer-god depicted on imitation samian ware pottery which was manufactured at an unidentified kiln probably in west Wiltshire (Fig. 8.6). He is clearly a native deity but may be represented by the classical Silvanus among the deities venerated at Nettleton.

Fig. 8.6 Archer-god on an imitation samian ware vessel, from Wiltshire, width 130mm; WHM

Gods originally from the eastern areas of the Roman empire or from Africa were introduced into Britain in the Roman period and the worship of some is attested in Wiltshire. There is ample evidence for the worship of Bacchus in Britain in Roman times particularly in the late Roman period at the time of the domination of Christianity. This included feasting and drinking, music and dancing in a celebration of the powers of nature. In Wiltshire, evidence for the veneration of Bacchus is slender. He is attested by two bronze objects from Littlecote, which show that there was a cult worship of the god at the villa and by a bronze figurine depicting him from the Southbroom deposit. All probably date

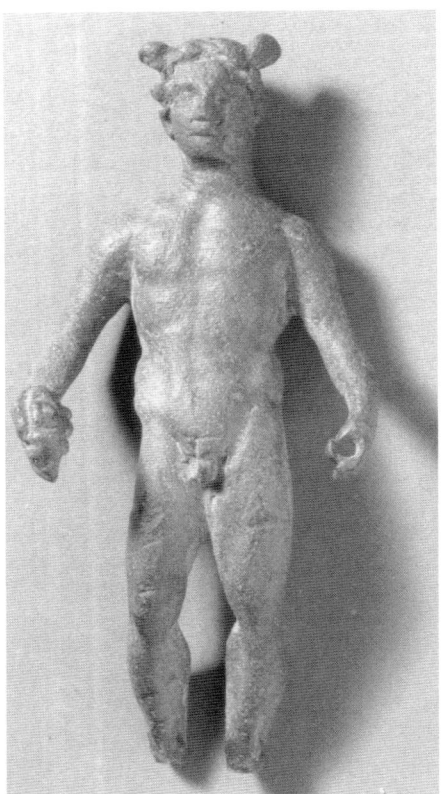 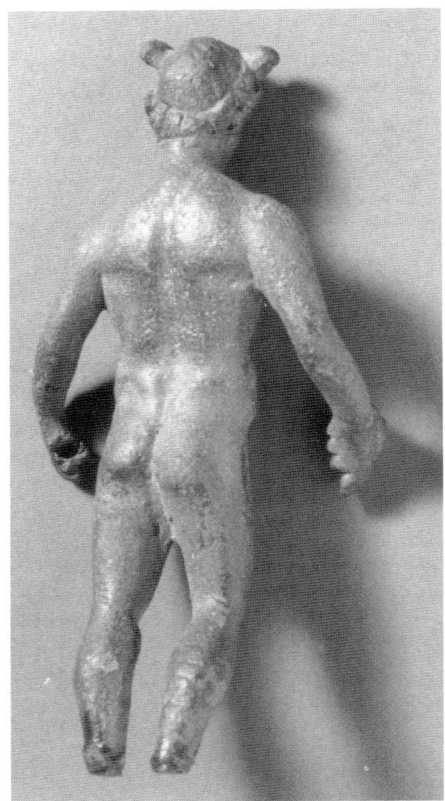

Fig. 8.7 Bronze figurine of Mercury, from near Cold Kitchen Hill, ht. 80mm; in private possession

from the 2nd to 3rd centuries. Of the other oriental mystery cults, there is no evidence for the worship of the goddess Cybele and her consort Attis. The bronze mount depicting Cybele said to have been found at Avebury (Cunnington and Goddard 1934, pl. lxiii, 1; incorrectly said to be from *Cunetio*) may now be seen to have been falsely given a Wiltshire findspot (Robinson forthcoming), while a sculpture from Froxfield which was formerly believed to depict Attis is now considered to depict Venus (Cunliffe and Fulford 1982, no. iii). Similarly there is no evidence for the worship of Isis and Serapis, two deities originally from Egypt. The bronze mount from Avebury depicting Serapis (Cunnington and Goddard 1934, pl. lxiii, 3) and the bust of the god found at Highworth carved from Egyptian porphyry are again both considered to have been falsely given Wiltshire findspots (Robinson forthcoming; Cunliffe and Fulford 1982, no. 113). On the whole this is the picture which one would expect to find in a rural area. Mystery cults of eastern origin would be expected only in the major towns or in the case of Bacchus in the more important villas.

Who then were the principal gods venerated in Wiltshire in Roman times? About 50 representations of gods have survived from the whole of the county. This is not a large number bearing in mind that about one third come from a single deposit, the cache of figurines found at Southbroom on the outskirts of Devizes in 1714 (Boon 1973). Among these the deities most commonly depicted in the county were Mercury, Mars, Venus and Hercules. Mercury (Fig. 8.7) should certainly be seen as an originally native Celtic god who, in Wiltshire, has been assimilated with the classical god. Mars again is known to have been assimilated with different Celtic gods in the west of England, particularly in the Cotswolds. In Wiltshire he possibly served more in his guise as a god of agriculture rather than of war. Both Venus and Hercules may have been venerated as purely classical deities in some instances, but at other times may refer rather to a native deity. The primacy of these gods is not untypical of other regions in southern Britain.

Of the other deities, Bacchus – as stated above – is represented in three instances, two of them at Littlecote, while Apollo is similarly represented only at Nettleton, where, also as noted above, he appears to have been the principal deity of the sanctuary. The god in fact is not commonly depicted in Britain at all. Minerva, Vulcan (Fig. 8.8), Fortuna and Diana have been recorded only twice in Wiltshire while those who, to date, have been recorded only once include the classical gods Jupiter and Neptune and the native gods Cernunnos, Epona, Rosmerta, the three mothers and the three-horned bull. Silvanus is mentioned once but if he is to be equated with the hunter-god depicted at Box and the archer depicted on imitation samian ware pottery, is perhaps to be seen as a native god of much greater significance in the county.

Fig. 8.8 Bronze figurine of Vulcan, from North Bradley, ht. 105mm; WHM

There remains, finally, an important number of representations of deities in stone sculpture or on bronze figurines that may not be identified at all. They include stone sculptures from Nettleton, Mildenhall (Fig. 8.9) and Easton Grey (Fig. 8.10); the cloaked Genius from Charlton Down, the pottery cult figurine head from Westbury Ironworks (Fig. 8.1) and whichever deities were intended by carved stone heads from Bradenstoke and Great Bedwyn.

Fig. 8.9 Votive relief of an unidentified female deity, from Cunetio, *ht. 300mm; WHM*

The discovery of votive objects which allude to specific gods provides additional information for their veneration in Wiltshire. Figurines of cockerels, as found at Great Bedwyn and Ashton Keynes, probably relate to the native Mercury and further stress his importance in the county. Plate brooches in the form of a horse and rider (Fig. 8.11), as found at Cold Kitchen Hill and Nettleton, are believed to allude specifically to a native war god, perhaps equated with Mars (Ferris 1985; Gurney 1986). Although one representation of Jupiter has been found in Wiltshire - one of the figurines from Southbroom - a bronze figurine of an eagle from Westbury Ironworks is probably also to be seen as an allusion to the god. Brooches in the form of a wheel, as found at Nettleton and perhaps also at Cold Kitchen Hill may allude to a Celtic sky god who was assimilated with Jupiter (Green 1983). If so, then the god may be seen from these ancillary objects of having been of greater importance in Wiltshire than might otherwise appear.

The extensive excavation of Nettleton illustrates in some detail both the size and extent of a provincial Roman religious complex in Wiltshire and its history. The complex

Fig. 8.10 Head of an unidentified goddess or attendant in a head-dress or cap, from Easton Grey, ht. 130mm; WHM

grew up by the side of the Fosse Way where it crosses the Broadmead Brook at the junction of two valleys. Altogether, apart from the shrine itself over 30 other buildings were identified apart from ancillary pits, enclosures and cemeteries, not all of which were, of course, contemporary (Corney this volume).

The first circular shrine, built in about AD 69 was 10.06m wide. Adjacent to it was a rectangular hall, 18.3 by 7.32m in size, identified as a meeting place for an association or brotherhood associated with the cult (building VII). Other contemporary buildings include a house for the temple priest (building VIII), a hostelry (building XI) and the house possibly for the overseer responsible for the care and supervision of the temple (building XIII). In the 3rd century the complex grew in wealth and importance. Around AD 250, an octagonal podium, 21.35m in diameter, was erected around the shrine with a pavement of fine limestone chippings; while a precinct wall was built around the settlement. A shop (building X) sold votives to worshippers as well as food and drink to travellers: a second hostelry (building XII) was built as well as several domestic buildings (XIV, XVI and XVII). After a fire in the later 3rd century the shrine was rebuilt as an octagonal building with an octagonal ambulatory. In the early 4th century, the shrine was at its peak, but went into decline in the course of the century. The shrine may have become a church while the settlement became a small scale industrial centre with evidence for the working of bronze,

Fig. 8.11 Bronze and enamel 'horse and rider' brooch from Cold Kitchen Hill, width 21mm; WHM

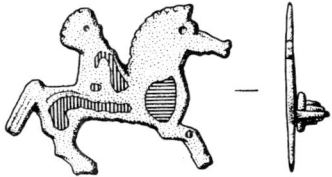

iron and pewter. In the time of Julian II the shrine had a short-lived religious revival before being sacked in the third quarter of the century.

Comparable evidence is lacking from other religious sites in Wiltshire. Aerial photographs suggest that the religious complex at Cold Kitchen Hill was a simple structure. The principal building was a rectangular shrine set towards the back of a rectangular enclosure opposite the entrance. Along one side of this was attached a second smaller rectangular enclosure with a separate entrance, while close by was an additional free standing sub-rectangular enclosure in the corner of which was a large mound, apparently an integral part of the complex. The history of the complex may have started in the Iron Age. The coin evidence suggests that it continued to flourish until about the mid 4th century. A minor peak of Valentinianic coins may be due to the revival of paganism under Julian. The total absence of the latest 4th-century coins suggest strongly that the temple had gone out of use well before AD 400.

The form and extent of most other Roman religious sites in Wiltshire are not well known. The temple at Marlborough was octagonal in form, similar to that at Nettleton in its later stage of construction and also to other Romano-Celtic temple sites. It is very much to be regretted that we know nothing of the number and nature of the buildings that made up Westbury Ironworks. Other features on this site evidently included a cemetery area (of which there were four at Nettleton) and a group of wells or shafts. These may be compared with the group of wells by the columned building south of Silbury Hill and those at another suspected religious site at Winterslow. They may have served a ritual purpose – such as either for communicating with, or making offerings to, the underworld. In contrast, a group of pits or basins excavated at Nettleton may have had a different function. At Winterslow a crescent-shaped earthwork has been identified as the remains of a religious theatre that was an integral part of the religious complex. A fragment of a spout in the form of a masked actor's head from Westbury Ironworks raises the intriguing if slender possibility that there may have been a religious theatre at that site too.

Of the rituals and cult practices that took place at the different religious sites in the Wiltshire we know relatively little. The temple allowed a worshipper the opportunity and place to approach the god as a petitioner, asking him to intercede on the petitioner's behalf in a matter that concerned him, whether a safe childbirth, the fecundity of farm or family or the return of lost or stolen property. In return for the intercession the petitioner would offer to the god devotional prayers and a real or symbolic gift.

Assemblages of votive objects which were offered to a god or to the gods at a shrine have been discovered at a number of religious sites in Wiltshire, notably at Nettleton and Cold Kitchen Hill, and they closely reflect similar assemblages of votive offerings from religious sites outside Wiltshire such as Uley and Lamyatt Beacon. In some instances it is the identification of a group of objects as probably votive which enables us to interpret the site where they were found as a religious one. At Winterbourne Monkton, the presence of a group of brooches under 12mm in length (Fig. 8.12) among an assemblage of jewellery, domestic objects and coins allows us to interpret the group as a collection of votive offerings and the site – of which no structures have been identified – as a religious one. At Stockton Earthworks, the presence of a miniature stone altar among objects found in a

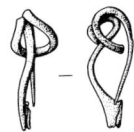

Fig. 8.12 Miniature bronze fibula, one of a group of votive offerings, from Winterbourne Monkton, actual size; WHM

not well recorded excavation undertaken in 1923 (Nan Kivell 1926b, pl. v, fig. 11), suggests that it was one of a group of votive objects and that the excavation may have extended into a religious area in the settlement, but whether a public temple or a domestic *lararium* is uncertain.

Votive objects have to be distinguished as far as possible from casually lost or discarded objects on the site, which may date from the period when the temple was no longer in use, and also from finds of religious paraphernalia and equipment, including temple furniture and lighting equipment and other items in everyday use such as perhaps pottery. Most often found are normal everyday objects such as food and presumably also drink, surviving today only in the form of animal bones and pottery platters or containers; coins, jewellery, particularly brooches, pins, finger rings, bracelets and glass bead necklaces; personal items, such as toilet articles, dress fittings; and finally cutlery, tools, weapons and other items of military equipment. Some of these everyday objects may have been made at or near the shrine in workshops that were part of the temple complex, to be sold to the worshippers at a shop or stall which was also a fundamental part of the complex. At Cold Kitchen Hill the large quantity of glass beads found, some of them in a segmented form which is almost restricted to the site, suggests that they were made at or near the shrine, specifically for deposit there, perhaps draped around the neck of the effigy of an as yet unidentified goddess. At Winterbourne Monkton, the inclusion among the assemblage of objects found of a group of La Tène III Nauheim type brooches of the same style, suggests either that they were made nearby or that a stall holder had acquired a consignment of brooches of one type to sell to worshippers at the shrine. Many of the everyday objects deposited as votives may have had a symbolic reference that at times escapes us today. For example, bone pins are believed to have been considered suitable offerings which should be made by women awaiting childbirth. They are common finds at Cold Kitchen Hill, suggesting that this was one reason for the shrine's importance.

Miniature versions of everyday objects are certainly among the most fascinating examples of votive offerings which have survived. The miniature brooches from Winterbourne Monkton (Fig. 8.12) reflect the great importance of full size brooches as votives at other religious sites such as Nettleton and Cold Kitchen Hill. Miniature socketed axes in bronze have also been found at Cold Kitchen Hill and, outside Wiltshire, at the temple at Lamyatt Beacon in Somerset (Robinson 1995). Although echoing the socketed axes of the later Bronze Age, rather than depicting archaic objects no longer in use, they probably copy socketed iron axeheads, still used in the Iron Age and Roman period as alternatives to shaft-hole axeheads. The miniature socketed bronze axes have also been found in groups at other places in Wiltshire including Calne Without and All Cannings, and although there is no other evidence, it is possible that the find spots are religious in purpose.

The most important or richest dedications at a shrine would have been the stone sculptures and the stone altars which complemented the principal cult statue of the god and the altar installed at the founding of the temple. Thus at Nettleton, the inscription on the altar to Apollo Cunomaglos shows that it was a gift to the god by 'Corotica, daughter of Iutus in fulfilment of her vow', while the altar to Silvanus and the *Numeni Augusti Nostri* was dedicated by Aur[elius?] Pu[   ]. Sadly there is no inscription to confirm that it was a dedication although the votive bronze plaque to Apollo is inscribed to the effect that it was dedicated to the god by Decimius. Figurines of bronze or pipe clay were also offered to the gods. They either depicted the god, such as the figures of Mercury from near Cold Kitchen Hill and Charlton Down, or his attributes, such as cockerel figurines alluding to Mercury from the domestic sites at Great Bedwyn and Ashton Keynes, and the figurine of an eagle probably alluding to Jupiter from Westbury Ironworks.

Jewellery can be in a form that relates specifically to a god and which would emphasise the devotion of the worshipper. Thus a finger ring from Nettleton bears an intaglio depicting Apollo to whom the shrine was dedicated, while horse and rider brooches and wheel brooches would be relevant to Mars and a sky deity respectively. Other religious items specifically made for depositing in a shrine include silver or bronze leaves, which are sometimes inscribed. The only examples from Wiltshire, however, are uninscribed bronze leaves without context from *Cunetio* and from near Malmesbury. Bronze bells as found at Cold Kitchen Hill and metal rings from the building south of Silbury Hill would both probably have been made solely as votive objects.

Lead 'curse tablets' are inscriptions offered to a temple in which the worshipper petitions the god to assist him against someone who has opposed him, such as a thief of his property, a rival in love, a rival in the courts or a contestant in the public games. Large numbers have been found at the temple of Sulis Minerva at Bath and in that of Mercury at Uley. To date two only have been recorded from Wiltshire, both fragmentary and difficult to read. Their contexts have not been published. In that from Marlborough Downs, the petitioner asks Mars to have returned to him a stolen pony requesting that a punishment be inflicted on the thief for nine years (Tomlin and Hassall 1999). In that from Wanborough the name of the god is lost. Again it seeks the return of stolen property begging that the god does not permit the thief 'to drink, nor eat, nor sleep, nor wait and that you do not allow any part to remain of him or of the family from which he springs' (Rea 1972).

The sculptured representations of the gods, the figurines and other votive objects enable us to identify the gods who were venerated at the shrines and on rare occasions the chief god to whom it was dedicated. At Nettleton, as we have seen, the number of items alluding to Apollo suggests that he was the god to whom the shrine was dedicated and that he was to be equated with a native god, Cunomaglos, the 'hound prince'. Apollo, who is only represented in Wiltshire at Nettleton, may have been worshipped as a healing god, perhaps associated with the stream running by the temple. Other deities whom worshippers might have venerated also at the shrine may have been Silvanus and Diana, the Romano-Celtic couple Mercury and Rosmerta and the spirit of the emperor.

Horse and rider and wheel brooches suggest that both Mars and Jupiter might also have been venerated at the shrine.

At Cold Kitchen Hill, the recent discovery nearby of a figurine depicting Mercury suggests that he was venerated there, but whether as the principal deity, as at Uley and Lamyatt Beacon, is uncertain. As at Nettleton there are finds of horse and rider brooches and perhaps wheel brooches too. The finds of glass bead necklaces and bone pins in some numbers suggest that a goddess worshipped there was of special importance.

Box, on the evidence above all of the discovery of a silver votive eye, may have been a building attached to a healing shrine, the curative powers lying in the spring on the site. A small fragment of sculpture found depicting Neptune may well allude to the waters of the spring. The finely carved block, noted above, probably from the entrance, depicts a hunter god, perhaps the same deity found elsewhere in the Cotswolds, but whether he is to be seen as the chief deity of the site is quite uncertain (Fig. 6.8).

The quality of the bronze plaque depicting Minerva, or a native deity assimilated with the goddess, found in an enclosure at Charlton Down, suggests the great importance of the goddess in this large and important rural settlement (Fig. 6.4). Unfortunately we cannot tell whether the other religious figures found at the settlement came from the same findspot. They include a bronze figurine of Mercury (Cunnington and Goddard 1934, pl. lxix, 3) and a cloaked 'Genius' in carved stone (Cunliffe and Fulford 1982, no. 103). A similar situation exists at Westbury Ironworks where the association of the finds is not confirmed. They include a pottery cult figure of a female goddess in a twisted rope headdress, a bronze bowl with escutcheons depicting a female goddess and a figurine of an eagle which probably alludes to Jupiter or his native equivalent. Two sculptured fragments from Easton Grey may come from a smaller wayside shrine on the Fosse Way that has not yet been defined (Cunliffe and Fulford 1982, nos 120, 136). One appears to depict Mars or a native god assimilated to Mars, accompanied either by three female attendants or perhaps by the Three Mothers. The other depicts an unidentified native goddess in a head-dress. The great importance of the Celtic Mars in the Cotswolds in Gloucestershire suggest that if these two are from a religious site, the dedication may have been to Mars with other female deities also venerated there.

Finally, the question whether the prehistoric monuments of Wiltshire were venerated in both Iron Age and Roman times is problematic. A number of individual finds of coins and artefacts of Roman date and of coin hoards have been found on or close to Neolithic or Bronze Age barrows. In some instances at least, we may suspect that hoards were concealed there for no other reasons than that a barrow makes an easily identifiable marker and that it may have been believed that the sanctity of the spot might help to protect the deposit. Stray finds of objects, such as the Roman brooch from the barrow West Overton G 19, may not necessarily be casual losses but could well be propitiatory offerings to the 'spirit' of the grave or the shades of the departed. Comparable evidence for the Iron Age is almost non-existent. We may, however, note that the earthworks of the Iron Age hill fort at Olivers Camp in Roundway skirt the barrows that lie in their path, which may illustrate a respect for the grave or a fear of the dead within it.

A few finds of Iron Age date have been made either on or close to the great henge monuments of Stonehenge and Avebury, but not Marden. Their contexts are in the main not recorded and they constitute weak evidence for any religious use of these sites in the Iron Age.

At Stonehenge a scatter of Roman objects, including coins, pottery and other objects has been found. They are as likely to have been casual losses by Roman sightseers or picnickers. A similar small number of Roman objects have been found at Avebury but again provide little indication that they might be votive in nature and that the site was revered in the Roman period in any way. However the probable presence of a small religious site at Winterbourne Monkton, close to Avebury may be relevant. Of greater interest is the essentially unexcavated Roman building immediately south of Silbury Hill with its possibly votive metal rings noted above. Why of all the prehistoric monuments of the county, Silbury Hill might have been singled out for continued or resumed veneration in the Roman period is difficult to guess at. The answer may lie in the fact that it was adjacent to the Roman road from London to Bath and that it may have developed as much as a wayside shrine as a temple to the veneration of a prehistoric monument.

Each important Roman house in Wiltshire would have had a domestic *lararium* or shrine in which the gods which were particularly important to the household were revered. The particular gods varied from house to house. Gods attested at some villas include:

North Wraxall villa	Hercules
Euridge Farm, Colerne villa	Hercules
Stanchester villa	Venus
Froxfield villa	Venus
Castle Combe villa (?)	Diana
Littlecote villa	Bacchus
Castle Copse villa	Mercury (?)

At Littlecote, the excavators have argued that a shrine to Orpheus as part of a domestic cult was built in the late Roman period. Others have argued that the celebrated Orpheus pavement was merely a demonstration by the owner of his classical sophistication in a room that may be alternatively interpreted as a purely secular dining room in a Mediterranean fashion. Here we must await a full discussion in the long-awaited excavation report.

The group of figurines from Southbroom has been regarded as a temple deposit. However the presence of a *genius familiaris* figurine among them suggests rather that they are domestic figures from a household shrine. The collection combines figures in a good classical style (Venus, Vulcan, Mars, Bacchus and the *genius familiaris*) with others which are of provincial Romano-Celtic style. Many cannot be identified for certain as their attributes are not clear. They may include Mars, Jupiter, Mercury and Minerva. A figure holding two serpents has variously been identified as representing Hercules, Dionysus/Bacchus or Mars, or, a little more convincingly, as the Celtic god Cernunnos (Fig. 6.3). Another Celtic deity depicted is the three-horned bull. Other animal figures include a horse and another unidentified animal, now lacking its rider. A bronze dog is a fragment from a lamp which may have illuminated the shrine.

We do not know for certain when Christianity reached Britain and how quickly and to what depth it permeated the rural countryside in places such as Wiltshire. The writer Tertullian (*c.* AD 160-240) wrote that '(even) places of the British not approached by the Romans were now made subject to the true Christ', and such an early dating for the arrival of Christianity in western Britain is confirmed by the SATOR etc. palindrome from *Corinium*, dated to the late 2nd century. Christianity became the official religion of the Roman Empire in AD 313 and the presence of British bishops at the Council of Arles in AD 314 confirms how established the church in Britain had become by that date.

Tangible evidence for Christianity in Wiltshire is however sparse. There are many fewer identifiable Christian objects dating from the Roman period from Wiltshire than in the neighbouring counties of Hampshire, Gloucestershire and Dorset, the reason perhaps being the absence of major towns in the county, which would have acted as foci for Christianity. A plate brooch in the form of a fish, found at Rotherley, and likely to date from the 2nd century, and a gold ring from the villa at Brail Wood, Great Bedwyn, decorated with a saltire and dated to the 3rd to 4th centuries (Mawer 1995, 80 and 69 respectively) would be the earliest Christian objects from Wiltshire. There is however doubt that they are truly Christian. There is in fact no certain evidence for Christianity in the county until the 4th century.

The decline and closure of the pagan temples in the 4th century is certainly as a result of the spread of Christianity. It has been suggested that shortly before AD 350 the octagonal shrine at Nettleton was adapted as a cruciform church by closing off four of the eight apses, while some of the 4th-century burials nearly aligned east–west and lacking grave goods may also be Christian. Objects which with more confidence can be said to be Christian are two late 4th-century strap-ends from Charlton Down and Monkton Deverill decorated with a peacock and a tree of life (Mawer 1995).

A number of medieval churches in Wiltshire such as Cherhill and Malmesbury Abbey are located on the sites of Roman villas and may show continuity between villas used as centres for Christian worship in the late and post-Roman period, and the establishment of medieval churches. Two bronze mounts from Nine Hills, Potterne, in the form of a fish may be either Roman or post-Roman in date. While their Christian nature is unconfirmed, they were found close to the spring from where, in the Middle Ages, the village church at Potterne obtained water for baptisms. They too may then reflect a continuity between the church in Roman times and that in the medieval period.

References

Boon, G. C., 1973, 'Genius and lar in Celtic Britain', *Jahr RGZM,* 20, 265-9

Cunliffe, B. W., and Fulford, M. G., 1982, *Corpus of Sculpture of the Roman World, 1(2), Bath and the Rest of Wessex,* Oxford

Cunnington, M. E., 1910, 'Notes on the Roman antiquities in the Westbury Collection at the museum, Devizes', *WANHM,* 36, 464-74

_____ , 1917, 'Lidbury Camp', *WANHM,* 40, 12-36

Cunnington, M. E., and Goddard, E. H., 1934, *Catalogue of Antiquities in the Museum of the WANHS at Devizes, Pt 2,* Devizes

Ferris, I. M., 1985, 'Horse and rider brooches in Britain: A new example from Rocester, Staffordshire', *Trans South Staffs Archaeol and Historical Soc,* 26, 1-10

Gingell, C., 1979, 'The bronze and iron hoard from Melksham and another Wiltshire find', in C. Burgess and D. Coombs (eds.), *Bronze Age Hoards. Some Finds Old and New*, BAR Brit Ser, 67, 245-51

Green, M. J., 1983, 'The Roman wheel brooch from Lakenheath (Suffolk) and a note on the typology of wheel brooches', *Bull Board Celtic Studies*, 30, 166-75

Gurney, D., 1986, '*Settlement, Religion and Industry on the Roman Fen Edge, Norfolk*', East Anglian Archaeol, 31

Henig, M., 1977/1978, 'Roman signet rings in Devizes Museum', *WANHM,*72/3, 178-9

_____ , 1979/80, 'A Roman ring from Potterne', *WANHM,* 74/5, 186-8

_____ , 1999, 'A Bronze appliqué mount from Westbury', *WANHM,* 92, 123-4

Hurst, H. R., Dartnall, D. L., and Fisher, C., 1987, 'Excavations at Box Roman villa, 1967-8', *WANHM,* 81, 19-51

Mawer, C. F., 1995, *Evidence for Christianity in Roman Britain. The Small-finds*, BAR Brit Ser, 243

Nan Kivell, R. de C., 1925, 'Objects found during excavations on the Roman-British site at Cold Kitchen Hill, Brixton Deverill, Wiltshire', *WANHM,* 43, 180-91

_____ , 1926a, 'Objects found during excavations on the Roman-British site at Cold Kitchen Hill, Brixton Deverill, Wiltshire', *WANHM,* 43, 327-32

_____ , 1926b, 'Objects found during excavations on the Roman-British site at Stockton Earthworks, 1923', *WANHM,* 43, 389-94

_____ , 1928, 'Objects found during excavations on the Roman-British site at Cold Kitchen Hill, Brixton Deverill, Wiltshire', *WANHM,* 44, 138-42

Piggott, S., Robinson, P., Corfield, M., 1985, 'Symposium papers on the Marlborough bucket', unpub., Devizes

Rea, J., 1972, 'A lead tablet from Wanborough, Wiltshire', *Britannia*, 3, 363-7

Robinson, P., 1977, 'A local Iron Age coinage in silver and perhaps gold in Wiltshire', *British Numismatic Journ*, 47, 1-20

_____ , 1995, 'Miniature socketed bronze axes from Wiltshire', *WANHM, 88,* 60-8

_____ , forthcoming, 'Falsely provenanced figurines from Avebury', *WANHM*

Stead, I. M., 1991, 'Many more Iron Age shields from Britain', *Antiq Journ*, 71, 1-35

Tomlin, R. S. O., and Hassall, M. W. C., 1999, 'Roman Britain in 1998. II Inscriptions', *Britannia* 30, 375-86

Walters, B., and Phillips, B., 1997, *An Archaeological Evaluation at Blunsdon St Andrew, Wiltshire*, Swindon

Webster, G., 1983, 'The function of Chedworth Roman villa', *Trans Bristol and Gloucester Archaeol Soc,* 101, 5-20

Wedlake, W. J., 1982, *The Excavation of the Shrine of Apollo at Nettleton, Wiltshire, 1956-1971*, Soc Antiq Res Rep, 40, London

9   ROMANO-BRITISH BURIALS IN WILTSHIRE

by Anne Foster

Introduction

Rowan Whimster's 1981 survey of burial practices in Iron Age Britain and Robert Philpott's similar 1991 study of Roman Britain for the first time furnished the basis for a comparison of burial practices throughout the country. Until recently much of the evidence for such practices in Wiltshire consisted of individual graves and often poorly recorded cemeteries excavated in the past. The publication in detail within the last decade of several small Romano-British cemeteries in Wiltshire has provided both the impetus and the purpose for a review of Romano-British burial practices specifically in this county. In order to make the paper more readable, the number of references has been kept to a minimum; only those authors directly quoted are referenced within the text. Full details for all sites mentioned are given in the gazetteer at the end of the paper.

Inhumations

The preferred pre-conquest burial rite in Wiltshire appears to have been inhumation (Whimster 1981, 195), and this form of burial continues, with modifications, throughout Roman times. There are some 389 Romano-British inhumations recorded from the county, a quarter of them single burials or with at most two individuals in close proximity. The majority of such burials are without grave goods. In many cases, the only dating evidence is the presence of Romano-British potsherds in or near the grave fill. The largest cemeteries (3+ burials) so far excavated include that at Winterbourne (37 cremations, 14 inhumations), and Boscombe Down Sports Field (36 inhumations and 1 cremation). Neither has been fully published. Smaller cemeteries linked to individual farmsteads or small settlements include those at Eyewell Farm (7 burials), Maddington Farm (9 burials) and Erlestoke Detention Centre (8 burials). A cemetery at Boscombe Down West and one 'west of Imber', both now destroyed, each contained at least 15 inhumations The sanctuary site at Nettleton produced 3 small cemeteries, some 27 burials, not all fully excavated. The small enclosed cemetery at North View Hospital, Purton (6 inhumations, 1 cremation) and the mausoleum at Truckle Hill villa (4 burials) are perhaps private family burial grounds. Other cemeteries with unknown numbers of burials are recorded at Coleman's Mead ('many'), Highworth ('numerous'), Covingham Farm, Yarnbury Castle and Teffont Quarry. Inhumation is the common factor in these cemeteries (Winterbourne apart) but there is much variety in details such as the use or non-use of coffins, the treatment of the body, the presence of grave goods, and so on.

Some individuals were simply buried coffinless in shallow graves. Others were placed in stone-lined cists, or coffins of wood, stone, or lead. Sometimes, as at Birchanger Farm, Westbury, a lead coffin was encased within an outer wooden one (Fig. 9.1). The lack of a coffin or the use of a wooden one may, of course, have some bearing on the number of skeletons recovered and give a biased picture of the distribution of Romano-British burials. As many of the larger groups of inhumations are not yet closely dated, it is difficult to determine whether there is a significant increase in coffined burials over time and if this reflects increasing Romanisation of an area. At Boscombe Down West, for example, only

Fig. 9.1 Lead coffin, from Birchanger Farm, Westbury, 1.8m by 0.4 to 0.5m by 0.5m deep; WHM

4 of the 17 inhumations were within coffins, in this case of wood. The cemetery was dated by the excavator to the late 3rd to 4th century AD. In the 3rd to 4th century cemetery at Nettleton, 'Cemetery A', 6 of the 15 graves were not fully excavated; in the remaining 9 all the burials were in wooden coffins. 'The majority' were in coffins at Boscombe Down Sports Field (Anon. 1997, 151-2). Most coffined burials are apparently late although it does not follow that uncoffined burials are early; at Figheldean, Grave 61 contained a dog skeleton and hobnails but no coffin in a 'probably late' Romano-British cemetery. Securely dated 1st to 2nd-century coffined burials are rare; at

Maddington Farm a middle-aged ?male was interred in a wooden coffin with a coin of Faustina in his mouth.

An unusual burial at Black Field, Mildenhall, in which (above the face of the occupant) a flap was cut in the lid of the lead coffin may be an instance of a pipe burial whereby the deceased could participate in memorial feasts. A further feature of this coffin was the casting of the lower portion containing the body in two sections welded in the middle, a practice repeated in at least seven other examples from the county. This may represent the work of a local industry (Annable 1980, 189). The body was apparently shrouded, a not uncommon practice in Roman burials.

Perhaps more prestigious are the eight inhumations in large timber-lined vaults, one of which lay within a small square enclosure, at Boscombe Down Sports Field. Small stone mausolea were apparently in use at Nettleton and Truckle Hill.

Secondary Romano-British inhumations in Bronze Age barrows are recorded although rare. Examples include the four crouched burials recorded in association with Romano-British pottery from Snail Down, and one extended burial associated with two 4th-century coins in a barrow at Beach's Barn. It may be that other crouched burials with no datable artifacts such as those at Idmiston and Mount Wood are Roman as well, for the deposition of crouched burials (see below) continued in Wiltshire well into the Roman period as at Maddington Farm. A possible primary Romano-British barrow inhumation was described at Codford St Peter as being extended, in a 'room, 11 foot deep' with 'two pieces of fine Roman pottery' (Hoare 1812, 78). Cunnington (1934, 158), however, includes it in her survey of Pagan Saxon Wiltshire as being more typical of Saxon than Roman practice.

Within the grave, the position of the body varies. Some are flexed or crouched, a relic of the Iron Age (Whimster 1981, 194). There are two crouched burials at Maddington Farm (Graves 1026 and 1177) in a cemetery associated with a farmstead of the 3rd to 4th century. Perhaps the retention of the crouched posture indicates the conservatism of the rural Romano-British population. Otherwise, the remains are generally extended and supine. There are some instances of prone burials, as in Grave 6 at Purton where a young female with six fingers on her left hand was buried face down, perhaps in some ritual intended to ensure she remained within the grave. The provision of a stone coffin and the placing of a 3rd-century coin near her jaw imply that no disrespect was intended to the deceased. The same is perhaps true of the prone burial of an adult male at Maddington Farm: he was furnished with a coin in his mouth and a canine companion. At Tan Hill, however, the prone burial of a male with his hands apparently tied behind his back may indicate some kind of execution. (The remains have now disappeared.) The prone inhumation of a young woman in marshy ground at Wilsford cum Lake is not yet conclusively dated although the grave was sealed by a peaty layer associated with Romano-British pottery. It is possible that the burial so close to water had a symbolic meaning. Prone burials are, however, not common in Wiltshire, nor elsewhere (Philpott 1991, 71).

Also unusual are instances where the body has been decapitated after death and the skull redeposited within the grave. There are three examples of this practice at Winterbourne, in two of which the head was placed at the feet of the deceased and once by the right elbow (D. Algar, pers. comm.). Two of these individuals are male, one female. In another instance, at Manton Down (Clatford Bottom), the head of the female buried was placed between her feet and a jar (sic) substituted. There is some suggestion that at Eyewell Farm an infant ?male was decapitated before burial. Three headless skeletons with Romano-British pottery in a pit at Ludgershall may have undergone the same procedure. Other post-mortem mutilations may have served a more practical purpose. In the case of the 3-4 year old child buried at Vancellettes Farm, where both feet had been detached and placed beside the lower legs, it appears that the body was simply too large for the coffin and was perhaps not the original occupant (Chandler 1989). The same might be true of the burial at Northwood Farm where the farm labourer responsible for the discovery described the skeleton as having 'the arms cut off and put down by the legs' (Grant King 1963, 224).

The practice of decapitation was not widespread in Wiltshire. Although three of the fourteen inhumations at Winterbourne were decapitated, none are recorded from Lyncroft (12 inhumations), Figheldean (9+ inhumations), Maddington Farm (8+ inhumations) nor Purton (6 inhumations). All are recent excavations and such information is unlikely to have been missed. Of course, the complete publication of the Boscombe Down Sports Field excavation could change this picture. Elsewhere the proportion of decapitations within cemeteries varies greatly but tends to be a predominantly rural practice: 7/439 at Lankhills, 15/100 at Cassington, 2/58 at Allington Avenue, Dorchester (Philpott 1991, 80).

The purpose of decapitation is not completely understood. It is suggested that the six adults (5 male, 1 female) decapitated and buried in the Bath Gate cemetery at Cirencester were executed (McWhirr *et al.* 1982, 108) while those at Lankhills (1 child, 3 males, 2 females) were perhaps the victims of sacrifice (Clarke 1979, 372, 193). There are three probable cases at Poundbury, two of them on the periphery of the cemetery perhaps denoting exclusion of some kind (Farwell and Molleson 1993, 227). On the other hand, Philpott argues that in many cases the care with which burials are laid out argues against the deceased being criminals or pariahs and that decapitation may in some cases be part of a regeneration ritual to ensure the well being of certain individuals in the afterlife (Philpott 1991, 88). This is perhaps especially true of infants or children. In any case it appears to have begun as a rural practice in late Roman times and to have substantially died out by the post-Roman period (Farwell and Molleson 1993, 227).

Sometimes items of jewellery, food, pottery or coins were deliberately placed within the grave. Of the 17 graves at Boscombe Down West, for example, grave goods were recovered from only three inhumations. Hobnails from footwear are the most common and occur in both male and female burials. They are mainly associated with the 3rd and 4th centuries. Eight out of nine graves at the late Roman cemetery at Figheldean contained hobnails; conversely one instance is reported from the six inhumations at the 3rd-century cemetery at Purton. Three of the seventeen graves at Boscombe Down west contained hobnails as did Grave 11 at Winterbourne. Although the introduction of hobnailed footwear is Roman, its inclusion in graves appears to be a largely rural practice growing out of a native rite. The distribution of hobnail burial is also largely in southern England (Philpott 1991, 71).

Coins are not common; there are only some twelve instances as yet recorded in Wiltshire of coins deliberately deposited as grave goods. Most are 3rd to 4th century. A coin of Vespasian was found in the fill of one grave at Nettleton and 2nd-century coins have come from Maddington Farm (Faustina), Amesbury (Antoninus Pius) and Broad Town Field (Marcus Aurelius). Most were near the face or actually in the mouth. At Westrop House a young female was interred with a 3rd-century coin between her legs and the coin of Marcus Aurelius at Broad Town was reportedly on the chest of the inhumation. It is not clear whether two 4th-century coins with the intrusive burial at Beach's Barn barrow were intentionally deposited. Clearly the need to pay Charon was not widely felt and appears mainly as a later practice.

Other articles deposited in graves include iron knives (Woodcock Farm and Winterbourne, for example), small glass vessels (Purton and Southbroom, Devizes), a bone comb (Boscombe Down West), brooches (Boscombe Down West, Amesbury, and Knowle Barn, among others) and pottery (the Kestrels, Easterton, for example). A ring was found above the coffin at Northwood Farm, and bronze tweezers, and an earpick in a burial at Honey Street. At Hamshill Ditches a coin of Claudius II and a lead weight accompanied the inhumation. It is unclear whether the quern recovered at the Masonic Hall, Swindon, was in the cist grave or the grave fill. An unusually rich burial near Southgrove Farm contained bone and iron crossbow fittings, a whetstone, bronze tweezers, an iron hammerhead, and two knife blades.

Animal remains are rare. One of the four inhumations at Blounts Court had a sheep jawbone at its left knee and a Late Iron Age to early Roman burial at Werg, associated with a sherd of Savernake ware, had an ox bone laid by his arm (Meyrick 1955, 20). However, dogs are fairly common companions in Romano-British burials (Philpott 1991, 204). Dog's teeth were found in a grave at Chantry Field and possible dog bones in a late 3rd to 4th-century stone coffin burial at Trinity School, Bradford-on Avon, where a man and a woman were enclosed in the same coffin. The skeleton of a small dog was included in Grave 1002 at Maddington Farm and in Grave 61 at Figheldean. The inhumation of a female with iron nails and a dog skeleton at Tilshead, although classed as Saxon (*VCH* 1957), is more typically Roman; the dating of the find is 'very uncertain' (Cunnington 1934, 170). It must be stressed that inclusion of any or some of these items is not widespread; while almost 30% of those buried singly had grave goods, the proportion decreased to approximately 17% for those in cemeteries (although once again publication of Boscombe Down Sports Field could change the picture).

The Roman proscription against burials within the boundaries of a settlement here, as elsewhere in the Empire, did not apply to infants and some of the over 30 infants buried in pits and ditches at Rotherley may well be Romano-British. Infant burials have been found in pits at Durrington Walls, Chapperton Down, and Butterfield Down among others and in the ditches at Woodhenge in strata with Romano-British pottery. None of these were reported to have been in coffins or accompanied by grave goods. Not all very young children were buried outside formal cemeteries, however. The possibly decapitated infant at Eyewell Farm was interred among adults in a cist grave and an 'infant' (sic) inhumation is included in Cemetery A at Nettleton. Two neonates are recorded from

Winterbourne, one with a small jar containing an iron pin between its legs. The inclusion of both adults and young children in a cemetery is sometimes taken as an indicator of Christian practice which is discussed later.

Older, pre-adolescent, children are accorded more ceremony than infants. At Churches Field a 9-month-old child was buried in a stone coffin and the child's stone coffin at Vancellette's Farm had a lead liner. Stone coffins for children have been found at Iford Manor, the Brewery site at Bradford (Fig. 9.2), and Parsonage Farm. As with adults, grave goods are infrequent, but the contents of a child's grave near Beckhampton included beads, rings and a fibula pin. A 3rd to 4th-century child/adolescent grave at Biss Bottom contained hobnails and a miniature pottery vessel. Occasionally, an adult and a child were interred together: at Sherston, a 35-year-old male was buried with a 'child' (no age given) lying across his left side and chest.

Fig. 9.2 Limestone coffin for a child, from Bradford-on-Avon, 0.96m by 0.51m by 0.23m deep; WHM

The difficulties of deducing religious beliefs from archaeological remains are clear; nevertheless, such factors as the orientation of the body within the grave are sometimes used as evidence of such beliefs. East–west orientation is often taken as an indicator of Christian ritual, for example. In Wiltshire such information has not often been recorded except for the more recently excavated cemeteries. Latterly, it has been argued (Farwell and Molleson 1993, 236; Woodward 1992, 96-7, among others) that several characteristics taken together are a more reliable pointer towards religious belief. The burial in the same cemetery of infants and adults, east–west orientation of the body, the absence of grave goods, and the separation of graves may suggest Christian practice. The deposition of coins, decapitation, the superimposition of graves, and the prone burial rite may point towards a pagan interment. But in many instances in late Roman Britain no discernible distinction can be made between pagan and Christian burials; inhumations laid east–west in rows and without grave goods are 'entirely typical' of a class of late Romano-British cemeteries (Philpott 1991, 239) which are not necessarily Christian. There are very few objects bearing unarguably Christian symbols from Wiltshire (Mawer 1995, 64) and none from cemetery contexts. Wedlake, in excavating the shrine of Apollo at Nettleton, suggested that the modification of the octagonal temple was intended to convert it into a Christian church (Wedlake 1982, 103-5). The evidence for this is not strong and there is some indication that the same building had pagan associations in the late 4th century (*ibid.* 1982, 79). The question of the prevalence of Christian belief in Roman Wiltshire is still largely unanswered and, perhaps, unanswerable.

Cremations

Although inhumation appears to have been the principle rite in Iron Age and Roman Wiltshire, there runs concurrently from at least the late Iron Age a tradition of cremation (e.g. the Marlborough bucket burial: Robinson 1998, 145-7). This practice can be followed in the archaeological record from the 1st through to the 4th centuries AD with cemeteries often containing both cremations and inhumations. At Cuffs Corner, nine inhumations were accompanied by nearby deposits of 'burnt bone', implying cremation. The cemetery is unfortunately not closely dated. 'Cemetery C' at Nettleton (7 cremations) also included one inhumation and unurned burnt bone. At the Lyncroft Estate site, four cremations in early 2nd-century pots shared a cemetery with twelve inhumations of apparently late Romano-British date (one with a coin of Magnus Maximus). Later cremations include the 37 at Winterbourne, one cremation among 36 inhumations at Boscombe Down Sports Field, and a cremation from Heywood, Westbury Ironworks, containing a coin of Constantine I (Fig. 9.3). At Parsonage Farm, the inhumation of a child in a stone coffin was 'almost certainly contemporaneous' (Annable 1964, 183) with a cremation in a late 3rd to 4th-century cooking pot laid against the head of the coffin. Three 'pyre debris pits' containing human bone at Maddington Farm were associated with a 3rd to 4th-century inhumation cemetery.

Until Winterbourne, Boscombe Down Sports Field, and Lyncroft Estate are fully published it is not possible to determine if cremations and inhumations at these sites are interspersed or whether there were separate sections within the cemeteries for the two different rites. At Poundbury (Farwell and Molleson 1993, 30), Lankhills (Clarke 1979, 128), and Cirencester (McWhirr *et al.* 1982, 99) where late cremations also occur, although rare they are not obviously separated from inhumations. The difficulties in recognising unurned deposits, especially in the past, may have contributed to a biased perception of the popularity of this rite, as does the low survival rate of unurned 'topsoil' cremations such as those at Lankhills (Clarke 1979, 129). Late cremations, at a time when almost all burials in Britain were inhumations, have sometimes been regarded as 'Germanic' (*ibid.* 1979, 351), but the absence of 'Germanic' objects and the presence in some cremations of common Romano-British objects such as hobnails suggest that cremation continued as a native rite well into the late Roman period in Britain, both on urban sites such as Lankhills and Poundbury and on rural sites like Owslebury as well (Collis 1977, 33). This certainly appears to have been the case in the Wiltshire cemeteries so far excavated and

Fig. 9.3 Cremation urn, Dorset Black-Burnished ware, ht. 120mm, and 'Charon's obol' a follis of Constantine I, diam. 25mm, from Westbury Ironworks; WHM

perhaps reflects the conservatism of certain families or professions (e.g. priests) within the province.

Because cremation can destroy much of the evidence of the age, sex, and physical condition of those buried, there is little information of this sort published for Wiltshire. At Winterbourne, both males and females, adults and juveniles were cremated. A cremated adult female and foetus were buried together. It is interesting, but perhaps not significant, that the two neonates in the cemetery were both inhumations.

As with inhumations, there is much variety in the actual details of the individual burials. Some ashes are simply deposited in shallow scoops or pits as at Weir Farm and Cuffs Corner. In 'Cemetery C' at Nettleton there are also unurned cremations. Others are in pots, sometimes with lids (Francis Meadows and Heywood, where a shallow dish served as a lid. The pot was inscribed with an 'M' the meaning of which is obscure). At Mildenhall the cremation was placed in an urn of 'black moulded pottery' under an 'arch of brick' (*VCH* 1957, 1, 88). The ashes were interred at Truckle Hill villa in a hollowed-out cavity in a stone block in a 'mausoleum' with three inhumations. The lion's head mount from East Coulston implies the use of a casket (Fig. 9.4); similar mounts have been found at Radnage (pre-Flavian, Skilbeck 1923, 334-8) and Fishbourne (pre-AD 75, Cunliffe 1971, 117-18). The cremation at Purton was enclosed within a glass vessel protected by a lead ossuary decorated with scallop shells and St Andrew crosses.

Fig. 9.4 Bronze stud in the form of a lion's head from a funerary casket, diam. 10mm, from East Coulston; WHM

Whether in a container or not, few cremation burials were accompanied by grave goods. None were noted, for example, in the Purton burial despite the richness of the containers used. However, an unurned burial at Milston Farm House contained in the burial pit an iron knife, bone pin and a 'thumb impressed clay object' (Cunnington 1932, 197). At Stanton St Quintin, a bronze dolphin brooch and a teardrop-shaped glass bead were deposited. The Heywood cremation contained, as noted above, a coin: such finds are extremely rare in Wiltshire.

The site at Winterbourne is perhaps unusual in that the majority of the cremations are associated with beakers or jars, many of them burnt. Additionally, Grave 16 contained an iron knife and Graves 19 and 32 unidentified iron objects. Grave 28 may be associated with a small pair of linked copper alloy discs, Grave 36 had a large cleat, Grave 38 hobnails (possibly from Grave 39, another cremation) and Grave 42, an iron goad.

There is some evidence that cremation burials in barrows occurred during the Roman period. At Lamb Down, Codford, an *in situ* cremation appears to have taken place: with one exception, all the finds are Roman. These include a small bronze fragment of a brooch or pendant, three iron studs, and a coin of AD 364-367 found in the weathered chalk below what remained of the old land surface. The sherds recovered were of 3rd to 4th-century date. About 45m north of the Roman road from *Cunetio* to *Verlucio* are the barrow-like remnants of three 2nd-century 'tombs' (West Overton 6, 6a, 7). Here the cremated remains were evidently enclosed within a circular ditch set with posts which could have risen 'at least 6 feet high' (Smith and Simpson 1964, 76) to form a drum-like appearance. Clearly such a construction was intended to be seen from the road. Among the finds from no. 7 are fragments of a bronze-mounted box possibly a funeral casket. It must be noted, however, that these 'mounds' had been twice previously excavated, once by Colt Hoare in the early 19th century and again by Thurnam in 1860 (Thurnam 1860, 350-1). Colt Hoare reported (1821, 91) that the mounds had been 'robbed' previous to his own excavations.

Late- and post-Roman evidence

The latest recorded cremations in Wiltshire are those in the cemetery at Winterbourne where coins of Constantius II and Valentinian I were found with two of the inhumations. There are no securely dated 5th-century Roman burials from Wiltshire and the question of the continuity of burial practice and the siting of cemeteries in the post-Roman period is still very much an open one (Eagles this volume). By the end of the 4th century unfurnished extended inhumation was almost universal in Britain (Philpott 1991, 226), practised by both Christians and pagans. As noted above it is very difficult to determine from such scant evidence the spread, or otherwise, of Christian belief. Anglo-Saxon intrusive burials have been found in the Overton 'tombs' but in no currently published Romano-British cemetery in Wiltshire is there unequivocal evidence of post-Roman burials. The inclusion of hobnailed footwear, a 3rd to 4th-century Romano-British practice, is not attested in the early 5th century in Wiltshire although Roman elements are found in a few Anglo-Saxon burials such as the Romano-British brooch in Grave 11 in the Anglo-Saxon cemetery at Collingbourne Ducis (Gingell 1978, 97) and the gaming pieces in an Anglo-Saxon barrow at Bishops Cannings (Roundway 40a: Cunnington 1869, 159-67). It has been suggested that the Romano-British practice of decapitation might have been borrowed by Anglo-Saxon incomers, perhaps married to native women (Clarke 1979, 375), but perhaps with a different purpose in mind. Just as when, during the Roman period, there was a time lag between the introduction and widespread adoption of new burial fashions (as seen, for example, in the late 4th-century cremations at Winterbourne) Romano-British burial customs must have continued for some time, especially in rural areas, after the influx of Anglo-Saxon ideas. Large groups of inhumation burials without grave goods and unfortunately now lost have been recorded from Fargo Plantation (30 individuals) and Swindon ('nearly 100'). Such groups could represent sub-Roman/Saxon Wiltshire but without more precise dating this can only remain speculation. The unexpected dating by radiocarbon to the middle Iron Age of a cemetery recently excavated at Yarnton, Oxon (Hey *et al.* 1999) demonstrates the pitfalls inherent in dating burials without any associated artefacts. It also illustrates the possible surprises awaiting further investigations of Romano-British burials.

Wiltshire sites with Romano-British burials

Amesbury	*WANHM,* 56, 411
Beach's Barn, Fittleton	*WANHM,* 36, 626
Beckhampton, Avebury	*WANHM,* 74/75, 205; WHM 1978.44.23
Birchanger Farm, Westbury	*WANHM,* 82, 156-7
Biss Bottom, Westbury/Upton Scudamore	WILTM Rpt 1993.067; *WANHM,* 87, 156
Blounts Court, Potterne	*WANHM,* 61, 95; 62, 135
Boscombe Down Sports Field, Amesbury	*WANHM,* 90, 151-2

Boscombe Down West, Idmiston/ Allington	*VCH* 1957, 1.26; *WANHM*, 54, 123-68; WILTM Rpt 1998.045
Brewery, Bradford on Avon	*VCH* 1957, 1.45; *WANHM*, 36, 509; 38, 208
Broad Town Field, Clyffe Pypard	*WANHM* 40, 353; 45, 183
Butterfield Down, Amesbury	*WANHM*, 89, 39
Chantry Field, Tisbury	SMR ST 92NW, 301
Chapperton Down, Chitterne	*VCH* 1957, 1.57; *WANHM*, 45, 182-3; 77, 139, 141; 91, 162; Hoare 1812, 89
Churches Field, Bradford on Avon	*WANHM*, 53, 137-8, 151
Codford barrow, Ashton Valley Group, Codford St Peter	*WANHM*, 58, 435; Hoare 1812, 78
Coleman's Mead/St Margaret's Mead	*WANHM* 22, 234-8
Covingham Farm, Wanborough	*WANHM*, 41, 279
Cricklade Road, Highworth	*WANHM*, 57, 247, 268
'Cross Roads', Tilshead	*WANHM*, 46, 170
Cuffs Corner, Clyffe Pypard	*WANHM*, 19, 55; 38, 227
'Cunetio', Mildenhall	*WANHM*, 22, 234-5; 41, 391-2; 55, 305; 72/73, 187-91; Hoare 1821, 71-2
Durrington Walls, Durrington	*WANHM*, 66, 87, 125-7
East Coulston	WHM 107.1981
Erlestoke Detention Centre, Erlestoke	WHM, Archaeol Archive
Eyewell Farm, Chilmark	*WANHM*, 85, 159-60; 91, 11-33; WILTM Rpt.1994.018
Fargo Plantation, Durrington	*WANHM*, 31, 331
Figheldean	*WANHM*, 86, 23-5, 41-2, 50-1; 92, 16-17, 31
Francis Meadows, West Overton	WHM, J.W. Brooke Notebook, 85, 184
Hamshill Ditches, Barford St Martin	*WANHM*, 62, 121
Heywood, Westbury Ironworks	*WANHM*, 36, 465, 477; 70/71, 135.86; *VCH* 1957, 1.77; *Archaeol Journ*, 137, 1980, 50-85
Honey Street, Alton	*WANHM* 37, 205; 38, 162
Iford Manor, Westwood	*WANHM*, 38, 341; 41, 171; 45, 208.
Imber	*WANHM*, 39, 500; *VCH* 1957, 1.79
The Kestrels, Easterton	*WANHM*, 45, 399, 483
Knowle Barn, Little Bedwyn	WHM, A.D. Passmore Notebook, 443
Lake House, Wilsford cum Lake	*WANHM*, 91, 158; WILTM Rpt 1996.033
Lamb Down, Codford	*WANHM*, 58, 434-6
Ludgershall	*WANHM*, 45, 196.112a
Lyncroft Estate/St Paul's Drive, Wanborough	*WANHM*, 67, 175; 68, 135
Maddington Farm, Shrewton	*WANHM*, 89, 44-72
Manton Down, Preshute	*VCH* 1957, 1.97; *WANHM*, 26, 412; 45, 216

Milston Farm House, Figheldean	*VCH* 1957, 1.89; *WANHM*, 45, 197
Nettleton (Shrine of Apollo)	Wedlake 1982
North View Hospital, Purton	*WANHM*, 82, 177; 83, 220; 84, 144; WILTM Rpt 1989.012
Northwood Farm, Colerne	*WANHM*, 58, 223-4; 59, 206; 65, 198-9; 66, 198
Overton Hill, West Overton	*VCH* 1957, 1.195; *WANHM* 6, 330; 59, 68-85; 60, 159; 80, 103-19
Parsonage Farm, Winsley	*WANHM*, 58, 450-1; 59, 182-3
Rotherley, Berwick St John	Pitt Rivers 1887-98
Sherston	*WANHM*, 85, 161
Snail Down Round Barrow, Collingbourne Ducis	*WANHM*, 56, 130-48; 92, 122
Southbroom Junior School, Devizes	*WANHM*, 58, 62, 222-3
Southgrove Farm, Burbage	*WANHM* 28, 87-90; 45, 180
Stanton St. Quinton	*VCH* 1957, 1.107; *WANHM*, 43, 334-5
Swindon	*WANHM* 38, 46, 329; 46, 156; 70/71, 136
Tan Hill, Bishops Cannings	*WANHM*, 54, 228
Teffont Evias Quarry, Teffont	*VCH* 1957, 1.113; *WANHM*, 35, 503; 36, 142; 38, 329; 45, 485-6
Trinity School, Bradford on Avon	*WANHM*, 56, 390
Truckle Hill, North Wraxall	*VCH* 1957, 1.57; *WANHM*, 7, 59-75; 72/73, 206; 74/75, 206; 80, 242
Vancellette's Farm, Sherston	WILTM Rpt 1989
Weir Farm, Broad Hinton	*VCH* 1957, 1.50; *WANHM*, 41, 390; 45, 178
Werg, Mildenhall	Meyrick 1955
Westrop House, Highworth	*VCH* 1957, 1.77; *WANHM*, 50, 99-100
Winterbourne Down, Winterbourne	D. Algar, pers. comm.; *WANHM*, 58, 470; *JRS* 53, 149
Woodcock Farm, Warminster	WANHM 48, 468-9
Woodhenge, Durrington	Cunnington 1929
Yarnbury Castle, Steeple Langford	*VCH* 1957, 1.38; *WANHM*, 39, 401; 46, 206, 214-16

References

Anon., 1997, 'Excavation and fieldwork in Wiltshire', *WANHM*, 90, 151-2

Annable, F. K., 1964, 'Romano-British interments at Parsonage Farm, Winsley', *WANHM*, 59, 182-3

_____ , 1980, 'A coffined burial of Roman date from Cunetio', *WANHM*, 72/73, 189-91

Chandler, C., 1989, 'The rescue excavation of a Romano-British child burial at Vancellette's Farm, Sherston, Wilts', WILTM Rpt

Clarke, G., 1979, *The Roman Cemetery at Lankhills*, Oxford

Collis, J., 1977, 'Owslebury (Hants) and the problem of burials on rural settlements', in *Burial in the Roman World* (ed. R. Reece), CBA Res Rep, 22, London, 26-34

Cunliffe, B., 1971, *Excavations at Fishbourne 1961-9, II: The Finds,* London

Cunnington, M.E., 1929, *Woodhenge,* Devizes

_____ , 1932, 'Romano-British Wiltshire', *WANHM,* 45, 166-216

_____ , 1934, 'Wiltshire in pagan Saxon times', *WANHM,* 46, 147-75

Cunnington W., 1860, 'Roundway Hill, account of Ancient British and Anglo-Saxon barrows', *WANHM,* 6, 159-67

Farwell, D. E., and Molleson, T. L., 1993, *Excavations at Poundbury 1966-80, II: The Cemeteries,* Dorchester

Gingell, C., 1978, 'The Excavation of an early Anglo-Saxon cemetery at Collingbourne Ducis', *WANHM,* 70/71, 61-98

Grant King, D., 1963, 'A Romano-British burial, Colerne', *WANHM,* 58, 224

Hey, G., Bayliss, A., and Boyle, A., 1999, 'Iron Age inhumation burials at Yarnton, Oxfordshire', *Antiquity,* 73, 551-62

Hoare, R. C., 1812, *The Ancient History of Wiltshire, Volume I,* London

_____ , 1821, *The Ancient History of Wiltshire, Volume II, The Roman Aera,* London

Mawer, C. F., 1995, *Evidence for Christianity in Roman Britain,* BAR Brit Ser, 243, Oxford

McWhirr, A., Viner, L., and Wells, C., 1982, *Romano-British Cemeteries at Cirencester,* Cirencester

Meyrick, O., 1955, 'Romano-British burials at Werg', *Marlborough College Nat Hist Soc Rep,* 1947-55, no. 96

Philpott, R., 1991, *Burial Practices in Roman Britain,* BAR Brit Ser, 219, Oxford

Pitt Rivers, A. H. L. F., 1888, *Excavations in Cranborne Chase, near Rushmore, II,* privately printed

Robinson, P. H., 1998, 'A late Iron Age or early Roman spout in the Stourhead collection', *WANHM,* 91, 145-8

Skilbeck, C. O., 1923, 'Notes on the discovery of a Roman burial at Radnage, Bucks', *Antiq Journ,* 3, 334-8

Smith I. F., and Simpson, D. D. A., 1964, 'Excavation of three Roman tombs and a prehistoric pit on Overton Down', *WANHM,* 59, 68-85

Thurnam, J., 1860, 'Examination of barrows on the downs of north Wiltshire', *WANHM,* 6, 317-36

VCH 1957, *Victoria County History, Wiltshire, I, (i),* London

Wedlake, W. J., 1982, *The Excavation of the Shrine of Apollo at Nettleton, Wiltshire 1956-1971,* Soc Antiq Res Rep, 40, London.

Whimster, R., 1981, *Burial Practices in Iron Age Britain,* BAR Brit Ser, 90, Oxford

Woodward, A., 1992, *Shrines and Sacrifice,* London

10 WANSDYKE IN THE WOODS:

AN UNFINISHED ROMAN MILITARY EARTHWORK FOR A NON-EVENT

by Peter Fowler

Dedication

Ken Annable was kind to me far beyond the call of duty in my early days in Wiltshire archaeology. An attractive streak of unconformity ran through his thoughts, and I hope it remains sufficiently strong to find diversion enough in the following mildly iconoclastic offering which, *inter alia*, suggests that Wiltshire's Wansdyke, precisely because it was abandoned unfinished, is much more directly a part of Romano-British archaeology than Anglo-Saxon history.

Introduction

'Archaeologists who have dealt with Wansdyke have acted generally on the assumption that it is a single work constructed at one time with one object' (Major and Burrow 1926, 135). My purpose, heavily trailed in the sub-title, is to suggest that Wansdyke, *sensu* East Wansdyke in Wiltshire alone, is indeed a single work constructed at one time with one object; and, further, that it was a military work in Roman mode, intended to face a military threat from the north. In arriving at that judgement independently, I am nevertheless only reviving a century-old idea, for Pitt-Rivers (1892, 25-6, 30) was clearly of similar mind and indeed saw close similarities between Wansdyke and Hadrian's Wall.

My addition to the continuing debate about Wansdyke is the observation that part of it at least was unfinished at the time construction work stopped, and that the work was never completed. The stoppage, I suggest, occurred because the anticipated military event did not happen. And because the threat evaporated, the work was not completed.

Wansdyke is unfinished in West Woods, in Overton and Fyfield parishes. They are the 'Woods' of my title, woods which existed in late and post-Roman times (Fowler 2000). Here we are concerned with but 4.5km of unfashionable dyke within them (Fig. 10.1). We largely ignore, therefore, East Wansdyke in all its grandeur to the west on the downs, and its on the whole rather pathetic and puzzlingly discontinuous remains to the east in and beyond present-day Savernake Forest. Pitt-Rivers himself, a military man, observed that 'the rampart diminishes in size, or is wanting, in places where forests may have existed,

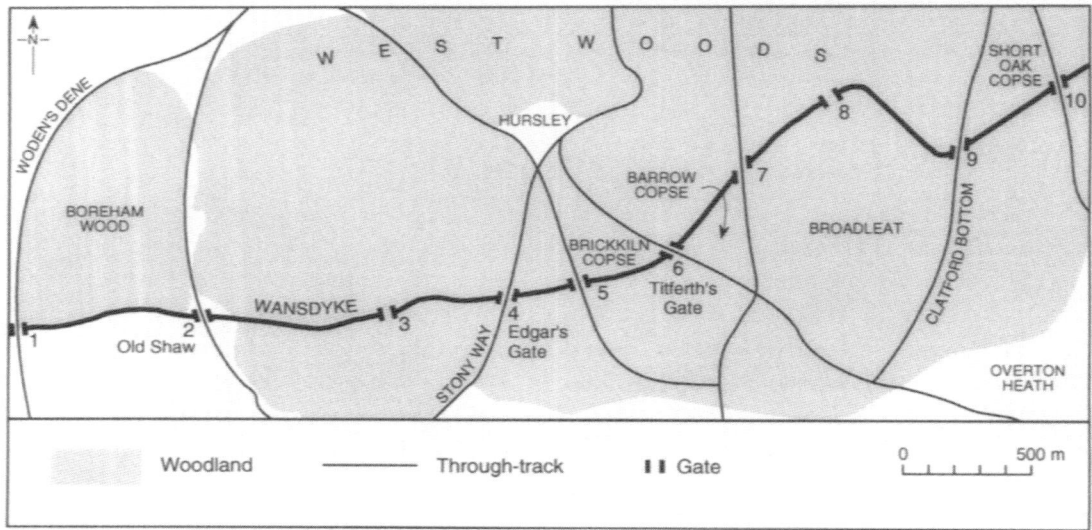

Fig. 10.1 Map of East Wansdyke in West Woods, showing probable contemporary woodland and, schematically, the positions of ten possible 'gates', 1-10 here, i-x in text Section 3, 'The Gateways', below.

and that it increases in places where forests are unlikely to have grown.' (1892, quoted by Major and Burrow, 1926, 152). But our point is that in West Woods the bank is lower, the dyke smaller, not because it was intentionally built smaller or because it is in the woods, but because it was not finished.

My observations to this effect have arisen in recent fieldwork on and along a monument which I honestly thought had been 'done' and consequently needed little attention during my landscape study of Fyfield and West Overton parishes (Fowler and Blackwell 1998; Fowler 2000). The latter contains the academic background and much of the detail behind this discussion, but is not repeatedly referenced here in what is meant to be a readable essay. This paper, originally written over Xmas 1998, is the result of a little exercise in 1997-8, a spin-off from the larger project.

OS maps apart, the only worthwhile publications specifically on East Wansdyke are Hoare (1821), Pitt-Rivers (1892), Crawford (1953), Fox and Fox (1958), Clark (1958) and Green (1971). 'Worthwhile' means publications which brought forward new primary evidence, as distinct from re-assessments of existing evidence.

East Wansdyke: new evidence from fieldwork in the woods

Our fieldwork has produced new evidence in West Woods in three respects:

1. On the nature of the bank;
2. On the nature of the ditch;
3. On the nature of the gateways.

We first treat them separately, working from west to east in each case. Our description can luxuriate in impressionistic terms like 'fairly low' because the earthwork is quite well-recorded in plan and profile throughout, notably on OS large-scale maps and in Fox and Fox 1958, 10-16, 20-25 (we refer as appropriate to their profiles as 'Fox D.7' etc.). We accept such records overall, and specify the particular points which we find inadequately recorded and those with which we disagree.

1. The bank

Wansdyke's impressive bank continues eastwards off the downs into Woden's Dene, where there may have been an original gateway (see below), and up to Shaw Farm (Fox D.6). Were it not for its covering of beech trees, it would be as well-known here as the length immediately to the west. After Shaw Farm, however, it never really regains that downland stature. It is first mangled by the site of Shaw Manor Farm: called 'Homestead' in 1734 (WRO 1553/109, the earliest map of this area), the Farm consisted of four buildings. The two largest – house and barn? – were actually on the bank. Wansdyke was also affected by the comings and goings to Shaw village, now deserted, immediately to its south. An ancient and important track passed through it by the Farm on its way south from the Marlborough Downs to the Vale of Pewsey (and *vice versa*). At the Wansdyke crossing itself, however, there is no clear evidence of an original gateway.

The bank re-emerges east of the Shaw disturbance as an upstanding earthwork (Fox D.7) to pass downhill to a narrow combe, where there is a break which continues a short distance up the eastern slope. The 1734 map shows Wansdyke as continuous over this length between 'Great Wood' and 'The Triangle', a cleared area, on the north and 'Church Lands' on the south. For some 400m as far east as the eastern corner of 'The Triangle', Wansdyke's ditch is the ancient boundary between Shaw (now West Overton Civil Parish) and Alton Priors (Huish CP), a rare co-incidence as Bonney has observed and ruminated upon (1966; 1972). The likelihood in this case is that the earthwork briefly followed, for convenience, the line of an existing estate boundary across a small dry valley before heading north east as it climbed again on to a ridge at the 220m contour. Here it turns with the contour through 55° to cross the ridge and start descending again across the contours to a track coming up from Hursley Bottom. This pattern of arrangements is closely mirrored 2km to the north-east at Daffy Copse and Clatford Bottom. The break in Wansdyke at this Hursley Bottom track is original and was called 'Edgar's gate' in the 10th century (Fig. 10.11a).

The bank restarts quite prominently east of Edgar's gate (Fig. 10.2, left hand side) but soon decreases up the slope until it fades out and stops just before reaching the 'Stone' marked on the OS 6 inch map at SU 15086501 (Fig. 10.3). The stone itself is a round-headed, late 19th-century boundary stone inscribed 'H.M.' (Henry Meux). In the gap before the bank starts again two tracks elide. One is another track climbing southwards from Hursley Bottom; the other is the modern farm track hitherto in front of the ditch but here switching to run eastwards behind the bank. The bank itself is stepped forward, its new departure point on the eastern side of the gap being in line with the ditch coming up from the west (Fig. 10.4).

Fig. 10.2 Edgar's gate: looking through from the north, showing the trackway through it, doing a 'dog-leg' left of the puddle (= end of the western ditch) in the foreground and then right this side of the left figure on the stub of the eastern bank and beneath the right figure standing in the slight 'holloway' at the foot of the western bank. The continuation of the track southwards in the middle distance is called stanihtan weg *('stony way') in the East Overton charter (AD 939).*

For the whole of the next stretch the bank is even lower that it appears, because it is overlaid by a boundary bank along its length (Figs. 10.5, 10.6). Such banks, boundaries of individual woods and copses which make up the silvicultural mosaic of West Woods, are common archaeological features in these woods. Here, the boundary is of the southern edge of what was generally Wells Copse and specifically Brickkiln Copse (see below) and Strawberry Ground.

The bank of Wansdyke here is actually a series of dumps which have joined together in line but still show their own tails fanned out at the back. Each heap is 2-3m in width but not more than 0.5-0.75m high – hardly a mighty earthwork. In front of them is a berm, the shoulder of the original ground surface on which they were dumped, back from the quarries which were the source of their material. The copse bank too very slightly undulates as it runs from heap to heap. Collectively, these heaps look as if they await another one or two heightenings and a final smoothing before the bank of which they were meant to be a part would have been completed. The bank, however, rises and expands as it approaches the next break so that, here apparently completed, it is up to 1.75m high as it becomes the western side of Titferth's gate (see below).

The bank continues north-eastwards at its grandest in the woods (Fowler and Blackwell 1998, colour pl. 27) – but it is still less than 2m high above the present ground surface when viewed from behind. But it does seem to have been completed, at least over a length of some 450m. More or less co-incidentally with being cut by a modern forestry track (but see gate vii below), the bank reverts to a lower and unfinished appearance. The Foxes provide no profile along the whole of this length and the Burrow water colour (no. 77) is a fanciful exaggeration. By the time we reach the parish boundary with Fyfield, the bank is barely a metre high.

The parish boundary is a low bank with a shallow ditch on its east, running north west–south east to cross Wansdyke more or less at a right angle. The whole is barely more than 2m in width, with each of its two components not more than 0.3-0.4m in relief. The role of this earthwork as the parish boundary is, however, secondary, for here we enter that part of Fyfield which was added to the parish in 1896 when it absorbed Clatford Park; and the earthwork is indeed the Park pale: hence the ditch on its east, the *inside* of the pale. And of course the ditch cuts through the top of Wansdyke's bank, because it is

Fig. 10.3 Wansdyke east of Edgar's gate as it begins to run out uphill towards the camera and the west side of the 'Meux gate'. The figure on the left stands on top of what has by here become a small as well as a low bank, with a clear berm between its front and the ditch's inner lip (marked by the coppiced hazel, centre). The scale provided by the right hand figure shows that the ditch is narrow and little more than a shallow scoop.

later, and then clearly proceeds southwards. Its course is mapped on OS maps as a continuous curving boundary looping round the south and east sides of Clatford Park Farm. We meet it again below.

Within a few metres of the banks' conjunction, Wansdyke's bank fades away and stops with a slight inward curve, arguably a last heap of soil. Then there is a significant difference between Wansdyke as mapped and the evidence on the ground, though the OS 1889 6 inch map, and – curiously – the recent Explorer 157 1:25000, show the situation correctly. Wansdyke is missing for some 70m. Across the gap from bank end to bank end runs a slight scarp; it falls *c.* 0.3m towards where the ditch should be but is not. It looks like the marking out line for the earthwork, here not covered over because work stopped before any ditch was dug. The gap might be accidental, where the bank had simply not been built when construction work stopped. On the other hand, it may be deliberate, for example a gap left for the insertion of a gate. Either way, it indicates incompleteness when work was abandoned.

When the bank begins again, it does so with a few low humps behind the line of the scarp. Then it becomes a proper bank again, across the line of the scarp, but it is never

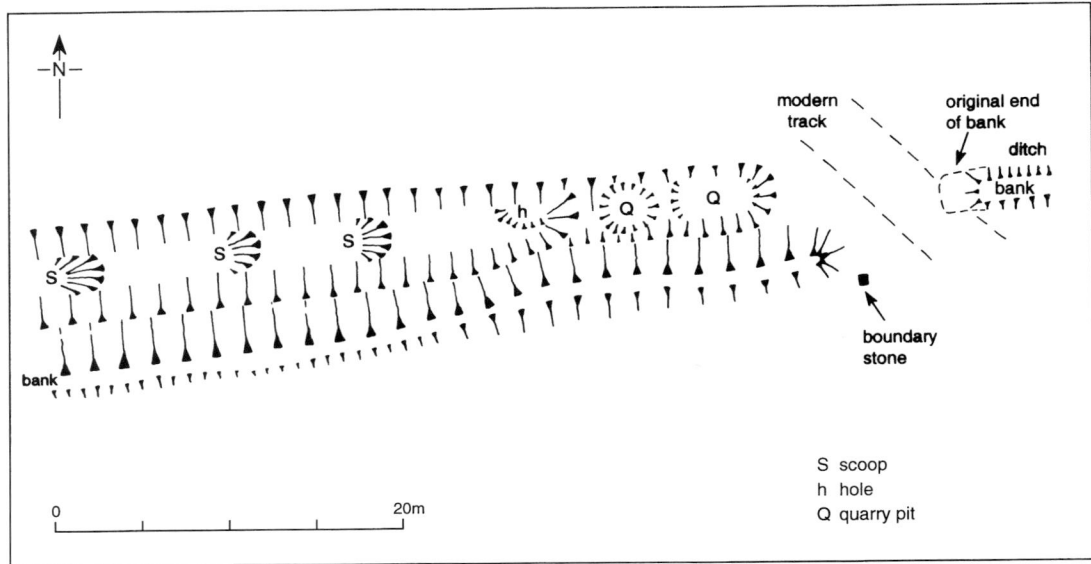

Fig. 10.4 Plan of 'Meux gate', with details of Wansdyke approaching from the west and stopping in an incomplete state, most marked in the ditch. Note the staggered entrance.

more than 1m high at the back until the corner of Daffy Copse where, its most north-easterly point in the woods, it was completed. By then the earthwork overall is once more at its woodland best, so that the sharp south-easterly turn of 70° is impressive. This would have been particularly so had a view of it from below in Clatford Bottom been clear of trees, as indeed was the case in medieval times. Even now in woodland, it seems like a salient deliberately jutting out over the lower ground, a façade meant to be seen. The most was made of military necessity, however, for the earthwork had to be turned south-east so as not to lose height to the north-east with the natural slope. So Wansdyke was turned to cross the combe side at right angles to its slope and then straightened up to cross the combe itself almost at a right angle. It is not difficult to recognise a military mind at work. And yet, all the way down the slope from the salient to the edge of the woodland north-west of Clatford Park Farm, Wansdyke is unfinished (Fig. 10.7).

Fig. 10.5 Wansdyke along the southern edge of Brickkiln Wood looking east. The ditch is out of sight to the left. The bank largely consists of a copse bank to the left of the left hand figure who is standing on top of a low irregular mound. The base of the back of the original, unfinished Wansdyke is marked by the right hand figure.

Fig. 10.6 Wansdyke in the same area as Fig. 10.5 but now looking west to show the ditch at its largest but still accompanied by a low, irregular bank. The left hand figure stands on a copse bank on top of Wansdyke's incomplete bank.

Briefly clear of woodland as it crosses Clatford Bottom, the dyke is momentarily quite impressive on the west side of the road (Fig. 10.8, essentially the same view as Burrow's accurate rendition no. 78); but the bank does not appear to start again until some 200m up the eastern slope. Even then the bank is minimal to begin with, though it may be larger beneath a superincumbent lynchet (Fig. 10.9). After that, all the way up past Short Oak Copse on the north to the north-west corner of the former Gore Copse on the south, the bank is continuous, a metre or so high at its rear and perched back from what is visibly the front edge of a berm marked by a break in slope (Fig. 10.10). At the south-east corner of the modern Short Oak Copse, the bank is destroyed in two places by two major holloways. It has been completely removed by the more easterly, a deeply scored track which has ascended from the north as a holloway diagonally across the slope from Clatford Bottom. It continues southwards in a tunnel of trees as a 'sunken way' towards Clench Common.

Fig. 10.7 Wansdyke, a shallow, irregular ditch with a low bank on its left in this view looking west just before the earthwork plunges behind the camera into Clatford Bottom. This is a rare length in which a parish boundary runs along the ditch where it also served as a post-medieval park pale (the parish boundary status is modern).

Along the western side of that holloway runs Clatford Park pale which sweeps round from the south to use Wansdyke as its boundary, now also Fyfield parish boundary, all the way back to that impressive salient in Daffy Wood. For the whole of that length, the earthwork, more specifically its ditch, is co-incident with the parish boundary between Fyfield and Preshute Civil Parishes. This is not historically significant in this case in terms of ancient estates, for Fyfield's medieval boundary did not come as far south as Wansdyke.

185

Fig. 10.8 Wansdyke down the slope from Fig. 10.7, here viewed looking east as it briefly emerges from the woodland to cross Clatford Bottom where there may have been a gate. The apparently impressive bank is only c. 1m high above the ground behind it, and indeed the dimensions of the earthwork overall, here quite clear out in the open, are typical of the tree-obscured bank and ditch for much of the length eastwards. The breaks in the bank are not original; the parish boundary runs along the ditch, here also that of a park pale. Clatford Park Farm is to the right.

It was Clatford Park, a creation of Elizabethan times, that followed the earthwork as part of its northern boundary. When the Park was added to Fyfield parish in 1896, therefore, it was Wansdyke, alias the Park pale, which became part of the south-eastern boundary of the new civil parish.

2. The ditch

Wansdyke's ditch is always on the north; but the ditch is no more continuous through the woods than is the bank. In some places, it is now impossible to be certain visually whether the ditch existed but has been filled in, or whether it was never dug; but that is a matter that nowadays could easily and speedily be resolved geophysically. Here the reader can assume that, except at the points commented on, the ditch is present throughout, normally in these woods *c.* 6-7m in width and only a metre or so deep below the present land surfac surface outside it (Fox D.7, D.8).

Fig. 10.9 Wansdyke at the equivalent position to Fig. 10.8 but on the eastern side of Clatford Bottom climbing up and eastwards towards Short Oak Copse. There is no sign of a ditch here - it begins again slightly uphill in the bushes on the left - and the line of the bank, if it existed, is indicated only by a break in slope at the edge of a ploughed field.

In fact, it crosses Woden's Dene and approaches Shaw in its downland guise, some 3m and 5.25m below, respectively, the outer ground surface and the bank top (Fox D.6). In the woods, between gates iv and v, uphill of Edgar's gate the ditch becomes progressively shallower going up the slope, then narrows, then comes to a rounded end as a continuous feature, and then its line is continued first by a quarry pit and then by two contiguous pits

Fig. 10.10 A typical length and profile of Wansdyke viewed looking east as it continues to climb along the south side of Short Oak Copse. The two coppiced hazels on the slope into the ditch are actually on a slight break in slope where the bank ends and the ditch cut begins. The bank is scarcely 1m high at its rear, and the ditch, still the parish boundary, is only a little deeper in relation to the slight bank on its outer edge. This could be of Clatford Park pale rather than an original feature of Wansdyke.

(Fig. 10.4). Then it stops altogether, just short of the end of the bank, which has correspondingly decreased. On the east side of the break, the ditch recommences, stepped forward from its line to the west; but it is now once more different. Its original end may well have been obliterated, for dug into it is a deep pit with baked clay debris around its northern rim and signs of structure immediately north again. This is presumably the brick kiln of 'Brickkiln Copse'; two buildings are positioned here in 1889 (OS 6 inch map). Further east, however, the ditch continues to be larger that might be expected from the small size of the bank (above), and it contains further, clearly secondary, pits as it passes along the south side of much-pitted woodland (Fig. 10.6). Its line is again staggered either side of Titferth's gate (see below and Fig. 10.11B).

After a good run where it seems to have been completed, the ditch is then obliterated by modern works on a forest ride following a much older track ('*readdan* gate' below). Immediately east of the Fyfield parish boundary/park pale, the ditch becomes shallower, ending in two pits, apparently quarry-pits. There is no ditch at all for the 70m gap where the bank is missing. Thereafter, though mechanically infilled where crossed by a wide, forestry ride at one point, the ditch picks up its 'normal', woodland proportions as far as the salient in Daffy Copse; but thereafter to just above the floor of Clatford Bottom, it is unfinished (Fig. 10.7).

At the complex intersection of Wansdyke, tracks and parish boundary at the south-east corner of Short Oak Copse, the ditch comes up the slope from the west (Fig. 10.9) and firmly stops in an original, rounded end. Its restart is obliterated by a later, very large, deep quarry (see 'gateway x' below).

3. The gateways

Documentary evidence for four 'geats' through Wansdyke in the 10th century does not, of course, necessarily make them original, for the earthwork was by then 400 and more years old. Nevertheless, here we propose that they were original gateways. In addition, we bring into consideration six other breaks which might also have been original features of the woodland Wansdyke. The ten possible original gateways through Wansdyke on this stretch are (Fig. 10.1):

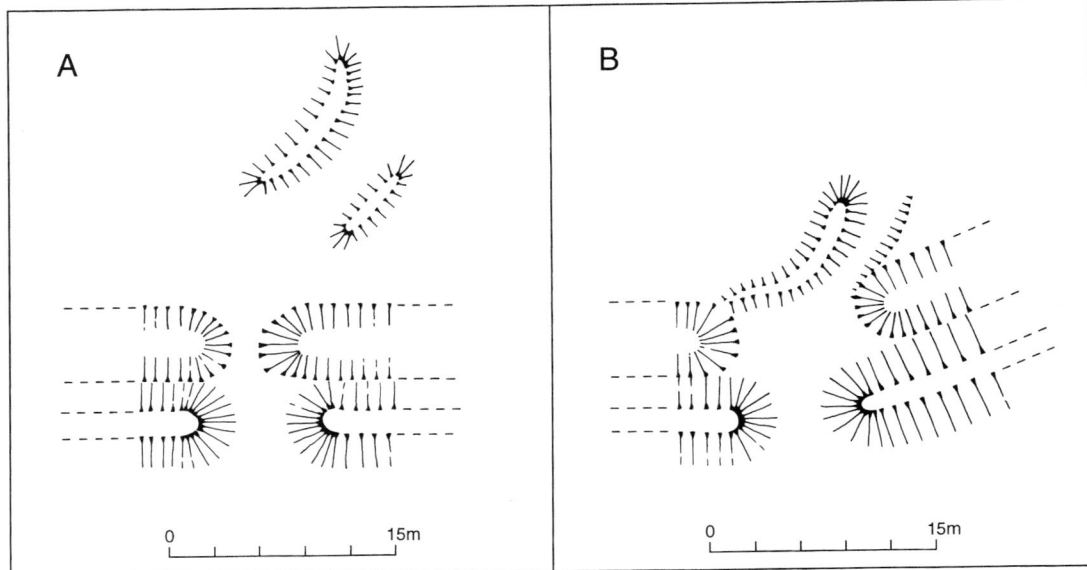

Fig. 10.11 Schematic plans from original field survey of two of the 'gates' through Wansdyke. A is Eadgardes gete *with outer earthworks apparently channeling access from the north on to a causeway narrowed by the end of the eastern ditch overlapping the end of the eastern bank;* B shows Titferthes geat *with a plan also incorporating outer earthworks and apparently attempting a similar effect but with a 'stagger' this time created by the eastern end of the bank overlapping the end of the ditch, cf. Fig. 10.4.*

i.   *Woddes geat*: a gate referred to in a spurious charter (S272, discussed by Fox and Fox 1958, 14, following Grundy, unaware of the charter's status) (SU 12746523)

ii.   Old Shaw on the way from Boreham to Huish (SU 13546534)

iii.   'Triangle gate', a name invented here, following a 1734 field name, for an otherwise unnamed possible break across a minor combe (SU 14236535)

iv.   *Eadgardes gete*: a 'charter gate' (AD 972, West Overton, S784) on the way from Hursley Bottom to Huish (SU 14766547; Fig. 10.11A)

v.   'Meux gate', a name invented here for a nameless break beside the 'HM' boundary stone on the track from Hursley Bottom to Heath Barn (SU 15076555; Fig. 10.4)

vi.   *Titferthes geat*: a 'charter gate' (AD 939, East Overton, S449) on the way from Hursley Bottom to Oare Hill and Martinsell hillfort (SU 15406568; Fig. 10.11B)

vii.   *'Readdan gate'*, a name invented here for a nameless break in the earthwork on the line of another old through-route, from Fyfield to Oare Hill, using a word from a descriptive phrase in the 9th-century Oare charter (S424; SU 15676604)

viii.   'Broadleat gate', a name invented here, taken from an adjacent block of woodland on the south, for an original, 70m gap in the earthwork (SU 15926629)

ix.   'Clatford Park gate', a name invented here for a possible, undocumented gate at the junction between Wansdyke and the track along Clatford Bottom from Clatford to Oare Hill and Martinsell hillfort (SU 165662)

x.   'Short Oak gate', an invented name to avoid making the assumption that this break, largely modern, is the site of the Oare charter's 'cripel' gate (S424), though the location is at least approximately correct, on the track through Wansdyke from Clatford Bottom to Clench Common and Martinsell hillfort (SU 16896642)

None of these are certainly original gateways; even if some are original, none are definitely built gateways, in the sense that there were such through Hadrian's Wall; and all may simply be gaps, original or otherwise. Four, however, provide primary field evidence of original structure, the criterion on which judgement is initially made in the following list.

i. *Woddes geat* occurs in a spurious charter but that does not alter the likelihood of there having been an original break in Wansdyke, gated or otherwise, at this junction between the Dyke and an ancient trackway along the bottom of Woden's Dene. There is no alternative location in the bottom or on the sides of the combe so we are happy to follow the Foxes (1958, fig. 28) even though no archaeological evidence is visible to help decide whether this break is original or not. The Foxes incline to suggest a late Saxon break had been made to accommodate the track (1958, 14); we are minded to suggest Wansdyke was built to control access along such a track (below) and would therefore expect the *geat* to be an original feature, perhaps with a built gateway. Probably original.

ii. The evidence on the ground at 'Old Shaw' on the way from Boreham to Huish is too confused to be useful. The case for an entrance here rests almost entirely on the judgement that the former north-south trackway passing through Wansdyke here was likely to have been in existence before Wansdyke was built (an idea elaborated in Fowler 1998). Existence unproven.

iii. 'Triangle gate' is merely a suggestion, based on the gap there today and the similarity on a smaller scale with the probable gates at Woden's Dene and Clatford Bottom (nos i and x). The bank and ditch come down into a small combe from the west, but no earthwork crosses the combe floor or starts up the slope to the east. Wansdyke is, however, shown as continuous here on the 1734 map. No ancient through-way up this combe is known, though a local track from Hursley Bottom is mapped. Dubious.

iv. *Eadgardes gete* is located reasonably securely by our reading of the West and East Overton charters (S784, S449), despite differing from the Foxes (1958, fig. 12) who were following Crawford (MS 6 inch map). The area of the *gete* is far more than a simple gap through the bank (Fig. 10.11A). The eastern ditch terminal projected across the entrance to narrow an original causeway to path-width, giving on to a way through between the bank terminals which was itself oblique and narrow (Fig. 10.2). In front, the slight remains of earthworks are now badly-damaged by farm traffic at a busy cross-tracks in the woods at a low point which collects water and is nearly always muddy. Two outworks are nevertheless discernible, with a suspicion that the outer and larger one continued obliquely across the entrance nearer, or actually to, the outer lip of the western ditch (that area is cut up by the east-west track *cf.* gate vi). The shorter, inner bank looks as if it was intended to funnel traffic obliquely into the 'gateway' from the north-east; the general effect anyway seems to have been to deflect to one side or both any direct approach up the track head-on to a gateway. The position is right at the head of a narrow combe, a natural line for a through-track which is again thought to be of considerable antiquity (the last centuries BC is suggested in Fowler 2000, chapter 16). That track continues southwards as one of the main through-routes to Pewsey Vale and beyond, initially as a fairly straight and apparently made-up road. Charter S449 refers to this length of track as *stanihtan weg*, 'stony way.' Markedly firm and dry even in wet weather, it is the southerly continuation of a through-track called 'ridgeway' high on northern Overton Down in the same charter (and so called the 'Overton Ridgeway' in Fowler 2000). The name, position, context and nature of this gap in Wansdyke make it almost certain that it is original and very probably a built gate of military character.

v.   The 'Meux gate' is only some 300m east and uphill of Edgar's gate, so another original proper gate here would seem unlikely; yet both bank and ditch coming up that slope diminish and then stop (Fig. 10.4). The existing track along the front of the dyke passes through that gap, continuing eastwards behind it. The bank and ditch east of the gap are stepped forward. In two important respects, then – the stepped and staggered relationships of bank and ditch on each of its sides, the plan of this gap (Fig. 10.4) resembles features of the two named gates to west and east (Fig. 10.11). The intended gate, with military characteristics in plan, was clearly unfinished.

vi.   *Titferth's geat*, another confident identification, is flanked by the two most impressive lengths of Wansdyke in the woods. Although damaged by modern usage, it is the best-preserved of the claimants to be an original gate. Its plan (Fig. 10.11B) shows its main characteristics: a change in Wansdyke's alignment; staggered and stepped earthwork terminals, with the ditch ends on both sides deliberately stopping short of the bank ends (or the bank ends deliberately overshooting the ditch ends on both sides); and a curved outwork, strongly indicating an intention to control passage coming from the north. No direct approach would have been possible and entrants would have been forced to pass through, in effect, on a path between the outwork and the end of the eastern ditch. The plan, and presumably the intention, were very similar to that at Edgar's gate (Fig. 10.11a); and indeed, one suspects that the plan at the latter, had it been better preserved, would have looked even more similar to that at Titferth's gate. And, as at Edgar's gate, these arrangements, interpreted as of an original, built military gate, were across an alternative track from Hursley Bottom on what was essentially the same, ancient through-route between the Marlborough Downs and the Vale of Pewsey. Almost certainly an original built gate.

vii.   '*Readdan gate*' is another intersection of Wansdyke and an ancient track, this time one from Fyfield past its animal pound and sheep-cote called *Attele* to *readdan sloh*, a point towards the south-east corner of the East Overton charter (S449). This track is another branch of the great north–south 'Ridgeway route' (Fowler 2000, fig. 16.4). The charter bounds in fact pass just to the west of this break, then run south-west along Wansdyke to Titferth's gate. It is the boundary of the Oare charter (S424) that may well have followed the track northwards from *readdan sloh* to our putative gate, turning at Wansdyke to the east or, expressed probably more correctly, then turning east along a line subsequently followed by Wansdyke. The 'gate' now looks like a completely modern flattening of the earthwork to facilitate recreational use of a bridleway. Merely a suggestion, but see below; unproven.

viii.   'Broadleat gate' is another suggestion only, occasioned by a genuine and apparently original 70m gap in Wansdyke. The dyke may merely have been left unfinished but it is conceivable that the gap was left deliberately for the insertion of a gateway which was never constructed. The point is not on any known track. Hypothetical, but see below.

ix.   'Clatford Park gate': no unequivocal evidence of a gate exists here but a break in the bank and ditch of Wansdyke seems to have occurred where it is intersected in Clatford Bottom by another ancient, north–south track. The track is now tarmacadamed. On its west, bank and ditch come right up to the road (Fig. 10.8), but on the east, where the ground starts rising immediately, there is no ditch and no clear sign of a bank for as much as 100m. Then its presence becomes apparent more as a lynchet than a free-standing bank (Fig. 10.9). The position and situation are very similar to those at *Woddes geat*, but no name exists here. Probable original gap but gate unproven.

x.   'Short Oak gate' at the south-east corner of the eponymous Copse is probably in the right location for the 'geat' referred to in the Oare charter (S424), but the area is markedly disfigured and the evidence for an actual gate slight. The two best pieces of evidence are that, here again, is an intersection between Wansdyke and another main branch of the north-south through-route and, secondly, the western ditch stops in a clearly-defined rounded terminal. There are no outworks. Probably an original break, possibly a built gate.

Interpretation

Construction

Our primary field evidence allows the following proposition as to how Wansdyke was built through the woods in five constructional stages (Fig. 10.12):

1.   The precise line of the bank was chosen using military criteria concerning topography, field of view especially overlooking and along combes, and the defensive qualities of the situation at intersections with combes and, above all, with existing tracks of the north–south Ridgeway through-route; and then marking out this line with a scarp dug into the topsoil indicating the line for the back of the bank (Fig. 10.12A).

2.   Material was scraped up from a line of separate, shallow scoops and dumped at the back of the intended bank, over the marking out line. The process was repeated, making small quarries along the line of what was to become the ditch while dumping material from them in heaps along the back of what was to become the bank (Fig. 10.12B).

3.   As the quarries enlarged, they joined up, at least near the ground surface, enabling the embryonic ditch to be deepened as a series of irregular pits producing the material for larger heaps which were also joining up (Fig. 10.12C).

4.   Penultimately the ditch-pits were joined up by knocking down the 'walls' between them and then by deepening the ditch to produce enough material for a continuous, if still somewhat humpy, bank (Fig. 10.12C).

5.   Finally, the ditch was finished off at its required depth as a continuous feature and its sides trimmed so that they were at the required angle; and the bank was smoothed off with a continuous slope into the ditch at the front and down to ground level at the rear. Whether a palisade was added to the bank top is unknown, for no excavation of Wansdyke in the woods has taken place. The existence of a palisade would help explain the inadequacy of Wansdyke's earthworks as a barrier even where it was completed in the woods (Fig. 10.12D).

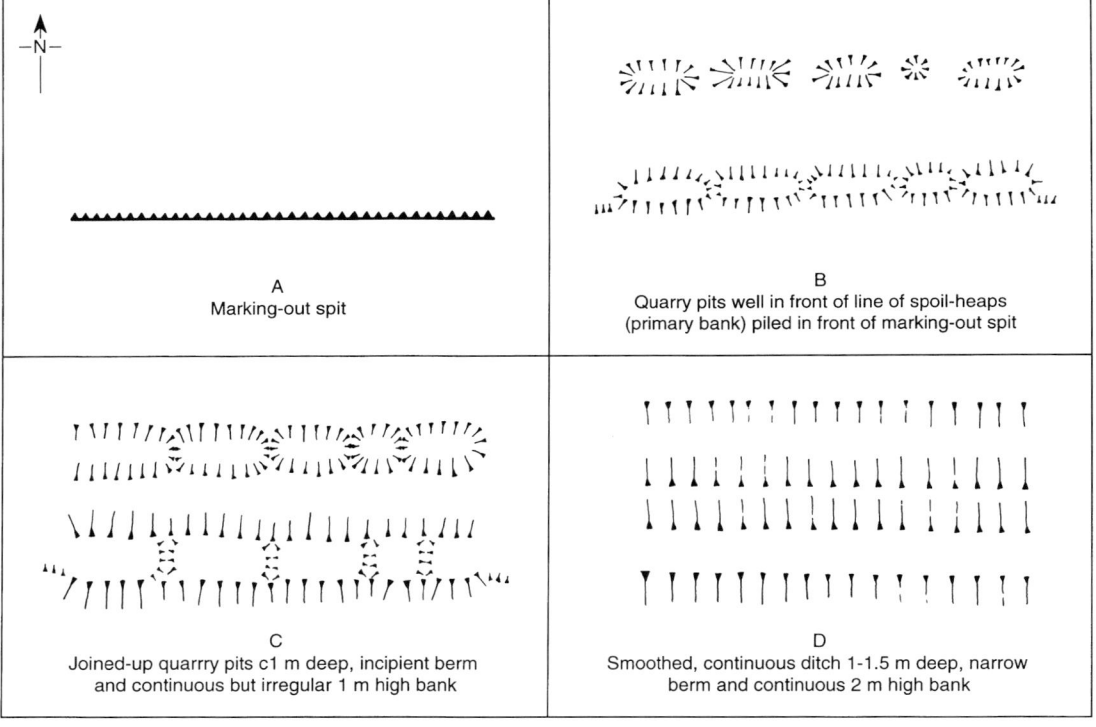

Fig. 10.12 Model of Wansdyke's construction in the Woods: four stages, all indicated by earthwork evidence: A at gate viii; B between gates vii and viii; C between gates iv and vi; D between gates i and ii and viii and x.

Such a sequence, independently inferred from newly-observed field evidence, is close to that proposed by Green (1971), based on his excavated evidence to both west and east of our length in the Woods. Little good evidence exists, however, from excavation or experiment to calculate accurately the sort of logistical input necessary to build Wansdyke in the woods as we have described it. Nevertheless, we have the original data from the Overton Down experimental earthwork study as modified by Atkinson and utilised by Renfrew and Startin (all references in Bell *et al.* 1995, 14.16). In addition, an engineer's estimate is available for the *vallum* behind Hadrian's Wall (Breeze and Dobson 1987, 81).

The imponderables are still too great for any certainty but the various approaches all point to an effort of the order of 20-30 days by 1000 men being required to build Wansdyke in the woods – had it been completed. The hint that the work could have been done in that sort of time, say between hay-making and cereal harvest or in September between harvest and ploughing, gives the wooded earthwork a human dimension while emphasising the scale of the undertaking across the downs.

Gateways

Ways through Wansdyke occurred at predetermined places, some of them with actual gates. As on Hadrian's Wall, for example, gates might have been built as free-standing structures, to which the earthwork later abutted (*cf.* Breeze and Dobson 1987, 46 in relation to Portgate; 70 in relation to milecastles and turrets). On Wansdyke, however, it is more likely that construction of the bank may have begun at the gates, with gangs of people working outwards from them in both directions as is strongly suggested at, and either side of, Titferth's gate; or gaps were left at pre-determined places during construction of the bank and ditch for the 'specialist gate-builders' to come along later and complete the work. The 'Broadleat gate' can be convincingly interpreted in this way, and to a lesser extent so too can the 'Meux gate'. Of course, various methods may have been used simultaneously in haste.

These 'pre-determined places' were at the earthwork's intersections with the pre-existing through-ways, all part of the bundle of tracks we have elsewhere argued to be the north–south transhumant 'Ridgeway route' (Fowler 2000, chapter 16; Fowler 1998). Such were sufficiently important to have needed accommodating by this new construction (rather as existing roads have to be accommodated with flyovers and underpasses when a modern by-pass is built). In general, we see all ten of our 'gates' as original gaps rather than later breaks, with some (nos. i, iv, v, vi, viii, ix?) also furnished with contemporary structures and possibly manned – or intended to be manned, – not just for defence but to control travellers, herdsmen and farmers on both sides of this new barrier. Functionally, an almost exact description of what we envisage of Wansdyke has already been written by others of another linear barrier 300 miles to the north: 'The purpose of the barrier was to control movement, not to prevent it, as the liberal provision of gateways demonstrates. Civilians, whether merchants, local farmers moving their cattle and sheep or simply local people visiting relatives on the other side of the Wall, would be allowed through the gateways ... movement on horseback, or in carts, or the driving of beasts, would only be possible through a controlled gateway' (Breeze and Dobson 1987, 40-41).

Conceivably, there is just the hint in the gateway arrangements on Wansdyke that a different, or double, set of intentions was in mind. Perhaps, as with Hadrian's Wall, a master-plan, or memories of the need for an overall design plan, were in existence, intending to place gates, especially deliberate military gates, at roughly fixed intervals as well as blocking and therefore controlling main, existing through-tracks. In fact, if such was in mind, it was not too difficult to meet both objectives.

It seems likely that the main through-ways within the Ridgeway route passed locally along Woden's Dene, through Hursley Bottom and up Clatford Bottom. That is, our study-length of Wansdyke forms a natural entity, with open downs to its west, Savernake Forest to its east, and woodland in between (Fig. 10.1). Overall, its length is 4.74km, that is 5184 yards, 2.95 miles or close to 3 Roman miles. Edgar's gate occurs roughly half way between the named gate in Woden's Dene and the probable gate in Clatford Bottom. Each of the lengths of Wansdyke respectively to west and east between it and the next major gate is then close to 1½ Roman miles, meaning that each length could be neatly subdivided into three lengths of half a Roman mile each. A unitary subdivision along such lines can in fact be perceived. In the eastern half of our length of Wansdyke, for example, it is half a Roman mile from Edgar's gate to Titferth's gate and then again to the possible 'Broadleat gate'. From there it is another half a Roman mile to the suggested gate in Clatford Bottom. This may be accidental; if not, questions have to be asked about the nature of Wansdyke.

All of the gates are across branches of the north-south Ridgeway route except for the 'Meux gate' and the 'Broadlet gate', both of which were unfinished and spaced out at the smallest unit of sub-division. They look as if they may have been inserted – or rather were intended to be inserted, – to meet some design requirement rather than a real need. One is reminded of the Poltross Burn milecastle, conventional in its spatial location according to the rules but actually in a locally ludicrous position topographically. The Wall of which it was a part, far to the north, may well have been in mind, in however imprecise a form, when Wansdyke was being conceived, designed and built: 'So many gates were provided that travellers had to walk no more than half a mile (0.8km) along the Wall to the nearest crossing point. But the gates were also provided to allow troops to move easily through the Wall to deal with an attack from the north ... the lavish provision of gates must have facilitated the maintenance of the wall and ditch ... there is a clear overprovision of gates ...' (Breeze and Dobson 1987, 40-41). On our wooded stretch of Wansdyke, with its similar 'lavish' provision of gates, the average distance between the principal gates, actual and intended but omitting 'designer gates' v and vii, is 0.73km (800 yards). The analogous gates on Hadrian's Wall were, of course, through the milecastles; the two turrets spaced between each milecastle at intervals of one third of a Roman mile (494m, 540 yards) were not gateways. Nevertheless, it is just possible that, however faintly, the Hadrianic pattern of milecastle > turret > turret > milecastle > turret > turret > milecastle may be echoed in the pattern of Wansdyke's gates through West Woods: main (*Woddes*) > minor > minor > main (Edgar's) > minor > minor > main (Clatford Bottom).

The three main gates provided the framework for a rough and ready metrical pattern of two gateways (which may well have looked like turrets if they were built with any sort of superstructure) within each 'half' of Wansdyke in the woods. In each half, one gateway was astride a probable 'ancient' through-track (Shaw and 'readdan') with the other ('Meux' and 'Broadleat') meeting a design requirement. Therein probably lies their incompleteness when work stopped: they were being left till last. The position of every one of the nine possible gates between *Woddes geat* and 'Clatford Bottom gate', including those two named ones at the ends, can be explained by the hypothesis that Wansdyke is based on Roman military thinking and design.

Purpose

Our interpretation overall is that the intention of Wansdyke in the woods was specifically to block the Ridgeway, but the Ridgeway as a route newly-developing in late Roman times. The concept is of a 5km-broad corridor stretching from Red Shore (which blocks the single track now alone called the Ridgeway) to Short Oak Copse containing a bundle of trackways which was increasingly being recognised as the main north-south route from Thames to Solent. Locally, these tracks offered a variety of ways for moving off the Marlborough Downs, across the Kennet valley and then down into the Vale of Pewsey and beyond. East of Red Shore, a big Wansdyke blocked the way but from Woden's Dene onwards a carefully contrived earthwork was, we propose, specifically designed to control those many ways by constructing gateways through it to which traffic was funnelled. Clearly it was not the intention to prevent ordinary traffic moving through; rather was Wansdyke designed to allow that to continue while being prepared for the arrival of less friendly visitors.

Indeed, taking a wider view and accepting the whole of East Wansdyke as a distinct and quite short length of bank and ditch 15 miles (24km) long centred on our study area (Yorke 1995, 26), we may have stumbled on the reason for its construction by looking at the gates. They were to allow normal, civilian passage within a linear zone of movement some 4km wide through a cross-country military barrier. That barrier was designed specifically to control movement along that broad route and, if necessary, to make the route itself defensible against hostile approaches along it from the north. The western and eastern 'wings' of Wansdyke either side of the central wooded length can readily be explained on this model as outreach portions intended to make access across the watershed from northern to southern Chalk even more difficult. They had the effect, should anyone try to gain entry to 'inner Wessex' by stepping off the Ridgeway route, of pushing would-be intruders off the Chalk altogether and away westwards into more wooded ground on the flanks of the Avon valley and eastwards into Savernake Forest.

That interpretation, of course, begs the larger question of why Wansdyke was built in the first place. People build such defining lines across the landscape for a number of reasons, rarely for a single one. Hadrian, we are told, did so '... to separate the Romans from the barbarians' (*Scriptores Historiae Augustae, Vita Hadriani*, 11, 2), but modern study suggests his reason was also very much to control movement, commercial as much as military, into and from the province (as with the Berlin Wall). Such lines could also have been built primarily for defence (as with the Maginot Line) but also as statements about power, image and perception of a legitimate frontier (as with the Great Wall of China). The actual building work itself might well have been started as a provocation to the opposition outside or possibly as a distraction inside to keep the local populace occupied and with a sense of something being done. Wansdyke's nearest analogue, Bokerly Dyke, seems to have been a late-Roman re-inforcement of an old boundary, military and defensive in one obvious and doubtless necessary sense at the time – blocking a Roman road – but also a re-drawing of a political frontier. It remains the county boundary between Hampshire and Dorset (Bowen 1991), whereas Wansdyke left no imprint in either woods or minds. That it was referred to Woden, meaning its namers clearly had no idea who built it or when or why, speaks volumes about the brevity of its career and local insignificance.

Overall, the field evidence clearly indicates that Wansdyke in the woods was incomplete at the time that work on it was abandoned. Was it again like Hadrian's Wall where 'Work was broken off so abruptly that sections of wall were left standing to a variety of heights ... (Breeze and Dobson 1987, 46)? Wansdyke would have looked like an earthen equivalent, rather like an unfinished, major pipeline where work had stopped over a Bank Holiday weekend, a raw and messy scar across the land. It is conceivable that the cessation of work on Wansdyke in the woods marks the passing of the emergency which created the need for it in the first place.

My suggestions arise independently and directly from new field observation but, more than half a century ago, Trelawney Dayrell Reed (1944, esp. chapter IV), working only from his desk and library, had arrived at exactly the same conclusion: 'Wansdyke and Bokerly Dyke are similar in construction and both are, of course, derived ultimately from the example of the Roman Wall' (*ibid.*, 150). Reed's highly plausible account inadvertently indicated that a direct link may lie in his version of Arthur's northern campaigns, along and on both sides of Hadrian's Wall (*ibid.*, 163-70). They could easily have provided the mechanism, were that necessary, to bring the requisite idea south in the 470-480s.

Date

According to Reed (*ibid.*, 154), however, Wansdyke was already built by then. He envisaged it as built *c.* 365 to mark an 'agreed boundary' negotiated under Ambrosius. His outside date-range is *c.* 365–515, with a preference for the shorter *c.* 365–390. At the other end of the chronological range, Reynolds (1999, 85) consciously flouts convention in proposing 'a Middle Anglo-Saxon context, as Wessex's equivalent to Offa's Dyke.' He correctly recognises both West and East Wansdykes as unfinished, but would explain both as the product of a hypothetical 'short-lived settlement between the West Saxons and the Mercians in the late eighth or early ninth century.' Were that so, presumably their ascription of their work to the pagan god Woden by the Christian West Saxon builders was some sort of joke. Can we suggest any more convincing historical circumstances in which such an intended major public work was unfinished? When, indeed, was Wansdyke built – and abandoned?

If our overall contention about Wansdyke's Roman inspiration is correct, then the later of commentators' two favourite dates is unlikely, i.e. around the mid-6th century (Myres 1964). So the often-mentioned earlier date in the late 5th century would seem preferable; and that could supply circumstances for a great construction effort and sudden abandonment. Another factor tilting the balance to this context is the clear evidence now from Somerset of renewed defence and gateway building at the Cadbury hill-forts. Indeed, at the one near Congresbury (Rahtz *et al.* 1992), one plausible interpretation has long been that the building occurred in response to the Saxon threat in the late 5th century, only to be disregarded in the decades after the decisive battle of Badon when, as Gildas relates, a generation of peace (and luxury and decadence) followed. We suggest that East Wansdyke, and specifically the length in the woods, was being hastily constructed in the 490s with Roman precedents in mind against what was feared to be an imminent invasion of Saxons from the Thames valley. Such an invasion would have had to come down the line of the Ridgeway route to enter the heartlands of the still Romanised Chalk country. A battle which proved to be decisive in that it halted the Saxons for a couple of generations took place, however, somewhere north of Wansdyke – perhaps Liddington Castle above Badbury village, perhaps outside Bath, perhaps elsewhere. The exact location does not matter for present purposes, though Liddington, only some 15km (9 miles) to the north-north-east, would fit neatly – close enough to be alarming, close enough to suck in most of the local, able male population, and close enough to hear quickly of the repulse of the invaders. Reed (1944) joins me in liking Badon at Liddington Hill. Wherever the encounter, its decisiveness was recognised immediately, as it was by all later writers. In this interpretation, then we see the duration of Wansdyke in the Woods as a matter of months in the mid-490s, say over 1-2 years at the most during construction, immediately before and only to within hours after the battle of Badon. Plausibly, Wansdyke became recognisably redundant that day. Dare we even imagine the British builders of Wansdyke at that moment, women, children and old men, downing tools, giving a resounding cheer, and walking off site away through the woods?

That romantic touch will not please the purist; but more serious is the objection that local knowledge in the late 5th-century Upper Kennet/Pewsey Vale area could not possibly embrace information about Roman-style defences, let alone the specifics of Hadrian's Wall. Yet current work is continually indicating the degree of Romanisation present in the 5th century in the locality (e.g. Corney 1997), and the Rudge cup, with its names of Wall forts, was found not a thousand miles away. In truth, however, the new field evidence does not require proof that a late Roman knowledge of military matters existed in central Wiltshire in the later 5th century. The evidence on the ground can stand without that, for it unambiguously indicates that Wansdyke in the woods was to an extent military yet was structurally not completed.

Bede, writing in the 720s and quoting a somewhat muddled Gildas, recounts how the Emperor 'decided to separate that portion of the island under his control from the remaining unconquered peoples, and he did this not with a wall, as some imagine, but with an earthwork. For a wall is built of stone, but an earthwork ... is constructed with sods cut from the earth and raised high above ground level, fronted by the ditch from which the sods were cut, and surmounted by a strong palisade of logs. [He] built a rampart and ditch of this type from sea to sea, and fortified it by a series of towers.' (Sherley-Price 1955, 1.5). If the 'series of towers' is envisaged as gate towers, these words, about something nearly four hundred years older than Wansdyke, written only about a generation after Wansdyke, and accurately quoted two hundred years after Wansdyke, could be a description of Wansdyke as we have found and interpreted it in the woods. There, at least, it is an earthwork firmly in the Roman tradition in thought, word and deed, built by Britons and nothing to do with Saxons who failed even to arrive for its opening.

Acknowledgements

Many people have quietly contributed to the infrastructure on which this essay has been created. Specific and critical help has been enjoyably forthcoming from Ian Blackwell, notably on Saxon charters and their bounds in the field, and from Gill Swanton and Mark Corney in fieldwork and survey, including being such elegant photographic scales. The author alone, however, is responsible for the argument and the suggestions.

References

Bell, M., Fowler, P. J., and Hillson, S., (eds.) 1995, *The Experimental Earthwork on Overton Down, Wiltshire, 1960-1992*, CBA Res Rep, 100, York

Bonney, D. J.,1966, 'Pagan Saxon burials and boundaries in Wiltshire', *WANHM*, 61, 25-30

_____ , 1972 'Early boundaries in Wessex', in P. Fowler (ed.) *Archaeology and the Landscape*, London, 168-86 (East Wansdyke, 174-76, fig. 19)

Bowen, H. C., 1991, *The Archaeology of Bokerley Dyke*, RCHME, Swindon

Breeze, D. J., and Dobson, B., 1987, *Hadrian's Wall*, 3rd edn, Harmondsworth

Clark, A. J., 1958, 'The nature of Wansdyke', *Antiquity*, 32, 89-96

Corney, M., 1997, 'The origins and development of the 'small town' of *Cunetio*, Mildenhall, Wiltshire', *Britannia*, 28, 337-50

Crawford, O. G. S., 1953, *Archaeology in the Field*, London

Fowler, P., 1998, 'Moving through the landscape', in T. Williamson and P. Evison (eds), *The Archaeology of Landscape*, Manchester, 25-41

_____ , 2000, *Landscape Plotted and Pieced. Landscape History and Local Archaeology in Fyfield and West Overton, Wiltshire*, Soc Ant Res Rep, 64, London

Fowler, P., and Blackwell, I., 1998, *The Land of Lettice Sweetapple. An English Countryside Explored*, Stroud

Fox, A., and Fox, C., 1958, 'Wansdyke reconsidered', *Archaeol Journ*, 115, 1-48

Green, H. S., 1971, 'Wansdyke, excavations 1966 to 1970', *WANHM*, 66, 129-46

Hoare, R. C., 1821, *The Ancient History of Wiltshire, Vol. II, The Roman Aera*, London

Major, A. F., and Burrows, E. J., 1926, *The Mystery of Wansdyke. Being the Record of Research and Investigation in the Field*, Cheltenham

Myres, J. N. L., 1964, 'Wansdyke and the origins of Wessex', in H. Trevor-Roper (ed.), *Essays in British History*, London, 1-27

Pitt-Rivers, A. H. L. F., 1892, *Excavations in Cranborne Chase III: Bokerly and Wansdyke*, privately printed

Rahtz, P. A., *et al.*, 1992, *Cadbury Congresbury 1968-73. A Late/Post-Roman Hilltop Settlement in Somerset*, BAR Brit Ser, 223, Oxford

Reed, T. D., 1944, *The Battle for Britain in the Fifth Century. An Essay in Dark Age History*, London

Reynolds, A., 1999, *Later Anglo-Saxon England. Life and Landscape*, Stroud

S = Sawyer, P. H., 1968, *Anglo-Saxon Charters: an Annotated List and Bibliography*, London

Sherley-Price, L., 1955, *Bede. A History of the English Church and People*, Harmondsworth

Yorke, B., 1995, *Wessex in the Early Middle Ages*, London

11 ANGLO-SAXON PRESENCE AND CULTURE IN WILTSHIRE *c*. AD 450 – *c*. 675

by Bruce Eagles

Summary

It is suggested that the initial Germanic immigration may have taken place within the framework of the former Romano-British *civitates*. The north-west and west, and possibly the north-east corner, and the extreme south-west of the county appear to have remained in British hands until the 7th century when Saxon conquest was finally completed. The major theme of the paper is the emergence and growth of a Saxon identity in the county. Archaeological information is derived almost entirely from burials and stray artifacts. Excavated settlements are few and knowledge of the location of habitations is enhanced only by the occasional scatter of potsherds, supplemented, in a more general way, by place-names. The Anglo-Saxon Chronicle, personal names in literary sources, the laws of Ine, and place-names afford other and important evidence of contact and intermingling between the indigenous population and immigrants in Wiltshire.

The wider background

British warlords and Saxon mercenaries

After the Roman withdrawal Gildas tells us that the British were soon divided, their leaders warlords (*tyranni*) involved in civil wars (Winterbottom 1978, cc. 19, 21; Dumville 1995, 179-81). It is at least possible that some of these warlords ruled territories based on the *civitates*, for among those denounced by Gildas himself (c. 28), in a later context, is Constantine, king of Dumnonia; and it had been to the leaders of the *civitates* that Honorius had addressed his famous rescript of AD 410 that the Britons must henceforth look to their own defence (Paschoud 1989, n. 133, 57-60). However, it should be noted that the extent to which the *civitas* may have provided an identity for any individual or group at this time is unknown. The fate of the towns is discussed by Wacher (1995, 408).

It is also possible that such British warlords soon employed some Saxon mercenaries (who came with their families), although Gildas (c. 23) refers to the Saxons only in the context of *foederati* defending the east coast against the Picts. Their employment elsewhere, however, may be suggested by the occurrence of inhumation burials and Germanic brooches, of the middle third of the 5th century, from a number of inland sites, including Dorchester-on-Thames (Hawkes 1986, 68; Welch 1999, 34) and Hod Hill hillfort in central Dorset (Eagles and Mortimer 1993). *'Multo tempore'*, Gildas says (c. 23), the Saxons rose in revolt and a contemporary Gallic Chronicle tells us that 'Britain' – whatever the chronicler meant by that – passed under the control of the Saxons (*in dicionem Saxonum*) in *c.* AD 441/2 (Muhlberger 1983; Wood 1998, 519).

The introduction into Britain of a new material culture and its impact

BACKGROUND

Novel styles of burial and types of buildings and artifacts, derived from the eastern, continental, littoral of the North Sea and from northern Gaul, become increasingly common in much of eastern and southern England from *c.* AD 475, that is, one or two generations after the arrival of the first immigrants. However, the degree to which this archaeological evidence is directly related to immigration from the continent or how far it marks the adoption of Germanic culture by the Britons, is the subject of considerable ongoing debate (Higham 1992, 8; Gelling 1993, 51; Scull 1993, 70); and there are problems in interpreting ethnicity from material culture (Jones 1997). The continuing arrival of newcomers from overseas is often difficult to demonstrate; an example is the prolonged contact between Issendorf in Lower Saxony and Spong Hill in Norfolk (Hills 1998, 148). In the 6th century a wide range of artifacts show strong insular development (Hawkes 1986, 81). Better farming conditions in England compared with those prevailing in north-west Europe, may also have been an incentive for migration (Zimmermann 1999).

SETTLEMENTS

The traditional north-west European aisled longhouse was not imported into England. However, by the mid 5th century this type of building was already obsolescent on the continent, being replaced by more modest 'farmhouses' (though little is known of their function) which do share many similarities with the structures found in this country. It has also been pointed out that the longhouse may well have been unsuited to the more restricted social groups which settlements in England appear to represent. Romano-British influence remains unclear, not least because of the very limited information available about late Roman wooden buildings. *Grubenhäuser*, small sunken-featured buildings, with a long history on the continent, now first appear, alongside the farmhouses, widely and immediately, throughout southern and eastern England. Some of these small buildings were craft workshops, others may have been used for storage (Hamerow 1997; 1999; Zimmermann 1999). Their apparent absence in areas to the west of Wiltshire, which did not come under Anglo-Saxon control until the 7th century and which display only very limited signs of 'Anglo-Saxon' cultural influence before that date, suggests that the new buildings went hand-in-hand with the novel burial rites. Posthole patterns found at, for instance, Poundbury,

Dorset (Sparey-Green 1996) and at Cadbury-Congresbury hillfort, Somerset (Rahtz *et al.* 1992, 193), point to sizeable, but apparently rather irregular, timber buildings. Furthermore, some small structures at Poundbury described as sunken-featured are in fact terraced into the slope and do not seem directly comparable to those in 'Anglo-Saxon' areas, although, it may be noted, the partially excavated building at Coombe Down (see below) seems similar as does evidence from Crickley Hill hillfort, Gloucestershire (Dixon 1988). The frequent new siting of settlements, many of which were probably small and may have accommodated family groups, is not necessarily significant, as relatively frequent shifts of site, within a generally dispersed pattern of settlement, is well known in the early Anglo-Saxon period.

Assemblages of artifacts from most settlements of this period are generally very limited, but often include handmade organic-tempered pottery, whether or not the sites lie within or without areas of 'Anglo-Saxon' influence. Where such pottery is the only evidence for post-Roman occupation in regions which otherwise exhibit clear signs of 'Anglo-Saxon' culture, it presumably either pre-dates the beginning of Saxon influence or, for some reason, 'Anglo-Saxon' products were not locally available (Eagles 1994, 18; Evans 1990).

BURIAL RITES

The suggestion has been put forward that the distinctive 'Anglo-Saxon' burial rites and dress, evidence for which derives chiefly from the disposition of artifacts within the grave, were being increasingly adopted by the British population (Dickinson 1982, 52; Scull 1992, 14). Ucko (1969) has demonstrated that burial rites are not necessarily conservative, and may even change very rapidly. The native inhabitants outside Kent, it is reasonably argued, were absorbed into, or indeed transformed by, a new, promoted, 'Saxon' or 'Anglian' identity in, respectively, southern and northern England (Dickinson 1991; 1993; Hines 1994, 52-4; Hamerow 1997). It may also be noted that imitation of the fearsome Saxons had occurred on the continent before their arrival in England; thus the early 5th-century equal-armed brooch from Hod Hill, Dorset, is a copy of a Saxon type, paralleled in Holland (Eagles and Mortimer 1993; Böhme 1999, 67). The homogeneity of cemeteries both in England and on the nearer parts of the continent, in terms of their general layout, the presence of both accompanied and unaccompanied burials (caution should be exercised in respect of the latter, in so far as artifacts of organic origin may have decayed without trace), the range of grave-goods, grave orientation, body posture and position, is striking. The emphasis in all of these burial grounds appears to be on the family or household, which in England could have included Britons (Crawford 1997; Härke 1995, 70). 'Created kinship', especially through the marriage of Anglo-Saxon men to British women is also a possibility (Charles-Edwards 1997). Burial practice therefore appears to mirror the small farmsteads noted above. If the wishes and custom of the kin were paramount, variation of rite is likely to have been both local and subtle, differing within as well as between cemeteries (Lucy 1998; Stoodley 1999, with particular reference to Wiltshire). Burial display may be especially evident at times of social stress, being used as a means of underlining a new legitimacy (Hedeager 1993, 128; Halsall 1995a, 43).

The long established and general practice in the countryside and the small towns of late Roman Britain was of unaccompanied inhumation burial on family plots. The unfurnished graves in the new cemeteries, and some others, for example those where the body is accompanied solely by a knife, cannot of themselves be differentiated from such burials (Philpott 1991, 126, 176). However, the 'Anglo-Saxon' cemeteries afford no evidence of particularly distinctive Romano-British burial rites, such as that with hob-nailed footwear, which is known to have been widespread in Wessex in the 4th century, although the date of its disuse is by no means clear (*ibid.*, 167). There may have been later burials in the cemetery at Wasperton, Warks, but the excavation there awaits full publication and the chronology of the site remains uncertain (Esmonde Cleary 1989, 201). This raises the possibility that native customs may have continued after the arrival of the Saxons and alongside the new-style largely furnished cemeteries.

Another, important, aspect of 'Anglo-Saxon' cemeteries, which are generally in new locations, is their frequent occurrence near prehistoric barrows. Indeed, such a position appears to have been deliberately selected in order to provide a focus for the new burials. The same phenomenon is known in north Germany (Thäte 1996). Furthermore, Anglo-Saxon style, accompanied inhumations are often found inserted into the barrows themselves. Although intrusive interments are also known in the Romano-British period, they are infrequent and may have been associated with cults of the dead (Williams 1998a, 76). It has been argued that the incoming Saxons deliberately chose to bury their deceased in this way as another means by which they could emphasise their newly acquired authority through links with a mythical past. The practice could then have been copied by some of the local population who had become identified with the new culture (Bradley 1987; Lucy 1992; Williams 1997; 1998b). In that way, the rite may have become another element in the development of a 'Saxon identity'. Barrows were also reused for high status burials in the 7th century (see below).

The adoption of Old English by the Britons

The paucity of Brittonic words which were borrowed into Old English demonstrates that the Britons consciously learned the language of the dominant Anglo-Saxons, who for their part clearly made little attempt to adopt the native tongue (Jackson 1953, 241). However, the process appears to have been long drawn out; in the early 8th century Bede considered it appropriate to give both English and British versions of some place-names. The thoroughness of the change in language mirrors the fundamental, in a sense almost aggressive, material cultural transformation which occurred from the later 5th century. Although the suggestion has been made that the scale of the adoption of the English language could have come about only as a result of the local presence of significant numbers of immigrant peasant farmers (Gelling 1993, 51), it has proved as difficult to explain the changes in language as those in the archaeology; either can be seen as an aspect of culture and thus equally subject to manipulation (Hines 1996a). The church may have played an important part in spreading the use of Old English (R. Coates, pers. comm.; Bazelmans 1999, 72). It has been pointed out that the language of the Britons had been of lower status than Latin throughout the period of the Empire, and its inferiority, now as the language of the defeated enemy, was maintained, but in relation to English (Charles-Edwards 1995, 729; Hines 1998, 286). Indeed, there is doubt about the extent to which, if at all, Latin borrowings into Old English occurred after the Anglo-Saxons had arrived in Britain (Wollman 1993). It seems that it is the role played by different languages, in an essentially oral world in which bilingualism was commonplace (Geary 1983, 20), especially amongst the elite, which should be the emphasis of further research.

Ethnicity

A number of recent studies have emphasised the shifting and subjective definition of so-called ethnic groupings in the ancient world, with particular reference to the barbarians who entered the late Roman empire. It can no longer be argued that the groups of people (*gentes*) who went by, for example, the name of Goths, Franks, Burgundians or Saxons were genetically related. The group names reflected the reality of new power and represent, essentially, a political ethnicity, manipulated by the elite, and were to that extent artificial. Indeed it seems clear that these groups could include Roman citizens, and in large numbers. In Gothic Italy, for instance, the terminology appears to have been applied to the army of Theoderic, which was very mixed and included Romans; on the other hand, non-combatants, of whatever origin or social group were termed 'Romans' (Amory 1997 *contra* Heather 1996, 299). The Burgundians seem to have been similarly distinguished (Amory 1993; 1994), as do the Franks (Halsall 1995b, 28). There are hints of a similar differentiation in England. A number of clauses in the Laws of Ine of Wessex (Wormald 1995, 977), which date to AD 688-694, make reference to the Britons (*wealas*) (Faull 1975). The criteria used to distinguish and, within the kingdom, to define a 'Briton' are by no means certain. However, the lawcode deals with individuals according to their status; Britons could be of some means, though they were always of inferior rank to their English counterparts. A straightforward ethnic distinction seems unlikely and, in the light of continental usage, it may be significant that in Ine's laws a *wilisc* was a tribute payer but that a *ceorl* of comparable status owed military service to the king (Barnwell forthcoming).

The new leaders sought to establish and consolidate their authority by reference to, even the creation of, Germanic origin myths which were intertwined with others from classical sources; the latter marked their acceptance into the western Roman world. Their claimed descent from mythical figures of the distant past could only be maintained through success, as showing divine approval (Wolfram 1994, 21). The ancient texts, as always, tell us only of the upper echelons of society. Individuals could hold more than one ethnicity at any one time, and use it to their own advantage (Halsall 1999, 140). Loyalty to a personal lord was normally of greater importance for the individual. This was particularly true of the personal following (*comitatus*) of a warlord, which cut across the demands of kin (Abels 1988, 16). Territorial dimensions of ethnicity, whereby not just people but their land too were subject to rule, were developing on the continent from the 6th century (Geary 1983, 23) but, it has been suggested, only from the 7th century in England (Kleinschmidt 1998, 84).

It is clear that the barbarian leaders and folk coming into Britain in the 5th century were of very diverse origin. Bede (*HE*: Colgrave and Mynors 1969, i.15 and v.9) says that there were Jutes, Saxons and Angles, the latter two tracing their ancestry amongst the continental Frisians, Rugians, Danes, Huns and Bructeri, peoples who lived in Germany and were therefore known collectively to the Britons as 'Garmani'. Bede's list is discussed by Wallace-Hadrill (1988, 22, 181). Archaeology shows that others, not necessarily Germans at all, arrived from the frontier region of northern Gaul (Evison 1965; Böhme 1986). In addition, any such groups are likely to have become mixed both during the crossings and after reaching Britain.

The literary traditions of the Anglo-Saxon conquest of Wiltshire in the 5th and 6th centuries

Introduction

The Anglo-Saxon Chronicle (Whitelock *et al*. 1961), which was compiled *c*. AD 890, purports to record the conquest of Wessex by the Woden-born Cerdicings, although descent from Woden may have been introduced only by Ine, AD 688-726 (Kleinschmidt 1998, 94). It therefore offers an origin myth for the foundation of the kingdom and claims to provide some very limited historical information for the 6th century. However, it has been shown that the material it contains was manipulated to suit the needs of Alfred's propaganda and the value of the entries before the 7th century is very uncertain, not least because only minimal independent checks can be made against them. Some entries may well have been influenced by the particular interests of some religious houses (Dumville 1985; Nelson 1991; Yorke 1993; 1995, 53).

The genealogies of the West Saxon kings which the Chronicle cites include several names – Cerdic, Ceawlin and Caedwalla – which are of British origin, and another, Cenwalh, the *-wahl* element of whose English name refers to a Briton (Hawkes 1986, 76; Coates 1989-90; Yorke 1990, 138; Parsons 1997). These names may represent English name borrowing from the Britons, or they may reflect either intermarriage with the Britons at the highest social level or the incorporation of some notable British leaders into the 'English' tradition. British names also occur in the genealogies of other kingdoms; they were not always those of members of local families but their recurrence in Wessex perhaps makes this more likely. Such dynastic marriages would have been one means by which new territories were brought under English control. However, Cerdic is said to have arrived from overseas, and was perhaps a returning emigré who had prospered in Gaul (Campbell 1982, 37).

The Wiltshire Avon near Salisbury

Annals in the Anglo-Saxon Chronicle recount the conquest by Cerdic and his son Cynric of the Avon valley and the Salisbury area, which was said to have been ultimately achieved following a victory at Charford in AD 519. The 6th-century dates given in the Chronicle are unreliable; as an example, Cerdic's reign has been recalculated as AD 538-554 (Dumville

1985, 51). Under the entry for AD 527, the Chronicle records that Cerdic and Cynric fought the British at *Cerdicesleag*, which is unknown; it also says Cerdic died in AD 534; and that Cynric defeated the Britons at Old Sarum in AD 552. Charford, 'Cerdic's ford', on the River Avon some 12km to the south of Old Sarum and on the Hampshire side of the present county boundary with Wiltshire, may once have lain at the northern limit of the territory of the Jutes in south Hampshire where, perhaps, it met the lands of the *Wilsaete*, the 'dwellers by the Wylye', recorded in the Chronicle s.a. 800 and 878. *Cerdices beorg*, the only other seemingly identifiable name – of a barrow – associated with Cerdic, is sited at the junction of the boundaries of the parishes of Andover, St Mary Bourne and Hurstbourne Priors in Hampshire (Yorke 1989, 91).

Central and northern Wiltshire

Under the annal for AD 556, the Anglo-Saxon Chronicle introduces Ceawlin and records that in that year he and Cynric fought alongside each other against the British at *Beranbyrg*, identified as Barbury, a hillfort on the Ridgeway 11km to the north of the Wansdyke. None of the events of Ceawlin's remarkable career – he is the only king of the Gewisse to appear in Bede's list of great overlords (HE, ii.5) – takes place south of Wansdyke. Bede (*HE*, iii.7) says that the West Saxons were formerly known as the Gewisse; Walker (1956, 183) and Yorke (1989, 92) suggest the change occurred under Caedwalla, AD 685/6-688, but Kleinschmidt (1998, 97) argues that the name Gewisse may not have been of long standing and furthermore may have been pertinent to only one branch of the West Saxon royal house, that of Ine. However, for the sake of convenience, the name is retained here in a general sense for the period from Cerdic to Caedwalla. Ceawlin's fighting alongside Cynric has been taken to indicate joint action for the first time by Anglo-Saxon kingdoms based on the Thames and in southern Wessex (Hawkes 1986, 86). Sims-Williams (1983, 28), however, points out that the sources do not present Ceawlin other than as a Cerdicing. The boundary between these kingdoms was marked, it may be suggested, militarily by Wansdyke (see below). The events reported for AD 556 may also define a decisive point towards the ultimate achievement of a single Wessex kingdom. There is no further mention of Cynric. In AD 560 the Chronicle states that Ceawlin succeeded to the 'kingdom of Wessex'; he fights alongside members of his own family, which may indicate that one or more of them was put in charge of areas to the south on his behalf. The result of the great battle at *Wodnesbeorg* in AD 592 was that Ceawlin 'was driven out'. *Wodnesbeorg* is the long barrow called 'Adam's Grave', which lies only 1.5km south of the point, at Red Shore, Alton Priors, where the Ridgeway passes through an original gap identified in the East Wansdyke (Green 1971). The Chronicle entry, which does not specify the combatants, has always been difficult to understand but the battle may have been fought between Ceawlin and 'Saxons' south of Wansdyke who now regained their independence (Eagles 1994, 27). If this interpretation is correct, the absorption of southern Wiltshire by the Gewisse occurred at some time after this event. However, as has been noticed, it is unclear how far rulership was yet seen in territorial terms and Cerdic and his early successors may have been leaders of a group or groups of 'Gewisse' and no more (but see also above). The distinct geographical locations evident in different sections of the Chronicle are notable and could relate to the traditions of once independent petty dynasts (Kirby 1991, 55). Whenever the absorption of southern Wiltshire did take place, the process of integration had presumably been accomplished by the time of the attack by Caedwalla (AD 685/6-688) on the Isle of Wight, when the mainland territory of the Jutes seems to have been in Gewissan hands (Yorke 1989, 92, with reference to Bede, HE, iv.16).

The appearance and spread of a new material culture in Wiltshire in the late 5th and 6th centuries (Fig 11.1)

The area around Old Sarum

To the east of Old Sarum, the burial ground at Winterbourne Gunner was in use in the 5th century (see below). The location of the associated settlement may be indicated by a few handmade organic-tempered sherds, which were found in limited excavation of the later settlement earthworks by the church of St Mary, only some 400m to the north of the burials (*WANHM*, 61, 108; finds in the Salisbury and South Wiltshire Museum). South of Old Sarum, a new cemetery, with furnished and some unfurnished burials (possibly two adjacent cemeteries, one with west–east, the other with south–north inhumations of the 5th century), was established at Petersfinger, east of the confluence of the Avon and the Bourne (Evison 1965, 38; Eagles 1994, 15). In 1860, in a gravel pit some 0.8km to the west, Dr Blackmore recovered Mesolithic flints, animal bones, charcoal and, again, organic-tempered pottery (Moore and Algar 1968). The latter included a distinctive, and well-known, type of plain 'Anglo-Saxon' pot with three small, pierced, lugs (Eagles 1979 (i), 85). No Roman wares were found, and this suggests a new settlement location. A third cemetery is known at Harnham (Evison 1965, 38; Eagles 1994, 15). A further such burial ground is known to the south, at Charlton, by the Avon (Davies 1984). Burial continued in all of these cemeteries in the 6th century. No 5th-century graves are known at Kelsey Road, St Edmunds Church and at East Harnham, all now within the limits of Salisbury (references to 'Anglo-Saxon' burial sites, unless specifically stated otherwise, will be found in Meaney 1964). Recent finds from metal-detecting suggest another 5th-century site in the Avon valley at Breamore in Hampshire just to the south of the county boundary (C. Gifford *et al.*, pers. comm.).

The Wiltshire Avon and its tributaries

In the chalklands of south Wiltshire, many burial sites occur in, or immediately overlook, the river valleys. Two of the major rivers, the Avon and the Wylye, retained their British names, as did the Nadder (references to British and English place-names are to Gover, Mawer and Stenton 1939 unless specifically stated otherwise). By the Avon, Walton (in Downton parish) may refer to the Britons (Fig. 11.2; Gelling 1997, 94). There are a host of new 6th-century sites and findspots. Recent finds here and elsewhere or records of them in the county are, unless noted otherwise, either in the collections of the Salisbury and South Wiltshire Museum (hereafter SM) or the Wiltshire Heritage Museum, Devizes

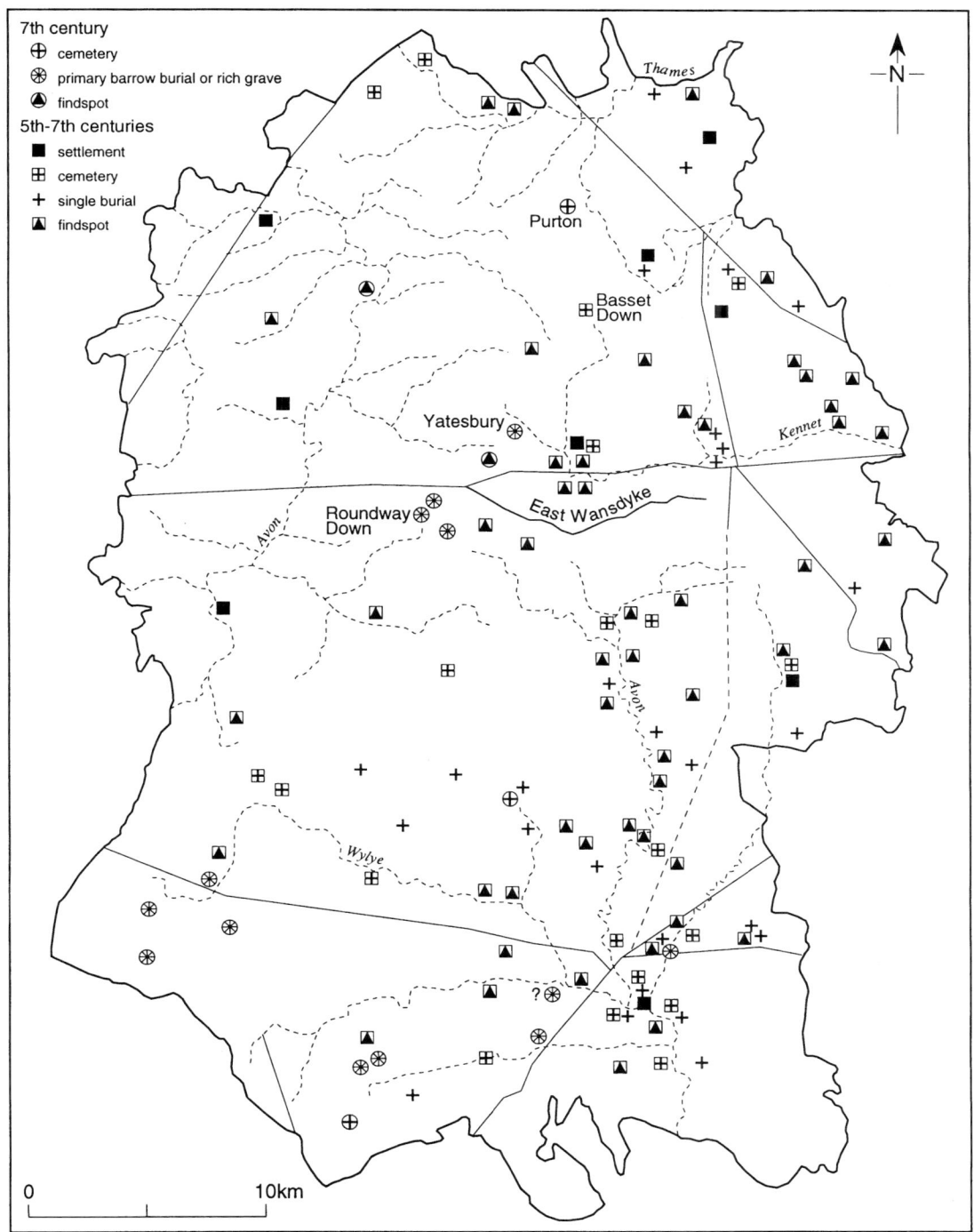

Fig. 11.1 'Anglo-Saxon' and other sites of the 5th to 7th centuries

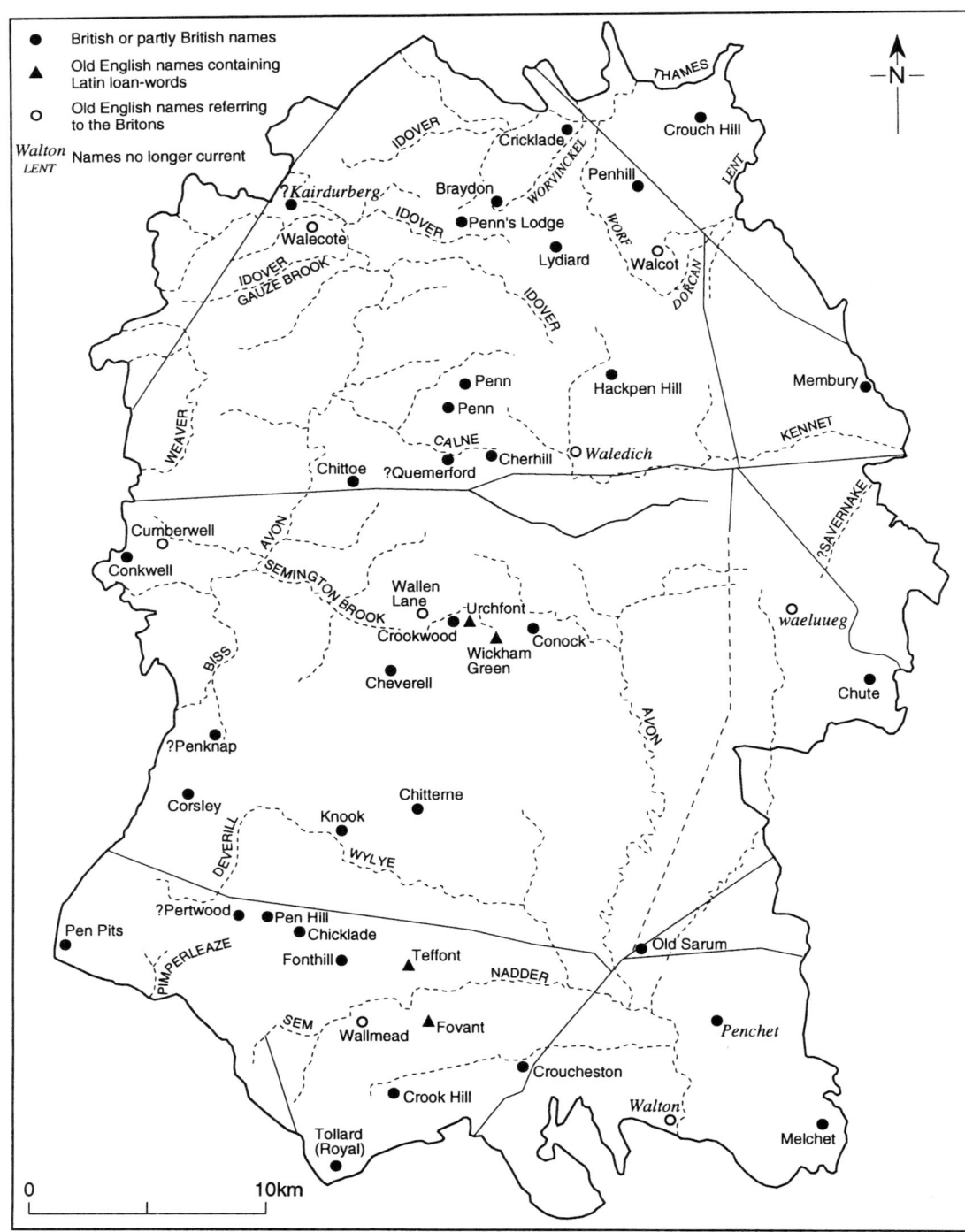

Fig. 11.2 British and related place names

(hereafter WHM). Particular attention may be drawn to a burial of high status, with sword, shield and spear, from below Witherington Ring, Alderbury. Several sites are recorded in Amesbury parish. Button brooches have been found in Upavon village and nearby at Widdington. The cemetery at Blacknall Field (known locally as Black Patch), Pewsey, lies on the Lower Chalk, on the south side of the upper Avon and on the southern slopes of Pewsey Vale. Excavations by Ken Annable between 1969 and 1976 uncovered 102 inhumations and three cremations (interim reports in *WANHM*; K. Annable, pers. comm.); the cemetery at Winterbourne Gunner is the only other early 'Anglo-Saxon' cemetery of comparable size in the county. The earliest graves at Blacknall Field include: (66) with applied saucer brooches decorated with a star; (104) with saucer brooches with five scrolls; (38, 44, 67) with button brooches; and (16) with a spearhead of Swanton's group E1, thought to date before rather than after the end of the 5th century (Swanton 1973, 79). The cemetery continued in use throughout the 6th century.

The Bourne, the Nadder and the Ebble are all tributary to the Avon, the Bourne on its left, the two others on its right bank. Croucheston by the Ebble has a name of British origin; along the Nadder such names occur only west of Teffont (see below). In the Bourne valley the cemetery at Winterbourne Gunner has already been noticed. A richly furnished late 7th or early 8th-century barrow on Ford Down is discussed below, in another context. A remarkable grave of the mid 6th century above the Bourne at Tidworth contained four adult male skeletons, each with weapons (Härke 1993). Excavations at Collingbourne Ducis in 1998 revealed a settlement with at least ten sunken-featured buildings and a possible post-built structure, beside the upper Bourne. One of the former dates between the 5th and late 7th century, the others being later (Pine 2001). The site lies only some 150m below a cemetery with 5th-century graves (Gingell 1975/76; Eagles 1994, 15). Along the Nadder, there is only one find from east of Teffont, a spearhead from Barford St Martin. Above and along the Ebble there are spearheads from Odstock Down and Bishopstone and a cemetery at Broadchalke.

The Wylye is another, but major, tributary of the Avon. In the valley the name Knook is probably Brittonic and Corton may be of Latin derivation (Gelling 1997, 79). Intrusive burials in long barrows at Sherrington and Warminster (King Barrow, Boreham), are notable; they included, respectively, one accompanied by a two-edged sword and one with a seax. The hanging-bowl from Wilton is noted below. The Wylye has two tributaries, the Winterbourne (its later and present name is the Till) and another in the Ashton valley, both of which rise on the southern flanks of Salisbury Plain. Chitterne, at the head of the Ashton valley, has a woodland name of British origin, though the landscape is now an open one. 'Anglo-Saxon' burials are known from both valleys. Grave-goods from a 7th-century cemetery at Shrewton on the upper Winterbourne are particularly distinctive and include openwork satchel fittings, paralleled at Winkelbury (see below), and a gold bracteate. The upper Wylye, or Deverill, is considered below.

Salisbury Plain

These generally dry chalk uplands are bisected, unequally, by the River Avon. It is possible that water conservation on the Plain continued after the Roman period (Field 1999).

Other sites lie by lesser streams on the fringes of the Chalk, as has been mentioned above. The Greensand fringing the northern escarpment of the Plain, where it overlooks the Vale of Pewsey, was equally favoured for settlement. At Urchfont – the name is comparable with Teffont (see below) – quantities of Late Iron Age metalwork and Roman coins may point to another shrine (WHM records); Wickham (Green) nearby also has a name of Latin derivation (Gelling 1997, 73, 74, 84). Crookwood (Farm), at Urchfont, and Conock and Cheverell, respectively to the east and west have Brittonic names. These 'groups' of British names recur throughout the county and require further study, here as elsewhere (Gelling 1997, 90). Excavations at Wellhead Lane, Westbury, produced quantities of unstratified Romano-British and handmade organic-tempered potsherds, the latter including a pierced lug of the type noticed above (Fowler 1966). The excavations in 1990 at Grove Farm, Market Lavington, uncovered a contiguous and apparently contemporary settlement and cemetery, the latter in use from the later 5th into the 7th century (Williams and Newman forthcoming). Although late Roman material was found in the vicinity, the settlement occupied a new site, near the top of a local ridge in the Upper Greensand, well served by streams, and overlooking the clay lowlands. The burials were on the slope below. Three probable sunken-featured buildings but no larger structures were identified. The surrounding landscape was predominantly open. Wheat, rye and barley were grown. The livestock included cattle (over 50%), sheep/goat (around 37%) and pig but the latter accounted for less than 10% of the total. The large size of some of the cattle, and the sheep, which were kept probably for their wool, points to a background of Roman husbandry, a feature noted at early 'Anglo-Saxon' sites elsewhere, such as Abbots Worthy, Hampshire (Coy 1991, 67).

The excavated cemetery comprised 42 inhumations, an unknown part of the whole; the burials were of men, women and children. The earliest of the women's graves appears to be (4), with a pair of ring-and-dot disc brooches. Grave (33) has just one of them, and is discussed below. Saucer brooches, reported upon by Dr T. Dickinson, in grave (26) date between the later 5th and the mid 6th century. The earliest weapon burials (17, 27, 31, 34) have spearheads of types H1-H3 and K2, of the late 5th century onwards. Burial (32) has a spearhead of hybrid C4/E4 type, of the mid 6th to mid 7th century. None of the graves intersected each other but some were cut into and others cut by settlement ditches. Thus one ditch cut a burial (11) with amber beads, usually regarded as indicative of the 6th century, but a ditch of a later phase was itself cut by grave (35) with, among other goods, a spearhead of group KI/K2.

On the high Chalk, a 'sunken-featured building', with which handmade organic-tempered and stamped pottery was associated, was cut into a hollow made by a negative lynchet and tracks at the Romano-British settlement at Coombe Down, Enford. The site lies on top of a local spur (Entwistle *et al.* 1993, 12). Its discovery was unexpected and it raises the possibility that other such places on the Plain may have continued in occupation or, less probably, were reoccupied. Scattered burials point to the likely existence of other settlements. Attention may be drawn to a group of seven small barrows, which may be of this period, on Netheravon Down (G. Brown, pers. comm.). Bronze Age barrows with unaccompanied intrusive interments, which, as elsewhere, may be of early Anglo-Saxon date, and stray finds of spearheads from Bulford are recorded along the Nine Mile River, a tributary of the Avon. Burials or casual finds are also known from Heytesbury (intrusive in Bowl's Barrow), Wilsford Down and Rushall Down.

Bedwyn and the Hundred of Kinwardstone

This large Hundred (see below) encompasses very varied terrain. At the south the Chalk of Salisbury Plain stretches into the parishes of Collingbourne Kingston and Ducis, where there was a settlement and cemetery (see above), but at the south-east corner there was Chute Forest, its name of British origin. A small-long brooch is known from Wilton, in the parish of Grafton. A burial in a Bronze Age disc barrow at Great Botley Copse at East Grafton belongs to the late 6th or early 7th century. Immediately to the east of Bedwyn, from Shalbourne, there is an assemblage of finds of 6th-century and later date. '*Waeluueg*' in a Bedwyn charter (Sawyer 1968, 756, hereafter S) and, in a slightly variant form (Grundy 1920, 78), in a charter for Burbage (S 688) may not refer to the Britons. At the north-west of the Hundred is the Forest of Savernake, in origin a British river-name, possibly of the Bedwyn stream (Gover *et al*. 1939, 15; Jackson 1953, 294). In this area, the southern slopes of the Kennet vale carry extensive spreads of clay-with-flints; on the south bank too are the Eocene Beds which offer poor soils of little use for agriculture. Another medieval forest, that of Barroc, which gave its name to the county of Berkshire (Gelling 1976, 801) may have been almost continuous with that of Savernake, stretching eastwards as far as Enborne (Hooke 1988, 150). The density and extent of the woodland within this large area at different periods is unknown and cannot be assumed (Eagles 1997).

The Kennet and its tributaries

North of Savernake Forest, the River Kennet, a major tributary of the Thames, affords easy access from and to the east. Furthermore, in terms of communications, major Roman roads from Old Sarum, Winchester, Silchester, Cirencester and Bath are focused upon a crossing of the river at the small town of *Cunetio* (Mildenhall). At some date after AD 354-8 the town was defended with a wall with external bastions; its function had clearly changed, and the place perhaps had a new role in the collection of the *annona* (Corney 1997; this volume). An inhumation grave located near Savernake Hospital (Marlborough) contained a spearhead of group K1. To the west, sites probably of the 6th century are known in Avebury parish, including a sunken-featured building by the winterbourne which feeds southwards into the Kennet which itself rises at Silbury Hill (Fowler and Blackwell 1998, 24). A burial is also recorded at Yatesbury in Cherhill parish (Meaney 1964, 279, Yatesbury I). A quantity of handmade pottery, including stamped sherds, came from excavations beside the Kennet itself (P. Robinson, pers. comm.). There are also finds from two locations at Ogbourne St Andrew beside the River Og, a tributary of the Kennet, which rises to the north on the Marlborough Downs and meets the Kennet at Marlborough. A Romano-British settlement site at Ogbourne St George has produced organic-tempered pottery (Fowler 1966). Lower down the Kennet, sites and stray finds are known from the parishes of Mildenhall and Ramsbury. On Poulton Downs (Mildenhall), north of the river, the altogether exceptional discovery was made of a woman who had been thrown into a Roman well. Excavations at Ramsbury have demonstrated large tracts of forest thereabouts in the Middle Saxon period (Haslam 1980).

The Marlborough and Wiltshire Downs

On the north side of the Vale of Pewsey, casual finds of brooches are known from Bishops Cannings and Allcannings. Further north, on the Chalk, there are 7th-century burials at Roundway and Heddington (see below). Beyond Wansdyke and the upper Kennet, inhumations, apparently intrusive in a barrow, are recorded from immediately above the outer escarpment of the Chalk at Clyffe Pypard. At Clyffe Pypard, too, organic-tempered pottery has been found on the site of a Roman building (*WANHM*, 70/71, 136). The cemetery at Basset Down, Lydiard Tregoze, is in a similar location, as is another, newly discovered, at Wroughton (R. Canham, pers. comm.; not mapped on Fig. 11.1). A brooch of gilded bronze and decorated with a row of punched circles down both the bow and the faceted foot, of probable 5th-century date, is among finds recorded from graves found there in 1822 (Evison 1965, 39-40; the brooch is in WHM). Grave-groups do not survive. Large saucer brooches point to the continued use of the cemetery until the later 6th century. Further north-east, a probable sunken-featured building has been partially excavated on the Greensand which edges the Chalk below Liddington Castle (*WANHM*, 74/75, 113).

At Avebury the Kennet cuts through the inner escarpment of the Chalk whose upper edge, north of the river, is followed closely by the Ridgeway, which then continues north-eastwards to the county boundary at Bishopstone, and beyond (see below for the burial at Lowbury Hill). Bronze Age barrows on Overton Hill, West Overton, were found to contain 'Saxon' intrusive burials; one may belong to the 5th century, but others are certainly of 6th-century date (Eagles 1986; White 1988, 17). They are sited immediately above the River Kennet and the point where the Ridgeway crosses the Roman road from Silchester to Bath. By the Ridgeway, to the north, there are finds from Barbury Castle. Burials at Foxhill and at Callas Hill, Wanborough, lie by the Roman road from Silchester to Cirencester, respectively 1km and 2.3km north of its intersection with the Ridgeway. To the south of the Ridgeway, in Bishopstone parish, a burial, intrusive in a Bronze Age barrow, is recorded from Hinton Downs; there are other findspots nearby (*WANHM*, 46, 173; *WANHM*, 72/73, 207). Further to the east and south on the Downs, artifacts, including the upper part of a cruciform brooch from a Romano-British site, have been recovered from locations at Aldbourne (Eagles 1997, 380). There is a wrist-clasp, the only one known in the county, from Baydon (Hines 1996b).

The *civitates* of the Roman administration and after (Fig. 11.3)

For the purposes of late Roman civil administration, the area that was later to become Wiltshire appears to have lain within the bounds of several self-governing *civitates*, which were centred upon Cirencester, in Gloucestershire (*Corinium Dobunnorum*), Silchester (*Calleva Atrebatum*) and Winchester (*Venta Belgarum*), both in Hampshire, and Dorchester, in Dorset (*Durnovaria Durotrigum*). Ilchester, in Somerset (*Lindinis Durotrigum*) may have been the capital of a subdivision of the Durotriges. These units, which were for the most part of pre-Roman tribal origin (Hanson 1988, 55), were themselves subdivided into *pagi*, about which little is known. The Roman name *Durocornovium*, which was given to a settlement on Ermine Street and beside the Dorcan stream (a Britonnic name: *VCH Wilts* 1973, I, ii, 482) near Wanborough in north-east Wiltshire, however, appears to mean the 'fort of the Cornovii', who perhaps occupied one of these lesser territories, probably within the *civitas Dobunnorum* (Rivet and Smith 1981, 350; Gelling 1988, 46; Burnham and Wacher 1990, 160; see also below).

There are hints of the boundaries of the *civitates* at certain places. Thus in the Roman period part of the eastern boundary of the Durotriges, dividing them from the Belgae, is likely to have followed the line of the east-facing Bokerley Dyke, on the present county division between Dorset and Hampshire (Bowen 1990). To the east, in the post-Roman period, the area which was later known as the New Forest appears to have been part of a Jutish kingdom in south Hampshire, the western limit of which is unknown, until the late 7th century (Yorke 1989, 92). Another point on the eastern boundary of the Durotriges is suggested by the Old English place-name Teffont, in the Nadder valley (south-west Wiltshire), whose name incorporates Latin **funta*, a spring or fountain, and means 'the spring on the boundary'. Gelling (1997, 83) has suggested that the terminology was precise, that the word may have been a direct loan from Latin speakers and that it may have referred specifically to a place where Roman constructions were evident. This may well be the case at Teffont where, on a knife-edge of Greensand, very limited excavation uncovered walling, and copious finds from the Late Iron Age onwards, including more than 200 coins, the latest of them of Honorius (AD 395-423), suggestive of a shrine; the site lies by the junction of the parishes of Teffont Magna, Teffont Evias and Chilmark (NMR records). Further support for an important boundary there is to be found in the contrasting dates and nature of the 'Anglo-Saxon' burial sites to the east and west of Teffont. For whereas furnished 6th-century cemeteries are well known eastwards, in the valleys of the Wylye, Nadder and Ebble, all the burials to the west, which are again of 'Anglo-Saxon' type, are of 7th-century date and furthermore include a remarkable number which display particularly distinctive rites and rich grave goods. This may suggest that the western area was part of a different territory from that to the east, and one which had remained in British hands until the 7th century, when it became subject to Saxon conquest.

Other bounds are more difficult to determine. Ptolemy says that Bath lay in the *civitas* of the Belgae. This attribution has always presented problems, for the distribution of Dobunnic coins would indicate that the place was situated firmly within their territory (Van Arsdell 1994). However, it has been noted that Ptolemy's statement may have been an error, in that he could have taken it from a partially misplaced entry on a map (Rivet and Smith 1981, 121). Indeed, the Bristol Avon at Bath may have divided the Dobunni from the northern group of the Durotriges, for the Late Iron Age archaeology south of that river looks to the south-west, rather than to south Gloucestershire, even though there is no break in the distribution of Dobunnic coins (Cunliffe 1991, 171). Attention may also be drawn to the route taken by West Wansdyke, which follows the high ground on the south bank of the Avon. The interpretation of Iron Age coin maps, as has long been known, must be undertaken only with the utmost caution, not least because so little is known of the coin issuers themselves, the probable acceptability of coinage (and therefore its loss or hoarding) outside the issuers' own territories and, most importantly, the continued and significant circulation of the coins in the early Roman period. However, in spite of these difficulties, the limit of Dobunnic coinage in south-western Wiltshire appears reasonably secure. It has also been suggested elsewhere that the north-facing East Wansdyke may have been built close to the boundary between the Belgae and the Dobunni (Eagles 1994, 24). The Dyke is designed to block access from the Ridgeway but it also cuts the Roman road from Silchester to Bath where the road meets the northern escarpment of the chalk downs at Morgan's Hill, Bishop's Cannings.

The important Romano-British temple site on the Chalk and above the source of the River Wylye at Cold Kitchen Hill (Brixton Deverill) may have lain near the limit between the Belgae, the Durotriges and the Dobunni. The road from Old Sarum (*Sorviodunum*) to the Mendips passes beside it and the shrine is also located at the southern end of the block of three parishes (the others are Longbridge and Hill Deverill) named from the River Deverill. The Deverill is the former, British, name of the upper Wylye. It is known that some temples were sited on pre-Roman bounds in Gaul, where they served a variety of inter-tribal needs (Rivet 1958, 134). To the west the Roman road crossed the Upper Greensand and Oxford Clay which supported the southern part of Selwood. The wood marked the eastern limit of the new bishopric of Sherborne in AD 705 (ASC s.a.709). Asser recorded its Welsh name, *Coit Maur* – 'the great wood' (Stenton 1971, 65). This wood most probably also defined, however vaguely, the earlier Roman cantons in this area. The precise extent of the woodland at an early date is far from clear but the county boundary with Somerset between Maiden Bradley and Dilton Marsh looks suspiciously straight and may be of relatively late origin (for Domesday woodland see *VCH Wilts* 1959, IV, 391, 414).

In eastern Wiltshire, coins of the Atrebates hint that the *civitas Atrebatum* may have intruded into the county. In this connection attention may be drawn to the Domesday Hundred of Kinwardstone. It is of exceptional size and incorporates the early 100-hide royal estate of Bedwyn and the hillfort of Chisbury. The tradition that Chisbury was the stronghold of the sub-king Cissa, who was said to have been a predecessor of Caedwalla (AD 685/6-688) and to have ruled Wiltshire and the greater part of Berkshire from this centre, may reflect the earlier separateness of the area and its connections eastwards (Stenton 1913, 8; Eagles 1997). The eastern termination of East Wansdyke just within the Hundred bounds in the modern parish of Savernake, a former extra-parochial area and detached portion of Savernake Forest, may be significant (A. Reynolds, pers. comm.). The Domesday Hundred was an amalgamation of royal estates, at least of Bedwyn and Pewsey (J. Pitt, pers. comm.). The British name of Membury, which means the hillfort on the boundary, in Ramsbury parish, may not relate to its present position on the county boundary with Berkshire but to an earlier location between the Atrebates and the Dobunni (P. Robinson, pers. comm.).

Civil wars?

The apparently widespread outbreak of violence following the Roman withdrawal (see above) may provide the context for the final, built-up phases of Bokerley Dyke and for East and West Wansdyke, all three of which, as noticed above, may have lain on or close to the boundaries of *civitates*. The careful reinstatement of Ackling Dyke soon after Bokerley Dyke had been cut through the Roman road may point to a date when Roman techniques of road building were still current or remembered (Bowen 1990, 39; Eagles 1994, 23). Reynolds (1999, 85) suggests a late 8th or early 9th-century context for East and West Wansdyke, while Fowler (this volume) also argues for a 5th-century date. These particular stretches of boundary were, presumably, re-asserted because they were disputed, whereas elsewhere there was no need to mark the limits in a particular way (T. Darvill, pers. comm.).

There is no evidence to hint that any part of either Wiltshire or Dorset was in Saxon hands by the middle of the 5th century. Indeed, a grave (VI), probably of the third quarter of the 5th century, in the cemetery at Winterbourne Gunner may also belong with an initial group of *foederati*. This burial ground is in a strategic location, where the Portway, the Roman road from Silchester to the major road junction at Old Sarum, which lies close by to the west, crosses the Bourne. The grave's contents include a francisca, brought in most probably from 'Frankish' Belgium or northern France, and a strapend decorated with a fantastic beast in late Roman style, which is likely to have been made in southern Britain (Evison 1965, 39, 60, 67; Eagles 1994, 13). The strapend, whose fine decoration shows no sign of wear, is paralleled locally at Gussage Cow Down, east Dorset (M. Corney, pers. comm.). Accelerator radiocarbon-dating of the skeleton in one of the unfurnished graves excavated subsequently in the same cemetery indicated that that burial occurred between cal AD 400-460 (1610+/-35 BP: OXA-8036; J. Richards, pers. comm.). The Romano-British name (*Sorviodunum*) for the roadside settlement beside Old Sarum was adopted by the Anglo-Saxons, who called the place *Searobyrg*. The transfer points to the continuing presence there of Brittonic speakers and could, perhaps, have come about in the context of the employment of Germanic mercenaries (Gelling 1997, 54). It has been suggested (R. Coates, pers. comm.) that *Sorviodunum* may mean 'the fortress of Sorwjos'.

The location of the earliest, 5th-century, 'Anglo-Saxon' sites in relation to the *civitates* (Fig. 11.3)

Suggestions have been made above as to some possible limits to those parts of the four or five late Roman *civitates* which lay within Wiltshire. Within such boundaries the earliest 'Anglo-Saxon' sites around Old Sarum would have been located in the former *civitas Belgarum*. The cemetery at Pewsey was perhaps close to the boundary between that *civitas* and that of the canton of the Atrebates. Collingbourne Ducis, in Kinwardstone Hundred, may have been within the former *civitas Atrebatum*. There is a saucer brooch with a star design,

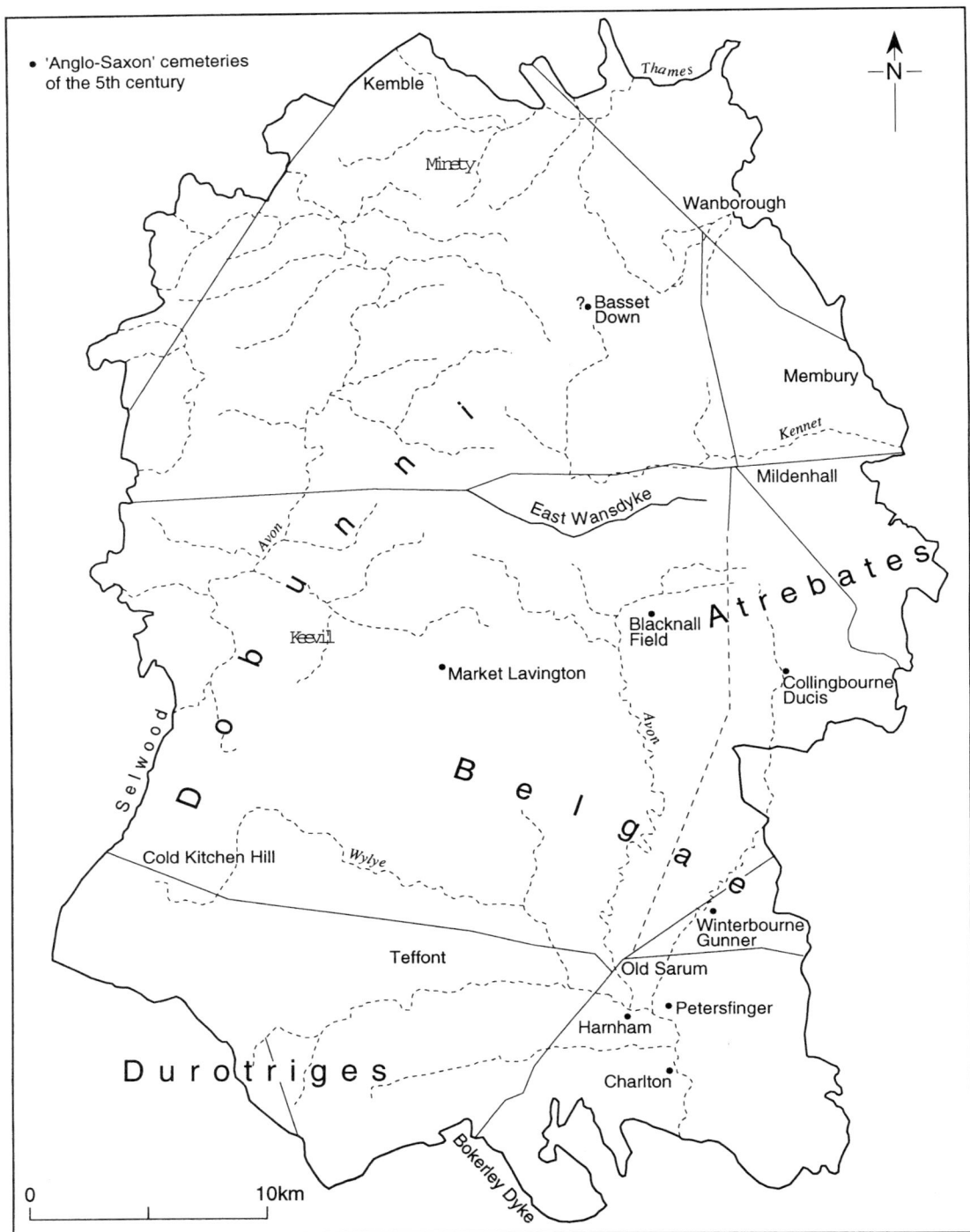

Fig. 11.3 The Romano-British civitates *and 'Anglo-Saxon' cemeteries of the 5th century*

of the second half of the 5th or the first half of the 6th century (Welch 1976), from the hillfort at Membury which was possibly on the border between the *civitates* of the Atrebates and the Dobunni (see above).

The situation of the settlement at Market Lavington, near the boundary shared by the *civitas Belgarum* and the *civitas Dubonnorum* and far to the west of the other 'Anglo-Saxon' sites, and on the west side of Salisbury Plain, requires comment. It raises the possibility that an immigrant community was planted there, at the limit of territory newly acquired in the late 5th century, perhaps to mark its new 'ownership'. Alternatively, it could be suggested that the settlement at Market Lavington was unplanned, and only one of perhaps a number which were thinly scattered in areas under British, even 'Saxonised' British, control in the latter part of the 5th century; if so, it may represent a small, intrusive but, initially at least, perhaps unimportant element amongst the native population. There are parallels for this in the 6th-century 'Anglo-Saxon' sites and artifacts scattered in Dorset and Somerset (Evison 1968). The location and early date of the cemeteries at Beckford, Hereford and Worcester, are also comparable (Evison and Hill 1996; Bassett 1997). Furthermore, the Market Lavington cemetery does not appear to have the strongly military character seen in the high proportion of weapon burials at Stretton-on-Fosse, Warks, regarded as belonging to a frontier community (Härke forthcoming). Whatever interpretation is put upon the site, the initial date of the Market Lavington burials coincides with the appearance of a number of 'Anglo-Saxon' burial grounds and settlements elsewhere in the county and is a part of that new phenomenon.

Gildas, who may have been writing *c.* AD 540 (Charles-Edwards 1986), describes (cc. 10, 26) a generation of peace following a British victory at *Mons Badonicus* and the partition of the country by treaty. Härke (1990, 28) has argued that the archaeological evidence also points to the late 5th and early 6th centuries as a time of relative peace. It is possible that there is some relationship between the extent of 'Anglo-Saxon' culture, as seen in its novel but unadulterated form in Wiltshire, at this time and this division with the barbarians. Any such conclusions should be treated with caution; there are many problems of relating distribution maps of material culture and ethnicity (Jones 1997, 123).

Styles of dress and personal display within the new material culture

The apparently conscious promotion of a 'Saxon' identity in the south of England in the 6th century has already been noticed. The great majority, by far, of the brooches of this date found in Wiltshire are circular, but of a range of types, even within cemeteries; their wearers seem to have identified with this widespread 'Saxon' culture. Notable forms represented are button brooches, plain and ring-and-dot decorated disc types, and a wide variety of cast and applied saucer brooches. The designs on many of the saucer brooches tend to be very individualistic and careful analysis of the cast type has resulted in the identification of a large number of small groups, whose members may be very widely scattered (Dickinson 1993). Thus Dr Dickinson's study of the examples from Market Lavington has shown that the closest parallels to the cast saucer brooch in grave (8) are from Alveston (Warks) and Woodston (Cambs), although an origin in Hampshire is possible for the group as a whole (Evison 1988, 47). The central field of a pair of these brooches in grave (7) is most closely matched at Mildenhall (Passmore 1934), and the pellets in the design at Blacknall Field, Pewsey, grave (21), both within the county. Other connections appear to have been more distant. General parallels to the outer field of the brooch in (24) are particularly evident in the Upper Thames region, while features of the decoration on the brooches in (26) share similarities with others in the East Midlands. It is suggested that these individual differences, within a general framework of potent symbolism, were deliberate and, perhaps, a means through which the elite were distinguished, generally and from each other, or each other's kin (Dickinson 1993, 39). A single saucer brooch in (8), worn at the left shoulder, fastened the usual tubular gown but represents a distinctive regional style of dress, found with children and young women in Berkshire and Wiltshire (Owen-Crocker 1986, 35), though Stoodley (pers. comm.) has noted that it occurs only infrequently in Wiltshire. The contents of grave (21) at Blacknall Field included a great square-headed brooch, an Anglian type as well as the pair of gilt cast saucer brooches noted above. Anglian artifacts are very unusual in Wiltshire; they include a cruciform brooch from Aldbourne and a wrist-clasp from Baydon, already noted. However, taken together and with others known to the east in nearby Berkshire they are sufficiently prominent to indicate direct communication with areas of Anglian culture, seen at its closest in Northamptonshire (Hines 1996b). The single disc brooch, of Roman type, on the right shoulder of the male in Collingbourne Ducis, grave 11, however, accords with Roman costume (Janes 1996, 127); the same grave contained an iron buckle with silver inlay. Roman-style dress may also have been worn by the person buried in Market Lavington (33); the sex of the adult skeleton could not be determined, but there was a disc brooch with ring-and-dot decoration, fastening an outer garment, at the right shoulder, over an inner garment with a belt. At Harnham the number of females who wore finger-rings and bracelets in the Romano-British fashion is notable (N. Stoodley, pers. comm.).

The mechanisms by which brooches, and their designs, travelled are still little understood. Local production seems most likely, itinerant craftsmen providing the necessary skills (Dickinson 1993, 36). A lead model for a five-spiral saucer brooch is a casual find from Ramsbury (in WHM; Mortimer 1994).

The 'Frankish' links which have already been noted at Winterbourne Gunner in the 5th century are also evident in the Salisbury area at Harnham and Petersfinger (Evison 1965, passim) and at Charlton (Davies 1984), and there is also, as noted above, a silver-inlaid buckle from Collingbourne Ducis. Similar associations are apparent in the 6th century. At Winterbourne Gunner, a perforated spoon was found in grave (VII), along with an 'Anglian' small-long brooch. Other costumes too appear to send a 'mixed' cultural message. Rogers has noted that the 'Saxon' gilded saucer brooch in Market Lavington (24) was worn at the right shoulder and appears to have fastened a sophisticated pattern-woven woollen undergown, with a woollen tabby outer garment of Frankish style fastened by a buckle (Rogers forthcoming). Three button brooches were associated with a local variant of a 'Frankish' bow brooch in Petersfinger grave XXV (Leeds and Shortt 1953; Arnold 1982, 50). A copy of a 'Frankish' bird brooch (Arnold 1982, 57;

brooch in SM) has been found recently at Milston, in the Avon valley to the north of Amesbury. Some of these fashions may have spread from Kent, where there were insular versions of continental Frankish dress (Parfitt and Brugmann 1997, 113). It is possible that some of these variations in costume resulted from competing, perhaps short-lived, ethnicities amongst the elite.

The western limit of 'Saxon' culture by the end of the 6th century

South of Salisbury Plain, Anglo-Saxon style burials are evident as far west as Teffont in the Nadder valley and Warminster on the Wylye by this date. They are absent from the extreme south-west of the county, including the valley of the upper Wylye or Deverill. Further north, such burials, and some 'Anglo-Saxon' settlements occur, generally, as far as the western and northern limit of the Chalk and Greensand, across Salisbury Plain (the most westerly find is a late 6th-century saucer brooch from Worton) and the Marlborough Downs. Finds from West Overton and Lydiard Tregoze possibly hint that an 'English' culture may have already penetrated to the western edge of the Marlborough Downs, considered to have belonged to the Dobunni, by AD 500. Cultural assimilation here, if anywhere, by communities farming the same chalkland landscape, might be thought likely; such a common purpose may well have been stronger than their links with their fellow farmers in the 'cheese' country to the north-west, where an 'Anglo-Saxon' material culture is not yet evident. The only known sites, of burials, are at Kemble and Castle Eaton (*WANHM*, 72/73, 207), beside the Thames. It is possible that the extent of this cultural zone changed little during the 6th century.

New conquests in the 7th century (Fig. 11.1)

The south-west of the county

It has been noticed above that the south-west corner of Wiltshire had, most probably, been part of the *civitas Durotrigum*, and reference was made to the appearance there of a number of notable 7th-century 'Anglo-Saxon' burials. Among them is a group of primary barrows, whose graves contain sugar-loaf shield bosses, which date to the second quarter of the 7th century (Dickinson and Härke 1992, 21, fig. 16). They occur on the high Chalk at Alvediston, Maiden Bradley and West Knoyle. The burial at Alvediston lies close to the elaborately accompanied late 7th-century female grave, cut into a Bronze Age barrow and with its distinctive bed-burial rite, at Swallowcliffe (Speake 1989; see below). Two other 7th-century burial grounds are known in this area, on Winkelbury Hill, Berwick St John (where the bed-burial practice recurs) and at Monkton Deverill, where the cemetery included another primary barrow (Rawlings 1995, 26; see below); and a richly furnished female grave of the second half of the 7th century has recently been excavated at Mere (Wessex Archaeology 1995). A grave with a prototype sugar-loaf boss, probably of much the same date as the others, has been recorded at Ebbesborne Wake, which lies south of Teffont, towards the north end of Bokerley Dyke.

The four parishes of the Deverills, which share the former, British, name of the upper Wylye, are likely to have lain within its bounds. There is a notable group of place-names of Latin origin, Fonthill, Fovant and Teffont, in the Vale of Wardour. British place- and river-names are relatively abundant. Romano-British and organic-tempered pottery have been found together at Swallowcliffe (NMR ST 92 NE 36). There was a minster (*'monasterium'*), with a *parochia*, of some standing at Tisbury in south-west Wiltshire by *c.* 700. A charter of AD 759 (S1256) refers to the acquisition by Tisbury of a 30 hide estate near the River Fontmell, some 14km to the south-west in Dorset, probably in the late 7th or early 8th century. A late 10th-century charter confirmed the gift of Tisbury to Shaftesbury, maintaining the strong association with Dorset (Edwards 1988, 229; J Pitt, pers. comm.).

The west and north of the county

By the end of the 5th century an 'Anglo-Saxon' culture is evident as far west as Market Lavington, which, it has been suggested, may have been close to the boundary between the former Roman *civitates* of the Belgae and the Dobunni, and also, perhaps, as far as Basset Down (Lydiard Tregoze) to the north of East Wansdyke and most probably well within former Dobunnic territory. The cultural limit was apparently similar a hundred years later.

Beyond this 'Anglo-Saxon' zone, there is little sign of 5th- and 6th-century occupation of any kind on the clays and limestone in the western and northern parts of the county. In the north-west, a site at Kington St Michael has produced unstratified organic-tempered pottery (*WANHM*, 83, 229) which also occurs, in the north-east, at the Romano-British settlement at Cleveland Farm, Ashton Keynes (Frere 1990, 353). There were notable stretches of woodland at Braydon, Chippenham and Melksham, all being considered parts of Selwood by Asser in the 9th century (*VCH Wilts* 1959, IV, 391). There are many British river and place-names (the river name Idover is marked selectively on Fig. 11.3; a full list is given in Gover *et al.* 1939, 2-4). These river names relate to the Avon and the Thames and to some of their many tributaries. A minor tributary of the Cole, which rises at Chiseldon, named in charters Dorcyn, Dorcan, or Dorternebrok, flows past *Durocornovium*. There is a similar absence of early 'Anglo-Saxon' sites in south Gloucestershire. Burials and finds are known only from Kemble and Chavenage (Avening). At Bath, the reservoir building around the sacred spring associated with the Roman temple was not finally destroyed until at least the 6th century; an enamelled penannular brooch from the votive deposit there may date between the mid 5th and mid 6th century AD (Youngs 1995). Occupation elsewhere in the town may possibly have lasted as long (Cunliffe and Davenport 1985, 45; Burnham and Wacher 1990, 175; Woodward 1992, 113). There were possible post-Roman deposits, perhaps of agricultural origin, at Bath Street, which leads westwards from the Roman baths. A 6th-century 'Anglo-Saxon' brooch and a knife of similar date were recovered from later contexts (Davenport 1999, 48, 59, 60).

An exceptional find in the north-west of the county is an unfinished Celtic hanging bowl mount of the mid to late 7th century from Seagry, in the upper Avon valley south of Malmesbury. This piece may point to a British workshop there – evidence for which is otherwise known only in Scotland (Youngs with Eagles 1998). Also significant are two large zoomorphic penannular brooches, an enamelled one from 'near Calne', and a plain one from Oldbury Castle, on the Calne/Cherhill boundary immediately above the chalk escarpment. Such brooches were worn by Celtic men and women, and could signal rank, though an 'Anglo-Saxon' context is also possible. The one from near Calne is of the same type as that from Bath referred to above, the other may perhaps date a little later (Youngs 1995). There are numerous British place-names in and around Calne.

It is possible that the area from Kemble southwards as far as Bath, and from the Bristol Channel in the west to Oldbury in the east, and just possibly the north-east of Wiltshire too (though the evidence from there is less clear), should perhaps be considered as a single territory in British hands until some date in the 7th century. The whole area may have lain within the former *civitas Dobunnorum* (see above). The names Kemble, Minety, and Keevil may refer to their position on a boundary, Kemble being a word of definite, and Minety and Keevil probable, British origin (Fig. 11.3; Coates and Breeze 2000, 112). Kemble is by the source of the Thames, a location likely of itself to have ensured ancient prominence. Its boundary position has endured, being transferred from Wiltshire to Gloucestershire only in 1897, and it lay within the Wiltshire Domesday Hundred of Chedglow. 'Anglo-Saxon' burials in the parish have been noted above. The entry in the Anglo-Saxon Chronicle s.a. 577 possibly recalls a memory of the former independence of Bath (but note Sims-Williams 1983, 33).

The Gewisse, Mercia and the Britons at war

The Anglo-Saxon Chronicle records that in AD 628 Cynegils and Cwichelm of the Gewisse fought against Penda at Cirencester and 'came to terms' (imposed by Penda). Stenton (1971, 45) noted that Penda's victory marked an important step in the emergence of the Hwicce; indeed, the archaeological evidence suggests that that part of Gloucestershire had long had close links with the Dorchester-on-Thames region, considered to lie in the Gewissan heartlands and where Cynegils was baptised in AD 635. The background to a battle at Bradford-on-Avon in AD 652 is particularly obscure, as it is variously recorded as fought against the British or as civil war in different sources (Whitelock *et al.* 1961, 20, n 2). It is therefore not at all clear that it relates to an onslaught against British territory and, indeed, the place may not be correctly identified. The first unambiguous reference to an advance south-westwards by the Gewisse is the battle of Peonnan, possibly at Penselwood, in AD 658 when the Britons were said to have been driven back to the Parrett, in west Somerset (Yorke 1995, 53). There is no mention of Dorset and the annal may relate only to the former northern part of Durotrigian territory, that based on Ilchester. The first charter for Glastonbury dates to AD 678, in the reign of Centwine (Yorke 1990, 137; Costen 1992, 102). In AD 682 Centwine (AD 676-685/6), whose successes may have been underestimated, put the Britons to flight as far as the sea (Yorke 1990, 136).

'Saxon' influence was particularly marked – there may have been conquest – in the south-east of Dorset by the late 6th century (Eagles 1994, 17). Elsewhere in the county, Cenwalh (AD 642-73) was said to have transferred a 100 hide estate from the British monastery at Lanprobus to new Sherborne in AD 671 (Finberg 1964, 98; O'Donovan 1988, 82); and a charter (S1164), datable between AD 669 and AD 675, of Cenred, presumably the father of Ine but at this date apparently only a minor king in Wessex, grants land in the county to Abbot Bectun (Edwards 1988, 229). There is reason, therefore, to believe that Dorset was in Gewissan hands early in the AD 670s. Although the Chronicle makes no explicit mention of the county at this time, military conquest (as opposed to some peaceful means of acquisition, such as a marriage settlement) of the area at around this date is possible, and the group of burials with sugar-loaf shield bosses might seem to support such a view. If the latest phases of Bokerley Dyke do not date to the immediate post-Roman period, as has been suggested above, these events in the 7th-century wars offer an alternative context (H. Williams, pers. comm.). In this connection, it is possible that the richly furnished bed-burial of a woman, intrusive in a long barrow which had been incorporated into a prehistoric linear earthwork, itself an element in the complex and multi-phase Bokerley boundary 'line', was deliberately so placed to 'mark' the appropriation of new territory (Bowen 1991, 5, Pentridge 23; Speake 1989, 107, 'Woodyates'). It may also be noted that some, at least, of the unaccompanied burials in Bokerley Dyke at Bokerley Junction are (later) deviant burials, probably relating to an execution site (Reynolds 1998, 149).

It appears to be only in the 7th century that sites of 'Anglo-Saxon' character first appear in the north-east corner of Wiltshire, although it may be noted that there is a 6th-century burial immediately across the boundary in Berkshire at Coleshill, and another, in Wiltshire, by the Thames at Castle Eaton (*WANHM*, 72/73, 207). A further record relates to a burial with a knife, quite possibly 7th century, at Stanton Fitzwarren; this site, and the 7th-century cemetery at Purton, are on the Coral Rag. A seax has been found at Ashton Keynes (*WANHM*, 69, 186). At Swindon, on the Portland Limestone which caps Old Swindon Hill, excavations in 1975-77 uncovered six sunken-featured buildings and one of timber. The wooden building was approximately 8.5m by 4.5m and had been destroyed by fire; more than 100 loomweights, many of them in line, together with lengths of timber, apparently from the loom itself, shears and large pots were found. The walls of this building were covered with a sophisticated plastering. It overlay a slightly larger building, of post-hole construction, with internal stake-holes; associated finds included bone pins, many of them decorated, yellow vessel glass, and a gold fragment with inset garnet (Canham and Phillips nd). A grave with a spearhead and knife has been recorded nearby, in Evelyn Street.

There are also signs of change at the western margin of the Chalk in the 7th century. As has been seen, Oldbury hillfort may have been in British hands at this time; if so, it overlooked 'Anglo-Saxon' territory to the north, east and south. The distribution and location of sites immediately to the south of Oldbury, beyond the point where the Roman road from Silchester to Bath (which is followed by the southern boundary of Calne Without) was blocked by East Wansdyke, affords some further suggestive evidence of the old

Belgic/Dobunnic boundary. For there is a notable group of 'Anglo-Saxon' burials, all certainly or probably of 7th-century date, on the Chalk in the parishes of Heddington and Roundway, to the east of Oliver's Camp, which is similarly sited to Oldbury hillfort. Two of them are primary barrow burials, one on the summit of King's Play Hill, Heddington, the other on the top of Roundway Hill. There is also a richly furnished grave of the later 7th century, possibly a bed-burial (Speake 1989, 107), intrusive in a round barrow on Roundway Down. The accompaniments of the latter included a pin-suite with a gold roundel with a blue glass setting in the form of a cross, which has been thought of probable Irish workmanship and to reflect the influence of the monastery at Malmesbury (Meaney and Hawkes 1970, 48; see further below). It may be noted that a Roman villa is located immediately below Oliver's Camp, to the south of Mother Anthony's Well, which lies at the head of a stream below the escarpment and at the junction of the parishes of Bromham, Rowde and Roundway; an earlier position on the Belgic/Dobunnic boundary is possible (*VCH Wilts* 1957, I. i, 51).

The richness of the intrusive burial on Roundway Down, and the probable recurrence there of the bed-burial rite, together with the local grouping and siting of 7th-century graves in that area, is reminiscent of the situation, noted above, in the south-west of the county, where it has been interpreted as reflecting new Anglo-Saxon conquest at much the same time. It may, perhaps, be argued that these burials also mark 'Anglo-Saxon' intrusion into new territory, in this case that which had once belonged to the Dobunni.

In the same vein, attention may also be drawn to the series of 'Anglo-Saxon' graves, of similar date, in what had probably been north Durotrigian territory in north Somerset. These burials occur at Buckland Dinham, Camerton, Evercreech, Queen Camel, Huish Episcopi and Keynsham (Geake 1997, passim; 1999a, passim). The latter was accompanied by a gold pendant with filigree decoration and dates to the late 7th or early 8th century (Geake 1997, 38). Its location immediately south of the Avon, between the river and the West Wansdyke, is perhaps comparable with the burial, noticed above, intrusive in a 'strand' of Bokerley Dyke (Eagles 1994, 18; Youngs with Eagles 1998, 40). The first charter for Glastonbury dates to AD 678, in the reign of Centwine of the Gewisse (Yorke 1990, 137; Costen 1992, 102).

Further, important, evidence for Anglo-Saxon control of north-west Wiltshire and north Somerset is provided by a series of charters which had been preserved in the monastic archives at Bath and Malmesbury. The foundation charter (S51) for the monastery at Bath dates to AD 675 and records the grant of 100 hides by Osric king of the Hwicce to Abbess Berta (Sims-Williams 1975, 2). Mercian control of the area was presumably secure by AD 679-80, when the Hwicce diocese was established (Plummer 1896, II, 246). The monastery at Malmesbury was possibly founded in the mid 7th century by the Irish hermit Maildub – perhaps, on the arguments used in this paper, when the area was still in British hands. Bede (HE, v.18) says the place was named after Maildub: see also Campbell (1987, 338) and Sims-Williams (1990, 108). Aldhelm, its first abbot, was said by William of Malmesbury to have been of West Saxon royal lineage, and the monastery appears always to have been in West Saxon hands (Sims-Williams 1990, 384). Charters show Aldhelm to have secured patronage from both Mercia and Wessex. From Mercia came land at Tetbury, *'iuxta Tettan monasterium'*, in AD 681, the earliest genuine and datable grant to Malmesbury (S71/73; Edwards 1988, 90), and an estate at Somerford Keynes in AD 685 (S1169; Edwards 1988, 93). Yorke (1990, 107) has noted that it was Mercian policy to support religious houses in areas they wished to take over. From Wessex came an exchange of land east of Braydon Wood (Forest) for an estate near the monastery in *c.* AD 676-686 (S1170; Edwards 1988, 94), and land at Kemble and east of Braydon Wood in AD 688 (S231/234; Edwards 1988, 97). Edwards (*ibid.*) suggests Caedwalla perhaps disposed of border areas to the Church.

West Saxon and Hwiccan rivalry in north-west Wiltshire in the later 7th century is therefore clear. As has been noted, the history of the monasteries shows the critical nature of the West Saxon border in the area (Sims-Williams 1990, 384). Aldhelm's concern for his monastery at Malmesbury is underlined by the privileges granted by Pope Sergius I, with the agreement of both Ine and Aethelred that Malmesbury should not suffer in wars between their kingdoms (Edwards 1988, 104).

The acquisition of new territories in the west may have resulted in the redrawing of some ancient and major boundaries. Ryme (Dorset) and Rimpton (Somerset) may both refer to the establishment of a new boundary, which became the northern limit of Dorset (Costen 1992, 85). Mere's name may have come about in the same way. Finally, it is possible that Martin, which probably means 'the boundary settlement', derives its (English) name from its location adjacent both to Bokerley Dyke and to the former southern boundary of the territory of the Wilsaete (Cole 1991/2, 39). The parish is now in Hampshire but was formerly in Wiltshire.

At Foxley, on the Corallian limestone west of Malmesbury, aerial photography has revealed a substantial settlement near the Fosse Way. A hall with external buttresses is comparable with one at Cowdery's Down in Hampshire but there is also a probable church (Hinchliffe 1986). The range of the only radiocarbon date available from this site (obtained from test excavation), of cal AD 555-665 (1430 +/- 80 BP: HAR-6216), poses many questions, for it covers a period from the time when the area was certainly still in British hands to well after the Anglo-Saxon conquest. Sunken-featured structures and timber-framed buildings have been excavated at Trowbridge (Graham and Davies 1993, 142), and there is another sunken-featured building at Chippenham (*WANHM*, 84, 143). It is quite possible that the sites at Foxley and Trowbridge, at least, date to a period after the area had been incorporated into the kingdoms of the Hwicce and the West Saxons.

Wiltshire and the emerging West Saxon kingdom

By the later 7th century, as has been seen, Wiltshire was no longer at the frontier of Wessex, which now stretched westwards into Devon. The military successes in the west were matched, under Caedwalla, in southern Hampshire and the Isle of Wight. His energetic successor, Ine (AD 688-726), was able to consolidate these gains. Ine's laws point to a king pro-active in law-making and profiting from his interference in the now greatly extended administration of justice (Wormald 1995). It is also possible that he developed

Hamwic and overseas trade (Morton 1992, 28); the self-confidence of Wessex at this time is discussed by Mayr-Harting (1991, 216). Christianity was now a force to be reckoned with, though since AD 635 when Cynegils had been baptised at Dorchester-on-Thames, the progress of Christianisation had been slow (Yorke 1990, 139) despite the advantages it brought to kings (Campbell 1986, 76). Pagan shrine place-names, it has been suggested, such as that of Thunresfeld (at Hardenhuish: 'open land, within woodland, of Thunor', the woodland here later known as Chippenham Forest) continued to be coined at the end of the 7th century (M. Gelling, pers. comm.; Gelling 1973, 121). Attention should also be drawn to the remarkable group of sites by the county boundary with Hampshire on the commanding top of Roche Court Down, Winterslow, whose name incorporates *hlaw*, the OE for tumulus (Gelling 1997, 134-6). There a pair of primary Anglo-Saxon barrows lie close to an inhumation cemetery with west–east burials; all are likely to belong to the 7th century. One barrow covered a male burial accompanied by a knife, whose grave-cut was aligned on a post-setting in the centre of the adjacent mound, which was of similar construction but lacked any interment. The arrangement may be of religious significance (Blair 1995; A. Reynolds, pers. comm.). Eighteen execution burials were in a nearby prehistoric linear ditch (Reynolds 1998, 151).

Archaeological evidence seems to reflect the growing coherence of the kingdom and increasing confidence and wide connections of its elite. A number of elaborately furnished burials of the second half of the 7th century have been noted above, in various contexts. Rites no longer appear to have essentially a local context but recur over wide areas. The distribution of the examples so far known of the bed-burial rite is remarkable; they occur only in Wiltshire (including Swallowcliffe), Cambridgeshire and the Peak District (Speake 1989, 109, fig. 90). Furthermore, the Swallowcliffe grave contains, clearly deliberately, items of both Celtic and Anglo-Saxon design as, for example, does the Lowbury Hill barrow in Oxfordshire (Härke 1994, 204). Parker Pearson (1982) has suggested that rich burials tend to be most noticeable at times when individuals needed to assert their position. In this connection, the insertion of rich burials through the primary grave in prehistoric barrows, as at Swallowcliffe and Roundway Down, suggests a deliberate attempt to replace the original burial and demonstrate the dominance of the new elite (N. Stoodley, pers. comm.).

The wish to be linked to the ancient Romans may also be seen in the location of three primary Anglo-Saxon barrows in the county close to Roman roads. One, of unusual form, with a penannular ditch with external bank, and beside a Bronze Age barrow, on Ford Down, was close to the road from Old Sarum to Winchester (Musty 1969). Another, on Salisbury Race Course and again by a Bronze Age barrow, was by the road from Old Sarum to Dorchester (Evison 1963). The third is at Monkton Deverill (Kingston Deverill parish) to the east of Cold Kitchen Hill and near the junction of the Roman road between Old Sarum and the Mendips with that from Hamworthy to Bath (Rawlings 1995, 37). The siting of these important burials presumably made a powerful statement; their position suggests that they were thought to provide protection for their people (Williams 1999, 80). Their location also indicates the continued significance of the Roman roads and the importance of controlling them – the same phenomenon is known elsewhere in England but requires further study. The association with through routes was clearly an important one, for the primary barrow at Alvediston, the burial at Swallowcliffe, and a third, with a relict box, at Yatesbury (Reynolds 1994, 193) all lie, not by Roman roads, but by herepaths.

Helen Geake (1997, passim; 1999b) has also drawn attention to the notable emphasis, not only in the burial record, in a number of the emerging kingdoms on a cultivated association with a Roman past and with the contemporary Mediterranean world. Such an outlook is likely to have been actively encouraged by the Church, whose role was so crucial in the formation of Wessex and of other new kingdoms (Wormald 1983, 124-6).

Conclusion

The period covered by this paper was one of dramatic change. It began when Roman officialdom had departed from Britain, never to return. Roman material culture suffered a rapid collapse. In spite of irregular contact with the disintegrating Roman world of northern Gaul, the initiative now lay not with the British warlords who inherited the old provinces but with the incoming Germanic peoples, many of whom had had only limited contact with the Roman empire. They brought with them new ways, new cultures and a new language. To all of these the native inhabitants had to adapt as best they might. It has been a central purpose here to try to tease out from a variety of meagre and ill understood evidence hints of these processes at work. It is not until some 150 years later that it is possible to see again, in Wessex as elsewhere, the establishment, with the aid of an enterprising and energetic Church, of robust political institutions which mark a new and important phase in the history of England.

Note Radiocarbon dates have been calibrated using Stuiver and Pearson 1986; the date ranges cited are given using the 68% confidence limits.

Acknowledgements

The writer would like to express his appreciation to Barry Ager, Graham Brown, Roy Canham and Lesley Freke (particularly with reference to the Wiltshire Sites and Monuments Record), Professor Richard Coates, Mark Corney, Mikael Dahlgren (Lund), Dr Tania Dickinson, Dr Margaret Gelling, Nick Griffiths, Dr Andrew Lawson and colleagues at Wessex Archaeology, Dr Sam Lucy, Dr Jonathon Pitt, Dr Andrew Reynolds, Dr Paul Robinson (who has kept me abreast with new finds and guided me in the interpretation of Iron Age coin finds), Peter Saunders and colleagues at the Salisbury and South Wiltshire Museum, and Howard Williams, for information and for much helpful discussion. Dr Paul Barnwell, Professor Tim Darvill, Professor John Hines, Dr Nick Stoodley, and Dr Barbara Yorke very kindly commented on the paper in draft and I have benefited greatly from their suggestions. The illustrations have been prepared by Alejandra Gutiérrez and to her too I offer my warm thanks.

References

Abels, R. P., 1988, *Lordship and Military Obligation in Anglo-Saxon England*, London

Amory, P., 1993, 'The meaning and purpose of ethnic terminology in the Burgundian laws', *Early Medieval Europe*, 2 (1), 1-28

_____ , 1994, 'Names, ethnic identity, and community in 5th- and 6th-century Burgundy', *Viator*, 25, 1-30

_____ , 1997, *People and Identity in Ostrogothic Italy, 489-554*, Cambridge

Arnold, C. J., 1982, *The Anglo-Saxon Cemeteries of the Isle of Wight*, London

Barnwell, P., forthcoming, 'Briton and warrior in post-Roman south-eastern England'

Bassett, S., 1997, 'Review of Evison and Hill 1996', *Medieval Archaeol*, 41, 330-1

Bazelmans, J., 1999, *By Weapons Made Worthy. Lords, Retainers and their Relationship in Beowulf*, Amsterdam

Blair, J., 1995, 'Anglo-Saxon pagan shrines and their prototypes', *Anglo-Saxon Studies in Archaeology and History*, 8, 1-28

Böhme, H. W., 1986, 'Das Ende der Römerherrschaft in Britannien und die angelsächsische Besiedlung Englands im 5 Jahrhundert', *Jahrbuch des Römisch-Germanischen Zentralmuseums*, 33, 469-574

_____ , 1999, 'Sächsische Söldner in römischen Heer. Das Land zwischen Ems und Niederelbe während des 4 und 5 Jahrhunderts', in F. Both and H. Aouni (eds) *Über allen Fronten. Nordwestdeutschland zwischen Augustus und Karl dem Grossen*, Archäologische Mitteilungen aus Nordwestdeutschland, Beiheft 26, Oldenburg, 49-73

Bowen, H. C., 1990, *The Archaeology of Bokerley Dyke*, London

_____ , 1991, *The Archaeology of Bokerley Dyke. Inventory*, London

Bradley, R., 1987, 'Time regained: the creation of continuity', *Journ British Archaeol Assoc*, 140, 1-17

Burnham, B. C., and Wacher, J. S., 1990, *The 'Small Towns' of Roman Britain*, London.

Campbell, J., (ed.), 1982, *The Anglo-Saxons*, Harmondsworth

_____ , 1986, 'Observations on the conversion of England', *Essays in Anglo-Saxon History*, London and Ronceverte, 69-84

_____ , 1987, 'The debt of the early English Church to Ireland', in P. Ní Chatháin and M. Richter (eds), *Irland und die Christenheit: Bibelstudien und Mission*, Stuttgart, 332-46

Canham, R., and Phillips, B., nd, *The Archaeology of Old Swindon Hill*, Swindon Archaeol Soc Report I

Chapman, J., and Hamerow, H., (eds), 1997, *Migrations and Invasions in Archaeological Explanation*, BAR Int Ser, 664, Oxford

Charles-Edwards, T., 1986, 'Review of *Gildas. New Approaches*', *Cambridge Medieval Celtic Studies*, 12, 115-20

_____ , 1995, 'Language and society among the insular Celts AD 400-1000', in M. Green (ed.), *The Celtic World*, London, 703-36

_____ , 1997, 'Anglo-Saxon kinship revisited', in J. Hines (ed) *The Anglo-Saxons from the Migration Period to the 8th Century. An Ethnographic Perspective*, Woodbridge, 171-210

Coates, R., 1989-90, 'On some controversy surrounding Gewissae/Gewissei, Cerdic and Ceawlin', *Nomina*, 13, 1-11

Coates, R., and Breeze, A., 2000, *Celtic Voices English Places. Studies of the Celtic Impact on Place-names in England*, Stamford

Cole, A., 1991-92, 'Distribution and use of the Old English place-name mere-tūn', *Journ English Place-Name Soc*, 31-41

Colgrave, B., and Mynors, R. A. B., (eds), 1969, *Bede's Ecclesiastical History of the English People*, Oxford

Corney, M., 1997, 'The origins and development of the 'small town' of *Cunetio*, Mildenhall, Wiltshire', *Britannia*, 28, 337-50

Costen, M., 1992, *The Origins of Somerset*, Manchester

Coy, J. P., 1991, 'The animal bones', in P. Fasham and R. Whinney, *Archaeology and the M3*, Hampshire Field Club and Archaeol Soc Monograph, 7, Winchester, 60-7

Crawford, S., 1997, 'Britons, Anglo-Saxons and the Germanic burial ritual', in Chapman and Hamerow 1997, 45-72

Cunliffe, B. W., 1991, *Iron Age Communities in Britain* (3rd edn.), London

Cunliffe, B. W., and Davenport, P., 1985, *The Temple of Sulis Minerva at Bath, Vol I(1), The Site*, Oxford

Davenport, P., 1999, *Archaeology in Bath. Excavations 1984-1989*, BAR Brit Ser, 284, Oxford

Davies, S. M., 1984, 'The excavation of an Anglo-Saxon cemetery (and some prehistoric pits) at Charlton Plantation, near Downton', *WANHM*, 79, 109-54

Dickinson, T. M., 1982, 'Fowler's Type G penannular brooches reconsidered', *Medieval Archaeol*, 26, 41-68

_____ , 1991, 'Material culture as social expression: the case of Saxon saucer brooches with running spiral decoration', *Studien zur Sachsenforschung*, 7, 29-70

_____ , 1993, 'Early Saxon saucer brooches: a preliminary overview', *Anglo-Saxon Studies in Archaeology and History*, 6, 11-44

Dickinson, T. M., and Härke, H., 1992, *Early Anglo-Saxon Shields*, London

Dixon, P., 1988, 'Crickley Hill 1969-1987', *Current Archaeology*, 110, 73-8

Dumville, D. N., 1985, 'The West Saxon genealogical Regnal List and the chronology of Wessex', *Peritia*, 4, 21-66

_____ , 1995, 'The idea of government in sub-Roman Britain', in G. Ausenda (ed.), *After Empire. Towards an Ethnology of Europe's Barbarians*, Woodbridge, 177-204

Eagles, B. N., 1979, *The Anglo-Saxon Settlement of Humberside*, BAR Brit Ser, 68, pts i and ii, Oxford

_____ , 1986, 'Pagan Anglo-Saxon burials at West Overton', *WANHM*, 80, 103-19

_____ , 1994, 'Evidence for settlement in the 5th to 7th centuries AD', in M. Aston and C. Lewis (eds), *The Medieval Landscape of Wessex*, Oxbow Monograph 46, Oxford, 13-32

_____ , 1997, 'The area around Bedwyn in the Anglo-Saxon period', in E. Hostetter and T. Howe (eds), *The Romano-British Villa at Castle Copse, Great Bedwyn*, Indiana, 378-97

Eagles, B. N., and Mortimer, C., 1993, 'Early Anglo-Saxon artefacts from Hod Hill Dorset', *Antiq Journ*, 73, 132-40

Edwards, H., 1988, *The Charters of the Early West Saxon Kingdom*, BAR Brit Ser, 198, Oxford

Entwistle, R., Fulford, M., and Raymond, F., 1993, *Salisbury Plain Project 1992-93 Interim Report*, Univ Reading

Esmonde Cleary, A. S., 1989, *The Ending of Roman Britain*, London

Evans, J., 1990, 'From the end of Roman Britain to the 'Celtic West', *Oxford Journ of Archaeol*, 9, 91-103

Evison, V. I., 1963, 'Sugar-loaf shield bosses', *Antiq Journ*, 43, 38-96

_____ , 1965, *The 5th-Century Invasions South of the Thames*, London

_____ , 1968, 'The Anglo-Saxon finds from Hardown Hill', *Procs Dorset Archaeol and Nat Hist Soc*, 90, 232-40

_____ , 1988, *An Anglo-Saxon Cemetery at Alton, Hampshire*, Hampshire Field Club and Archaeol Soc Monograph, 4, Winchester

Evison, V. I., and Hill, P., 1996, *Two Anglo-Saxon Cemeteries at Beckford, Hereford and Worcester*, CBA Res Rep, 103, York

Faull, M. L., 1975, 'The semantic development of Old English *wealh*', *Leeds Studies in English*, 8, 20-44

Field, D., 1999, 'Ancient water management on Salisbury Plain', in P. Pattison, D. Field and S. Ainsworth (eds), *Patterns of the Past. Essays in Landscape Archaeology for Christopher Taylor*, Oxford and Oakville, 29-35

Finberg, H. P. R., 1964, *Lucerna. Studies of Some Problems in the Early History of England*, London

Fowler, P. J., 1966, 'Two finds of Saxon domestic pottery in Wiltshire', *WANHM*, 61, 31-7

Fowler, P., and Blackwell, I., 1998, *The Land of Lettice Sweetapple. An English Countryside Explored*, Stroud

Frere, S. S., 1990, 'Roman Britain in 1989, I, sites explored', *Britannia*, 21, 303-64

Fulford, M. G., and Rippon, S. J., 1994, 'Lowbury Hill, Oxon: a re-assessment of the probable Romano-Celtic temple and the Anglo-Saxon barrow', *Archaeol Journ*, 151, 158-211

Geake, H., 1997, *The Use of Grave-goods in Conversion-Period England, c.600-c.850*, BAR Brit Ser, 261, Oxford

_____, 1999a, 'When were hanging bowls deposited in Anglo-Saxon graves?', *Medieval Archaeol*, 43, 1-18

_____, 1999b, 'Invisible kingdoms: the use of grave-goods in 7th-century England', in T. Dickinson and D. Griffiths (eds), 'The making of kingdoms', *Anglo-Saxon Studies in Archaeology and History*, 10, 203-15.

Geary, P. J., 1983, 'Ethnic identity as a situational construct in the early middle ages', *Mitteilungen der Anthropologischen Gesellschaft in Wien*, 113, 15-26

Gelling, M., 1973, 'Further thoughts on pagan place-names', in F. Sandgren (ed.), *Otium et Negotium. Studies in Onamatology and Library Science presented to Olof von Feilitzen*, Stockholm, 109-28

_____, 1976, *The Place-names of Berkshire. Part III*, English Place-Name Society, vol. 51, Cambridge

_____, 1993, 'Why aren't we speaking Welsh?', *Anglo-Saxon Studies in Archaeology and History*, 6, 51-6

_____, 1997, *Signposts to the Past. Place-names and the History of England*, 3rd edn., Chichester

Gingell, C. J., 1975/76, 'The excavation of an early Anglo-Saxon cemetery at Collingbourne Ducis', *WANHM*, 70/71, 61-98

Gover, J. E. B., Mawer, A., and Stenton, F. M., 1939, *The Place-names of Wiltshire*, English Place-Name Society, vol. 16, Cambridge

Graham. A. H., and Davies, S. M., 1993, *Excavations in Trowbridge, Wiltshire, 1977 and 1986-88. The Prehistoric, Saxon and Saxo-Norman Settlements and the Anarchy Period Castle*, Wessex Archaeology Report no. 2, Salisbury

Green, H. S., 1971, 'Wansdyke, excavations 1966 to 1970', *WANHM*, 66, 129-46

Grundy, G. B., 1920, 'Saxon land charters of Wiltshire. Second series', *Archaeol Journ*, 78, 8-126

Halsall, G., 1995a, 'The Merovingian period in north-east Gaul: transition or change?' in J. Bintliff and H. Hamerow (eds), *Europe Between Late Antiquity and the Middle Ages. Recent Archaeological and Historical Research in Western and Southern Europe*, BAR Int Ser, 617, 38-49

_____, 1995b, *Settlement and Social Organization. The Merovingian Region of Metz*, Cambridge

_____, 1999, 'Movers and shakers: the barbarians and the fall of Rome', review article *Early Medieval Europe*, 8(1), 131-45

Hamerow, H., 1997, 'Migration theory and the Anglo-Saxon identity crisis', in Chapman and Hamerow 1997, 33-44

_____, 1999, 'Anglo-Saxon timber buildings; the continental connection', in Sarfatij *et al.* 1999, 119-28

Hanson, W. S., 1988, 'Administration, urbanisation and acculturation in the Roman West', in D. Braund (ed.), *The Administration of the Roman Empire (241BC-AD193)*, Exeter, 53-68

Härke, H., 1990, "Warrior graves'? The background of the Anglo-Saxon weapon burial rite', *Past and Present*, 126, 22-43

_____ , 1993, 'Digging stiffs', *Reading Archaeol Newsletter*, I, 7

_____ , 1994, 'A context for the Saxon barrow', in Fulford and Rippon 1994, 202-6

_____ , 1995, 'Weapon burials and knives' in A. Boyle, A. Dodd, D. Miles and A. Mudd, *Two Oxfordshire Anglo-Saxon Cemeteries: Berinsfield and Didcot*, Thames Valley Landscapes Monograph no. 8, Oxford, 67-75

_____ , forthcoming, 'Immigrants and natives: a provisional model of Anglo-Saxon ethnogenesis'

Haslam, J., 1980, 'A middle Saxon iron smelting site at Ramsbury, Wiltshire', *Medieval Archaeol*, 24, 1-68

Hawkes, S. C., 1986, 'The early Saxon period', in G. Briggs, J. Cook and T. Rowley (eds), *The Archaeology of the Oxford Region*, Oxford, 64-114

Heather, P., 1996, *The Goths*, Oxford

Hedeager. L., 1993, 'The creation of Germanic identity. A European origin-myth', in P. Brun, S. van der Leeuw and C. Whittaker (eds), *Frontières d'Empire. Nature et Signification des Frontières Romaines*, Mémoires du Musée de Préhistoire d'Ile-de-France, 5, Nemours, 121-31

Higham, N., 1992, *Rome, Britain and the Anglo-Saxons*, London

Hills, C., 1998, 'Did the people of Spong Hill come from Schleswig-Holstein?', *Studien zur Sachsenforschung*, 11, 145-54

Hinchliffe, J., 1986, 'An early medieval settlement at Cowage Farm, Foxley, near Malmesbury', *Archaeol Journ*, 143, 240-59

Hines, J., 1994, 'The becoming of the English: identity, material culture and language in early Anglo-Saxon England', *Anglo-Saxon Studies in Archaeology and History*, 7, 49-59

_____ , 1996a 'Language and culture in an archaeological perspective', *Archaeologia Polona*, 34, 183-97

_____ , 1996b 'An early Anglo-Saxon wrist-clasp from the parish of Baydon', *WANHM*, 89, 130-2

_____ , 1998, 'Archaeology and language in a historical context: the creation of English', in R. Blench and M. Spriggs (eds), *Archaeology and Language II. Correlating Archaeological and Linguistic Hypotheses*, London and New York, 283-94

Hooke, D., 1988, 'Regional variation in southern and central England in the Anglo-Saxon period and its relationship to land units and settlement', in D. Hooke (ed.), *Anglo-Saxon Settlements*, Oxford, 123-51

Jackson, K., 1953, *Language and History in Early Britain. A Chronological Survey of the Brittonic Languages. 1st to 12th Century A.D*, Edinburgh

Janes, D., 1996, 'The golden clasp of the Late Roman state', *Early Medieval Europe*, 5(2), 127-53

Jones, S., 1997, *The Archaeology of Ethnicity. Constructing Identities in the Past and Present*, London and New York

Kirby, D. P., 1991, *The Earliest English Kings*, London

Kleinschmidt, H., 1998, 'The Geuissae and Bede: on the innovativeness of Bede's concept of the Gens', in J. Hill and M. Swan (eds), *The Community, the Family and the Saint. Patterns of Power in Early Medieval Europe*, Turnhout, 77-102

Leeds, E. T., and Shortt, H. de S., 1953, *An Anglo-Saxon Cemetery at Petersfinger, near Salisbury, Wilts*, Salisbury

Lucy, S., 1992, 'The significance of mortuary ritual in the political manipulation of the landscape', *Archaeol Review from Cambridge*, 11 (1), 93-103

_____ , 1998, *The Early Anglo-Saxon Cemeteries of East Yorkshire. An Analysis and Reinterpretation*, BAR Brit Ser, 272, Oxford

Mayr-Harting, H., 1991, *The Coming of Christianity to Anglo-Saxon England*, 3rd edn., Pennsylvania

Meaney, A. L. S., 1964, *A Gazetteer of Early Anglo-Saxon Burial Sites*, London

Meaney, A. L. S., and Hawkes, S. C., 1970, *Two Anglo-Saxon Cemeteries at Winnall, Winchester, Hampshire*, Soc Medieval Archaeol Monograph, 4, London

Moore, C. N., and Algar, D. J., 1968, 'Saxon 'grass-tempered ware' and Mesolithic finds from near Petersfinger, Laverstock', *WANHM*, 63, 103-5

Mortimer, C., 1994, 'Lead-alloy models for three early Anglo-Saxon brooches', *Anglo-Saxon Studies in Archaeology and History*, 7, 27-33

Morton, A. D., (ed.) 1992, *Excavations at Hamwic. Vol I: Excavations 1946-83, Excluding Six Dials and Melbourne Street*, CBA Res Rep, 84, London

Muhlberger, S., 1983, 'The Gallic Chronicle of 452 and its authority for British events', *Britannia*, 14, 23-33

Musty, J., 1969, 'The excavation of two barrows, one of Saxon date, at Ford, Laverstock, near Salisbury, Wiltshire', *Antiq Journ*, 49, 98-117

Nelson, J., 1991, 'Reconstructing a royal family: reflections on Alfred, from Asser, chapter 2', in I. Wood and N. Lund (eds), *People and Places in Northern Europe 500-1600. Essays in honour of Peter Hayes Sawyer*, Woodbridge, 47-66

O'Donovan, M. A., (ed.) 1988, *Charters of Sherborne. Anglo-Saxon Charters III*, British Academy, Oxford

Owen-Crocker, G. R., 1986, *Dress in Anglo-Saxon England*, Manchester

Parfitt, K., and Brugmann, B., 1997, *The Anglo-Saxon Cemetery on Mill Hill, Deal, Kent*, Soc Medieval Archaeol Monograph, 14, London

Parker Pearson, M., 1982, 'Mortuary practices, society and ideology: an ethnoarchaeological study', in I Hodder (ed.), *Symbolic and Structural Archaeology*, Cambridge, 99-113

Parsons, D., 1997, 'British *Caraticos..., Old English Cerdic', *Cambrian Medieval Celtic Studies*, 33, 1-8

Paschoud, F. (ed.), 1989, *Zosime, Histoire nouvelle*, tome III, 2e partie, (Livre VI and index), Paris

Passmore, A. D., 1934, 'A Saxon saucer brooch from Mildenhall', *WANHM*, 46, 393

Philpott, R., 1991, *Burial Practices in Roman Britain. A Survey of Grave Treatment and Furnishing AD 43-410*, BAR Brit Ser, 219, Oxford

Pine, J., 2001, 'The excavation of a Saxon settlement at Cadley Road, Collingbourne Ducis, Wiltshire', *WANHM*, 94, 88-117

Plummer, C., 1896, *Venerabilis Baedae Opera Historica*, 2 vols, Oxford

Rahtz, P. A., *et al.*, 1992, *Cadbury Congresbury 1968-73. A Late/Post-Roman Hilltop Settlement in Somerset*, BAR Brit Ser, 223, Oxford

Rawlings, M., 1995, 'Archaeological sites along the Wiltshire section of the Codford-Ilchester water pipeline', *WANHM*, 88, 26-49

Reynolds, A. J., 1994, 'The Compton Bassett area research project-first interim report', *Institute of Archaeology Bulletin*, 31, 169-98

_____ , 1998, 'Anglo-Saxon law in the landscape. An archaeological study of the Old English judicial system', unpub. PhD thesis, Univ London

_____ , 1999, *Later Anglo-Saxon England. Life and Landscape*, Stroud

Rivet, A. L. F., 1958, *Town and Country in Roman Britain*, London

Rivet, A. L. F., and Smith, C., 1981, *The Place-names of Roman Britain*, London

Rogers, P. W., forthcoming, 'The textiles', in Williams and Newman forthcoming

Sarfatij, H., Verwers, W. J. H., and Woltering, P. J., (eds), *In Discussion with the Past. Archaeological Studies Presented to W A van Es*, Amersfoort

Sawyer, P. H., 1968, *Anglo-Saxon Charters. An Annotated List and Bibliography*, Royal Hist Soc Handbook 8, London

Scull, C. J., 1992, 'Before Sutton Hoo: structures of power and society in early East Anglia', in M. Carver (ed.), *The Age of Sutton Hoo: the 7th Century in North-western Europe*, Woodbridge, 3-23

_____ , 1993, 'Archaeology, early Anglo-Saxon society and the origins of Anglo-Saxon kingdoms', *Anglo-Saxon Studies in Archaeology and History*, 6, 65-82

Sims-Williams, P.,1975, 'Continental influence at Bath monastery in the 7th century', *Anglo-Saxon England*, 4, 1-10

_____ , 1983, 'The settlement of England in Bede and the Chronicle', *Anglo-Saxon England*, 12, 1-41

_____ , 1990, *Religion and Literature in Western England 600-800*, Cambridge.

Sparey-Green, C., 1996, 'Poundbury, Dorset: settlement and economy in late and post-Roman Dorchester', in K Dark (ed.), *External Contacts and the Economy of Late Roman and Post-Roman Britain*, Woodbridge, 121-52

Speake, G., 1989, *A Saxon Bed Burial on Swallowcliffe Down. Excavations by F de M Vatcher*, HBMCE Archaeol Rep, 10, London

Stenton, F. M., 1913, *The Early History of the Abbey of Abingdon*, Reading

_____ , 1971, *Anglo-Saxon England*, 3rd edn, Oxford

Stoodley, N., 1999, 'Communities of the dead: the evidence for living populations from early Anglo-Saxon cemeteries', in D. Mowbray, R. Purdie and I. P. Wei (eds), *Authority and Community in the Middle Ages*, Stroud, 1-17

Stuiver, M., and Pearson, G. W., 1986, High-precision calibration of the radiocarbon timescale, AD 1950-500 BC, *Radiocarbon*, 28, no. 2B, 805-38

Swanton, M. J., 1973, *The Spearheads of the Anglo-Saxon Settlements*, Royal Archaeol Institute, London

Thäte, E., 1996, 'Alte Denkmäler und frühgeschichtliche Bestattungen: ein sächsisch-angelsächsischer Totenbrauch und seine Kontinuität. Eine vergleichende Studie', *Archäologische Informationen* 19/1 and 2, 105-16.

Ucko, P. J., 1969, 'Ethnography and archaeological interpretation of funerary remains', *World Archaeology*, 1 (2), 262-80

Van Arsdell, R. D., 1994, *The Coinage of the Dobunni. Money Supply and Coin Circulation in Dobunnic Territory. With a Gazetteer of Findspots by P de Jersey*, Oxford

Wacher, J. S., 1995, *The Towns of Roman Britain*, 2nd edn, London

Walker, H. E., 1956, 'Bede and the Gewissae: the political evolution of the Heptarchy and its nomenclature', *Cambridge Historical Journ*, 12, 174-86

Wallace-Hadrill, J. M., 1988, *Bede's Ecclesiastical History of the English People. A Historical Commentary*, Oxford

Welch, M. G., 1976, 'Disc, gilt bronze, from an applied brooch', in B. Cunliffe, *Excavations at Portchester Castle. Vol 2, Saxon*, Soc Antiq Res Rep, 33, London, 206-11

_____ , 1999, 'Relating Anglo-Saxon chronology to continental chronologies in the 5th century AD', in U. von Freeden, U. Koch and A. Wieczorek (eds), *Völker an Nord- und Ostsee und die Franken*, Akten des 48. Sachsensymposiums in Mannheim vom 7. bis 11. September 1997. Kolloquien zur Vor- und Frühgeschichte, Band 3. Mannheimer Geshichtsblätter, Neue Folge, Beiheft 2, 31-8

Wessex Archaeology 1995, *9 Barnes Place, Mere, Wiltshire. Archaeological Report on Human Burial*, Trust for Wessex Archaeol, Report no. 39535

White, R. H., 1988, *Roman and Celtic Objects from Anglo-Saxon Graves. A Catalogue and an Interpretation of Their Use*, BAR Brit Ser, 191, Oxford

Whitelock, D., with Douglas, D. C., and Tucker, S. I. (eds), 1961, *The Anglo-Saxon Chronicle. A Revised Translation*, London

Williams, H., 1997, 'Ancient landscapes and the dead: the reuse of prehistoric and Roman monuments as early Anglo-Saxon burial sites', *Medieval Archaeol*, 41, 1-32

_____ , 1998a, 'The ancient monument in Romano-British ritual practices', in C. Forcey, J. Hawthorne and R. Witcher (eds), *TRAC 97. Proceedings of the 7th Annual Theoretical Roman Archaeology Conference, Nottingham, 1997*, Oxford, 71-86

_____ , 1998b, 'Monuments and the past in early Anglo-Saxon England', *World Archaeology*, 30(1), 90-108

_____ , 1999, 'Placing the dead: investigating the location of wealthy barrow burials in 7th century England', in M. Rundkvist (ed.), *Grave Matters. Eight Studies of 1st Millennium AD Burials in Crimea, England and Southern Scandinavia*, BAR Int Ser, 781, 57-86

Williams, P., and Newman, R., forthcoming, *Excavations at Grove Farm, Market Lavington, Wilts, 1986-90*

Winterbottom, M. (ed.), 1978, *Gildas. The Ruin of Britain and Other Works*, Chichester

Wolfram, H., 1994, 'Origo et religio. Ethnic traditions and literature in early medieval texts', *Early Medieval Europe*, 3(1), 19-38

Wollman, A., 1993, 'Early Latin loan-words in Old English', *Anglo-Saxon England*, 22, 1-26

Wood, I. N., 1998, 'The barbarian invasions and first settlements', in A. Cameron and P. Garnsey (eds), *The Cambridge Ancient History, XIII, The Late Empire, AD 337-425*, Cambridge, 516-37

Woodward, A., 1992, *Shrines and Sacrifice*, London

Wormald, P., 1983, 'Bede, the Bretwaldas and the origins of the gens Anglorum', in D. Bullough and R Collins (eds), *Ideal and Reality in Frankish and Anglo-Saxon Society: Studies Presented to J M Wallace-Hadrill*, Oxford, 99-129.

_____ , 1995, "Inter cetera bona... genti suae': law-making and peace-keeping in the earliest English kingdoms', *Settimane di studio del centro italiano di studi sull'alto medioevo*, 42, 963-93

Yorke, B., 1989, 'The Jutes of Hampshire and Wight and the origins of Wessex', in S. Bassett (ed.), *The Origins of Anglo-Saxon Kingdoms*, Leicester, 84-96

_____ , 1990, *Kings and Kingdoms of Early Anglo-Saxon England*, London

_____ , 1993, 'Fact or fiction? The written evidence for the 5th and 6th centuries AD', *Anglo-Saxon Studies in Archaeology and History*, 6, 45-50

_____ , 1995, *Wessex in the Early Middle Ages*, Leicester

Youngs, S., 1995, 'A penannular brooch from near Calne, Wiltshire', *WANHM*, 88, 127-31

Youngs, S., with Eagles, B., 1998, 'Medieval hanging bowls from Wiltshire', *WANHM*, 91, 35-41

Zimmermann, W. H., 1999, 'Favourable conditions for cattle farming, one reason for the Anglo-Saxon migration over the North Sea? About the byre's evolution in the area south and east of the North Sea and England', in Sarfatij *et al.* 1999, 129-44

INDEX *by Peter Ellis*